Rajasthan,
Delhi & Agra

Delhi
p30

Agra & the
Taj Mahal
p78

Rajasthan
p102

...ED BY

Paul Clammer
Abigail Blasi, Kevin Raub

Contents

PLAN YOUR TRIP

ON THE ROAD

JAIPUR P103

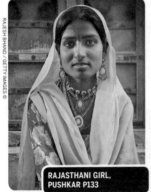

RAJASTHANI GIRL,
PUSHKAR P133

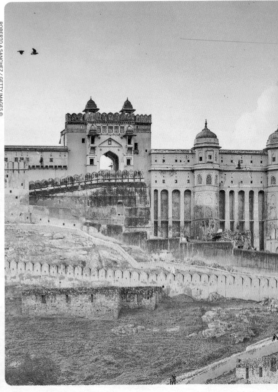

PRITI BHATT / GETTY IMAGES ©

RAJESH BHAND / GETTY IMAGES ©

ROBERTO A SANCHEZ / GETTY IMAGES ©

Contents

AMBER FORT P122

Welcome to Rajasthan, Delhi & Agra

Rajasthan, Delhi and Agra are the jewels in India's crown. From fairy-tale palaces and epic forts to dizzying festivals and wildlife encounters, this is India at its unbeatable Bollywood best.

The Golden Triangle

The famous Golden Triangle is a traveller's survey of Indian icons. It starts at the daunting mega-metropolis of Delhi with its majestic Mughal heritage, and then directs you to Agra, where one of the world's most famous tombs, the Taj Mahal, defines a city. The third point is Jaipur – a city painted pink with the Hawah Mahal and some of the most colourful bazaars in India. Jaipur is the gateway to Rajasthan, one of India's major drawcards; once you've stepped into a palace, stared up at a fort or swayed on the back of one of its camels, you'll readily understand why.

Magnificent Monuments

Most travellers to this region will arrive by air in the nation's capital. Delhi is an overwhelming, bursting-at-the-seams city that still manages to charm visitors with its magnificent heritage and heady cocktail of old Mughal architecture and the new of an India striding into the 21st century. A short train journey to the south, the Taj Mahal lives up to its hype with its perfect proportions and marble tones. In Rajasthan, it's the forts that grab you, from Jaisalmer's fairy-tale desert outpost, to the grandeur of Mehrangarh, which overlooks Jodhpur from its imposing hill-top setting.

Royal Heritage

Rajasthan is literally the Land of the Kings. It is home to the chivalrous Rajputs, and its battle-scarred heritage has bestowed legacies of pride and tradition. The upper echelons of this medieval society built magnificent palaces and forts, many of which are now glorious hotels and museums. In addition, stunning handicrafts and fine arts were developed and nurtured through patronage of the maharajas. Village life remains steeped in tradition but, just like the rest of India, the pace of change is ever accelerating. Turbaned men still barter for decorated camels, but now they relay the successful deal home via a smart phone.

Festival of Colour

The colours of this region are impossible to ignore and the effect of emerald green, canary yellow and fire-engine red turbans and saris is simply dazzling. The lucky might even see a flash of orange while tiger-spotting in Ranthambhore National Park. Easier to collect are the bright hues of Rajasthan's many festivals, from brightly decorated mounts at the camel and elephant festivals in Pushkar and Jaipur respectively, to the colourful explosions of Diwali and Holi, celebrated across the region.

Why I Love Rajasthan, Delhi & Agra

By Paul Clammer, Writer

Is there any better way to see Rajasthan unfold before you than through India's railways – tucked up in your berth and watching village life pass through the window, refreshed by the chai-wallah who passes through the carriage with an urn of sweet steaming tea? And when you arrive at your destination, you'll tumble through the backstreets by autorickshaw to the real magic – astounding fortresses and palaces, camel safaris and elephant rides. This is the India of the imagination made real. Noise, spice, heat and colour: what's not to love?

For more about our writers, see page 288.

Above: Boy dressed as Shiva during the Pushkar Camel Fair (p136)

Rajasthan, Delhi & Agra

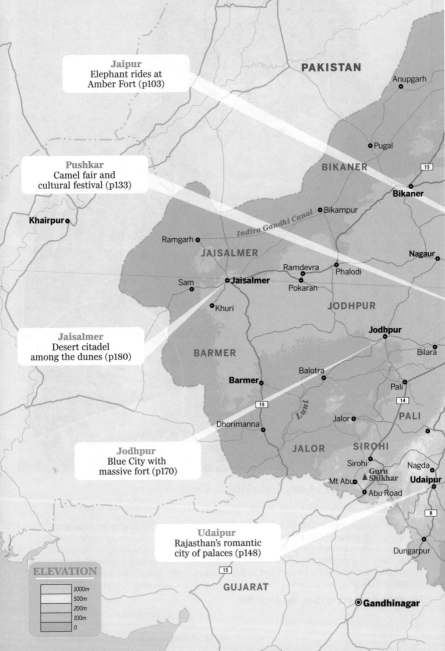

Jaipur
Elephant rides at
Amber Fort (p103)

Pushkar
Camel fair and
cultural festival (p133)

Jaisalmer
Desert citadel
among the dunes (p180)

Jodhpur
Blue City with
massive fort (p170)

Udaipur
Rajasthan's romantic
city of palaces (p148)

PAKISTAN

Anupgarh

Pugal

BIKANER

15

Bikaner

Khairpur

Bikampur

Indira Gandhi Canal

Ramgarh

JAISALMER

Nagaur

Ramdevra

Phalodi

Sam

Jaisalmer

Pokaran

Khuri

JODHPUR

Jodhpur

Bilara

BARMER

Balotra

Pali

Barmer

Luni

15

PALI

14

Dhorimanna

Jalor

Nagda

JALOR

SIROHI

Sirohi

Guru
▲ Shikhar

Mt Abu

Udaipur

8

Abu Road

Dungarpur

ELEVATION

	1000m
	500m
	200m
	100m
	0

15

GUJARAT

◎ **Gandhinagar**

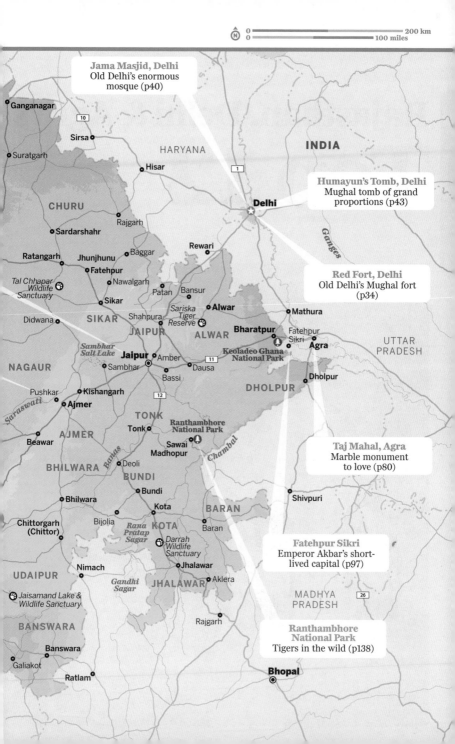

Jama Masjid, Delhi
Old Delhi's enormous mosque (p40)

Humayun's Tomb, Delhi
Mughal tomb of grand proportions (p43)

Red Fort, Delhi
Old Delhi's Mughal fort (p34)

Taj Mahal, Agra
Marble monument to love (p80)

Fatehpur Sikri
Emperor Akbar's short-lived capital (p97)

Ranthambhore National Park
Tigers in the wild (p138)

0 200 km
0 100 miles

INDIA

HARYANA

Delhi

Ganganagar
Sirsa
Suratgarh
Hisar
Rewari
CHURU
Rajgarh
Sardarshahr
Baggar
Ratangarh
Jhunjhunu
Fatehpur
Nawalgarh
Tal Chhapar Wildlife Sanctuary
Patan
Bansur
Mathura
Sikar
Shahpura
Sariska Tiger Reserve
Alwar
Didwana
SIKAR
JAIPUR
ALWAR
Bharatpur
Fatehpur Sikri
Agra
UTTAR PRADESH
Sambhar Salt Lake
Jaipur
Amber
Keoladeo Ghana National Park
Ganges
NAGAUR
Sambhar
Bassi
Dausa
Pushkar
Kishangarh
DHOLPUR
Dholpur
Saraswati
Ajmer
TONK
AJMER
Tonk
Ranthambhore National Park
Beawar
Deoli
Sawai Madhopur
Chambal
BHILWARA
BUNDI
Banas
Bundi
Bhilwara
Kota
BARAN
Shivpuri
Chittorgarh (Chittor)
Bijolia
Rana Pratap Sagar
KOTA
Baran
Darrah Wildlife Sanctuary
Nimach
Jhalawar
MADHYA PRADESH
UDAIPUR
Gandhi Sagar
JHALAWAR
Aklera
Jaisamand Lake & Wildlife Sanctuary
BANSWARA
Rajgarh
Banswara
Galiakot
Ratlam
Bhopal

10
1
11
12
26

Rajasthan, Delhi & Agra's
Top 12

Taj Mahal, Agra

1 Framed in its arched gateway, the full-frontal vision of the Taj Mahal (p80) is stunning – a painting somehow made real for you to enter. Even the maddening crowds don't spoil this vision of proportion and symmetry reflected in the mirror-like watercourses of the surrounding Mughal garden. Translucent white marble softly glows at dawn, dusk and under moonlight. Closer inspection reveals delicate designs and beautiful calligraphy inlaid with coloured stone, and the two cenotaphs, one of Mumtaz Mahal, the inspiration for the Taj Mahal, and the second of Shah Jahan, its creator.

Jaisalmer Fort

2 The 12th-century Jaisalmer Fort (p181) defiantly rises from the flat desert lands, a vision from childhood memories of tales such as 'Ali Baba and the Forty Thieves'. The reality is no less romantic. Castellated stone bastions and elephant-size doors protect a warren of narrow bazaars and Jain and Hindu temples, all bustling with life – a quarter of the city's population lives inside the fort. Overseeing the bazaars is the former Maharaja's seven-storey palace, now a fascinating museum.

DOUGLAS PEARSON / GETTY IMAGES ©

RUDI SEBASTIAN / GETTY IMAGES ©

Jodhpur

3 The ancient capital of the kingdom of the Marwar, Jodhpur (p170) rewards the traveller with Rajasthan's most spectacular fort, and from its ramparts one of India's iconic views. From this elevated perch the old city of Jodhpur, a maze of blue-block houses, is like an ocean surrounding an island fortress. Beyond the teeming city, jeep safaris explore the home of the desert-dwelling Bishnoi, a people who have been protecting the natural environment for aeons. Below: View of Jodhpur from Mehrangarh (p171)

Red Fort, Delhi

4 The massive Red Fort (p34) of Delhi is the heart of Shahjahanabad, the walled city constructed by Shah Jahan and now known as Old Delhi. Though little remains of the glorious interiors, the massive Mughal architecture and geometric gardens evoke the centuries-old magnificence of this imperial throne. From Lahore Gate, through which the visitor can easily imagine the grand processions of days past, you can wander the covered market, trimmed gardens, water features and elegant buildings, and then take in a sound and light show.

BRIAN FURBUSH PHOTOGRAPHY / GETTY IMAGES ©

DAMIEN SIMONIS / GETTY IMAGES ©

Camel Safari, Thar Desert

5 For an unbeatable cultural experience, hop aboard a ship of the desert for an extended safari or simple overnight jaunt into the windswept dunes of Rajasthan's Thar Desert (p234). From a camel's back you can see herds of gazelles and meet desert-dwelling villagers. At the end of the day you can make chapatis over an open fire, witness a cultural performance and fall blissfully asleep under a Persian carpet of glittering stars. You can organise a camel safari in Jaisalmer, as well as Bikaner and Osian.

Ranthambhore National Park

6 There are only a few places left where you can see the magnificent tiger in the wild. Ranthambhore National Park (p138) is one such place and your chances of spotting a tiger are good. This former hunting reserve of the maharajas of Jaipur is a majestic setting for a tiger safari. There are lush ravines and crocodile-infested lakes, and a crumbling fort straight out of the *Jungle Book*. Spotted deer graze in the dappled light of an open wood, their eyes, nostrils and ears twitching for the sight, smell or sound of a striped predator.

Amber Fort, Jaipur

7 Before the capital was moved to Jaipur, the fort palace of Amber (p122) was the capital of the Kachwaha. The honey-coloured citadel rises from a sloping ridge surrounded by higher ridges capped with battlements and watchtowers. From the beautiful geometric gardens and Maota Lake, you can ride an elephant to the main square, Jaleb Chowk. From here, wander freely through the palace grounds, halls of audience, the magnificent three-storey Ganesh Pol, the once-taboo *zenana* (women's quarters), and the still-glittering Jai Mandir.

POWEROFFOREVER / GETTY IMAGES ©

SIHASAKPRACHUM / GETTY IMAGES ©

TIM MAKINS / GETTY IMAGES ©

Fatehpur Sikri, Agra

8 Not far from Agra, on a rocky ridge where a Sufi saint had lived in a cave, Emperor Akbar built his new capital of Fatehpur Sikri (p97). This move from Agra was short-lived, however. Wandering the beautiful complex you can only be amazed that after just 14 years the great sandstone metropolis was abandoned, probably due to a lack of water. Dominating the palace complex is the expansive Jama Masjid, fronted by the immense Buland Darwaza (Victory Gate) commemorating Akbar's victory in Gujarat. Above: Diwan-i-Khas (p97), Fatehpur Sikri

Humayun's Tomb, Delhi

9 The splendid Humayun's tomb (p43) graciously sits on a multi-arched plinth rising from the neat lawns of its extensive *charbagh* (formal Persian garden), of which this was the first example in India. The garden is a perfect escape from Delhi's crowds. Sparkling water features, tidy cypresses and swaying palm trees are set against the symmetrical pink sandstone tomb built for Humayan, the second Mughal emperor, by his Persian-born senior wife, Haji Begum, who also lies here.

Udaipur

10 Following the fall of Chittorgarh, Maharana Udai Singh II moved the Mewar capital to Udaipur (p148) in 1568. The city is dominated by the sprawling City Palace that hugs the eastern shoreline of Udaipur's centrepiece, Lake Pichola. The enormous complex houses a museum, a couple of swish heritage hotels and the erstwhile royals. The mirror-surfaced lake, in turn, hosts one of Rajasthan's most renowned palaces, the wedding-cake Lake Palace, now also an exclusive five-star hotel and occasional movie set. City Palace (p149)

Jama Masjid, Delhi

11 The largest mosque in India, the red-sandstone Jama Masjid (p40) dominates the bazaars of Old Delhi with its towering 40m-high twin minarets and trio of marble domes. Grand flights of stairs lead up from the street to the imposing gates that separate the secular from the sacred. The vast, enclosed courtyard of Emperor Shah Jahan's last architectural extravagance can host more than 20,000 worshippers at a single prayer session. Climb the southern minaret for an unforgettable view.

Pushkar Camel Fair

12 Some come for the camels, some come to bathe away their sins, some come just for the fun. Pushkar's extraordinary camel fair (p136) is Rajasthan's signature event, combining Hindu spiritulism, camel commerce and cultural celebration. The camels, cattle and Mawari steeds arrive early so that the dealing can be done before the frivolity of the fair takes over, and before the full-moon ceremony of Kartik Purnima, when pilgrims bathe and set candles afloat in a holy lake.

Need to Know

For more information, see Survival Guide (p239)

Currency
Indian rupee (₹)

Language
Hindi and English. There are five regional dialects of Hindi spoken in Rajasthan.

Visas
Thirty-day visas on arrival are becoming more common for many nationalities, otherwise travel on the standard six-month tourist visa. Tourist visas are valid from the date of issue, not the arrival date.

Money
Most urban centres have ATMS. Carry cash or travellers cheques as back-up. MasterCard and Visa are the most widely accepted credit cards.

Mobile Phones
Getting connected can involve time-consuming identity checks. Avoid high roaming costs by hooking up to a local network.

Time
India Standard Time (GMT/UTC plus 5½ hours)

When to Go

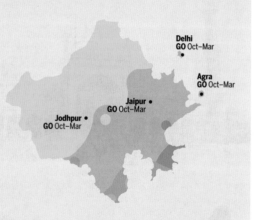

Warm to hot summers, mild winters
Tropical climate, wet & dry seasons
Dry climate
Desert, dry climate

Delhi
GO Oct–Mar

Agra
GO Oct–Mar

Jaipur
GO Oct–Mar

Jodhpur
GO Oct–Mar

High Season
(Dec–Feb)

➡ Pleasant daytime temperature, but can get cold at night.

➡ Peak tourists, peak prices – pre-book all flights and accommodation.

➡ Domestic flights often get delayed owing to fog.

Shoulder Seasons
(Sep–Nov & Feb–Mar)

➡ Warm nights suit many visitors fleeing colder climes.

➡ Ranthambhore National Park opens in October and the migratory birds arrive at Keoladeo Ghana National Park.

Low Season
(Apr–Aug)

➡ By April it's warming up and June is very hot, awaiting the monsoon, which brings the rain in July and August.

➡ Ranthambhore National Park closes at the end of June.

Useful Websites

Festivals of India (www.festivalsofindia.in) All about Indian festivals.

Incredible India (www.incredibleindia.org) Official India tourism site.

IndiaMike (www.indiamike.com) Popular travellers forum.

Lonely Planet (www.lonelyplanet.com/india) Destination information, the popular Thorn Tree Travel Forum and more.

Rajasthan Tourism Development Corporation (www.rtdc.in) Rajasthan government tourism site.

Important Numbers

To dial numbers from outside India, dial your international access code, India's country code then the number (minus the '0' used for dialling domestically).

Country code	☏91
International access code (in India)	☏00
Ambulance	☏102
Police	☏100

Exchange Rates

Australia	A$1	₹50
Canada	C$1	₹52
Euro zone	€1	₹71
Japan	¥100	₹53
New Zealand	NZ$1	₹47
Pakistan	PKR100	₹62
UK	£1	₹99
US	US$1	₹64

For current exchange rates see www.xe.com

Daily Costs

Budget:
Less than ₹2000

➡ Accommodation: less than ₹1000 for a double

➡ Thalis: a healthy way to eat on a budget

➡ Bottled beer: drink as an occasional treat

Midrange:
₹2000–8000

➡ Accommodation: ₹1000–5000 (allows for occasional stays in heritage hotels)

➡ Consider hiring a car and driver for short sightseeing jaunts

Top End:
More than ₹8000

➡ Palatial accommodation fit for a maharaja: ₹5000 plus

➡ Hire a car and driver, or hop on the Palace on Wheels luxury train

➡ Go shopping

Opening Hours

Official business hours are 10am to 5.30pm Monday to Friday, with many offices closing for a lunch hour around 1pm. Many sights are open from dawn to dusk.

Banks 9.30am or 10am to 2pm or 4pm Monday to Friday, to noon or 1pm Saturday

Restaurants lunch: noon–2.30pm/3pm; dinner: 7pm–10pm/11pm

Shops 10am–7pm, some closed Sunday

Arriving in New Delhi

Indira Gandhi International Airport (p72) There is a prepaid-taxi booth at Delhi airport where you can book a taxi for a fixed price (including luggage), thus avoiding commission scams. Many hotels will arrange airport pick-ups with advance notice – these are often complimentary at top-end hotels but for a fee at others. Because of the late-night arrival of many international flights, a hotel-room booking and airport pick-up is advised.

Getting Around

Transport in India is reasonably priced, quick and efficient.

Train Extensive coverage of the country, inexpensive and heavily used: advance booking is recommended.

Car Hiring a car with a driver doesn't cost a fortune, and is recommended over driving yourself.

Bus Cheaper and slower than trains, but a useful and practical alternative. Overnight sleeper buses are best avoided.

For much more on **getting around**, see p257

If You Like...

Wildlife

If you are interested in India's wildlife then Rajasthan should be high on your list. Its national parks started out as hunting reserves for the maharajas. In later years, with modern weapons, this turned into wholesale slaughter and led to a conservation ethos and establishment of national parks.

Ranthambhore National Park This remains one of the best places to spot a wild tiger in India and has amazing scenery and a spooky fort. (p138)

Keoladeo Ghana National Park An internationally recognised wetland attracting scores of seasonal migrants – a birdwatchers paradise. (p124)

Sariska Tiger Reserve Tigers were reintroduced here after it lost its own population to poaching – Sariska is at the sharp end of tiger conservation. (p128)

Bazaar Shopping

Rajasthan is one of the easiest places to spend money, with its bustling and vibrant bazaars, colourful arts and crafts, gorgeous fabrics, miniature paintings, blue pottery, magic carpets and much more. The cardinal rule is to bargain hard.

Delhi The capital has it all, from modern shopping malls with international designer goods down to the pestering purveyors of Chandni Chowk. (p68)

Agra Artisans create marble inlaid with coloured stones in the pietra dura technique used on the Taj Mahal. (p93)

Jaipur A shopper's dream – arts and crafts abound in the bazaars of the Old City and top of the list is the amazing jewellery. (p103)

Pushkar Explore the cluttered Sadar Bazaar, chock-a-block with arts and crafts, from exquisite embroidered textiles to hippie paraphernalia. (p133)

Fancy Festivals

Rich in religion and tradition, Rajasthan has many vibrant festivals. Most festivals follow either the Indian lunar calendar or the Islamic calendar, and therefore change annually relative to the Gregorian calendar.

Diwali The liveliest festival of the Hindu calendar, celebrated on the 15th day of Kartika (October/November), featuring crazy amounts of fireworks. (p20)

Holi Probably the most exuberant Hindu festival – people celebrate spring (February/March) by throwing coloured water and *gulal* (powder) at one another. (p18)

Pushkar Camel Fair Rajasthan's biggest event – part agricultural show, part cultural festival and part Hindu pilgrimage. (p136)

Jaipur Elephant Festival A celebration of all things pachyderm: elephants are decorated and games include elephant-versus-human tug-of-war. (p18)

Sleeping in a Palace

The phenomenal wealth of the feudal kings and princes was as exclusive as it was vast. At that time, only by luck of birth or special invitation could one have experienced the splendid interiors. But now the erstwhile royals rely on tourism, and the palaces have become luxury hotels.

Jaipur Regional nobles built palaces around this city, so you'll find several palatial digs – the former maharaja's own palace, the Rambagh, is one of India's best hotels. (p115)

Udaipur This ticks all the boxes for the most romantic setting, with the Lake Palace, a floating wedding-cake hotel. (p148)

Jodhpur Boasts one of the last palaces to be built before the royals lost their gravy trains – the Umaid Bhawan Palace is an art deco colossus with stunning rooms. (p173)

Deserts & Camels

Rajasthan's great Thar Desert is criss-crossed by ancient trade routes and dotted with traditional villages where life continues in a fashion very similar to more romantic times. Camels remain an important method of transport, and they remain integral to traditional desert culture.

Jaisalmer Home to the overnight camel safari – sand dunes, traditional dance and food, and a charpoy under the stars. (p180)

Jodhpur The centre for exploring the desert homelands of the Bishnoi, a people who hold all animals sacred, particularly the blackbuck, India's desert antelope. (p170)

Bikaner Travel in a traditional camel cart, while visiting villages and sleeping on dunes. (p190)

Mighty Forts

The feudal past of Delhi, Agra and Rajasthan has left a legacy of fortresses. These buildings evoke the past and are the focus of tourists and would-be time travellers.

Delhi The home of Shah Jahan's Red Fort, where Peacock Throne once resided. (p34)

Agra View the older and bigger red sandstone fort that was started by Akbar and became the prison of his grandson Shah Jahan. (p81)

Chittorgarh A massive citadel capping a mountain plateau – its bastions embrace palaces, temples and towers. (p145)

Jodhpur A blue city spread beneath the ramparts of the hulk of Mehrangarh, Rajasthan's most commanding fort. (p171)

Jaisalmer Travellers are rewarded with a golden sandstone castle that drifts in the desert and is still inhabited. (p181)

Top: Mehrangarh (p171)
Bottom: Pushkar Camel Fair (p136)

Month By Month

January

Mid-winter cool lingers throughout the north, and it's downright cold in the desert night air. Pleasant daytime weather and several festivals make it a popular time to travel, so book ahead.

🪁 Kite Festival

Sankranti, the Hindu festival marking the sun's passage across the Tropic of Capricorn, is celebrated in many ways throughout India. In Jaipur it's the mass kite-flying that steals the show.

🪁 Jaipur Literature Festival

In just a handful of years the Jaipur Literature Festi-val (jaipurliteraturefestival. org) has grown into the world's biggest free lit-erature festival, attracting local and international au-thors and poets. Readings, debates, music and even the odd controversy keep it energised.

🪁 Jaisalmer Desert Festival

A three-day celebration of desert culture, with many events taking place in the Sam sand dunes. Camel races, turban-tying con-tests, traditional puppetry, folk dances and the famous Mr Desert competition are part of the fun. It may fall in February.

🪁 Vasant Panchami

Hindus dress in yellow and place books, musical instruments and other educational objects in front of idols of Saraswati, the goddess of learning, to receive her blessing. The holiday may fall in February.

February

The weather remains comfortable in Delhi and Rajasthan, with very little rain and plenty of festivals. The days are getting marginally warmer but it's still ideal travelling weather.

🪁 Shivaratri

This day of Hindu fast-ing recalls the *tandava* (cosmic dance of fury) of Lord Shiva. Temple proces-sions are followed by the chanting of mantras and anointing of linga (phallic images symbolising Shiva). Shivaratri can also fall in March.

🪁 Jaipur Elephant Festival

Taking place on the day be-fore Holi (and so both can fall in March), the Jaipur Elephant Festival celebrates the pachyderm's place in Indian culture. There are elephant dress parades and competitions such as polo and tug-of-war.

🪁 Holi

One of North India's most exuberant festivals; Hindus celebrate the beginning of spring, in either Febru-ary or March, by throwing coloured water and *gulal* (powder) at anyone within range. On the night before Holi, bonfires symbolise the demise of the demoness Holika.

March

The last month of the main travel season, March sees the last of the cool days of winter as daytime temperatures creep above 30°C.

Wildlife-Watching

As the weather warms up and water sources dry out, animals tend to congregate at the few remaining sources of water. This can improve your chances of spotting tigers and leopards.

Rama's Birthday

During Ramanavami, which lasts anywhere from one to nine days, Hindus celebrate the birth of Rama with processions, music, fasting and feasting, readings and enactments of scenes from the Ramayana and ceremonial weddings of Rama and Sita idols.

May

The region heats up with daytime temperatures over 40°C. Life slows down as the humidity builds up in anticipation of the monsoon.

Summer Festival

Rajasthan's very own hill station, the delightful Mt Abu, celebrates summer (or perhaps the town's climatological defiance of summer) with a three-day carnival. There are boat races on Nakki Lake, fireworks and traditional music and dances.

Mango Madness

Mangoes are indigenous to India, which might be why they're so ridiculously good here. The season starts in March, but in May the fruit is sweet, juicy and everywhere. A hundred varieties grow here, but the Alphonso is known as 'king'.

Ramadan (Ramazan)

Thirty days of dawn-to-dusk fasting mark the ninth month of the Islamic calendar. Muslims traditionally turn their attention to God, with a focus on prayer and purification. Ramadan begins around 7 June 2016, 27 May 2017 and 16 May 2018.

July

Now it's really raining, with many a dusty road becoming an impassable quagmire. But you may be tempted by the reduced accommodation rates and smaller crowds.

Brothers & Sisters

On Raksha Bandhan (Narial Purnima), girls fix amulets known as *rakhis* to the wrists of brothers and close male friends to protect them in the coming year. Brothers reciprocate with gifts and promises to take care of their sisters.

Eid al-Fitr

Muslims celebrate the end of Ramadan with three days of festivities, starting 30 days after the start of the fast.

August

It's very much monsoon season and the relief is palpable. In a good season there's copious but not constant rainfall, and temperatures are noticeably lower, but still steamy.

Independence Day

This public holiday on 15 August marks the anniversary of India's independence from Britain in 1947. Celebrations are a countrywide expression of patriotism, with flag-hoisting ceremonies (the biggest one is in Delhi), parades and patriotic cultural programs.

Teej

The festival of Teej celebrates the arrival of the monsoon, and the marriage of Parvati to Shiva. Three-day celebrations across Rajasthan, particularly Jaipur, culminate in a street procession of the Teej idol.

September

The rain begins to ease, though temperatures are still high. By the end of September, Rajasthan and Delhi are all but finished with the monsoon.

Ganesh's Birthday

Hindus celebrate Ganesh Chaturthi, the birth of the elephant-headed god, with verve, particularly in Ranthambhore Fort. Thousands gather at the abandoned fort and clay idols of Ganesh are paraded. Ganesh Chaturthi may also be in August.

PLAN YOUR TRIP MONTH BY MONTH

PLAN YOUR TRIP MONTH BY MONTH

★ Navratri

This Hindu 'Festival of Nine Nights', leading up to Dussehra celebrates the goddess Durga in all her incarnations. Special dances are performed, and the goddesses Lakshmi and Saraswati are also celebrated. Navratri may fall in October.

★ Dussehra

Colourful Dussehra celebrates the victory of the Hindu god Rama over the demon-king Ravana and the triumph of good over evil. Dussehra is big in Kota, where effigies of Ravana are ritually burned. This festival may fall in October.

October

Occasional heavy showers aside, this is when North India starts to get its travel mojo on. October brings festivals, national park openings and more comfortable temperatures, with post-monsoon lushness.

★ Gandhi's Birthday

The national holiday of Gandhi Jayanti is a solemn celebration of Mohandas Gandhi's birth, on 2 October, with prayer meetings at his cremation site in Delhi (Raj Ghat). Schools and businesses close for the day. (p41)

★ Diwali

In the lunar month of Kartika, in October or November, Hindus celebrate Diwali for five days, giving gifts, lighting fireworks, and burning lamps to lead

JEREMY RICHARDS / GETTY IMAGES ©

CHRISTER FREDRIKSSON / GETTY IMAGES ©

Top: Jaipur Elephant Festival (p18)
Bottom: Birdwatching, Bharatpur's Keoladeo National Park (p124)

Lord Rama home from exile. This is India's main holiday time and it is hard to get a transport seat or a hotel room without a booking.

November

The climate is blissful, with warm days and cooler nights. The peak season is getting into full swing. Lower temperatures mean higher prices and more tourist buses.

✨ Pushkar Camel Fair

Rajasthan's premier cultural event takes place in the Hindu lunar month of Kartika (October or November). As well as camel trading, there is horse and cattle trading and an amazing fairground atmosphere. It culminates with ritual bathing in Pushkar's holy lake. (p136)

December

December is peak tourist season for a reason: the daytime weather is glorious, the humidity is low and the nights are cool. The mood is festive and it seems everyone is getting married.

⊙ Weddings

Marriage season peaks in December, and you may see a *baraat* (bridegroom's procession), replete with white horse and brass band, on your travels. Across the country, loud music and spectacular parties are the way they roll, with brides in *mehndi* (ornate henna) and pure gold.

🏃 Birdwatching

Many of India's spectacular winter migrants complete their travels and set up nesting colonies. Keoladeo Ghana National Park is an internationally renowned wetland and birdwatching mecca. (p124)

🏃 Camel Treks in Rajasthan

The cool winter (November to February) is the time to mount a camel and ride through the Rajasthani sands. See the Thar Desert from a whole new perspective: observe gazelles, make dinner over an open fire and camp out in the dunes.

✨ Prophet Mohammed's Birthday

The Islamic festival of Eid-Milad-un-Nabi celebrates the birth of the Prophet Mohammed with prayers and processions. It falls in the third month of the Islamic calendar: around 24 December 2015, 12 December 2016 and 1 December 2017.

Itineraries

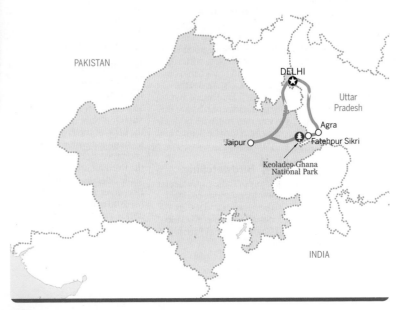

PAKISTAN

DELHI

Uttar
Pradesh

Agra

Jaipur

Fatehpur Sikri

Keoladeo Ghana
National Park

INDIA

1 WEEK **The Golden Triangle**

One route is so well loved it even has a name: the Golden Triangle. This classic Delhi–Agra–Jaipur trip can be squeezed into a single week.

Spend a day or two in **Delhi**, finding your feet and seeing the big-draw sights, such as the magnificent Mughal Red Fort and Jama Masjid, India's largest mosque. Then catch a convenient train to **Agra** to spend a day being awed by the world's most extravagant monument to love, the Taj Mahal, and exploring the mighty Agra Fort. Only an hour away is **Fatehpur Sikri**, a beautiful Mughal city dating from the apogee of Mughal power. It is amazingly well preserved and deserves a full day of exploring.

If you have time, take a rural respite at **Keoladeo Ghana National Park**, one of the world's foremost bird reserves. Having relaxed at this beautiful and rewarding place, you can then take a train to **Jaipur**. Spend a couple of days in and around Rajasthan's hectic, dusky-pink capital, seeing the City Palace and Amber Fort, and stocking up on blue pottery, dazzling jewellery and Rajasthani puppets before heading back to Delhi.

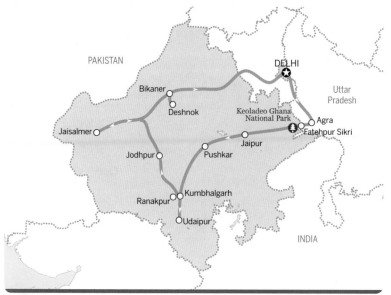

 **Royal Rajasthan**

With a fortnight to spare, you can forget triangles and go all out for a multifaceted loop taking in Rajasthan's most spectacular cities, all erstwhile capitals of former princely states, boasting fairy-tale palaces and stern fortresses.

You will most likely start from the nation's capital of **Delhi** to see the Mughal monuments, such as the massive Red Fort. No trip to India is complete without a visit to the Taj Mahal at **Agra**. Spend two days here viewing the Taj during the day, at night and from the maze-like Agra Fort. Spend a day exploring the ghost city of **Fatehpur Sikri**, before heading to the birdwatching mecca that is **Keoladeo Ghana National Park**. Next stop is the pink city of **Jaipur**, where you will want to spend two or three days exploring the palaces of Jaipur and Amber.

From Jaipur, take a short trip to the sacred lake of **Pushkar**, where you can release your inner hippie or attend the camel fair. Move on to the romantic lake-town of **Udaipur**, visiting the fine City Palace and the impressive Jagdish Temple as well as doing some shopping and relaxing on rooftops while peering at the lake and its famous palace. From Udaipur head towards the extraordinary, bustling, blue city of Jodhpur. Take time to stop at the milk-white Jain temple complex of **Ranakpur** and the isolated, dramatic fortifications of **Kumbhalgarh** – as they are fairly close together, you can visit them en route to Jodhpur within a day. In **Jodhpur**, visit the spectacular Mehrangarh, a fort that towers protectively over the city like a storybook fortress.

Next take an overnight train to the Golden City, **Jaisalmer**, a giant sandcastle in the desert, with its beautiful Jain temples and exquisite merchants' *havelis* (traditional, ornately decorated mansions). Take a short camel safari through the bewitching landscape of sweeping dunes and sleep under the stars. If you have the time, break your journey back to Delhi with a stop in the desert city of **Bikaner**, home of the impregnable Junagarh Fort, and nearest city to the famous rat temple of **Deshnok**.

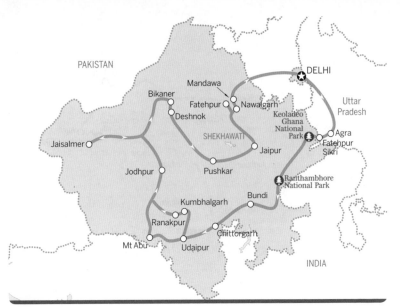

A Month-Long Sojourn

A month will allow you to explore Delhi, Agra and Rajasthan to their fullest extent, with plenty of time to linger along the way whenever a particular destination takes your fancy.

After arriving in **Delhi** and exploring the city sights, take the train down to **Agra** to gaze at the picture-perfect Taj Mahal, explore Agra Fort and have a day-trip out to the abandoned Mughal city of **Fatehpur Sikri**. To experience Rajasthan's wild side, first head to the World Heritage–listed birdwatching paradise of **Keoladeo Ghana National Park**, where the sheer numbers of nesting birdlife will astound you. This can be followed by a tiger safari or three at **Ranthambhore National Park**, one of your best bets of spotting a tiger in all India.

Take a Kota-bound train southwest for a stop at the charming small town of **Bundi**, to explore the crumbling palace. From here, it is a short train ride to **Chittorgarh**, where one of Rajasthan's most impressive fortresses occupies a mountain plateau. Next stop is **Udaipur**, where you can relax from your travels with a few easy days of sightseeing, elegant dining and souvenir shopping.

From Udaipur it's worth side-tripping to **Mt Abu** to see the magnificent Delwara Temples before going north to Jodhpur. Alternatively, head north to Jodhpur, stopping on the way to see the magnificent fort at **Kumbhalgarh** and the Jain temples of **Ranakpur**. From **Jodhpur** it's an easy train or bus ride to **Jaisalmer**, the desert town with a romantic picturesque fort rising from the golden sands. Here you can spend a few days exploring *havelis* and palaces, before taking an overnight camel trek into the desert. After Jaisalmer, head to **Bikaner**.

Travel south from Bikaner, stopping at the fascinating rat temple of **Deshnok** before coming to rest at the sacred pilgrimage town of **Pushkar**. At Pushkar you may be in time for the famous camel festival; otherwise, just relax for a few days and soak in the serenity.

From Pushkar it's a short hop to **Jaipur**, with its fabulous citadel at Amber and great shopping. Head north to Shekhawati for a few days, inspecting *havelis* at **Mandawa**, **Nawalgarh** and **Fatehpur**, before returning to Delhi.

Plan Your Trip

Travel with Children

Fascinating, frustrating, thrilling and fulfilling – India is as much of an adventure for children as it is for parents. Though the sensory overload may be, at times, overwhelming for younger kids, the colours, scents, sights and sounds of India more than compensate by setting young imaginations ablaze.

India for Kids

Being a family-oriented society, India is a very child-friendly destination. That doesn't necessarily translate into a child-friendly travel destination, however. Smaller children, in particular, will be constantly coddled, offered treats and smiles and warm welcomes. And while all this is fabulous for outgoing children it may prove tiring, or even disconcerting or frightening, for those of a more retiring disposition. Remember, though, that the attention your children will inevitably receive is almost always good-natured; kids are the centre of life in many Indian households, and your own will be treated – usually for better rather than worse – just the same.

Eating

Feeding your brood is fairly easy in the well-touristed parts of India and you'll find Western dishes with a bit of searching. Look out for multicuisine restaurants, should your little one be saying 'not curry again'.

Adventurous eaters will delight in experimenting with a vast range of tastes and textures: paneer (unfermented cheese) dishes, simple dhal (curried lentil dish), creamy korma, buttered naan (tandoor-baked bread), pilau (rice) and

Best Regions for Kids

Agra & Fatehpur Sikri

Give them a few stories of the *Arabian Nights* before they lay eyes on the Taj Mahal and let their imaginations soar. A visit to nearby Fatehpur Sikri will also please the creative young mind.

Keoladeo Ghana National Park

Here, the kids can let go of your hand and jump on a bike. Let them ride along the car-free road and tick off as many feathered species as they can.

Ranthambhore National Park

What kid won't be thrilled to see a wild tiger? And there's a mesmerising jungle fortress straight out of Kipling's *The Jungle Book* to explore.

Amber

Riding the elephants up to Amber Fort is great – and topped only by spending time feeding and caring for them afterwards at a nearby elephant camp.

Sam Sand Dunes

Riding a camel across the sand dunes should be easy after mastering an elephant...surely?

momos (steamed or fried dumplings) are all firm favourites. Few children, no matter how culinarily unadventurous, can resist the finger-food fun of a vast South Indian *dosa* (rice pancake).

Sleeping

India offers such an array of accommodation – from budget boxes to former palaces of the maharajas – that you're bound to be able to find something that will appeal to the whole family. Hotels will almost always come up with an extra bed or two for a nominal charge. Most places won't mind fitting one or maybe two children into a regular-sized double room along with their parents. Any more is pushing your luck – look for two rooms that have an adjoining door.

On the Road

Travel in India can be arduous for the whole family. Plan fun, easy days to follow longer car, bus or train rides, and pack plenty of diversions. An iPod, iPad or laptop with a stock of movies downloaded make invaluable travel companions, as do books, light toys and games. The golden rule is to expect your best-laid plans to take a hit every now and then. Travelling on the road with kids in India requires constant vigilance. Be especially cautious of road traffic – pedestrians are at the bottom of the feeding chain and road rules are routinely ignored.

Health

Health care of a decent standard, even in the most traveller-frequented parts of India, is not as easily available as you might be used to. The recommended way to track down a doctor at short notice is through your hotel. In general, the most common concerns for on-the-road parents include heat rash, skin complaints such as impetigo, insect bites or stings and diarrhoea. If your child takes special medication, bring along an adequate stock in case it's not easily found locally.

Children's Highlights

Fortress Splendours

Jaipur (p122) Take an elephant ride into the majestic citadel of Amber.

Jaisalmer (p181) Re-create the *Arabian Nights* in Jaisalmer's desert fortress.

Jodhpur (p171) Amaze their imaginations with the story-book fort and palace.

Cats & Birds

Ranthambhore National Park (p138) Tigers, jungles, jeep safaris and an abandoned mountain-top fort.

Keoladeo Ghana National Park (p124) The chance to go cycling on car-free roads.

Planning

Before You Go

Remember to visit your doctor to discuss vaccinations, health advisories and other health-related issues involving your children well in advance of travel. For helpful hints, see Lonely Planet's *Travel with Children*, and the Kids To Go section of Lonely Planet's Thorn Tree forum (lonelyplanet.com/thorntree).

What to Pack

If you're travelling with a baby or toddler, there are several items worth packing in quantity: nappies, nappy rash cream, extra bottles, wet wipes, infant formula and jars or dehydrated packets of favourite foods. You can get these items in many parts of India too, but often at premium prices, and brands may be unfamiliar. Another good idea is a fold-up baby bed; a pushchair, though, is superfluous, since there are few places with pavements even enough to use it. For older children, make sure you bring sturdy footwear, a hat, child-friendly insect repellent and sun lotion.

Regions at a Glance

Rajasthan, Delhi and Agra are India in microcosm. Its history rises out of the landscape, from the monuments of the Mughal empire to the forts and palaces of the Rajput maharajas. In a colourful country, Rajasthan might be the most dazzling of India's regions – there are festivals galore, tigers to spot, desert vistas to explore by camel, and enough arts and crafts to make you wish you had a bigger luggage allowance.

Delhi

Mughal Sites
Bazaars
Food

Monumental History

Wander around Delhi's sprawling Red Fort and Jama Masjid, and the streets of labyrinthine Old Delhi, and you'll soon gain a sense of the glories of the Mughal empire. Humayan's domed tomb was the precursor to the Taj Mahal.

Shopping

All of India's riches sparkle in Delhi's bazaars and emporiums but you need to be prepared to haggle. You can also browse designer boutiques, old musical instrument shops and some of the country's best bookstores.

Local Cuisine

Delhi is one of the better places in India to taste everything from cutting-edge creative Indian cuisine in luscious five-star hotels, to fresh-from-the-fire, delectable *Dilli-ka-Chaat* (Delhi street food).

p30

Agra & the Taj Mahal

Architecture
History
Shopping

Romantic Locations

The Taj Mahal is as breath-takingly proportioned and serenely beautiful as the brochures would have you believe. Follow its moods throughout the day and into the night with a viewing under a full moon.

Mughal Heritage

Peering at the Taj from where Shah Jahan was imprisoned in Agra Fort gives a whole new perspective on the famous tomb, while wandering the empty spaces of Fatehpur Sikri, Emperor Akbar's spectacular but poorly sited city is also stunningly evocative.

Crafts

Agra is renowned for marble items inlaid with semi-precious stones, recreating the amazing pietra dura work that embellishes the Taj Mahal.

p78

Rajasthan

Forts & Palaces
Animal Encounters
Festivals

Rajput Grandeur

The splendid palaces of Rajasthan demonstrate the wealth and power of the royal Rajputs, who once dominated the region. They boast magnificent architecture, from Jaipur's Hawa Mahal to the graceful lakeside glories of Udaipur.

On Safari

Rajasthan is a great place to get closer to nature. Track tigers through Ranthambhore National Park, go bird-spotting by bicycle in Keoladeo or sail into the sands on your ship of the desert with a camel safari from Jaisalmer or Bikaner.

Holidays & Celebrations

Heading the list is the celebrated camel fair in the tiny Hindu pilgrimage town of Pushkar. Other show-stoppers include Jaipur's famous literature and elephant festivals, and the Urs, the anniversary of the death of a sufi saint in nearby Ajmer.

p102

On the Road

Delhi
p30
⭐

Agra & the Taj Mahal
p78
○

Rajasthan
p102

Delhi

📋 011 / POP 25 MILLION / ELEV 293M

Best Places to Eat

➡ Hotel Saravana Bhavan (p62)

➡ Bukhara (p64)

➡ Indian Accent (p65)

➡ Alkauser (p63)

➡ Sodabottleopenerwala (p63)

Best Places to Stay

➡ Lodhi (p58)

➡ Hotel Amax Inn (p55)

➡ Devna (p59)

➡ Bloom Rooms (p57)

Why Go?

Mystery, magic, mayhem. Welcome to Delhi, City of Djinns, and 25 million people. Like an eastern Rome, India's capital is littered with the relics of lost empires. A succession of armies stormed across the Indo-Gangetic plain and imprinted their identity onto the vanquished city, before vanishing into rubble and ruin. Modern Delhi is a chaotic tapestry of medieval fortifications, Mughal mausoleums, dusty bazaars, colonial-era town planning, and mega malls.

Travellers sometimes leave Delhi underwhelmed, after ticking off the sights and tussling with the touts. But give the city a chance and you might fall in love. It's often the lesser-known corners that are most rewarding, such as Lodi Gardens at dusk, the *qawwali* (Islamic devotional singing) at Nizamuddin or the great fort of Purana Qila. A recommended way to glimpse beneath the surface is to take one of the city's tours, from a former street child's view of Old Delhi to a cycle tour along the Yamuna.

When to Go
Delhi

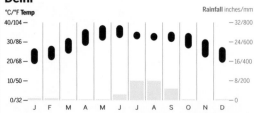

Oct–Mar Delhi at its best: warm with clear skies. Morning fog can play havoc with flight schedules.

May–Aug The months to avoid – hot, humid and uncomfortable.

Jun–Sep Monsoon season sees high temperatures and regular rain – a sticky combination.

History

Hindus claim Delhi as the site of ancient Indraprastha, home of the Pandavas in the Mahabharata, and excavations near the Purana Qila have revealed evidence of human habitation dating back 3000 years. The name Delhi is linked to the Maurya king Dhilu, who ruled the region in the 1st century BC, but for most of its existence, the city has been known by the names given to it by its conquerors.

The first city for which clear archaeological evidence remains was Lal Kot, or Qila Rai Pithora, founded by the Hindu king Prithvi Raj Chauhan in the 12th century. The city fell to Afghan invaders in 1191, and for the next 600 years, Delhi was ruled by a succession of Muslim sultans and emperors. The first, Qutub-ud-din Aibak, razed the Hindu city and used its stones to construct Mehrauli and the towering Qutb Minar.

Qutub-ud-din Aibak's Mamluk (Slave) dynasty was quickly replaced by the Khilji dynasty, following a coup. The Khiljis constructed a new capital at Siri, northeast of Mehrauli, supplied with water from the royal tank at Hauz Khas. Following another coup, the Tughlaq sultans seized the reins, creating a new fortified capital at Tughlaqabad, and two more cities – Jahanpanah and Ferozabad – for good measure.

The Tughlaq dynasty fell after Tamerlane stormed through town in 1398, opening the door for the Sayyid and Lodi dynasties, the last of the Delhi sultanates, whose tombs are scattered around the Lodi Gardens. The scene was set for the arrival of the Mughals. Babur, the first Mughal emperor, seized Delhi in 1526, and a new capital rose at Shergarh (the present-day Purana Qila), presided over by his son, Humayun.

Frantic city building continued throughout the Mughal period. Shah Jahan gained the Peacock Throne in 1627 and raised a new city, Shahjahanabad, centred on the Red Fort. The Mughal city fell in 1739, to the Persian Nadir Shah, and the dynasty went into steep decline. The last Mughal emperor, Bahadur Shah Zafar, was exiled to Burma (Myanmar) by the British for his role in the 1857 First War of Independence (Indian Uprising); there were some new rulers in town.

When the British shifted their capital to Delhi from increasingly rebellious Calcutta in 1911, it was time for another bout of construction. The architect Edwin Lutyens drew up plans for a new city of wide boulevards and stately administrative buildings to accommodate the colonial government – New Delhi was born.

Delhi has faced numerous challenges since Independence, from the violence of Partition to the deepening gulf between rich and poor, but the city on the Yamuna continues to flourish, with its new satellite cities adding ever increasing skyscrapers to the city's outskirts.

DELHI'S TOP FESTIVALS

To confirm dates contact India Tourism Delhi (p71).

Republic Day (⊘ 26 Jan) A spectacular military parade in Rajpath.

Beating of the Retreat (⊘ 29 Jan) More military pageantry in Rajpath.

St.Art (⊘ Jan/Feb) Street-art festival.

Independence Day (⊘ 15 Aug) India celebrates Independence from Britain and the prime minister addresses the nation from the Red Fort.

Dussehra (Durga Puja; ⊘ Sep/Oct) Hindus celebrate the victory of good over evil with parades of colourful effigies.

Ananya Dance Festival (⊘ Oct) Free classical Indian dance festival takes place at Purana Qila.

Qutb Festival (⊘ Oct/Nov) Several days of Sufi singing and classical music and dance at the Qutb Minar complex.

Diwali (⊘ Nov/Dec) Fireworks across the city for the festival of light.

Delhi International Arts Festival (DIAF; ⊘ Dec) Three weeks of exhibitions, performing arts, films, literature and culinary events at venues Delhi-wide.

Delhi Highlights

1 Seeing how Mughals lived in the **Red Fort** (p34), the sandstone palace of the last emperors of Delhi

2 Wandering in peace around the architectural perfection of **Humayun's Tomb** (p43), inspiration for the Taj Mahal

3 Standing at the base of the magnificent **Qutb Minar** (p76), then plunge into the overgrown ruins of neighbouring **Mehrauli Archaeological Park** (p77)

4 Losing yourself in the mazelike **bazaars** (p68) of Old Delhi

5 Experiencing a living piece of Islamic history while hearing *qawwali* (Islamic devotional singing)

Dr KB Hedgewar Marg

Yamuna River

Anand Vihar ISBT (3km)

Indraprastha Marg

Hapur Bypass

MANJU KA TILA

SEELAMPUR

Welcome Ⓜ

Seelampur Ⓜ

Shastri Park Ⓜ

Marginal Bandh Rd

Akshardham Ⓜ

Aksardham Temple Ⓦ

Yamuna Bank Ⓜ

Vidhan Sabha Ⓜ

CIVIL LINES

Civil Lines Ⓜ

Tis Hazari Ⓜ

Kashmere Gate Ⓜ

Delhi Train Station (Old Delhi) Ⓡ

Lothian Cemetery

Red Fort

OLD DELHI

PARDA BAGH

Hindi Park

Ring Rd (MG Rd)

GANDHI DARSHAN

Indraprastha Ⓜ

Pragati Maidan Train Station Ⓡ

Tilak Bridge Train Station Ⓡ

Pragati Maidan Ⓡ

PRAGATI MAIDAN

Boating Lake

See Old Delhi Map (p38)

KAMLA NAGAR

Delhi University

Sabzi Mandi Train Station Ⓡ

Pratap Nagar Ⓜ

SABZI MANDI

Kishan Ganj Train Station Ⓡ

Saral Rohilla Train Station Ⓡ

SADAR BAZAAR

Sadar Bazaar Train Station Ⓡ

RAM NAGAR

Chandni Chowk Ⓜ

Old Delhi's Bazaars ④

Chawri Bazar Ⓜ

New Delhi Train Station

New Delhi Ⓜ

Minto Bridge Train Station

Shivaji Bridge Train Station Ⓡ

DARYAGANJ

NEW DELHI

Rajiv Chowk Ⓜ

Barakhamba Road Ⓜ

Mandi House Ⓜ

India Gate

Khan Market Ⓜ

KAKA NAGAR

SUNDER NAGAR

Qutb Rd

PAHARGANJ

Jhandewalan Ⓜ

Karol Bagh

See Paharganj Map (p56)

State Emporiums Ⓜ

Imperial ⑧

Connaught Place

See Connaught Place Map (p42)

Central Secretariat Ⓜ

MEENA BAGH

Motilal Nehru Place

Prithviraj Rd

Grand Trunk Rd

KAROL BAGH

Rajendra Place Ⓜ

RAJENDRA NAGAR

Pusa Rd

Pusa Hill Forest

Upper Ridge Rd

See New Delhi & Around Map (p46)

PRESIDENT'S ESTATE

Mughal Gardens

Willingdon Cres

Udyog Bhawan Ⓜ

Delhi Polo Club

Mahavir Jayanti Park

ASHOK VIHAR

Keshav Puram Ⓜ

Kanhiya Nagar Ⓜ

Inderlok Ⓜ

Ring Rd

New Rohtak Rd

Shastri Nagar

Daya Basti

PATEL NAGAR

Patel Nagar Train Station Ⓡ

Shadipur Ⓜ

Patel Nagar Ⓜ

Patel Rd

Kirti Nagar Ⓡ

Kirti Train Station Ⓡ

NEW RAJENDRA NAGAR

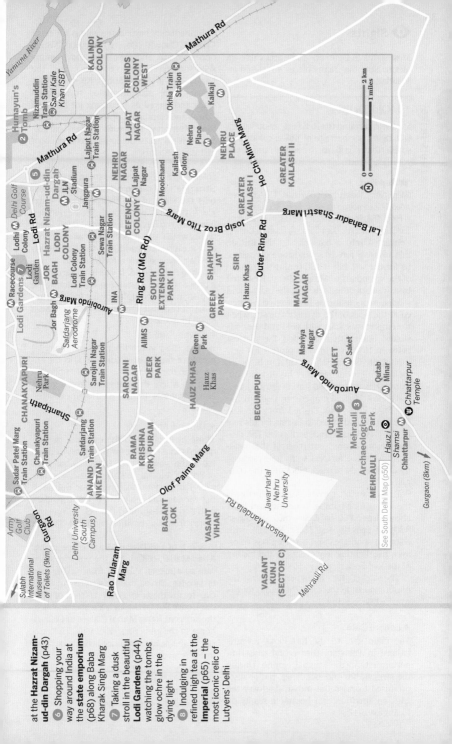

◉ Sights

Most sights in Delhi are easily accessible via metro. Note that many places are closed on Monday.

◉ Old Delhi

Sprawling around the Red Fort, medieval-era Old Delhi is a barrage of noise, colour and smells that bombard the senses and make your head whirl.

★ Red Fort
FORT

(Map p38; Indian/foreigner/child ₹10/250/free, video ₹25, combined museum ticket ₹5, audio guide in Hindi ₹68, English or Korean ₹113; ⊘ dawn-dusk Tue-Sun, museums 9am-5pm; Ⓜ Chandni Chowk) Converted into a barracks by the British, this massive fort is a sandstone carcass of its former self, but it still conjures a picture of the splendour of Mughal Delhi. Protected by a dramatic 18m-high wall, the marble and sandstone monuments here were constructed at the peak of the dynasty's power, when the empire was flush with gold and precious stones. Shah Jahan founded the fortress between 1638 and 1648 to protect his new capital city of Shahjahanabad, but he never took up full residence, after his disloyal son, Aurangzeb, imprisoned him in Agra Fort.

The last Mughal emperor of Delhi, Bahadur Shah Zafar, was flushed from the Red Fort in 1857 and exiled to Burma for his role in the First War of Independence. The new conquerors cleared out most of the buildings inside the fortress walls and replaced them with ugly barrack blocks for the colonial army.

Every evening, except Monday, the fort is the setting for a bombastic **sound-and-light show** (Tue-Fri ₹60, Sat & Sun ₹80; ⊘ in English 8.30pm & 9pm May-Aug, 7.30pm Nov-Jan), with coloured spotlights and a portentous voice-over, highlighting key events in the history of the Red Fort.

The ticket for foreigners covers the museums inside the fort. The audio tour is worthwhile to bring the site to life.

➡ Lahore Gate

The main gate to the fort looks towards Lahore in Pakistan, the second most important city in the Mughal empire. During the struggle for Independence, nationalists promised to raise the Indian flag over the gate, an ambition that became a reality on 15 August 1947.

Immediately beyond the gate is the regal **Chatta Chowk** (Covered Bazaar), which once sold silk and jewels, but now mainly sells souvenirs. At the eastern end of the bazaar, the arched **Naubat Khana** (Drum House) once accommodated royal musicians and served as a parking lot for royal horses and elephants. Upstairs is the **Indian War Memorial Museum** (⊘ 8am-5pm Tue-Sun), with a fearsome-looking collection of historic weaponry.

A short stroll north, housed in a colonial-era block, the **Museum on India's Struggle for Freedom** (⊘ 9am-5pm Tue-Sun) tells the story of the Independence struggle. If you walk on through the dilapidated barracks, you'll reach a deserted *baoli* (stepwell), which the British used as a prison, and a causeway leading to the **Salimgarh** (⊘ 10am-5pm Tue-Sun), a fortress built by Salim Shah Suri in 1546. It was likewise used as a prison, first by Aurangzeb, and later by the British; it's still occupied by the Indian army, but you can visit the ruined mosque and a small museum.

➡ Diwan-i-Am

Beyond the Naubat Khana, a monumental arcade of sandstone columns marks the entrance to the Diwan-i-Am (Hall of Public Audience), where the emperor greeted guests and dignitaries from a pietra-dura covered balcony.

➡ Diwan-i-Khas

Those in favour with the emperor, or conquered rivals begging for peace, were admitted to the white marble Diwan-i-Khas (Hall of Private Audience). This delicate, wedding cake–like pavilion features some outstanding carving and inlay work. The legendary gold and jewel-studded Peacock Throne was looted from the pavilion by Nadir Shah in 1739.

South of the Diwan-i-Khas is the dainty **Khas Mahal**, containing the emperor's private apartments, shielded from prying eyes by lace-like carved marble screens. An artificial stream, the *nahr-i-bihisht* (river of paradise), once flowed through the apartments to the adjacent **Rang Mahal** (Palace of Colour), home to the emperor's chief wife. The exterior of the palace was once lavishly painted; inside is an elegant lotus-shaped fountain.

➡ Mumtaz Mahal

South of the Rang Mahal, this pavilion once contained the quarters for other women of the royal household. Today it houses the **Museum of Archaeology** (⊙9am-5pm Tue-Sun), with royal vestments, miniature paintings, astrolabes, Mughal scrolls and a shirt inscribed with verses from the Quran to protect the emperor from assassins.

➡ **Royal Baths & Moti Masjid**

North of the Diwan-i-Khas are the royal baths, which once contained a sauna and hot baths for the royal family, and the Moti Masjid (Pearl Mosque), an elegant private place of worship for the emperor. The outer walls align with the fort walls, while the inner walls are slightly askew to correctly align with Mecca. Both are closed to visitors, but you can peer through the screen windows.

➡ **Shahi Burj**

North of the royal baths is the Shahi Burj, a three-storey octagonal tower, where Shah Jahan planned the running of his empire. In front of the tower is what remains of an elegant formal garden, centred on the Zafar Mahal, a sandstone pavilion surrounded by a deep, empty water tank.

Chandni Chowk AREA

(Map p38; Ⓜ Chandni Chowk) Old Delhi's main thoroughfare is a chaotic shopping street, mobbed by hawkers, motorcycles, stray dogs and porters and with narrow lanes running off it offering the full medieval bazaar experience. In the time of Shah Jahan, a tree-lined canal ran down its centre, reflecting the moon, hence the name Chandni Chowk, or 'moonlight place'.

Digambara Jain Temple JAIN TEMPLE

(Map p38; Chandni Chowk; ⊙6am-noon & 6-9pm; Ⓜ Chandni Chowk) In the cluster of temples at the Red Fort end of Chandni Chowk, the scarlet Digambara Jain Temple houses a fascinating **bird hospital** (by donation; ⊙10am-5pm) established to further the Jain principle of preserving all life, with a capacity of 10,000. Only vegetarian birds are admitted (up to 60 per day), though predators are treated as outpatients. Remove shoes and leather items before entering the temple.

Nearby, the 18th-century **Sisganj Gurdwara** marks the the martrydom site of the ninth Sikh guru, Tegh Bahadur, executed by Aurangzeb in 1675 for resisting conversion to Islam.

Fatehpuri Masjid MOSQUE

(Map p38; Chandni Chowk) The western end of Chandni Chowk is book-ended by the mid-17th-century Fatehpuri Masjid, built by one of Shah Jahan's wives; it was sold to a Hindu nobleman by the British for ₹19,000 and returned to Muslim worship in exchange for four villages in 1877.

Small green buses shuttle between Digambara Jain Temple and Fatehpuri Masjid (₹5).

(Continued on page 40)

DELHI'S MIGHTY MEN

Wander the districts north of Kashmere Gate in Old Delhi and you may notice a disproportionately high number of muscular men. No, it's not your imagination. This dusty quarter is the favoured stomping ground for Delhi's traditional mud wrestlers. *Kushti*, or *pehlwani*, is a full-contact martial art, fusing elements of yoga and philosophy with combat and intense physical training.

Young men enrol at *akharas* (training centres) in their early teens, and follow a strict regimen of daily exercise, climbing ropes, lifting weights and hauling logs to build up the necessary muscle bulk for this intensely physical sport. Even diet and lifestyle is strictly controlled; sex, tobacco and alcohol are forbidden, and wrestlers live together in rustic accommodation under the supervision of a coach who doubles as spiritual guide.

Bouts take place on freshly tilled earth, adding an extra element of grit to proceedings. As with other types of wrestling, the aim is to pin your opponent to the ground, but fights often continue until one wrestler submits or collapses from exhaustion. At regional championships, wrestlers compete for golden *gadas* (ceremonial clubs), a tribute to the favoured weapon of Hanuman, patron deity of wrestling.

Most *akharas* welcome spectators at the daily dawn and dusk training sessions, so long as this doesn't interfere with training. Seek permission first to avoid offending these muscle-bound gents – the blog www.kushtiwrestling.blogspot.com is a good introduction to the sport and the main *akharas*. Indomania Cultural Tours (p54) has Yamaya tours that also take in an *akhara*.

Red Fort

HIGHLIGHTS

The main entrance to the Red Fort is through **Lahore Gate** ❶ – the bastion in front of it was built by Aurangzeb for increased security. You can still see bullet marks from 1857 on the gate.

Walk through the Chatta Chowk (Covered Bazaar), which once sold silks and jewellery to the nobility; beyond it lies **Naubat Khana** ❷, a russet-red building, which houses Hathi Pol (Elephant Gate), so called because visitors used to dismount from their elephants or horses here as a sign of respect. From here it's straight on to the **Diwan-i-Am** ❸, the Hall of Public Audiences. Behind this are the private palaces, the **Khas Mahal** ❹ and the **Diwan-i-Khas** ❺. Entry to this Hall of Private Audiences, the fort's most expensive building, was only permitted to the officials of state. Nearby is the **Moti Masjid (Pearl Mosque)** ❻ and south is the **Mumtaz Mahal** ❼, housing the Museum of Archaeology, or you can head north, where the Red Fort gardens are dotted by palatial pavilions and old British barracks. Here you'll find the **baoli** ❽, a spookily deserted water tank. Another five minutes' walk – across a road, then a railway bridge – brings you to the island fortress of **Salimgarh** ❾.

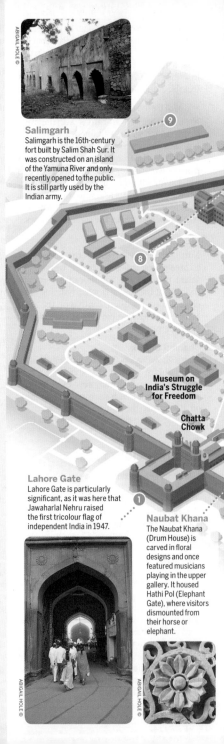

Salimgarh
Salimgarh is the 16th-century fort built by Salim Shah Sur. It was constructed on an island of the Yamuna River and only recently opened to the public. It is still partly used by the Indian army.

Museum on India's Struggle for Freedom

Chatta Chowk

Lahore Gate
Lahore Gate is particularly significant, as it was here that Jawaharlal Nehru raised the first tricolour flag of independent India in 1947.

Naubat Khana
The Naubat Khana (Drum House) is carved in floral designs and once featured musicians playing in the upper gallery. It housed Hathi Pol (Elephant Gate), where visitors dismounted from their horse or elephant.

TOP TIPS

» **To avoid crowds**, get here early or late in the day; avoid weekends and public holidays.

» **An atmospheric way** to see the Red Fort is by night; you can visit after dark if you attend the nightly Sound-&-Light Show.

Baoli
The Red Fort step well is seldom visited and is a hauntingly deserted place, even more so when you consider its chambers were used as cells by the British from August 1942.

Moti Masjid
The Moti Masjid (Pearl Mosque) was built by Aurangzeb in 1662 for his personal use. The domes were originally covered in copper, but the copper was removed and sold by the British.

Diwan-i-Khas
This was the most expensive building in the fort, consisting of white marble decorated with inlay work of cornelian and other stones. The screens overlooking what was once the river (now the ring road) were filled with coloured glass.

Baidon Pavilion

Zafar Mahal

Hammam

6

5

4

3

2

Rang Mahal

Mumtaz Mahal

7

PIT STOP
To refuel, head to Paratha Gali Wali, a foodstall-lined lane off Chandni Chowk noted for its many varieties of freshly made paratha (traditional flat bread).

Delhi Gate

← NORTH

Diwan-i-Am
These red sandstone columns were once covered in shell plaster, as polished and smooth as ivory, and in hot weather heavy red curtains were hung around the columns to block out the sun. It's believed the panels behind the marble throne were created by Florentine jeweller Austin de Bordeaux.

Khas Mahal
Most spectacular in the Emperor's private apartments is a beautiful marble screen at the northern end of the rooms; the 'Scales of Justice' are carved above it, suspended over a crescent, surrounded by stars and clouds.

Old Delhi

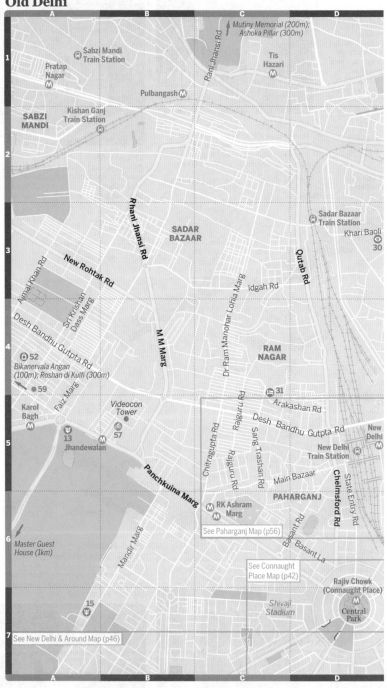

DELHI

Mutiny Memorial (200m);
Ashoka Pillar (300m)

Rani Jhansi Rd

Sabzi Mandi
Train Station

Pratap
Nagar Ⓜ

Tis
Hazari Ⓜ

Pulbangash Ⓜ

Kishan Ganj
Train Station Ⓡ

SABZI
MANDI

Sadar Bazaar
Train Station Ⓡ

Khari Baoli
◎
30

Rhani Jhansi Rd

SADAR
BAZAAR

Qutab Rd

New Rohtak Rd

Ajmal Khan Rd

Idgah Rd

Dr Ram Manohar Lohia Marg

Sri Krishan Das Marg

Desh Bandhu Gutpta Rd

M M Marg

RAM
NAGAR

Ⓐ 52
Bikanervala Angan
(100m); Roshan di Kulfi (300m)
● 59

Faiz Marg

Ⓐ 31

Arakashan Rd

Desh Bandhu Gutpta Rd

New
Delhi Ⓜ

Karol
Bagh Ⓜ

Videocon
Tower

Chitragupta Rd

Rajguru Rd

Pyaru Rd

Sang Trashan Rd

New Delhi
Train Station Ⓡ

Ⓜ

Ⓦ
13
Jhandewalan

Ⓐ
57

Rajguru Rd

Main Bazaar

PAHARGANJ

Chelmsford Rd

State Entry Rd

Panchkuina Marg

RK Ashram
Marg Ⓜ

See Paharganj Map (p56)

Mandir Marg

Basant Rd

Basant La

See Connaught
Place Map (p42)

Master Guest
House (1km)

Rajiv Chowk
(Connaught Place) Ⓜ

Shivaji
Stadium

Central
Park

Ⓦ
15

See New Delhi & Around Map (p46)

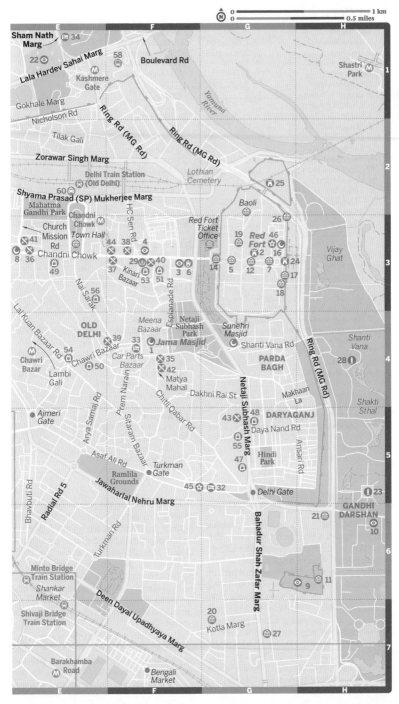

0 1 km
0 0.5 miles

Sham Nath Marg
34
22
Lala Hardev Sahai Marg
58
Boulevard Rd
Shastri Park
Kashmere Gate
Gokhale Marg
Nicholson Rd
Ring Rd (MG Rd)
Tilak Gali
Yamuna River
Ring Rd (MG Rd)
Zorawar Singh Marg
Delhi Train Station (Old Delhi)
Lothian Cemetery
25
60
Shyama Prasad (SP) Mukherjee Marg
Mahatma Gandhi Park
Chandni Chowk
Baoli
26
Red Fort Ticket Office
19
Red Fort
46
Church Mission Rd
Town Hall
HC Sen Rd
41
44 38 4
2
16
Vijay Ghat
8 36
Chandni Chowk
29 40
14 5
12 7
24
49
37 53 51
3 6
17
Kinari Bazaar
18
56
Nai Sarak
Meena Bazaar
Netaji Subhash Park
Sunehri Masjid
Shanti Vana
OLD DELHI
Esplanade Rd
Jama Masjid
Shanti Vana Rd
Lal Kuan Bazaar Rd
39
33
1
PARDA BAGH
28
54
Chawri Bazaar
Car Parts Bazaar
35
Chawri Bazar
50
Lambi Gali
42
Matya Mahal
Netaji Subhash Marg
Makhaan La
Shakti Sthal
Prem Narain
Dakhni Rai St
Arya Samaj Rd
Chitli Qabar Rd
48
DARYAGANJ
Ajmeri Gate
43
Daya Nand Rd
Sitaram Bazaar
Asaf Ali Rd
Turkman Gate
55
Hindi Park
Ansari Rd
Bhabuti Rd
Radial Rd 5
Ramlila Grounds
47
Jawaharlal Nehru Marg
45 32
Delhi Gate
23
GANDHI DARSHAN
21
Turkman Rd
10
Bahadur Shah Zafar Marg
Minto Bridge Train Station
Shankar Market
11
Shivaji Bridge Train Station
Deen Dayal Upadhyaya Marg
9
20
Barakhamba Road
Bengali Market
Kotla Marg
27

Old Delhi

(Continued from page 35)

★ **Jama Masjid** MOSQUE
(Map p38; camera & video each ₹300, tower ₹100; ☉ non-Muslims 8am-dusk, minaret 9am-5.30pm; Ⓜ Chawri Bazaar) A calm respite from the surrounding mayhem, India's largest mosque can hold 25,000 people. Towering over Old Delhi, the 'Friday Mosque' was Shah Jahan's final architectural opus, built between 1644 and 1658. It has three gateways, four angle towers and two minarets standing 40m high, and is constructed of alternating vertical strips of red sandstone and white marble. You can enter from gate 1 or 3. The only prayer session where non-Muslims may be present is at 7.45am.

Buy a ticket at the entrance to climb 121 steps up the narrow southern minaret (notices say that unaccompanied women are not permitted, but they may be allowed up with a 'guide' who'll expect a tip). From the top of the minaret, you can see one of the features that architect Edwin Lutyens incorporated into his design of New Delhi – the Jama Masjid, Connaught Place and Sansad Bhavan (Parliament House) are in a direct line.

Visitors should remove their shoes at the top of the stairs. There's no charge to enter the mosque, but you'll have to pay the camera charge whether you want to use your camera or not. Once you buy a camera ticket, you should be allowed to go out and re-enter later that day if you choose.

Raj Ghat
MONUMENT

(Map p38; ⊘6am-6pm) South of the Red Fort, situated on the banks of the Yamuna River, a simple black-marble platform marks the spot where Mahatma Gandhi was cremated following his assassination in 1948. It's a thought-provoking spot, inscribed with what are said to have been Gandhi's final words, *Hai Ram* (Oh, God). Across Kisan Ghat Rd is the **Gandhi Darshan** (⊘10am-5pm Mon-Sat) FREE, a huge pavilion displaying photos relating to the Mahatma.

Shanti Vana
MONUMENT

(Forest of Peace; Map p38) Jawaharlal Nehru, the first Indian prime minister, was cremated just to the north of Raj Ghat, at Shanti Vana, in 1964. The cremation sites of Nehru's daughter, Indira Gandhi, and grandsons Sanjay and Rajiv are lined up along the riverbank in their own memorial parks.

National Gandhi Museum
MUSEUM

(Map p38; ☑23311793; Raj Ghat; ⊘9.30am-5.30pm Tue-Sun) FREE A small but moving museum displaying historic photos and items such as Gandhi's spinning wheels and the dhoti (long loincloth) he was wearing at the time of his murder.

Feroz Shah Kotla
HISTORIC SITE

(Map p38; Bahadur Shah Zafar Marg; Indian/foreigner ₹5/100, video ₹25; ⊘dawn-dusk; Ⓜ Pragati Maidan) Ferozabad, the fifth city of Delhi, was built by Feroz Shah in 1354 as a replacement for Tughlaqabad. Ringed by crumbling fortifications are a huge mosque, a *baoli* (step-well), and the pyramid-like **Hawa Mahal**, topped by a 13m-high sandstone **Ashoka Pillar** inscribed with Ashoka's edicts. There's an otherworldly atmosphere to the ruins, which are still a place of worship – on Thursday afternoon, crowds gather to light candles and incense and leave bowls of milk to appease Delhi's *djinns* (invisible spirits). Shoes should be removed when entering the mosque and Hawa Mahal.

Shankar's International Dolls Museum
MUSEUM

(Map p38; ☑23316970; www.childrensbooktrust.com; Nehru House, Bahadur Shah Zafar Marg; adult/child ₹17/6; ⊘10am-6pm Tue-Sun) From tacky Spanish bullfighting figurines to graceful Japanese geisha dolls, this cutesy but engaging museum has a collection of 6500 dolls from 85 countries, from Brazil to Japan.

National Bal Bhavan
MUSEUM

(Map p38; www.nationalbalbhavan.nic.in; Kotla Marg; adult/child ₹5/free; ⊘9am-5.30pm Tue-Sat) Delhi's museum for children is a disorderly affair, with a toy train, animal enclosures, an exhibition on astrology and astronomy, and some delightful mini-dioramas showing key events in Indian history.

Nicholson Cemetery
CEMETERY

(Map p38; Lala Hardev Sahai Marg; ⊘8am-6pm summer, 9am-5pm winter; Ⓜ Kashmere Gate) Close to Kashmere Gate, this forgotten cemetery is the last resting place for hundreds of Delhi's colonial-era residents, many of whom perished in childhood. One famous (ex-)resident is Brigadier General John Nicholson, who died from injuries sustained while storming Delhi during the 1857 First War of Independence (Indian Uprising). At the time he was hailed as the 'Hero of Delhi,' but author William Dalrymple has described him as an 'imperial psychopath'.

Take the metro to nearby Pulbangash station to see the British-erected **Mutiny Memorial** (Rani Jhansi Rd) and an **Ashoka Pillar** (Rani Jhansi Rd), transported here by Feroz Shah.

Coronation Durbar Site
MONUMENT

(Shanti Swaroop Tyagi Marg; Ⓜ Model Town) In a desolate field, around 10km north of Old Delhi, a lone obelisk marks the site where King George V was declared emperor of India in 1911, and where the great *durbars* (fairs) were held to honour India's British overlords in 1877 and 1903. Take an autorickshaw from Model Town metro station.

Lakshmi Narayan Temple
HINDU TEMPLE

(Birla Mandir; Map p38; Mandir Marg; ⊘6am-9pm; Ⓜ Ramakrishna Ashram Marg) West of Connaught Place, the busy-looking, Orissan-style Lakshmi Narayan Temple was erected by the wealthy industrialist BD Birla. Gandhi inaugurated the complex in 1938 as a temple for all castes; a sign on the gate says, 'Everyone is Welcome'.

DELHI SIGHTS

Connaught Place

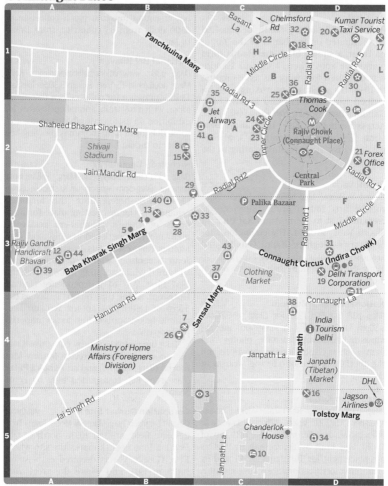

⊙ Connaught Place Area

Connaught Place   AREA
(Map p42; Ⓜ Rajiv Chowk) New Delhi's colonial heart is Connaught Place, named after
George V's paternal uncle, and fashioned
after the colonnades of Cheltenham and
Bath to assuage British homesickness. Its
whitewashed, grey-tinged streets radiate out
from the central circle of Rajiv Chowk, lined
with shops and restaurants. The outer circle
(divided into blocks G to N) is technically

called Connaught Circus, and the inner circle (divided into blocks A to F) is Connaught
Place, but locals call the whole area 'CP.'

Almost every visitor to Delhi comes here,
which partly explains the rampant touts.

Jantar Mantar   HISTORIC SITE
(Map p42; Sansad Marg; Indian/foreigner ₹5/100,
video ₹25; ⊙9am-dusk; Ⓜ Patel Chowk) The most
eccentric-seeming of Delhi's historic sites,
Jantar Mantar (derived from the Sanskrit
word for 'instrument') is an odd collection
of curving geometric buildings that are care-

◎ New Delhi & Around

★ Humayun's Tomb   HISTORIC BUILDING

(Map p46; Mathura Rd; Indian/foreigner ₹10/250, video ₹25; ⊘dawn-dusk; Ⓜ JLN Stadium) The most perfectly proportioned and captivating of Delhi's mausoleums, Humayun's tomb seems to float above the gardens that surround it. Built in the mid-16th century by Haji Begum, the Persian-born senior wife of the Mughal emperor Humayun, the tomb brings together Persian and Mughal elements, creating a template that strongly influenced the Taj Mahal.

Following six years of restoration, completed in 2013, the tomb, other monuments and gardens are looking bright and beautiful. The arched facade is inlaid with bands of white marble and red sandstone, and the building follows strict rules of Islamic geometry, with an emphasis on the number eight. The surrounding gardens are alive with green parakeets and contain the tombs of the emperor's favourite barber and Haji Begum. This was where the last Mughal emperor, Bahadur Shah Zafar, took refuge before being captured and exiled by the British in 1857.

To the right as you enter the complex, **Isa Khan's tomb** is a fine example of Lodi-era architecture, constructed in the 16th century. Further south is the monumental **Khan-i-Khanan's tomb** (Indian/foreigner ₹5/100; ⊘dawn-dusk), plundered in Mughal times to build Safdarjang's tomb.

A new visitor centre is due to be added to the site.

★ Hazrat Nizam-ud-din Dargah   SHRINE

(Map p46; off Lodi Rd; ⊘24hr; Ⓜ JLN Stadium) Hidden away in a tangle of bazaars selling rose petals, *attars* (perfumes) and offerings, the marble shrine of the Muslim Sufi saint Nizam-ud-din Auliya offers a window through the centuries, full of music and crowded with devotees. The ascetic Nizam-ud-din died in 1325 at the ripe old age of 92, and his mausoleum became a point of pilgrimage for Muslims from across the empire. Later kings and nobles wanted to be buried as close to Nizam-ud-din as possible, hence the number of nearby Mughal tombs.

Other tombs in the compound include the graves of Jahanara (daughter of Shah Jahan) and the renowned Urdu poet Amir Khuysru. It's one of Delhi's most extraordinary pleasures to take a seat on the marble floor

fully calibrated to monitor the movement of the stars and planets. Maharaja Jai Singh II constructed the observatory in 1725.

Agrasen ki Baoli   MONUMENT

(Map p42; Hailey Lane; ⊘dawn-dusk; ⓂBarakhamba Road) A remarkable thing to discover among the office towers southeast of Connaught Place, this atmospheric 14th-century step-well was once set in rural land, till the city grew up around it; 103 steps descend to the bottom, flanked by arched niches.

Connaught Place

and listen to Sufis singing rousing *qawwali* (Islamic devotional singing) at sunset. These are most spectacular on Thursday, but it's worth visiting on other evenings for a more intimate experience. Scattered around the surrounding alleyways are more tombs and a huge *baoli*. Entry is free, but visitors may be asked to make a donation.

A tour with the Hope Project (p54), which ends at the shrine, is recommended for some background.

Lodi Gardens   PARK
(Map p46; Lodi Rd; ☺ 6am-8pm Oct-Mar, 5am-8pm Apr-Sep; Ⓜ Khan Market or Jor Bagh) This peaceful park is Delhi's favourite escape, popular with everyone from power-walking politicians to amorous teens. The gardens are dotted with the crumbling tombs of Sayyid and Lodi rulers, including the impressive 15th-century **Bara Gumbad tomb** (Map p46) and mosque, and the strikingly different tombs of **Mohammed Shah** and **Sikander Lodi**. There's a lake crossed by the Athpula

(eight-piered) bridge, which dates from Emperor Akbar's reign.

Rajpath   AREA
(Ⓜ Khan Market) The focal point of Edwin Lutyens' plan for New Delhi was Rajpath (Kingsway), a grand parade linking India Gate to the offices of the Indian government. Constructed between 1914 and 1931, these grand civic buildings, reminiscent of Imperial Rome, were intended to spell out in stone the might of the British empire – yet just 16 years later, the British were out on their ear and Indian politicians were pacing the corridors of power.

Shielded by a wrought-iron fence at the western end of Rajpath, the official residence of the president of India, Rashtrapati Bhavan (p45), is flanked by the mirror-image, dome-crowned **North Secretariat** (Map p46) and **South Secretariat** (Map p46), housing government ministries. The Indian parliament meets nearby at the **Sansad**

Bhavan (Parliament House; Map p46), a circular, colonnaded edifice at the end of Sansad Marg.

At Rajpath's eastern end, and constantly thronged by tourists, is **India Gate** (Map p46). This 42m-high stone memorial arch, designed by Lutyens, pays tribute to around 90,000 Indian army soldiers who died in WWI, the Northwest Frontier operations, and the 1919 Anglo-Afghan War.

Rashtrapati Bhavan   HISTORIC BUILDING

(President's House; Map p46; ☑ 23012960; www. presidentofindia.nic.in; 1hr tour ₹50; ☉ 9am-4pm Fri-Sun; Ⓜ Central Secretariat) You have to book ahead online, but it's worth it to peek inside the grandiose President's House. Formerly home to the British Viceroy, it has 340 rooms, with 2.5km of corridors. However, visits are limited to the domed Durbar Hall, the presidential library and the gilded Ashoka Hall.

You'll have to leave cameras and phones at the entrance, but there's a chance to take pictures close up of the outside before/after your visit.

Rashtrapati Bhavan Museum   MUSEUM

(Map p46; ☑ 23013287; www.presidentofindia.nic. in; gate No 30, Mother Teresa Crescent Rd; tours ₹25; ☉ 9am-4pm Fri-Sun; Ⓜ Central Secretariat) Housed in the palace's former stables (opposite Talkotara Stadium), this museum houses an array of the extravagant gifts received by the president, some of architect Lutyens' plans for the palace, and a few touch-screen exhibits about its history. Visits are by tour only and advance online bookings are required.

Mughal Gardens   GARDENS

(Map p46; ☉ Tue-Sun Feb-Mar; Ⓜ Central Secretariat) FREE Rashtrapati Bhavan's incredible, manicured gardens are open to the public for only two months a year, when they are in flower. If you're in town then, go see them. Lord Louis Mountbatten, India's last viceroy, was said to have employed 418 gardeners to care for the fabulous Mughal-style arrangements.

National Museum   MUSEUM

(Map p46; ☑ 23019272; www.nationalmuseumindia.gov.in; Janpath; Indian/foreigner ₹10/300, audio guide English, French or German ₹400, Hindi ₹150, camera Indian/foreigner ₹20/300; ☉ 10am-5pm Tue-Sun; Ⓜ Central Secretariat) Offering a compelling if not always coherent snapshot of India's last 5000 years, this museum is not overwhelmingly large, but full of splendours. Exhibits include rare relics from the Harappan Civilisation, Buddha's 4th to 5th century BC effects, antiquities from the Silk Route, exquisite miniature paintings (look out for the hand-painted playing cards), woodcarvings, textiles, statues, musical instruments, and an armoury with gruesomely practical weapons and a suit of armour for an elephant.

Allow at least two hours, preferably half a day. Bring identification to obtain an audio guide (worthwhile as labelling is minimal).

Next door is the **Archaeological Survey of India** (☑ 011-23010822; www.asi.nic.in; Janpath; ☉ 9.30am-1pm & 2-6pm Mon-Fri), which stocks publications about India's main archaeological sites.

National Gallery of Modern Art   ART GALLERY

(Map p46; ☑ 23382835; www.ngmaindia.gov.in; Jaipur House, Dr Zakir Hussain Marg; Indian/foreigner ₹10/150; ☉ 10am-5pm Tue-Sun; Ⓜ Khan Market) Delhi's flagship art gallery displays a remarkable collection of paintings, from colonialera landscapes and 'Company Paintings', created by Indian artists to suit their new British rulers, to the primitive-inspired artworks of Nobel Prize–winner Rabindranath Tagore. Photography prohibited.

Gandhi Smriti   MUSEUM

(Map p46; ☑ 23012843; 5 Tees Jan Marg; ☉ 10am-5pm Tue-Sun, closed 2nd Sat of month; Ⓜ Racecourse) FREE This poignant memorial is where Mahatma Gandhi was shot dead by a Hindu zealot on 30 January 1948, after campaigning against intercommunal violence. Concrete footsteps lead to the spot where Gandhi died, marked by a small pavilion. Video prohibited.

The adjacent house, where the Mahatma spent his last 144 days, contains rooms preserved as Gandhi left them, a detailed account of his last 24 hours, and vivid dioramas depicting scenes from Gandhi's life, set in boxes like 1950s TVs. Upstairs is the interpretative exhibition **Eternal Gandhi**.

In the room where Gandhi lodged, you can see his meagre possessions – not much more than a walking stick, spectacles, a spinning wheel and a pair of *chappals* (sandals).

Indira Gandhi Memorial Museum   MUSEUM

(Map p46; ☑ 23010094; 1 Safdarjang Rd; ☉ 9.30am-4.45pm Tue-Sun; Ⓜ Racecourse) FREE The former residence of Indira Gandhi is now a museum dedicated to the former

New Delhi & Around

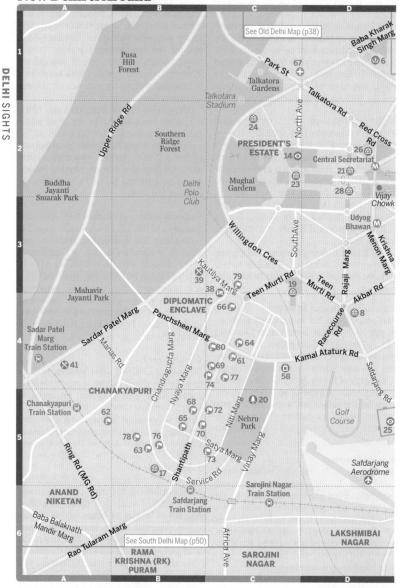

prime minister's life and family, India's Kennedys. It displays her personal effects, including the blood-stained sari she was wearing when she was assassinated in 1984. Many rooms are preserved in state, offering a window onto the elegant lives of Delhi's

political elite. An exhibit at the rear charts the similarly truncated life of Indira's son, Rajiv, assassinated in 1991. In the garden, an enclosed crystal pathway marks Indira Gandhi's final footsteps.

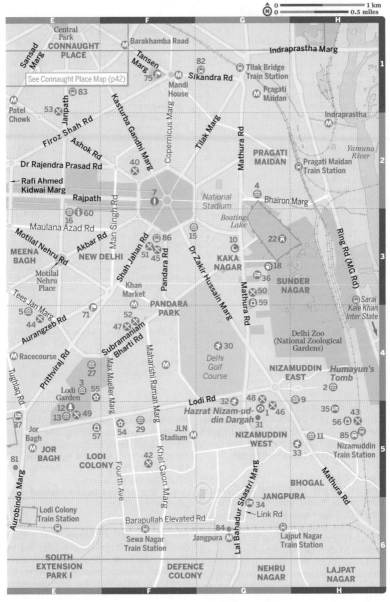

Nehru Memorial Museum MUSEUM
(Map p46; ☑ 23016734; www.nehrumemorial.nic. in; Teen Murti Rd; ☺ 8am-5.15pm Tue-Sun; Ⓜ Udyog Bhawan) FREE The stately Teen Murti Bhavan was the official residence of Jawaharlal Nehru (India's first prime minister), and before that, the official residence of the British commander-in-chief. As well as documents and photos relating to Nehru's life and work, there are several of his rooms preserved as if he's just popped out.

New Delhi & Around

In the grounds is an old-fashioned **plane-tarium** (Map p46; ☑23014504; www.nehruplanetarium.org; 45min show ₹50; ⊙Hindi 1.30pm & 4pm, English 11.30am & 3pm), which has shows about the stars in Hindi and English.

Purana Qila FORT
(Old Fort; Map p46; ☑24353178; Mathura Rd; Indian/foreigner ₹5/100, video ₹25, sound & light show ₹80; ⊙dawn-dusk; ⓂPragati Maidan) With its towering walls and dramatic gateways, Purana Qila was constructed by Afghan ruler Sher Shah (1538-45), who briefly seized control of Delhi from the emperor Humayun, and the monumental gatehouse opens onto a peaceful garden studded with ancient monuments. The graceful octagonal, red-sandstone **Sher Mandal** was used by Humayun as a library; it was a fall down its stairs that ended his reign, and life, in 1556. Beyond is the intricately patterned **Qila-i-Kuhran Mosque** (Mosque of Sher Shah). Across busy Mathura Road are more relics

from the city of Shergarh, including the **Khairul Manazil mosque**, still used by local Muslims. A popular **boating lake** has been created from the former moat, with pedalos for hire. There's a **sound & light show** (⊙in English 8.30pm Feb-Apr, Sep & Oct; 9pm May-Aug & 7.30pm Nov-Jan) at the fort.

The free **Ananya Dance Festival** takes place here in October.

Crafts Museum MUSEUM
(Map p46; ☑23371641; Bhairon Marg; ⊙10am-5pm Tue-Sun; ⓂPragati Maidan) FREE Set up like a traditional village, this captivating, rambling museum aims to preserve the traditional crafts of India, from handloom weaving to Mithila wall painting. Highlights include an enormous carved temple rath (chariot), a mock-up of a Gujarati *haveli* (traditional, ornately decorated residence) and a shrine made from giant terracotta figures. In the rear courtyard, artisans sell their products. There's a good cafe.

DELHI SIGHTS

National Rail Museum MUSEUM
(Map p46; ☎26881816; Service Rd, Chanakyapuri; adult/child ₹20/10, video ₹100; ◷9.30am-5.30pm Tue-Sun) Trainspotters and kids will adore this recently renovated museum, with its collection of steam locos and carriages spread across 4.5 hectares. Among the venerable bogies are the former Viceregal Dining Car, the Maharaja of Mysore's rolling saloon, and the Fairy Queen locomotive, dating from 1855. The indoor gallery displays Indian Railways memorabilia, including the skull of an elephant that charged the *UP Mail* in 1894. A **miniature train** (adult/child ₹20/10) chuffs around the grounds.

National Zoological Gardens ZOO
(Map p46; ☎24359825; www.nzpnewdelhi.gov.in; Mathura Rd; Indian/foreigner ₹40/200, camera/video ₹50/200; ◷9am-4.30pm Sat-Thu, to 4pm Oct-Mar; Ⓜ Pragati Maidan) Popular with families and couples, India's biggest zoo is set in 86 hectares. In fact, the grounds are so extensive you may have trouble finding the an-

imals. Kept in reasonably considerate conditions are lions, tigers, elephants, hippos, rhinos, spectacular birds and monkeys who periodically take leave of their enclosures.

Safdarjang's Tomb TOMB
(Map p46; Aurobindo Marg; Indian/foreigner ₹5/100, video ₹25; ◷dawn-dusk; Ⓜ Jor Bagh) Built by the Nawab of Avadh for his father, Safdarjang, this grandiose mid-18th-century tomb was erected during the twilight of the Mughal empire. With not enough funds to pay for all-over marble, that which is on the dome was taken from the nearby mausoleum of Khan-i-Khana, and it was finished in red sandstone.

Tibet House MUSEUM
(Map p46; ☎24611515; 1 Lodi Rd; admission ₹10; ◷9.30am-5.30pm Mon-Fri; Ⓜ JLN Stadium) Tibet House has a small museum displaying sacred manuscripts, votive carvings and historic *thangkas* (Tibetan cloth paintings), brought out of Tibet following the Chinese occupation. Photography prohibited.

South Delhi

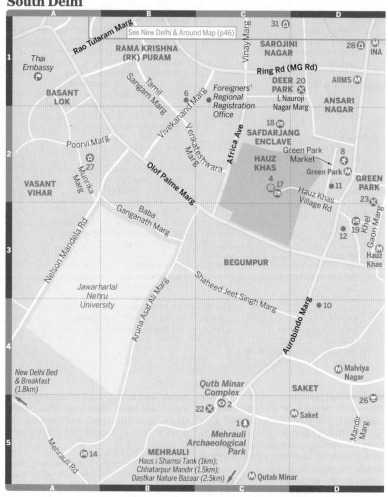

See New Delhi & Around Map (p46)

Nehru Park PARK

(Map p46; Vinay Marg; ⊙5am-8pm Apr-Sep, 6am-8pm Oct-Mar; ⓂRacecourse) On the edge of the Diplomatic Enclave, this green and pleasant park is a calm place to unwind away from the hubbub. In the centre is a statue of Lenin, revealing India's political sympathies during the Cold War.

Gurdwara Bangla Sahib SIKH TEMPLE

(Map p46; Ashoka Rd; ⊙4am-9pm; ⓂPatel Chowk) Topped by golden domes, this handsome white-marble gurdwara was constructed at the site where the eighth Sikh guru,

Harkrishan Dev, stayed before his death in 1664. Despite his tender years, the six-year-old guru tended to victims of Delhi's cholera and smallpox epidemic, and the waters of the gurdwara tank are said to have healing powers. Sikh pilgrims flock here at all hours, and devotional songs waft over the compound, adding to the contemplative mood.

◎ South Delhi

Hauz Khas AREA

(Map p50; ⓂGreen Park) The lake at Hauz Khas, meaning 'royal tank,' was built by

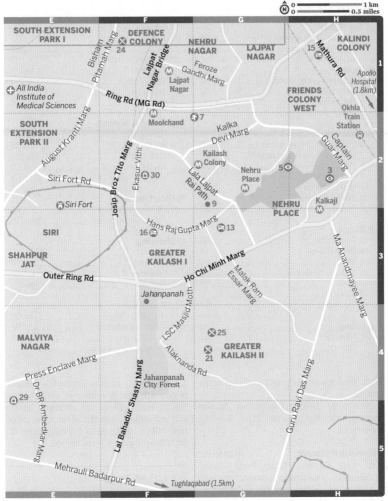

Sultan Ala-ud-din Khilji in the 13th century to provide water for Siri Fort. Thronged by birds and fringed by parkland, it is fronted by the ruins of Feroz Shah's 14th-century madrasa (religious school) and **tomb**, with a magnificent calligraphy-covered incised plaster ceiling.

To reach the lake shore, cut through the adjacent **Deer Park** (daylight hours), which has more ruined tombs, a well-stocked deer enclosure and a popular drumming circle. There are numerous Lodi-era tombs scattered along the access road to Hauz Khas Village, and in nearby Green Park.

Bahai House of Worship BAHAI TEMPLE
(Lotus Temple; Map p50; ☑26444029; www.ba haihouseofworship.in; Kalkaji; ☺9am-7pm Tue-Sun, to 5.30pm winter; ☎; Ⓜ Kalkaji Mandir) Designed by Iranian-Canadian architect Fariburz Sahba in 1986, Delhi's Bahai temple is a wonderful place to enjoy silence – a rare experience in Delhi. Styled after a lotus flower, with 27 immaculate white-marble petals, the temple was created to bring faiths together; visitors are invited to pray or meditate silently according to their own beliefs. The attached visitor centre tells the story of the Bahai

South Delhi

faith. Photography is prohibited inside the temple.

Nearby is Delhi's flamboyant **Iskcon temple**, operated by the Hare Krishna movement.

Chhatarpur Mandir　　　　HINDU TEMPLE
(Shri Adya Katyayani Shakti Peeth Mandir; ☑ 26802360; www.chhattarpurmandir.org; Main Chhatarpur Rd; ⊘ 4am-midnight; Ⓜ Chhatarpur) India's second-largest temple (after Akshardham), the Shri Adya Katyayani Shakti Peeth Mandir is dedicated to the goddess Katyayani (one of the nine forms of Parvati). There are dozens of shrines with towering South Indian *gopurams* (gateway towers), and an enormous statue of Hanuman stands guard over the compound. Weekdays tend to be fairly sedate, but the complex gets crowded at weekends and during the Navratri celebrations in September/October.

Kiran Nadar Museum of Art　　MUSEUM
(☑ 49160000; www.knma.in; 145 DLF, South Court Mall, Saket; ⊘ 10.30am-6.30pm Tue-Sun; Ⓜ Saket) A fine private museum devoted to contemporary art, this is a drop of culture amid Saket's malls. There are excellent temporary exhibitions, but the permanent collection will be displayed to full effect once the 80,000-sq-ft gallery is completed.

◉ Other Areas

★ **Akshardham Temple**　　HINDU TEMPLE
(☑ 22016688; www.akshardham.com; National Hwy 24, Noida turning; temple admission free, exhibitions ₹170, fountains ₹30; ⊘ 9.30am-6.30pm Tue-Sun; Ⓜ Akshardham) Rising dramatically over the eastern suburbs, the Hindu Swaminarayan group's controversially ostentatious Akshardham Temple draws elements from traditional Orissan, Gujarati, Mughal and Rajasthani architecture.

Surrounding this spiritual showpiece is a series of Disneyesque exhibitions, including a boat ride through 10,000 years of Indian history, animatronics telling stories from the life of Swaminarayan, and musical fountains.

The interior offers an almost psychedelic journey through Hindu mythology, with 20,000 carved deities, saints and mythical beings. Allow at least half a day to do the temple justice (weekdays are less crowded).

Sulabh International Museum of Toilets   MUSEUM

(☑ 25031518; www.sulabhtoiletmuseum.org; Sulabh Complex, Mahavir Enclave, Palam Dabri Rd; ⊙10am-5pm summer, 10.30am-5pm winter) **FREE** Run by a pioneering charity that has done extraordinary work bringing sanitation to the poor of India, this quirky museum displays toilet-related paraphernalia dating from 2500 BC to modern times. It's around 20km west of Connaught Place. Take the metro to Janakpuri West, then take a rickshaw.

🏃 Activities

Lodhi Spa   SPA

(Map p46; ☑ 43633333; www.thelodhi.com; Lodhi Hotel, Lodi Rd, New Delhi; 1hr massage from ₹3800; Ⓜ JLN Stadium) The fragrant, rarified world of the Lodhi Spa is open to nonguests who book treatments, such as massages, facials, and traditional ayurvedic treatments.

Aura   SPA

(Map p46; ☑ 8800621206; www.aurathaispa.com; Middle Lane, Khan Market; 1hr oil massage ₹2400; ⊙10am-9pm; Ⓜ Khan Market) Glitzy spa offering Thai-inspired massages and treatments. There are also branches at Karol Bagh, GK1, GK2 and Green Park.

Delhi Golf Club   GOLF

(Map p46; ☑ 24307100; www.delhigolfclub.org; Dr Zakir Hussain Marg; 18 holes weekdays/weekends ₹3050/4550; ⊙dawn-dusk; Ⓜ Khan Market) Founded in 1931, with beautiful, well-tended fairways, peacocks and Mughal pavilions. Weekends are busy.

Kerala Ayurveda   AYURVEDA

(Map p50; ☑ 41754888; www.keralaayurveda.biz; E-2 Green Park Extn; 1hr massage ₹1500; ⊙8am-8pm; Ⓜ Green Park) Treatments from *sarvang ksheerdhara* (massage with butter milk) to *sirodhara* (warm oil poured on the forehead).

Park Hotel   SWIMMING

(Map p42; ☑ 23743737; 15 Sansad Marg; per person ₹850; ⊙7am-7pm; Ⓜ Rajiv Chowk) The Park Hotel pool, handily convenient for Connaught Place, is surrounded by sunbeds and cabanas, and overlooked by the funky Aqua bar (p66).

Volunteering

There are plenty of ways to assist Delhi's less fortunate residents. The Salaam Balaak Trust (p54) in Paharganj, the Hope Project (p54) in Nizamuddin, and **Torch** (www.torchdelhi.org; 30D Nizamuddin Basti, Nizamuddin West) often have openings for volunteers. Mother Teresa's Missionaries of Charity run projects in Delhi that may accept volunteers – contact its Kolkata office (p459). **Concern India Foundation** (Map p50; ☑ 26210998; www.concernindiafoundation.org; A-52 Amar Colony, Lajpat Nagar IV) can also arrange placements for volunteers.

📚 Courses

Hush Cooking   COOKING

(Vasant Vihar; 3hr lesson ₹3200) The lovely Prabeen Singh, a former development worker, offers 1½-hour cookery lessons in her home, in a suburb close to the airport. After the lesson, you eat your creations.

Nita Mehta   COOKING

(☑ 26141185; www.nitamehta.com; Block TU, Uttari Pitampura, North Delhi; 3hr lesson ₹2000) Cookery writer, teacher and TV chef Nita Mehta offers Indian cookery courses.

Central Hindi Directorate   LANGUAGE

(Map p50; ☑ 26178454; www.hindinideshalaya.nic.in; West Block VII, RK Puram, Vivekanand Marg; 60hr basic course ₹6000) Runs certificate and diploma courses in Hindi; the basic course lasts 60 hours with three classes a week.

Sivananda Yoga   YOGA

(Map p50; www.sivananda.org.in; A41 Kailash Colony; classes ₹400; Ⓜ Kailash Colony) Excellent yoga ashram, with beginners and advanced courses, plus drop-in classes.

OFF THE BEATEN TRACK

SHAHPUR JAT

A 1km rickshaw ride northeast from Hauz Khas metro, the urban village of Shahpur Jat was a focus of Delhi's 2014 street-art festival so has plentiful wall paintings; the enclave is also full of boutiques selling beautiful high-end, handmade dresses, jewellery, shoes and homewares. **Little Black Book** (www.littleblackbookdelhi.com) offers street-art walking tours.

Sri Aurobindo Ashram MEDITATION, YOGA
(Map p50; ☑ 26567863; www.sriaurobindoashram.
net; Aurobindo Marg; M Hauz Khas) Yoga and
meditation for serious practitioners rather
than hobbyists.

Studio Abhyas MEDITATION, YOGA
(Map p50; ☑ 26962757; www.abhyastrust.org; F-27
Green Park; M Green Park) Yoga and meditation
classes and Vedic chanting in a comfortable
suburban home. Prior experience preferred.

Tushita Meditation Centre MEDITATION
(Map p50; ☑ 26513400; www.tushitadelhi.com; 9
Padmini Enclave; M Hauz Khas) Tibetan/Bud-
dhist meditation sessions – call or email for
details. Donations are appropriate.

👉 Tours

Tours are an excellent way to explore Delhi.
Admission fees and camera/video charges
aren't included, and rates are per person.
Book several days ahead.

★ DelhiByCycle BICYCLE TOUR
(☑ 9811723720; www.delhibycycle.com; per person
₹1850; ⊙ 6.30-10am) Run by a Dutch journalist, these tours are a fantastic way to explore
Delhi. Tours focus on specific neighbour-
hoods – Old Delhi, New Delhi, Nizamuddin,
and the banks of the Yamuna – and start early
to miss the worst of the traffic. The price includes chai and a Mughal breakfast. Child
seats are available.

Salaam Baalak Trust WALKING TOUR
(SBT; Map p56; ☑ 23584164; www.salaambaalak
trust.com; Gali Chandiwali, Paharganj; suggested
donation ₹200; M Ramakrishna Ashram Marg) 🎗
This charitable organisation offers two-hour
'street walks' guided by former street children, who will show you first-hand what life
is like for Delhi's homeless youngsters. The
fees help the Trust assist children on the
streets.

Street Connections WALKING TOUR
(www.walk.streetconnections.co.uk; 3hr walk ₹500)
🎗 This fascinating walk through Old Delhi
is guided by former street children who have
been helped by the Salaam Baalak Trust. It
explores the hidden corners of Old Delhi,
starting at the Jama Masjid and concluding
at one of the SBT shelters.

Hope Project WALKING TOUR
(Map p46; ☑ 24353006; www.hopeprojectindia.
org; 127 Hazrat Nizamuddin; 1½hr walk suggested
donation ₹200; M JLN Stadium) 🎗 This charity

runs fascinating walks around the Muslim
basti (slum) of Nizamuddin. Take the walk
in mid-afternoon to end at the *qawwali*
at the Hazrat Nizam-ud-din Dargah, or at
the more intimate session at the shrine of
Hazrat Inayat Khan on Friday. Wear modest
clothing.

Indomania Cultural Tours TOUR
(☑ 8860223456; www.indomaniatours.com;
half-day tours per person ₹2000) 🎗 Excellent tours by the knowledgeable Priyush,
exploring the parts of Delhi others don't
reach. Visit a Rajasthani pottery village on
Delhi's outskirts, cultural groups along the
Yamuna River, or Delhi's Tibetan enclave,
in tours that operate in association with
local NGOs.

**Delhi Tourism & Transport
Development Corporation** BUS TOUR
(DTTDC; Map p42; www.delhitourism.nic.in;
Baba Kharak Singh Marg; AC tours half-/full day
₹350/200; ⊙ 7am-9pm; M Rajiv Chowk) Offers
bus tours of New Delhi (9am to 1.30pm) and
Old Delhi (2.15pm to 5.45pm) visiting all the
big sights (avoid Monday, when most are
shut). It also runs the air-conditioned Ho
Ho (Hop-on, Hop-off) Dilli Dekho bus service, which circuits the major sights every
45 minutes or so from 8.30am to 6.30pm
(Indian/foreigner ₹350/700, two-day ticket
₹600/1200) – buy tickets from the booth
near the office.

Also runs rushed tours to Agra, Jaipur
and Haridwar.

Intach WALKING TOUR
(☑ 24641304; www.intachdelhichapter.org; tour
s ₹100) Intach runs walking tours with expert guides, exploring different areas, such
as Chandhi Chowk, Nizamuddin, Hauz Khas
and Mehrauli. Custom walks can also be
arranged.

**Delhi Transport
Corporation Tours** BUS TOUR
(Map p42; ☑ 23752774; www.dtc.nic.in; Scindia
House, Connaught Place; tour ₹200; ⊙ Tue-Sun;
M Rajiv Chowk) Inexpensive full-day air-con
bus tours to the top sights from Connaught
Place, leaving at 9.15am and returning at
5.45pm.

🛏 Sleeping

Delhi has plenty of choice, but it's wise to
book ahead, as popular places can fill up in
a flash. Reconfirm your booking 24 hours

before you arrive. Most hotels offer pick-up from the airport with advance notice. Homestays are becoming an attractive alternative to hotels, and there's also an array of options on airbnb.com. For details of government-approved places contact India Tourism Delhi (p71), or check www.incredibleindianhomes.com and www.mahindrahomestays.com.

Hotels with a minimum tariff of ₹1000 charge luxury tax (10% at the time of research) and service tax (7.42% at the time of research), and some also add a service charge (up to 10%). Most hotels have a noon checkout and luggage storage is usually possible.

🛏 Old Delhi

Most hotels in the old town see few foreign visitors.

Hotel New City Palace HOTEL $
(Map p38; ☎ 23279548; www.hotelnewcitypalace.in; 726 Jama Masjid; r ₹700; ❄; ⓂChawri Bazaar) A palace it's not, but this mazelike hotel has an amazing location overlooking the Jama Masjid. Rooms are small, but some have windows and views; the bathrooms could do with a good scrub, but staff are friendly.

Hotel Broadway HOTEL $$
(Map p38; ☎ 43663600; www.hotelbroadwaydelhi.com; 4/15 Asaf Ali Rd; s/d incl breakfast ₹2300/4000; ❄@; ⓂNew Delhi) A surprising find in the old city, Broadway was Delhi's first high-rise when it opened in 1956. Today it combines comfort with charm and eccentricity and has a great restaurant and bar. Some rooms have old-fashioned wood panelling, while others have been quirkily kitted out by French designer Catherine Lévy. Ask for one with views over Old Delhi.

Maidens Hotel HOTEL $$$
(Map p38; ☎ 23975464; www.maidenshotel.com; 7 Sham Nath Marg; r from ₹12,000; ❄@🛜🏊; ⓂCivil Lines) Set in immaculate gardens, Oberoi-owned Maidens is a graceful wedding cake of a hotel, built in 1903. Lutyens stayed here while supervising the building of New Delhi, and the enormous high-ceilinged rooms have a colonial-era charm that is combined with contemporary comforts. There are two restaurants, a pool and a bar.

🛏 Paharganj & Around

With bumper-to-bumper budget hotels and a deserved reputation for hassle and dodgy characters, Paharganj isn't everyone's cup of chai. However, it's convenient for New Delhi train station, a great place to plug into the traveller grapevine, and the mayhem can grow on you. Note that if you're paying peanuts, you're in for a sun-starved, grimy cell. Splash a bit extra and you'll get more cleanliness and comfort. There are also better, more midrange rooms for not much more on nearby Arakashan Rd. Be warned that street noise can be diabolical – keep ear plugs handy.

Because of the pedestrian congestion, taxi-wallahs may be reluctant to take you right to the doorstep of your hotel, but if it's on the Main Bazaar or Arakashan Rd, they can make it. You can walk to everywhere from New Delhi train station or metro (for Arakashan Rd) or the Ramakrishna Ashram Marg metro stop. However tired you are when you get off the Airport metro or bus, don't believe rickshaw drivers or anyone who tells you differently. To avoid commission scams when you first arrive, ask rickshaws to drop you at Chhe Tooti Chowk and complete your journey on foot.

★**Hotel Amax Inn** HOTEL $
(Map p38; ☎23543813; www.hotelamax.com; 8145/6 Arakashan Rd; s/d from ₹750/850; ❄@🛜) Set back from chaotic Arakashan Rd, the Amax offers fairly standard, good-value budget rooms, with bullet-hard pillows, but the friendly staff run the place with the globetrotting traveller in mind. The rooftop terrace is a great spot to swap travel stories and there's wi-fi in reception.

Hotel Namaskar HOTEL $
(Map p56; ☎ 23583456; www.namaskarhotel.com; 917 Chandiwalan, Main Bazaar; r ₹400-650, with AC

DELHI SLEEPING

DELHI SLEEPING

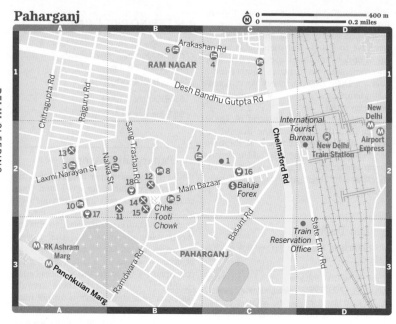

Paharganj

₹650; ✳ 🛜) Up the alleyway opposite Dayal Boot House, this old favourite is run by two amiable brothers. It's not the Ritz (it's humid and noisy), but the simple rooms are usually freshly painted, the colour scheme will tickle you pink, and wi-fi works in the rooms.

Hotel Rak International HOTEL $

(Map p56; ☎ 23562478; www.hotelrakinternational. com; off Main Bazaar; s/d ₹550/650, with AC ₹800/900; ✳) Tucked off the Main Bazaar and overlooking a scruffy courtyard, the modest rooms at this popular hotel have marble floors and bathrooms, chintzy built-in beds, including, unusually, twin rooms and...windows!

Cottage Yes Please HOTEL $

(Map p56; ☎ 23562300; www.cottageyesplease. com; 1843 Laxmi Narayan St; d from ₹950; ✳ @) One street north of Main Bazaar, this calm, comfortable place offers a selection of agreeable, if tired-looking, rooms. Rooms have TVs and fridges, and the decor runs to wood panelling and stained glass.

★**Bloom Rooms** HOTEL **$$**
(Map p56; ☑40174017; www.bloomrooms.com; 8591 Arakashan Road; s/d from ₹2200/2800; ☎) Sunny lemon-yellow and gleaming white, designer Bloom Rooms is sparklingly and clean, with soft pillows, white linen, great wi-fi and nice outdoor seating areas. This New Delhi branch is in a busy area but a haven inside. There's another balmy branch in **Jangpura** (Map p46; ☑41261400; 7 Link Rd) in South Delhi. Both have Amici restaurants (good pizza).

Hotel Grand Godwin HOTEL **$$**
(Map p56; ☑23546891; www.godwinhotels.com; 8502/41 Arakashan Rd; d incl breakfast from ₹2500; ✳@☎) Located north of Main Bazaar, on the hotel strip of Arakashan Rd, the Grand Godwin is firmly midrange, and the glitzy feel of the lobby extends to the smart rooms. Run by the same owners, the nearby Godwin Deluxe offers similar facilities for similar prices.

Hotel All iz Well HOTEL **$$**
(Map p56; ☑23580014; www.hotelallizwell.com; 4781 Main Bazaar; s/d ₹1300/1500; ✳☎) All iz Well offers clean, good-value, reasonably smart rooms, with room service, efficient wi-fi and reasonably helpful, unhassly staff. A calm and laid-back deal in Paharganj.

Jyoti Mahal Guesthouse GUESTHOUSE **$$**
(Map p56; ☑23580523; www.jyotimahal.net; 2488-2490 Nalwa St; s/d ₹2200/2500; ✳@☎) Full of Rajasthani carvings and antiques, Jyoti is a cut above other places in Paharganj, with some genuine character: it feels like a traditional *haveli* home. Arranged around a central atrium, rooms have handmade furniture, marble floors and some have four-poster beds.

Hotel Ajanta HOTEL **$$**
(Map p56; ☑42350000; www.ajantahotel.com; 8647 Arakashan Rd; d/ste ₹2640/4650; ✳@☎) Some rooms are better than others at Ajanta; pay the higher rates and you'll be in for a more spacious room with a grand, polished-wood look. Some have private balconies. The downstairs Vagabond restaurant serves quality Mughlai food.

Metropolis Tourist Home HOTEL **$$**
(Map p56; ☑23561794; www.metropolistourist-home.com; 16345 Main Bazaar; r from ₹2000; ✳@☎) A slightly haphazard but charac-terful lobby gives way to rooms with mood lighting, shiny bedspreads and slightly tired decor. The rooftop restaurant (mains ₹300 to ₹1000), hung with plants, is a tranquil retreat.

🛏 Connaught Place & Around

Sunny Guest House GUESTHOUSE **$**
(Map p42; ☑23312909; sunnyguesthouse1234@hotmail.com; 152 Scindia House, Connaught Lane; r ₹800, without bathroom ₹400-600; Ⓜ Rajiv Chowk) Sunny Guest House is light on the pocket for the location, but this comes at a price – tiny, dingy rooms.

Prem Sagar Guest House GUESTHOUSE **$$**
(Map p42; ☑23345263; www.premsagarguest-house.com; 1st fl, 11 P-Block, Connaught Place; s/d from ₹3520/4110; ✳@; Ⓜ Rajiv Chowk) A reliable, long-standing choice, with 12 snug rooms that aren't flash but are clean and relatively cheap for the location. There's a pot-plant-filled rear terrace, and internet in reception.

★**Imperial** HOTEL **$$$**
(Map p42; ☑23341234; www.theimperialindia.com; Janpath; r from ₹17,000; ✳@☎☲; Ⓜ Rajiv Chowk) The inimitable, Raj-era Imperial marries colonial classicism with gilded art deco. Rooms have high ceilings, flowing curtains, French linen and marble baths, and the hallways and atriums are lined with 18th- and 19th-century paintings and prints. The 1911 bar (p66) is highly recommended, and the Atrium cafe (p65) serves the perfect high tea.

Hotel Palace Heights HOTEL **$$$**
(Map p42; ☑43582610; www.hotelpalaceheights.com; 26-28 D-Block; s/d ₹7150/8250; ✳@☎; Ⓜ Rajiv Chowk) This boutique hotel is cool enough to wear shades, offering Connaught Place's nicest rooms with gleaming white linen, black lampshades and caramel and amber tones. There's an excellent restaurant, Zāffrān (p63).

Hotel Alka HOTEL **$$$**
(Map p42; ☑23344328; www.hotelalka.com; P-Block, Connaught Place; s/d from ₹3500/5500; ✳@☎; Ⓜ Rajiv Chowk) Hotel Alka has an old-fashioned charm, with lots of wooden furnishings. Rooms are small, but the pricier ones have some unique decor, including cheetah murals. There's a good pure veg (no onion or garlic) restaurant.

DELHI'S LITTLE LHASA

Home to Delhi's refugee Tibetan population, Majnu-ka-Tila takes a little effort to get to, but it's good for the little Lhasa vibe, and a good alternative traveller hub if the hustle of Paharganj is not your scene. This mellow enclave is packed with travel agents, restaurants and glittering trinket vendors and centres on a square with two colourful temples. You'll rub shoulders with maroon-clad Buddhist monks, local Tibetans and rather a lot of beggars; however, the streets have a peaceful, safe, small-town vibe.

Friendly **Wongdhen House** (☑ 23816689; 2wongdhenhouse@gmail.com; 15-A New Tibetan Colony; r ₹700-750, without bathroom ₹450; ✴) has simple, shabby, slightly overpriced rooms, and a good restaurant; next door **Lhasa House** (☑ 2393 9888, 2393 9777; lhasahouse@rediffmail.com; 16 New Aruna Nagar; r ₹350-550) is better value. **Ama** (H 40, New Aruna Nagar; snacks ₹20-95; ◷ 7am-9.30pm; ☎) is a splendid cafe hang-out, and there's the gorgeous, fantastic-value **Amala** (◷ 9am-8.30pm) boutique downstairs, selling everything from prayer flags to felt toys. Two good restaurants are **Tee Dee** (32 New Aruna Nagar; dishes ₹60-200; ◷ 8.30am-10.30pm) and **Dolma House** (Block 10, New Tibetan Colony; dishes ₹40-100; ◷ 8.30am-10.30pm).

To get here, take the metro to Vidhan Sabha, then one of the plentiful cycle-/autorickshaws (₹20/40) to the enclave on KB Hedgewar Marg.

🛌 West Delhi

Master Guest House   GUESTHOUSE $$
(☑ 28741089; www.master-guesthouse.com; R-500 New Rajendra Nagar; s/d incl breakfast from ₹3250/4250; ✴@☎; Ⓜ Rajendra Place) Around 5km west of Connaught Place, but a few minutes from Rajendra Place metro station, this smart and polished suburban home has three tastefully furnished rooms with spotless bathrooms. There's a leafy rooftop terrace.

Shanti Home   HOTEL $$$
(☑ 41573366; www.shantihome.com; A-1/300 Janakpuri; s/d incl breakfast from ₹5500/6500; ✴@☎; Ⓜ Uttam Nagar East) Deep in West Delhi, around 17km from Connaught Place, this delightful small hotel is close to the metro and offers beautifully decorated rooms that get gradually swisher the more you spend. There are spacious lounge areas, an excellent rooftop restaurant, a gym and a reasonably priced steam and ayurvedic massage service (₹1500/1800 for a 60-/90-minute facial).

🛌 New Delhi

Youth Hostel   HOSTEL $
(Map p46; ☑ 26116285; www.yhaindia.org; 5 Nyaya Marg, Chanakyapuri; dm/d ₹300/900, with AC ₹600/1612; ✴@; Ⓜ Udyyog Bhawan) The dormitory here is a great deal if you're looking for somewhere quiet and cheap, but you'll get better rooms elsewhere at these prices.

The obligatory one-month temporary YHA membership costs ₹150.

★ Lodhi   HOTEL $$$
(Map p46; ☑ 43633333; www.thelodhi.com; Lodi Rd; r from ₹27,000; ✴☎✉; Ⓜ JNL Stadium) Formerly the Aman, the Lodhi is one of Delhi's finest luxury hotels, with only 40 huge, lovely rooms and suites and acres of space. Each room has a balcony with private plunge pool, and those on the upper floors have great views, some over to Humayun's Tomb. Attention to detail is superb and the general managers greet everyone personally. There's also a top-notch spa.

Lutyens Bungalow   GUESTHOUSE $$$
(Map p46; ☑ 24611341; www.lutyensbungalow.co.in; 39 Prithviraj Rd; s/d incl breakfast from ₹5500/7000; ✴@☎✉; Ⓜ Racecourse) This great rambling house is an atmospheric green oasis, ideal if you're travelling with kids and perfectly located for exploring New Delhi. The garden is great – lawns, flowers and fluttering parrots – but rooms are a little stuffy and overpriced, though looking much better since recent renovations.

🛌 South Delhi

Moustache Hostel   HOSTEL $
(Map p50; www.facebook.com/moustachehostel; S25, GK1, M-Block Market Main Rd; dm ₹600, d ₹2500, incl breakfast; ✴☎; Ⓜ Kailash Colony) This cheerful hostel has appealing, nicely kept small dorms, a few doubles decorated with bright prints, and a funky, welcoming

vibe. It's a 15- to 20-minute walk from the metro. There's a book-lined common room and lots of local info. It's a great place to chat to other 20-something travellers.

Bed & Chai
HOSTEL $$

(Map p50; www.bedandchai.com; R55 Hans Raj Gupta Marg; dm ₹850, d with/without bathroom from ₹3000/2200) This French-owned guesthouse has simple, stylish rooms, decorated with flashes of colour and lamps made out of teapots. There's a sparkling clean dorm as well, a roof terrace and, of course, excellent chai. The owners also run Bed & Chai Masala, which has cheaper dorm beds.

Treetops
GUESTHOUSE $$

(Map p50; ☎ 9899555704; baig.murad@gmail.com; R-8b Hauz Khas Enclave; s/d incl breakfast ₹3500/4000; ❀ @ ☎; Ⓜ Hauz Khas) Cookery writer Tannie and journalist Murad have a gracious home and to stay here feels rather like visiting distant, upper-crust relatives. Treetops offers two large rooms opening onto a leafy rooftop terrace overlooking the park. Evening meals are available.

★ Devna
GUESTHOUSE $$$

(Map p46; ☎ 41507176; www.tensundernagar.com; 10 Sunder Nagar; s/d ₹5700/6000; ❀ @ ☎) Fronted by a pretty courtyard garden, and run with panache by the charming Atul and Devna, this is one of Delhi's prettiest guesthouses. The walls are lined with photos of maharajas and works of art (yes, those are original Jamini Roys) and the rooms are decked out with quirky antiques. The upstairs rooms front onto tiny terraces.

Manor
HOTEL $$$

(Map p50; ☎ 26925151; www.themanordelhi.com; 77 Friends Colony West; d incl breakfast from ₹12,000; ❀ @) A more intimate alternative to Delhi's five-star chains, this 16-room boutique hotel oozes privacy and elegance. Set amid lush lawns off Mathura Rd, the Manor offers the kind of designer touches normally found in the homes of Bollywood stars. There's a colonial air to the opulent rooms and the restaurant, Indian Accent (p65), is one of Delhi's finest.

Bnineteen
GUESTHOUSE $$$

(Map p46; ☎ 41825500; www.bnineteen.com; B-19 Nizamuddin East; s/d incl breakfast from ₹7500/9000; ❀ @; Ⓜ JNL Stadium) Located in posh and peaceful Nizamuddin East, with views over Humayun's tomb from the rooftop, this gorgeous place is owned by archi-

tects, and it shows. Rooms are modern and refined, and there is a state-of-the-art shared kitchen on each floor.

Scarlette
GUESTHOUSE $$$

(Map p50; ☎ 8826010278; www.scarlettenewdelhi.com; B2/139 Safdarjung Enclave; d ₹8000; ❀ ☎; Ⓜ Green Park) In a serene residential area, close to the Deer Park and Hauz Khas, Scarlette is a lovely boutique *maison d'hotes* (guesthouse) with just four rooms and a large sitting room filled with books and interesting *objets*. It's French-owned and popular with French speakers. A set menu dinner (rather pricey at ₹900 to ₹1200) is served nightly.

Rose
HOTEL $$$

(Map p50; ☎ 65680444; www.therosenewdelhi.com; T40 Hauz Khas Village; s ₹3750-8000, d ₹4250-8750; ❀ ☎; Ⓜ Green Park) This is a stylish guesthouse set in one of Delhi's most bohemian districts (packed with bars and boutiques, and good for live music), which sits alongside monument-scattered parkland. It's worthwhile paying for the more expensive rooms, as the cheaper ones have windows opening only onto the walkway.

🛌 Airport Area & Beyond

Delhi's brand-new Aerocity area is a bland but convenient conglomeration of hotels, only 4km from the airport. It's served by the Delhi Aerocity metro stop. Take your pick from brands such as JW Marriott, Red Fox and Lemon Tree; the cheapest option is the Ibis, which also offers a free 24-hour shuttle

OFF THE BEATEN TRACK

ESCAPE FROM DELHI

Tikli Bottom (www.tiklibottom.com; Manender Farm, Gairatpur Bas, Gurgaon; s/d full board ₹10,900/18,500) Less than 50km south of central Delhi, this peachy Lutyens-style bungalow surrounded by wooded hills is run by a British couple. The house and the owners seem to come from another era, one of toasted teacakes, lawns and chintz. There are four high-ceilinged guest rooms and spacious lounges, plus a beautiful pool overlooked by a pagoda and with hill views.

pick-up from either terminal. There are also a few choices in nearby Vasant Kunj.

There are also several options for sleeping at the airport, including Eaton Smart and SAMS sleeping pods; see www.newdelhiairport.in for details.

New Delhi Bed & Breakfast HOMESTAY $$
(☎26894812; www.newdelhibedandbreakfast.com; C8/8225 Vasant Kunj; s/d ₹3000/3500; ✳@) A proper homestay: Renu Dayal is warm and welcoming and has two double rooms (one en suite) in her elegant house in a leafy enclave, only 10 minutes' drive from the airport.

Chhoti Haveli HOMESTAY $$
(Map p50; ☎26124880; www.chhotihaveli.com; A1006, Pocket A, Vasant Kunj; s/d ₹3500/4000; ✳@⚡; MChhatarpur) Set in a block of low-rise apartments, in a quiet, leafy area near the airport, this well-kept place offers tastefully decorated rooms. Potted plants and scattered petals on the doorstep show a personal touch.

🍴 Eating

Delhi is a foodie paradise, and locals graze throughout the day, from the city's famous *Dilli-ka-chaat* (street-food snacks and salads) to indulgent feasts at Delhi's fine-dining restaurants.

Midrange and upmarket restaurants charge a service tax of around 10%; drinks taxes can suck a further 20% (alcoholic) or 12.5% (nonalcoholic) from your money belt. Many restaurants also levy a 10% service charge, in lieu of a tip. Taxes haven't been included here unless indicated.

Reservations may be required for popular and high-end restaurants.

🍴 Old Delhi

★Karim's MUGHLAI $
(Map p38; Gali Kababyan; mains ₹45-460; ⊗9am-12.30am; MChawri Bazaar) Just off the lane leading south from the Jama Masjid, Karim's has been delighting carnivores since 1913. Expect meaty Mughlai treats such as mutton *burrah* (marinated chops), delicious mutton mughlai, and the breakfast mutton and bread combo *nahari* (₹125 half portion). There's a second branch in **Nizamuddin West** (Map p46; 168/2 Jha House Basti).

Gali Paratha Wali STREET FOOD $
(Map p38; Gali Paratha Wali; parathas ₹15-35; ⊗7am-11pm; MChandni Chowk) Head to this

food-stall-lined lane off Chandni Chowk for delectable *parathas* (traditional flatbread) fresh off the *tawa* (hotplate). Choose from a spectacular array of stuffings, from green chilli and paneer to lemon and banana.

★Jalebiwala SWEETS $
(Map p38; Dariba Corner, Chandni Chowk; jalebis per 100g ₹30; ⊗8.30am-9.45pm; MChandni Chowk) Century-old Jalebiwala does Delhi's – if not India's – finest *jalebis* (deep-fried, syrupy fried dough), so pig out and worry about the calories tomorrow.

Natraj Dahi Balle Wala STREET FOOD $
(Map p38; 1396 Chandni Chowk; plate ₹50; ⊗10.30am-11pm; MChandni Chowk) This hole-in-the-wall with the big red sign and the big crowds is famous for its *dahi bhalle* (fried lentil balls served with yoghurt and garnished with chutney) and deliciously crispy *aloo tikki* (spiced potato patties).

Jain Coffee House STREET FOOD $
(Map p38; Raghu Ganj, Chawri Bazaar; sandwiches ₹60; ⊗9am-7.30pm; MChawri Bazaar) In a tiny lane, once Delhi's main granary, off Chawri Bazaar (Raghu Ganj is a tiny turning just before Nai Sarak), one grain trading family operates a sideline in delicious seasonal fruit sandwiches.

Kake di Hatti INDIAN $
(Map p38; 654-655 Church Mission Rd; mains ₹40-130; ⊗10am-11pm; MChawri Bazaar) This long-standing *dhaba* (snack bar) has been open since 1942 and is famous for its huge, delicious, stuffed (with peas and cheese, chili, cheese and onions, and many other combos) naans and *parathas,* which you can eat with various types of fragrant dhal. Look out for the hordes of people and the Hindi sign in red.

Haldiram's FAST FOOD $
(Map p38; 1454/2 Chandni Chowk; mains ₹68-178; ⊗10am-10.30pm; MChandni Chowk) This clean, bright cafeteria cum sweet shop is a popular stop for its top-notch dosas (large South Indian savoury crepe), *idli* (South Indian spongy, round, fermented rice cake) and thalis, and it also sells delectable *namkin* (savouries) and *mithai* (sweets) to eat on the hoof. There's a popular branch on **Connaught Place** (Map p42; 6 L-Block Connaught Place; ⊗10am-10.30pm; MRajiv Chowk).

Bikanervala FAST FOOD $
(Map p38; 382 Chandni Chowk; snacks ₹42-170; ⊗8am-10.30pm; MChandni Chowk) This bright

little canteen offers tasty snacks such as *paratha* and *channa bhatura* (fried bread with chickpeas). There's a handy branch among the state emporiums on **Baba Kharak Singh Marg** (Map p42; ; M Rajiv Chowk).

Ghantewala
SWEETS $
(Map p38; 1862A Chandni Chowk; mithai per 100g from ₹25; ◷8am-10pm; M Chandni Chowk) Delhi's most famous sweetery, 'the bell ringer' has been churning out *mithai* (Indian sweets) since 1790. Try some *sohan halwa* (ghee-dipped gram flour biscuits).

Moti Mahal
MUGHLAI $$
(Map p38; ☑ 23273661; 3704 Netaji Subhash Marg; mains ₹170-540; ◷11am-midnight) The original, much-copied Moti Mahal has been open for six generations – the food is much more impressive than the faded surroundings. Delhiites rate the place for its superior butter chicken and dhal makhani. There's live *qawwali* (Islamic devotional singing) Wednesday to Monday (8pm to 11.30pm).

Al-Jawahar
MUGHLAI $$
(Map p38; Matya Mahal; mains ₹100-275; ◷7am-midnight; M Chawri Bazaar) South of the Jama Masjid, Al-Jawahar serves up tasty Mughlai cuisine at laminate tables in an orderly dining room, and you can watch breads being freshly made at the front. Kebabs and mutton curries dominate the menu, but it also does good butter chicken and korma.

Chor Bizarre
KASHMIRI $$$
(Map p38; ☑ 23273821; Hotel Broadway, 4/15 Asaf Ali Rd; mains ₹305-675; ◷7.30-10.30am, noon-3.30pm & 7.30-11.30pm; M New Delhi) A dimly lit cavern filled with bric-a-brac, including a vintage car, Chor Bizarre (meaning 'thieves market') offers delicious and authentic Kashmiri cuisine, including *wazwan* (preparations of mutton and chicken), the traditional Kashmiri feast. It offers an old-town walking tour combined with lunch for ₹2500.

✕ Paharganj & West Delhi

Paharganj's restaurants are a reflection of the globetrotting backpackers who eat here. As well as Indian staples, you'll find everything from banana pancakes to Israeli falafel...executed with varying degrees of success. There are more cheap eats in the bazaars at Karol Bagh.

★ Sita Ram Dewan Chand
INDIAN $
(Map p56; 2243 Chuna Mandi; half/full plate ₹25/45; ◷8am-6pm; M Ramakrishna Ashram Marg) A family-run hole-in-the-wall, serving inexpensive portions of just one dish – *chole bhature* (spicy chickpeas), accompanied by delicious, freshly made, puffy, fried bread. It's a traditional breakfast but you can feast on it any time of day.

Brown Bread Bakery
ORGANIC $
(Map p56; Ajay Guesthouse, 5084-A, Main Bazaar; snacks ₹65-150; ◷7am-11pm; ☎; M Ramakrishna Ashram Marg) With a rustic, wicker-heavy interior and a long menu of largely organic breads, cheeses, jams, soups, teas and more, the Brown Bread is a nice relaxing place to hang out among other travellers from all over the place. You can also buy ayurvedic products here.

Sonu Chat House
INDIAN $
(Map p56; 5045, 46 Main Bazaar; dishes ₹60-160; ◷8am-1am; M Ramakrishna Ashram Marg) Perhaps Paharganj's most palatable *dhaba* (snack bar), this sunken small hive of activity is popular with foreign tourists and locals and serves up tasty thalis (from ₹70) and *masala dosa* (₹70).

Bikanervala Angan
FAST FOOD $
(82 Arya Samaj Rd, Karol Bagh; mains ₹80-170; ◷8am-midnight; M Karol Bagh) From the Bikanervala stable, this small but buzzing Karol Bagh canteen is a useful pit stop for South Indian treats, fast food and snacks. Thalis start at ₹135.

Roshan di Kulfi
ICE CREAM $
(Ajmal Khan Rd, Karol Bagh; kulfi ₹70-80; ◷8.30am-9.30pm; M Karol Bagh) A Karol Bagh institution for its scrumptious special *pista badam kulfi* (frozen milk dessert with pistachio, almond and cardamom). It's around 500m northeast of Karol Bagh metro.

★ Shimtur
KOREAN $$
(Map p56; 3rd fl, Navrang Guest House, Tooti Galli; meals ₹240-500; ◷10am-11pm; M Ramakrishna Ashram Marg) It's a mini-adventure to find this place, off the main drag and on top of the Navrang Guest House. Follow the stairs up several floors and you'll find a neat little bamboo-lined rooftop. The Korean food is fresh, authentic and delicious. Try the *bibimbap* (rice bowl with a mix of vegetables, egg and pickles; ₹240).

Tadka
INDIAN $$

(Map p56; 4986 Ramdwara Rd; mains ₹140-160; ⊙9am-10.30pm; Ⓜ Ramakrishna Ashram Marg) Named for everyone's favourite dhal, Tadka serves up tasty paneer dishes and other veg treats (thalis ₹170) under whirring fans, to an appreciative clientele of vegetarians and meat-avoiders.

Malhotra
MULTICUISINE $$

(Map p56; 1833 Laxmi Narayan St; mains ₹100-600; ⊙7am-11pm; Ⓜ Ramakrishna Ashram Marg) One street back from the Main Bazaar, Malhotra is smarter than most, with a good menu of set breakfasts, burgers, Indian and spirited attempts at continental dishes.

Cafe Fresh
CAFE $$

(Map p56; Laxmi Narayan St; dishes ₹100-200; ⊙8am-11pm; 🛜) This vegetarian cafe has reasonably good food and is an appealingly calm place to retreat (down a few steps) from the busy streets. Free wi-fi.

Metropolis Restaurant & Bar
MULTICUISINE $$

(Map p56; Metropolis Tourist Home, Main Bazaar; mains ₹300-1000; ⊙11am-11pm) On the rooftop at Metropolis Tourist Home, this energetic travellers' haunt is a cut above the competition, with prices to match, proffering cold beer and tasty tandoori chicken.

✗ Connaught Place

★ Hotel Saravana Bhavan
SOUTH INDIAN $

(Map p42; 15 P-Block, Connaught Place; mains ₹65-165; ⊙8am-11pm; Ⓜ Rajiv Chowk) Delhi's best thali is served up in unassuming surroundings – a simple Tamil canteen on the edge of Connaught Place. There are queues every meal time to sample the splendid array of richly spiced veg curries, dips, breads and condiments that make it onto every thali plate. There's a second branch on Janpath (Map p42; 46 Janpath; Ⓜ Rajiv Chowk).

Nizam's Kathi Kabab
FAST FOOD $

(Map p42; 5 H-Block, Connaught Place; kebabs ₹75-265; ⊙11.30am-11pm; Ⓜ Rajiv Chowk) This takeaway eatery creates masterful kebabs, biryani and *kati* rolls (kebabs wrapped in a hot *paratha*). It's always busy with meat-loving hordes, but there are also paneer, mushroom and egg options available so vegetarians don't have to miss out.

Coffee Home
INDIAN $

(Map p42; Baba Kharak Singh Marg; meals ₹35-70; ⊙11am-8pm; Ⓜ Rajiv Chowk) Popular with local workers, this has a lovely shady garden eating area, under the boughs of a peepal tree. It's always busy with locals feasting on South Indian snacks such as *masala dosa* (₹70), and is handily located next to the government emporiums.

Wenger's
BAKERY $

(Map p42; 16 A-Block, Connaught Place; snacks ₹30-90; ⊙10.45am-7.45pm; Ⓜ Rajiv Chowk) Legendary Wenger's has a wonderfully stuck-in-time feel having been baking since 1926. Come for cakes, sandwiches, biscuits and savoury patties. Around the corner you can eat in at Wenger's Deli (Map p42), which has the most delicious milkshakes, including mango (₹90).

Sagar Ratna
SOUTH INDIAN $$

(The Ashok, 50 B, Diplomatic Enclave; dishes ₹240-345; ⊙8am-11pm; Ⓜ Rajiv Chowk) Considered best of all the Sagar Ratna's around town, this venerable South Indian restaurant is always buzzing with families, couples and kitty parties, and does a great line in dosas, *idlis*, uttapams (savoury rice pancakes) and thalis. There are other branches in Connaught Place (Map p42; 15-K Block; dishes ₹100-250; ⊙8am-11pm; Ⓜ Rajiv Chowk) and Defence Colony Market (Map p50; Defence Colony Market; Ⓜ Lajpat Nagar).

Kake-da-Hotel
MUGHLAI $$

(Map p42; ☑9136666820; 67 Municipal Market; mains ₹140-530; ⊙noon-11.30pm; Ⓜ Rajiv Chowk) This simple *dhaba* (snack bar) is a basic hole in the wall that's popular with local workers for its famous butter chicken (₹180) and other Mughlai Punjabi dishes.

★ Rajdhani
INDIAN $$$

(Map p42; ☑43501200; 1/90 P-Block, Connaught Place; thalis ₹395, dinner & weekends ₹445; ⊙noon-4pm & 7-11pm; Ⓜ Rajiv Chowk) This pristine, nicely decorated two-level place serves up excellent-value food-of-the-gods vegetarian thalis with a fantastic array of Gujarati and Rajasthani dishes. It's the same, sumptuous thali daily.

Véda
INDIAN $$$

(Map p42; ☑41513535; 27 H-Block, Connaught Place; mains ₹400-1300; ⊙12.30-11.30pm; Ⓜ Rajiv Chowk) Fashion designer Rohit Baal created Véda's sumptuous interior, making for Connaught Place's most dimly lit eatery, a dark boudoir with swirling neo-Murano chandeliers and shimmering mirror mosaics. The menu proffers tasty classic Mughlai dishes (butter chicken, dhal makhani and the like) and they mix a mean Martini.

Swagath
SOUTH INDIAN $$$

(Map p46; ☑ 23366761; Janpath Hotel, Janpath; mains ₹195-1395; ☺ noon-11.45pm; ☏; Ⓜ Patel Chowk) Serving supremely scrumptious Indian seafood (especially crab, prawns, lobster and fish), Swagath will take you on a culinary tour through the fishing villages of South India. There are several branches, including at **Defence Colony Market** (Map p50; ☺ noon-11.45pm; Ⓜ Lajpat Nagar) and **M Block Market** (Map p50; ☺ noon-11.45pm).

Zäffrän
MUGHLAI $$$

(Map p46; ☑ 43582610; Hotel Palace Heights, 26-28 D-Block; mains ₹435-800; ☺ noon-3.30pm & 7pm-midnight) An excellent restaurant serving Mughlai cuisine, with a lovely, calm bamboo-shuttered, glass-covered terrace and plenty of light.

United Coffee House
MULTICUISINE $$$

(Map p42; ☑ 23416075; 15 E-Block, Connaught Place; mains ₹345-1000; ☺ noon-midnight; Ⓜ Rajiv Chowk) Not a coffee shop, but an upscale, high-ceilinged, chandeliered restaurant, with an old-world dining room full of characters who look as elderly as the fixtures and fittings. The menu covers everything from butter chicken to English high tea. Serves alcohol (a pint of Kingfisher costs ₹225).

Zen
CHINESE $$$

(Map p42; ☑ 23357444; 25 `B-Block, Connaught Place; mains ₹189-635; ☺ 11am-11pm; Ⓜ Rajiv Chowk) A high-ceilinged place with walls quilted like a Chanel handbag, Zen offers a more authentic take on Chinese cuisine than most Delhi eateries. Look out for dishes such as claypot tofu and spicy shredded lamb among the familiar standards.

🍴 New Delhi & Around

To dine in style, head to Delhi's upmarket hotels or the posh enclaves around Khan Market, Lodi Rd and Mathura Rd. Shoppers at Khan Market, in particular, will be spoilt for choice.

Lodi Colony Kebab Stands
STREET FOOD $

(Map p46; Hazrat Nizam-ud-din Dargah; kebabs from ₹30; ☺ noon-11pm; Ⓜ JLN Stadium) The alley in front of Hazrat Nizam-ud-din Dargah becomes a hive of activity every evening as devotees leave the shrine in search of suste-

nance. Canteen-style kebab houses cook up lip-smacking beef, mutton and chicken kebabs at bargain prices, with biryani and roti as filling side orders.

Andhra Pradesh Bhawan Canteen
SOUTH INDIAN $

(Map p46; 1 Ashoka Rd; breakfast ₹60, thalis ₹110; ☺ 7.30-10.30am, noon-3pm & 7.30-10pm; Ⓜ Patel Chowk) A hallowed bargain, the canteen at the Andhra Pradesh state house serves cheap and delicious unlimited South Indian thalis to a seemingly unlimited stream of patrons. Come on Sunday for the Hyderabadi biryani (₹180).

Nathu's
SOUTH INDIAN $

(Map p46; Sunder Nagar Market; dishes & snacks ₹60-100; ☺ 7am-11pm) A much-loved sweeterie serving up yummy *chaat* (Indian snacks), such as *golgappas* (crispy spheres with spicy filling, like eating a delicious water bomb), and filling 'mini meals.' Upstairs is Navanda's, with a broad menu of veg and nonveg Indian and Chinese treats.

Comesum
FAST FOOD $

(Map p46; Nizamuddin Train Station; dishes ₹180-300; ☺ 24hr) Fast food, from dosas to *kadhai* (metal pot) curries, served in double-quick time at all hours. There are branches at all the main train stations, but the biggest and best is at Nizamuddin.

★ Alkauser
STREET FOOD $$

(Map p46; www.alkausermughlaifood.com; Kautilya Marg; kebabs from ₹130, biryani from ₹250; ☺ 6-10.30pm) The family behind this hole-in-the-wall takeaway earned their stripes cooking kebabs for the Nawabs of Lucknow in the 1890s. The house speciality is the *kakori* kebab, a pâté-smooth combination of lamb and spices, but other treats include biryani (cooked *dum pukht* style in a *handi* pot sealed with pastry) and perfectly prepared lamb *burra* (marinated chops) and *murg malai tikka* (chicken marinated with spices and paneer). There are several branches, including one in the **Safdarjand Enclave market** (Map p50; ☺ 6-10.30pm; Ⓜ AIIMS).

★ Sodabottleopenerwala
PARSI $$

(Map p46; Khan Market; dishes ₹125-500; ☺ 11am-11.15pm; Ⓜ Khan Market) Suggesting a typical Parsi surname (taken from a trade), this place emulates the Iranian cafes of Mumbai and the food is authentic Persian. The upstairs terrace has a good deal more charm. The menu includes Iranian cakes and

'Bombay specials' including delicious *kanda bhaji* (crispy onion fritters).

Kitchen Cafe
MULTICUISINE **$$**

(Map p46; ☑ 41757960; Khan Market; mains ₹400-600; ⊙11am-11pm; Ⓜ Khan Market) A buzzing small cafe offering an informal alternative to the glam eateries. The menu trots from Italy (pasta) to Thailand (pad thai) to England (fish and chips).

Khan Chacha
FAST FOOD **$$**

(Map p46; Khan Market; snacks ₹170-240; ⊙noon-11pm; Ⓜ Khan Market) A simple eatery serving lip-smacking roti-wrapped mutton, chicken and paneer kebabs to a youthful crowd who appreciate the moderate prices and no-fuss attitude.

Mamagoto
ASIAN FUSION **$$**

(Map p46; ☑ 45166060; Middle Lane, Khan Market; mains ₹300-500; ⊙12.30-11.30pm; Ⓜ Khan Market) The name means 'to play with food' in Japanese, and the kidult theme extends to the funky manga art on the walls. The eclectic menu spans Japan, China and Southeast Asia – including some authentically spicy hawker-style Thai food.

Amici
ITALIAN **$$**

(Map p46; ☑ 43587191; 47 Khan Market; pizzas ₹300-400; ⊙11am-11pm; Ⓜ Khan Market) Calm and unpretentious, Amici actually pays some attention to the way they make pizzas in Italy. The pulled pork sandwich is also recommended.

★ Bukhara
INDIAN **$$$**

(Map p46; ☑ 26112233; ITC Maurya, Sadar Patel Marg; mains ₹750-2400; ⊙12.30-2.45pm & 7-11.45pm) Widely considered Delhi's best restaurant, this glam hotel eatery serves Northwest Frontier–style cuisine at low tables, with delectable melt-in-the-mouth kebabs and its famous Bukhara dhal. Reservations are essential.

Dhaba
PUNJABI **$$$**

(Map p46; ☑ 39555000; The Claridges, 12 Aurangzeb Rd; dishes ₹425-1295; ⊙12.30-2.30pm & 7-11.30pm; Ⓜ Racecourse) Set in the ritzy Claridges hotel, Dhaba is a fun and tasty choice, offering a posh take on Punjabi highway cuisine, including delicious dhal, *b¶alti* (curry cooked in a small dish called a *kadhai*) and *kulfi* (frozen milk dessert with pistachio, almond and cardamom), in a room that looks like a Punjabi highway, with half a Tata truck on the wall and Bollywood hits on the stereo.

Lodi Garden Restaurant
MEDITERRANEAN **$$$**

(Map p46; ☑ 24652808; Lodi Rd; mains ₹400-1700; ⊙12.30pm-12.45am; Ⓜ Jor Bagh) Set in a funky garden with lanterns dangling from the trees and tables in curtained pavilions and wooden carts, this is the most romantic dinner spot in New Delhi. Although not quite as impressive as the surroundings, the menu traverses Europe and the Middle East, and there's a popular Sunday brunch.

Pandara Market
INDIAN **$$$**

(Map p46; Pandara Rd; mains ₹365-700; ⊙noon-1am; Ⓜ Khan Market) Less a market than a strip of upmarket restaurants, this is a good option for night owls – some eateries here are open to 1am or later. Prices, standards and atmosphere are very similar along the strip. For quality Mughlai and North Indian food, try **Gulati** (mains ₹150-500; ⊙noon-1am), **Havemore** (mains ₹160-390; ⊙noon-2am), nicely made-over **Pindi** (mains ₹150-500; ⊙noon-midnight), or the surpisingly glitzy **Chicken Inn** (mains ₹150-500; ⊙noon-1am). For Indian-style Chinese and Thai food, head to **Ichiban** (mains ₹150-500; ⊙noon-12.30am).

✗ South Delhi

South Delhi's best eateries are tucked away in the southern suburbs of Hauz Khas, Greater Kailash II, Saket, Vasant Vihar and further afield.

★ Coast
SOUTH INDIAN **$$**

(Map p50; above Ogaan, Hauz Khas; set meals ₹340-440; ⊙noon-midnight; Ⓜ Green Park) A beautifully light, bright restaurant on several levels, with wonderful views over the parklands of Hauz Khas, Coast serves delicious, elegant cuisine, with light southern Indian dishes, such as *avial* (vegetable curry) with pumpkin *erisheri* (with black lentils) or European cuisine, such as salad with orange and walnuts.

Potbelly
BIHARI **$$**

(Map p50; 116C Shahpur Jat Village; mains ₹190-350; ⊙12.30-11pm; Ⓜ Hauz Khas) In the hip, boutique-filled urban village of Shahpur Jat: climb several flights of higgledy piggledy stairs to reach Potbelly, a rooftop cafe with good views and a lovely artsy mix of painted watering cans and cane furniture. The food is delicious – try the Bihari burger or *keema goli* (mutton meatballs).

Not Just Parathas INDIAN $$
(Map p50; 84 M-Block, Great Kailash II; dishes ₹90-625; ⊙ noon-midnight) They don't just serve *parathas* (stuffed flatbread), they serve 120 types of *parathas!* Try them stuffed with kebabs, veg curries, shredded chicken and untold other fillings.

★ **Indian Accent** INDIAN $$$
(Map p50; ☑ 26925151; Manor, 77 Friends Colony; tasting menu veg/nonveg ₹2595/2695) Overlooking lush lawns at the Manor hotel (p59), this exclusive restaurant serves inspired modern Indian cuisine. Familiar and unfamiliar ingredients are thrown together in surprising and beautifully creative combinations. The tasting menu is recommended, though its portions are remarkably small. But the food is delicious: sample delights such as *cheeni ki roti* (a hard bread stuffed with jaggery), and bacon-stuffed *kulcha* (soft-leavened Indian-style bread).

Olive MEDITERRANEAN $$$
(Map p50; ☑ 29574443; One Style Mile, Mehrauli; dishes ₹450-1350; ⊙ noon-midnight; Ⓜ Qutab Minar) Uberchic Olive with its uberchic clientele creates a little piece of the Mediterranean in the suburbs. The *haveli* setting, combined with beach-house colours, is unlike anywhere else in Delhi. Come for inventive Mediterranean dishes, such as scallops with mascarpone, quinoa, amaranth, pumpkin seeds and apricot-orange purée, and astoundingly good pizza.

Punjab Grill MUGHLAI $$$
(Map p50; ☑ 41572977; Select Citywalk, Saket; mains ₹420-1200; ⊙ 11am-11.30pm; Ⓜ Malviya Nagar) Don't be put off by the shopping-mall setting. This sleek eatery offers superior Mughlai food – kebabs, *kadhai* (metal pot) curries and unleavened breads – in classy surroundings. Take your pick from the gleaming dining room or the open-air terrace.

🍸 Drinking & Nightlife

Whether it's cappuccino and pastries for breakfast or beer and bites in the evening, Delhi has plenty of places to wet your whistle. For the latest places to go at night, check the hip and informative **Little Black Book** (www.littleblackbookdelhi.com) or **Brown Paper Bag** (http://bpbweekend.com/delhi). For gigs, check **Wild City** (www.thewildcity.com).

Cafes

Chain coffee shops abound – Café Coffee Day is the most prolific, but there are also numerous branches of Costa and Barista.

★ **Imperial** CAFE
Raise your pinkie finger! High tea at the Imperial (p57) is perhaps the most refined way to while away an afternoon in Delhi. Sip tea from bone-china cups and pluck dainty sandwiches and cakes from tiered stands, while discussing the latest goings-on in Shimla and Dalhousie. High tea is served in the Atrium from 3pm to 6pm daily (weekday/weekend ₹1100/1400 plus tax).

Café Turtle CAFE
(Map p46; Full Circle Bookstore, Khan Market; ⊙ 9.30am-9.30pm; Ⓜ Khan Market) Allied to the Full Circle Bookstore, this boho cafe ticks all the boxes when you're in the mood for coffee, cake and a calm reading space. There are branches in **N-Block Market** (Map p50; Greater Kailash Part I) and **Nizamuddin East** (Map p46).

Cha Bar CAFE
(Map p42; Oxford Bookstore, N81 Connaught Place; ⊙ 10am-9.30pm Mon-Sat, 11am-9.30pm Sun; Ⓜ Rajiv Chowk) Connaught Place's smart Oxford Bookstore contains the swish cafe Cha Bar, with more than 75 types of tea to choose from, as well as cakes and snacks, including a respectable fish and chips.

Kunzum Travel Cafe CAFE
(Map p50; www.kunzum.com; T49 Hauz Khas Village; ⊙ 11am-7.30pm Tue-Sun; 🛜; Ⓜ Green Park) Run by the team of travel writers behind the informative *Delhi 101* guidebook, Kunzum has a pay-what-you-like policy for the self-service French-press coffee and tea. There's free wi-fi and books and magazines to browse. They also run heritage walks.

Indian Coffee House CAFE
(Map p42; 2nd fl, Mohan Singh Place, Baba Kharak Singh Marg; ⊙ 9am-9pm; Ⓜ Rajiv Chowk) Stuck-in-time Indian Coffee House has lots of faded (to the point of dilapidation) charm. The roof terrace is a popular hang-out thanks to the staggeringly cheap menu of snacks (₹20 to ₹50) and it serves up South Indian coffee; there is a 'ladies and families' section.

Big Chill CAFE
(Map p46; Khan Market; ⊙ noon-11.30pm; Ⓜ Khan Market) There are two branches of this film-poster-lined cafe at Khan Market, packed

with chattering Delhi-ites. The menu is a directory of continental and Indian dishes. There's a branch at the DLF Place mall (Map p50; Ⓜ Malviya Nagar) in Saket.

Keventer's Milkshakes CAFE

(Map p42; 17 A-Block, Connaught Place; milkshakes ₹50-80; ⊙9am-11pm; Ⓜ Rajiv Chowk) If you want to find the best cheap treats, follow the teenagers. Keventer's has a cult following for its legendary milkshakes, slurped out of milk bottles on the pavement in front of the stand.

Bars

The nightlife scene in Delhi is fairly low-key, but a party mood prevails from Wednesday to Saturday, particularly in the bar-rammed enclave of Hauz Khas. There are also increasing numbers of bars in Paharganj.

A smart-casual dress code (no shorts, vests or flip-flops) applies at many places. Taxes can pack a nasty punch (alcoholic 20%, nonalcoholic 12.5%); they are not included here unless indicated. Most bars have two-for-one happy hours from around noon till 8pm.

★ Monkey Bar BAR

(Map p42; P3 Connaught Circus; ⊙noon-12.30pm; Ⓜ Rajiv Chowk) With exposed brick walls and piping, Monkey Bar is CP's coolest choice, with a friendly, buzzy vibe, and a '90s neo-industrial look. It's the kind of place the cast of *Friends* might have hung out, if they lived in Delhi. Try the excellent buffalo burgers with Gruyère, Gouda, whisky glaze, Bloody Mary tomatoes and umami ketchup and sample out-there cocktails (goat cheese as an ingredient?).

Hauz Khas Social BAR

(Map p50; 9A & 12 Hauz Khas Village; Ⓜ Green Park) Enter down a muralled passageway and through an unsigned door, which opens onto several large rooms with plate-glass windows, overlooking Hauz Khas' lush park. There's a space for the local hipster clientele to work or have laid-back meetings, lots of room for cocktails (served in measuring jugs) and snacks, and a busy smokers' terrace. There's also regular live music and DJs.

★ 1911 BAR

(Map p42; Imperial Hotel, Janpath; cocktails ₹750-1200, beer from ₹400; ⊙noon-12.45am; Ⓜ Rajiv Chowk) The elegant bar at the Imperial is the ultimate neocolonial extravagance. Sip perfectly prepared cocktails in front of murals of cavorting maharajas.

Barsoom BAR

(Map p50; 3rd fl, 26 Hauz Khas Village; Ⓜ Green Park) Barsoom was the dying Mars created by American pulp fiction author Edgar Rice Burroughs, and this bar has a cool, extra-terrestrial vibe, with mid-century-modern-style furniture upholstered in funky Aztec prints, and delectable snacks on the menu. It's a good place to catch live music, with eclectic sounds such as psychedelic sitar from Al Cometo.

Aqua BAR

(Map p42; Park Hotel, 15 Sansad Marg; ⊙11am-midnight; Ⓜ Rajiv Chowk) If you feel the need for some five-star style after visiting Jantar Mantar or shopping in Connaught Place, Aqua is a good place to flop, forget the world outside, and sip cocktails by the pool.

My Bar BAR

(Map p56; Main Bazaar, Paharganj; ⊙10am-12.30pm; Ⓜ Ramakrishna Ashram Marg) A dark and dingy bar, this is lively, loud and fun, with a cheery, mixed crowd of backpackers and locals, who'll even come here from outside Paharganj. There are several other branches, in CP and Hauz Khas, but this is the one to go for.

Sam's Bar BAR

(Map p56; Main Bazaar, Paharganj; ⊙noon-midnight; Ⓜ Ramakrishna Ashram Marg) This sophisticated (for Paharganj) addition to the Vivek Hotel empire on the Main Bazaar is a good choice for a drink and a chat, with a mixed crowd of men and women, locals and foreigners. On the menu you'll find plentiful snacks and a choice of local (Kingfisher ₹100) or international beers or spirits. The best seats are by the plate-glass windows overlooking the street.

Gem BAR

(Map p56; 1050 Main Bazaar, Paharganj; ⊙9am-midnight; Ⓜ Ramakrishna Ashram Marg) This dark, wood-panelled dive is a good, if seedy place to hang out with locals and other travellers; bottles of local beer cost from ₹100. The upstairs area has more atmosphere.

⭐ Entertainment

To access Delhi's dynamic arts scene, check local listings. October and March is the 'season', with shows and concerts (often free) happening nightly.

Music & Cultural Performances

Blues — LIVE MUSIC

(Map p42; 18 N-Block, Connaught Place; ☺noon-1am; Ⓜ Rajiv Chowk) A dark den with reasonably priced beers and random photos of rock stars on its brick walls. It's a lively, snob-free zone with a live band daily from 6.30pm.

Attic — CULTURAL PROGRAM

(Map p42; ☑23746050; www.theatticdelhi.org; 36 Regal Bldg, Sansad Marg; Ⓜ Rajiv Chowk) Small arts organisation set up to promote textiles and arts and crafts, with regular free or inexpensive exhibitions, music and dance lectures and workshops.

Habitat World — CULTURAL PROGRAM

(Map p46; ☑43663333; www.habitatworld.com; India Habitat Centre, Lodi Rd; Ⓜ Jor Bagh) Temporary art shows at the Visual Arts Gallery, and plays and arty performances in the public courtyards.

India International Centre — CULTURAL PROGRAM

(Map p46; ☑24619431; www.iicdelhi.nic.in; 40 Max Mueller Marg; Ⓜ Khan Market) This cultural centre holds regular free exhibitions, talks and cultural performances.

Cinemas

Delite Cinema — CINEMA

(Map p38; ☑23272903; 4/1, Asaf Ali Rd; Ⓜ New Delhi) Founded in 1955, the Delite was renovated in 2006 but still has a resolutely old-school, grandiose feel. It's a great place to see a masala picture (full-throttle Bollywood, a mix of action, comedy, romance and drama), with famous extra-large samosas available in the interval.

Big Cinemas Odeon — CINEMA

(Map p42; www.bigcinemas.com/in; 23 D-Block, Connaught Place; Ⓜ Rajiv Chowk) A smart modern cinema screening Bollywood blockbusters and Hollywood hits.

PVR Plaza Cinema — CINEMA

(Map p42; www.pvrcinemas.com; H-Block, Connaught Place; Ⓜ Rajiv Chowk) Glossy chain cinema, screening the latest Bollywood releases as well as high-profile Hollywood imports. There are branches on Baba Kharak Singh

Marg (Map p42; Ⓜ Rajiv Chowk) and at Basant Lok Community Centre (Map p50; Vasant Vihar; ; Ⓜ Hauz Khas) and Select Citywalk mall (Map p50; www.pvrcinemas.com; ; Ⓜ Malviya Nagar) in Saket.

🛍 Shopping

Delhi is a fabulous place to shop, from its glittering, frenetic bazaars to its gleaming boutiques and amazing regional craft outlets. Away from government-run emporiums and other fixed-price shops, haggle like you mean it. Many taxi and autorickshaw drivers earn commissions (via your inflated purchase price) by taking travellers to dubious, overpriced places – don't fall for it.

🏛 Old Delhi

As well as the many shops and markets to explore, it's worth browsing the myriad music shops (Map p38; Netaji Subhash Marg; ☺Mon-Sat) along Netaji Subhash Marg for sitars, tabla sets and other beautifully crafted Indian instruments.

Main Bazaar — HANDICRAFTS, CLOTHING

(Paharganj; ☺10am-9pm Tue-Sun; Ⓜ Ramakrishna Ashram Marg) The backpacker-oriented bazaar that runs through Paharganj is lined with shops and stalls selling everything from incense and hippy kaftans to religious stickers and cloth printing blocks. Haggle with purpose. The market is officially closed on Monday, but most stores stay open.

Aap Ki Pasand (San Cha) — DRINK

(Map p38; www.sanchatea.com; 15 Netaji Subhash Marg; ☺9.30am-7pm Mon-Sat) An elegant tea shop selling a full range of Indian teas, from Darjeeling and Assam to Nilgiri and Kangra. You can try before you buy, and teas come lovingly packaged in drawstring bags. There's another branch Santushti Shopping Complex (Chanakyapuri, Racecourse Rd; ☺10am-6.30pm Mon-Sat; Ⓜ Racecourse).

Karol Bagh Market — MARKET

(Map p38; ☺around 10am-7pm Tue-Sun; Ⓜ Karol Bagh) This brash middle-class market shimmers with all things sparkly, from dressy *lehanga choli* (skirt-and-blouse sets) to princess-style shoes, spices, fruit and nuts packed in shiny paper, and chrome motorcycle parts.

OLD DELHI'S BAZAARS

Old Delhi's bazaars are a head-spinning assault on the senses: an aromatic barrage of incense, spices, rickshaw fumes, body odour and worse, with a constant soundtrack of shouts, barks, music and car horns. This is less retail therapy, more heightened reality. The best time to come is midmorning, when you actually move through the streets.

Whole districts here are devoted to individual items. **Chandni Chowk** (Map p42; Old Delhi; ⊙10am-7pm Mon-Sat; Ⓜ Chandni Chowk) is all clothing, electronics and break-as-soon-as-you-buy-them novelties. For silver jewellery, head for **Dariba Kalan** (Map p38), the alley near the Sisganj Gurdwara. Off this lane, the **Kinari Bazaar** (Map p38), literally 'trimmings market', is famous for *zardozi* (gold embroidery), temple trim and wedding turbans. Running south from the old Town Hall, **Nai Sarak** (Map p38) is lined with stalls selling saris, shawls, chiffon and *lehanga* (long skins with waist cords), while nearby **Ballimaran** (Map p38) has sequined slippers and fancy, curly-toed *jootis*.

Beside the Fatehpuri Masjid, on Khari Baoli, is the nose-numbing **Spice Market** (Gadodia Market; Map p38; Khari Baoli), ablaze with piles of scarlet-red chillies, ginger and turmeric roots, peppercorns, cumin, coriander seeds, cardamom, dried fruit and nuts. For gorgeous wrapping paper and wedding cards, head to **Chawri Bazaar** (Map p38), leading west from the Jama Masjid. For steel cooking pots and cheap-as-chapattis paper kites, continue northwest to **Lal Kuan Main Bazaar** (Map p38).

🛍 Connaught Place

★**State Emporiums**   HANDICRAFTS, CLOTHING
(Map p42; Baba Kharak Singh Marg; ⊙11am-7pm Mon-Sat; Ⓜ Rajiv Chowk) Nestling side by side are the treasure-filled official emporiums of the different Indian states. Shopping here is like taking a tour around India – top stops include Kashmir, for papier mâché and carpets; Rajasthan, for miniature paintings and puppets; Uttar Pradesh, for marble inlaywork; Karnataka, for sandalwood sculptures; Tamil Nadu, for metal statues; and Odisha (Orissa), for stone carvings.

★**Kamala**   HANDICRAFTS
(Map p42; Baba Kharak Singh Marg; ⊙10am-6.45pm Mon-Sat; Ⓜ Rajiv Chowk) Upscale crafts and curios, designed with real panache, from the Crafts Council of India.

Central Cottage Industries Emporium   HANDICRAFTS
(Map p42; ☎ 23326790; Janpath; ⊙10am-7pm; Ⓜ Rajiv Chowk) This government-run, fixed-price multilevel Aladdin's cave of India-wide handicrafts is a great place to browse. Prices are higher than in the state emporiums, but the selection of woodcarvings, jewellery, pottery, papier mâché, *jootis* (traditional slip-on shoes), brassware, textiles, beauty products and miniature paintings is superb.

Khadi Gramodyog Bhawan   CLOTHING
(Map p42; Baba Kharak Singh Marg; ⊙10am-7.45pm Mon-Sat; Ⓜ Rajiv Chowk) 🏷 Known for its excellent *khadi* (homespun cloth), including good-value shawls, plus handmade paper, incense, spices, henna and lovely natural soaps.

Oxford Bookstore   BOOKS
(Map p42; N81 Connaught Place; ⊙10am-9.30pm Mon-Sat, 11am-9.30pm Sun; Ⓜ Rajiv Chowk) The newly located CP Oxford Bookstore is a beautifully designed, swish bookshop where you could browse for hours, though staff are not as knowledgeable as at other Delhi bookshops. It also sells good gifts, such as handmade paper notebooks. The attached Cha Bar (p65) is a great meeting spot.

Janpath & Tibetan Markets   HANDICRAFTS
(Map p42; Janpath; ⊙10.30am-7.30pm Mon-Sat; Ⓜ Rajiv Chowk) These twin markets sell the usual trinkets: shimmering mirrorwork embroidery, colourful shawls, Tibetan bric-a-brac, brass oms and dangly earrings. There are some good finds if you rummage through the junk. Haggle hard.

The Shop   CLOTHING, HOMEWARES
(Map p42; 10 Regal Bldg, Sansad Marg; ⊙10am-7.30pm Mon-Sat; Ⓜ Rajiv Chowk) Lovely homewares and clothes (including children's clothes) from all over India in a chic boutique with fixed prices.

People Tree HANDICRAFTS, CLOTHING
(Map p42; Regal Bldg, Sansad Marg; ⊘10.30am-7pm Mon-Sat; Ⓜ Rajiv Chowk) ✐ Teeny tiny fair-trade vedors People Tree sells cool T-shirts with funky Indian designs and urban attitude, as well as bags, jewellery and books. There's a branch in Hauz Khas village (Map p50; Ⓜ Hauz Khas).

Fabindia CLOTHING, HOMEWARES
(Map p42; www.fabindia.com; 28 B-Block, Connaught Place; ⊘11am-8pm; Ⓜ Rajiv Chowk) Reasonably priced ready-made clothes in funky Indian fabrics, from elegant kurtas and dupattas to Western-style shirts, plus stylish homewares. There are branches at Green Park (Map p50; Ⓜ Green Park), Khan Market (Map p46; Ⓜ Khan Market), N-Block Market (Map p50; Greater Kailash I; Ⓜ Kailash Colony) and Select Citywalk (Map p50, Saket; Ⓜ Malviya Nagar).

Godin Music MUSIC
(Map p42; Regal Bldg, Sansad Marg; ⊘11am-8pm; Ⓜ Rajiv Chowk) Fine musical instruments, from guitars to sitars, displayed in a modern showroom, though Godin has been going since 1940 and was once the tuner for Mountbatten's pianos.

M Ram & Sons CLOTHING
(Map p42; ☏23416558; 21 E-Block, Connaught Place; ⊘10.30am-8pm; Ⓜ Rajiv Chowk) A popular Delhi tailor, offering suits from ₹8000 (including material).

Marques & Co MUSIC
(Map p42; 14 G-Block, Connaught Place; ⊘noon-5pm Mon-Sat; Ⓜ Rajiv Chowk) This vintage music shop (since 1918) sells guitars, tabla sets, harmonicas and sheet music, in stuck-in-time glass cabinets.

🔒 New Delhi

⭐Khan Market MARKET
(Map p46; ⊘around 10.30am-8pm Mon-Sat; Ⓜ Khan Market) ✐ Favoured by expats and Delhi's elite, Khan Market's boutiques focus on fashion, books and homewares. For handmade paper, check out Anand Stationers, or try Mehra Bros for cool papier-mâché ornaments and Christmas decorations. Literature lovers should head to Full Circle Bookstore and Bahrisons (www.booksatbahri.com). For ethnic-inspired fashions and homeware, hit Fabindia, Anokhi and Good Earth, and for elegantly packaged ayurvedic remedies, browse Kama.

Good Earth HOMEWARES
(Map p46; www.goodearth.in; 9 ABC Khan Market; ⊘11.30am-8.30pm; Ⓜ Khan Market) Stuck for ideas for how to fill your designer apartment? Look no further than Good Earth, Delhi's most chichi homewares store. The see-and-be-seen Latitude 28° cafe is upstairs. There are branches at the Santushti Shopping Complex (Map p46; Ⓜ Racecourse) and Select Citywalk (Map p50; Saket; Ⓜ Malviya Nagar).

Full Circle Bookstore BOOKS
(Map p46; www.fullcirclebooks.in; 23 Khan Market; ⊘9.30am-9.30pm; Ⓜ Khan Market) Delhi's most welcoming bookstore, with racks of specialist books on the city, plus novels and kids' books. Relaxing Café Turtle is upstairs. There are branches at N-Block Market (p70; Ⓜ Kailash Colony) and Nizamuddin East (Map p46; Ⓜ JLN Stadium).

Meher Chand Market BOUTIQUES
(Map p46; Lodhi Colony; Ⓜ JLN Stadium) This enclave has recently emerged as a hot place to shop, with independent shops selling homewares and clothes; it's a particularly good place to pick up beautifully designed childrenswear. To eat, try chic Chez Nini (79-80, Meher Chand Market).

Anokhi CLOTHING
(Map p46; www.anokhi.com; 32 Khan Market; ⊘10am-8pm; Ⓜ Khan Market) Anokhi specialises in blockprint clothes and homewares, showcasing traditional designs that have a modern design sensibility. There are branches at the Santushti Shopping Complex (Map p46; ⊘10am-7pm Mon-Sat; Ⓜ Racecourse), N Block Market (Map p50; Greater Kailash I; ⊘10am-8pm; Ⓜ Kailash Colony) and a discount store in Nizamuddin East (Map p46; ⊘10am-8pm Mon-Sat; Ⓜ JLN Stadium).

DARYAGANJ SUNDAY BOOK MARKET

Daryaganj Kitab Bazaar (Book Market; Map p38; ⊘8am-6pm Sun) It's wonderful rummaging for gems here, from first editions to Mills and Boon, many at rock-bottom prices. It takes place for around 2km from Delhi Gate, northwards to the Red Fort, and a shorter distance west along Jawaharlal Nehru Marg.

Delhi Metro Map

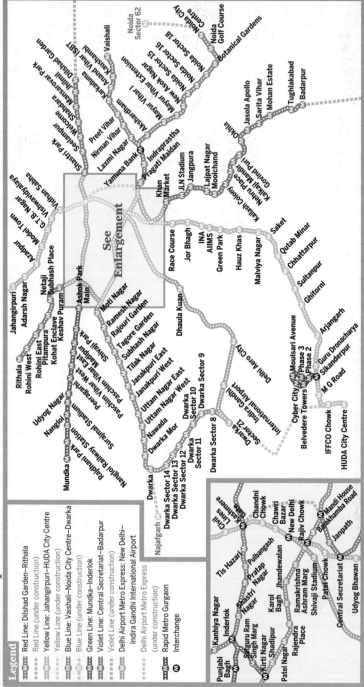

Legend

- Red Line: Dilshad Garden–Rithala
- Red Line (under construction)
- Yellow Line: Jahangirpuri–HUDA City Centre
- Yellow Line (under construction)
- Blue Line: Vaishali–Noida City Centre–Dwarka
- Blue Line (under construction)
- Green Line: Mundka–Inderlok
- Violet Line: Central Secretariat–Badarpur
- Violet Line (under construction)
- Delhi Airport Metro Express: New Delhi–Indira Gandhi International Airport
- Delhi Airport Metro Express (under construction)
- Rapid Metro Gurgaon
- Interchange

Sunder Nagar Market HANDICRAFTS
(Map p46; Mathura Rd; ⊙around 10.30am-7.30pm Mon-Sat; MPragati Maidan) This genteel enclave specialises in Indian and Nepali handicrafts, replica 'antiques', and furniture, and has two outstanding tea shops, selling fine Indian teas.

Santushti Shopping Complex HOMEWARES, CLOTHING
(Map p46; Kamal Ataturk Rd, Santushti Enclave; ⊙10am-7pm Mon-Sat; MRacecourse) Diplomats frequent this exclusive and serene complex facing the Ashok Hotel. Housed inside are stores such as Anokhi and Good Earth.

C Lal & Sons HANDICRAFTS
(Map p46; 9/172 Jor Bagh Market; ⊙10.30am-7.30pm; MJor Bagh) After sightseeing at Safdarjang's tomb, drop into Mr Lal's 'curiosity shop' for cute Christmas-tree decorations, papier mâché and carvings.

🏛 South Delhi

Delhi's glitziest malls are lined up along Press Enclave Marg in Saket. Here you'll find the full air-con shopping experience, plus soft play for kids. **Select Citywalk** has a PVR cinema (p67), branches of Fabindia and Good Earth, and lots of big-name eateries. **DLF Place** has the Kiran Nadar Museum of Art (p52), plus more of the same, including a branch of Bahrisons bookstore, while nearby **MGF Metropolitan** has several showy bars.

★**Hauz Khas Village** HANDICRAFTS, CLOTHING
(Map p50; ⊙11am-7pm Mon-Sat; MGreen Park) The tight alleyways of this arty little enclave are crammed with boutiques selling designer Indian-clothing, handicrafts, handmade furniture and old Bollywood movie posters.

★**Dilli Haat** HANDICRAFTS
(Map p50; Aurobindo Marg; admission ₹20; ⊙10.30am-10pm; MINA) Located opposite the colourful INA Market, this open-air food-and-crafts market is a cavalcade of colour, selling regional handicrafts. There are some gorgeous bits and pieces on offer; bargain hard. It's also a good place to sample cheap, delicious regional specialities, with lots of food stands.

Dastkar Nature Bazaar MARKET
(📋26808633; Andheria Modh; ⊙Tue-Sun; MChattarpur) Dastkar, a joint venture between an NGO and Delhi Tourism, holds

JHANDEWALAN HANUMAN TEMPLE

Jhandewalan Hanuman Temple (Map p38; Link Rd, Jhandewalan; ⊙dawn-dusk; MJhandewalan) While visiting the markets at Karol Bagh, it's worth making a detour to the surreal Jhandewalan Hanuman temple near Jhandewalan metro station. As well as a 34m-high Hanuman statue that soars above the train tracks, you can follow passageways through the mouths of demons to a series of atmospheric, deity-filled chambers.

monthly 12-day craft exhibitions. Each has a different theme and showcases cutting-edge regional culture, craft and food. There are also 15 permanent craft stalls.

N-Block Market MARKET
(Map p50; Greater Kailash I; ⊙10.30am-8pm Wed-Mon) Swanky boutiques and posh eateries, including popular branches of Fabindia, Anokhi and Full Circle Bookstore, complete with a Café Turtle.

Sarojini Nagar Market CLOTHING
(Map p50; ⊙around 11am-8pm Tue-Sun; MINA) Rummage here for cut-price Western-style clothes, with minor faults or blemishes, at bargain prices.

ℹ Information

DANGERS & ANNOYANCES

Shop & Hotel Touts Taxi-wallahs at the international airport and around tourist areas frequently act as touts for hotels, claiming that your chosen hotel is full, poor value, overbooked, dangerous, burned down or closed, or that there are riots in Delhi, as part of a ruse to steer you to a hotel where they will get a commission. Insist on being taken to where you want to go – making a show of writing down the registration plate number and phoning the autorickshaw/taxi helpline may help. Drivers and men who approach you at Connaught Place run a similar scam for private souvenir emporiums and tourist agents.

Travel Agent Touts Many travel agencies in Delhi claim to be tourist offices, even branding themselves with official tourist agency logos. There is only one tourist office – at 88 Janpath – and any other 'tourist office' is just a travel agency. Should you legitimately need the services of a travel agent, ask for a list of recommended agents from the bona-fide tourist office. Be wary of booking a multistop trip out of Delhi, particularly to Kashmir. Travellers are often hit for extra charges, or find out the class of travel and accommodation is less than they paid for.

Train Station Touts Touts (often dressed in official-looking uniform) at New Delhi train station endeavour to steer travellers away from the legitimate International Tourist Bureau (p74) and into private travel agencies where they earn a commission. An increasing problem is touts telling people that their tickets are invalid or that there's a problem with the trains, then helpfully assisting them in booking expensive alternative taxis or 3rd-class tickets passed off as something else. As a rule of thumb: don't believe anyone who approaches you trying to tell you anything at the train station.

INTERNET ACCESS

Most hotels offer free wi-fi access these days. At cafes offering free access, you'll probably have to show ID.

MEDIA

To check out what's on, see **Little Black Book** (www.littleblackbookdelhi.com) or **Brown Paper Bag** (www.bpbweekend.com/delhi). For printed listings see the weekly calendar pamphlet *Delhi Diary* (₹30), which is available at local bookshops.

MEDICAL SERVICES

Pharmacies are found on most shopping streets and in most suburban markets.

All India Institute of Medical Sciences (IIMS; Map p50; ☑ 40401010; www.aiims.edu; Ansari Nagar; Ⓜ AIIMS)

Apollo Hospital (☑ 29871090; www.apollo-hospdelhi.com; Mathura Rd, Sarita Vihar)

Dr Ram Manohar Lohia Hospital (Map p46; ☑ 23365525; www.rmlh.nic.in; Baba Kharak Singh Marg; Ⓜ Patel Chowk)

East West Medical Centre (☑ 24690429; www.eastwestrescue.com; 37 Prithviraj Rd)

MONEY

Banks with ATMs are everywhere you look in Delhi. Foreign exchange offices are concentrated along the Main Bazaar in Paharganj and around Connaught Place. Travel agents and moneychangers offer international money transfers.

Baluja Forex (Map p56; 4596 Main Bazaar, Paharganj; ⊗ 9am-7.30pm; Ⓜ New Delhi)

Thomas Cook (Map p42; ☑ 66271900/23; C33, 335 Inner Circle, Connaught Circus; ⊗ 9.30am-6.30pm Mon-Sat; Ⓜ Rajiv Chowk)

POST & TELEPHONE

Delhi has tons of telephone kiosks where you can make cheap local, interstate and international calls. Look for the STD ISD PCO signs.

DHL (Map p42; ☑ 23737587; ground fl, Mercantile Bldg, Tolstoy Marg; ⊗ 8am-8pm Mon-Sat; Ⓜ Rajiv Chowk)

Post Office (Map p42; 6 A-Block, Connaught Place; ⊗ 8am-7pm Mon-Sat; Ⓜ Rajiv Chowk)

TOURIST INFORMATION

India Tourism Delhi (Government of India; Map p42; ☑ 23320008; www.incredibleindia. org; 88 Janpath; ⊗ 9am-6pm Mon-Fri, to 2pm Sat; Ⓜ Rajiv Chowk) This is the only official tourist information centre outside the airport. Ignore touts who (falsely) claim to be associated with this office. Anyone who 'helpfully' approaches you is certainly not going to take you to the real office. It's a useful source of advice on Delhi, getting out of Delhi, and visiting surrounding states. Has a free Delhi map and brochures, and publishes a list of recommended travel agencies and B&Bs. Come here to report tourism-related complaints.

ⓘ Getting There & Away

AIR

Indira Gandhi International Airport is about 14km southwest of the centre. International and domestic flights use the gleaming new Terminal 3. Ageing Terminal 1 is reserved for low-cost carriers. Free shuttle buses (present your boarding pass and onward ticket) run between the two terminals every 20 minutes, but can take an hour or more. Leave at least three hours between transfers to be safe.

The arrivals hall at Terminal 3 has 24-hour forex, ATMs, prepaid taxi and car-hire counters, tourist information, bookshops, cafes and a **Premium Lounge** (☑ 61233922; 3hr s/d ₹2350/3520) with short-stay rooms.

You'll need to show your boarding pass to enter the terminal. At check-in, be sure to collect tags for all your carry-on bags and ensure these are stamped as you go through security.

Delhi's airport can be prone to thick fog in December and January (often disrupting airline schedules) – it's wise to allow a day between connecting flights during this period.

Air India (Indian Airlines; Map p46; ☑ 24622220; www.airindia.in; Aurobindo Marg; ⊗ 8.30am-7pm; Ⓜ Jor Bagh)

Jagson Airlines (Map p42; ☑ 23721593; Vandana Bldg, 11 Tolstoy Marg; ⊗ 10am-6pm Mon-Sat; Ⓜ Rajiv Chowk)

Jet Airways (Map p42; ☑ 39893333; www. jetairways.com; 11/12 G-Block, Connaught Place; ⊗ 10am-9pm; Ⓜ Rajiv Chowk)

SpiceJet (☑ 1800 1803333; www.spicejet.com)

BUS

Most travellers enter and leave Delhi by train, but buses are a useful option to some destinations and if the trains are booked up.

Most state-run services leave from the **Kashmere Gate Inter State Bus Terminal** (ISBT; Map p38; ☑ 23860290) in Old Delhi, accessible by metro. The ISBT has undergone major renovations over the last few years, which makes travelling from here an altogether more pleasant experience, with sales and information offices for the bus companies as you enter the terminal building. The **Anand Vihar Inter State Bus Terminal** (ISBT) has some services to Nainital and Kumaun in Uttarakhand. Some cheaper buses to destinations in Uttar Pradesh, Madhya Pradesh and Rajasthan leave from the **Sarai Kale Khan ISBT** on the ring road near Nizamuddin train station.

Arrive at least 30 minutes ahead of your departure time. You can avoid the hassle by paying a little more for private deluxe buses that leave from locations in central Delhi – enquire at travel agencies or your hotel for details. You can also book tickets or check information on **Cleartrip** (www.cleartrip.com), **Make My Trip** (www.makemytrip.com) or **Goibibo** (www.goibibo.com).

There are buses to Agra, but considering the traffic at either end, you're better off taking the train. **Himachal Pradesh Tourism Development Corporation** (HPTDC; Map p46) runs a bus from Himachal Bhawan on Sikandra Rd (near Mandi House) to Dharamsala (deluxe non-AC, ₹700, 12 hours) at 5.30pm, Shimla (Volvo AC; ₹900, nine hours) at 8.30pm and Manali (Volvo AC, ₹1300, 10 hours) at 6.30pm. Tickets are sold at Himachal Bhawan and **Chanderlok House** (Map p42; 36 Janpath; Ⓜ Rajiv Chowk).

HRTC (Himachal Road Transport Corporation) also has buses starting from Himachal Bhawan: Shimla (Volvo, ₹847, five daily) and one to Manali at 7pm (Volvo;,₹1305). These stop at the ISBT Kashmiri Gate 30 to 90 minutes later, from where it's ₹20 less.

Rajasthan Tourism (Map p46; ☑ 23381884; www.rtdc.com; Bikaner House, Pandara Rd) runs deluxe buses from Bikaner House, near India Gate, to the following destinations. (Women receive a discount of 30%):

Ajmer Volvo, ₹1092, nine hours, three daily

Jaipur super deluxe/Volvo ₹590/815, six hours, every one to two hours

Jodhpur super deluxe/Volvo ₹815/1490, 11 hours, two daily

Udaipur Volvo, ₹1625, 15 hours, one daily

State bus companies operating out of Delhi include the following:

Delhi Transport Corporation (Map p42; ☑ 23370210; www.dtc.nic.in)

Haryana Roadways (☑ 23868271; www.hartrans.gov.in)

Himachal Road Transport Corporation (☑ 23868694; www.hrtc.gov.in)

Punjab Roadways (☑ 23867842; www.punbusonline.com)

Rajasthan State Road Transport Corporation (☑ 23864470; www.rsrtc.rajasthan.gov.in)

Uttar Pradesh State Road Transport Corporation (☑ 23235367; www.upsrtc.com)

TRAIN

There are three main stations in Delhi: (Old) Delhi train station (aka Delhi Junction) in Old Delhi; New Delhi train station near Paharganj; and Nizamuddin train station, south of Sunder

BUSES FROM DELHI (KASHMERE GATE)

DESTINATION	FARE (₹)	DURATION (HR)	FREQUENCY
Amritsar	420-905	10	hourly, 6am-9.30pm
Chandigarh	215-520	5	half-hourly, 6.30am-midnight
Dehra Dun	257-713	7	nine daily, 6am-midnight
Dharamsala	520-1150	12	6.30am, 5.30am & 11pm
Haridwar	213-542	6	hourly, 5am-11pm
Jaipur	196-655	6	hourly, 24hr
Manali	651-1285	15	6.40am, 7.45am, 11.30am, hourly 3.45-10pm
Rishikesh	770	10	9.30am, 9pm
Shimla	380-827	10	5am, 12.30pm, hourly 4.50-10.30pm

Nagar. Make sure you know which station your train is leaving from.

There are two options for foreign travellers: you can brave the queues at the main **reservation office** (Map p56; Chelmsford Rd; ☉ 8am-8pm, to 2pm Sun), or visit the helpful **International Tourist Bureau** (ITB; Map p56; ☎ 23405156; 1st fl, New Delhi Train Station;

☉ 8am-8pm Mon-Sat, to 2pm Sun).The entrance to the ITB is before you go onto platform 1, via a staircase just to the right of the entrance to the platform. Do not believe anyone who tells you it has shifted, closed or burnt down! Walk with confidence and ignore all 'helpful' or 'official' approaches. The ITB is a large room with about

MAJOR TRAINS FROM DELHI

DESTINATION	TRAIN NO & NAME	FARE (₹)	DURATION (HR)	FREQUENCY	DEPARTURES & TRAIN STATION
Agra	12280 Taj Exp	100/365 (A)	3	1 daily	7.05am NZM
	12002 Bhopal Shatabdi	505/1000 (B)	2	1 daily	6am NDLS
Amritsar	12029/12013 Swarna/Amritsar Shatabdi	865/1690 (B)	6	1-2 daily	7.20am/ 4.30pm NDLS
Bengaluru	12430 Bangalore Rajdhani	2895/4020/6675 (C)	34	4 weekly	8.50pm NZM
Chennai	12434 Chennai Rajdhani	2795/3860/6355 (C)	28	2 weekly	5.55pm NZM
	12622 Tamil Nadu Exp	780/2020/2970 (D)	33	1 daily	10.30pm NDLS
Goa (Madgaon)	14854 Marudhar Exp	2605/3630/6075 (C)	26	3 weekly	10.55am NZM
	12432 Trivandrum Rajdhani	170/535/735 (D)	27	1 daily	3pm NZM
Haridwar	12017 Dehradun Shatabdi	585/1175 (B)	4½	1 daily	6.45am NDLS
Jaipur	12958 ADI Swama Jayanti Rajdani	795/1055/1695 (C)	4½	1 daily	7.55pm NDLS
	12916 Ashram Exp	235/590/820(D)	5	1 daily	3.20pm DLI
	12015 Ajmer Shatabdi	635/1280 (B)	4½	1 daily	6.05am NDLS
Kalka (for Shimla)	12011 Kalka Shatabdi	635/1280 (B)	4	2 daily	7.40am & 5.15pm NDLS
Khajuraho	12448 UP Sampark Kranti Exp	365/950/1340 (D)	10½	1 daily	8.10pm NZM
Lucknow	12004 Lucknow Swran Shatabdi	875/1830 (B)	6½	1 daily	6.15am NDLS
Mumbai	12952 Mumbai Rajdhani	2030/2810/4680 (C)	16	1 daily	4.45pm NDLS
	12954 August Kranti Rajdani	2030/2810/4680 (C)	17½	1 daily	4.50pm NZM
Udaipur	12963 Mewar Exp	415/1085/1545 (D)	12½	1 daily	6.55pm NDLS
Varanasi	12560 Shivganga Exp	415/1095/1555 (D)	12½	1 daily	6.55pm NDLS

Train stations: NDLS – New Delhi; DLI – Old Delhi; NZM – Hazrat Nizamuddin
Fares: (A) 2nd class/chair car; (B) chair car/1st-class AC; (C) 3AC/2AC/1AC; (D) sleeper/3AC/2AC

10 or more computer terminals – don't be fooled by other 'official' offices.

When making reservations here, you can pay in cash (rupees) only. Bring your passport.

When you arrive, take a ticket from the machine that gives you a place in the queue. Then complete a reservation form – ask at the information counter to check availability. You can then wait to complete and pay for your booking at the relevant counter. This is the best place to get last-minute bookings for quota seats to popular destinations, but come prepared to queue.

If you prefer to brave the standard reservation office, check the details for your journey (including the train number) in advance on the **Indian Railways** (www.indianrail.gov.in) website or **Erail** (www.erail.in), or in the publication *Trains at a Glance* (₹45), available at newsstands. You'll need to fill out a reservation form and queue – after 7pm is the quietest time to book.

ⓘ Getting Around

TO/FROM THE AIRPORT

International flights often arrive at ghastly hours, so it pays to book a hotel in advance and notify staff of your arrival time. Organised city transport runs to/from Terminal 3; a free shuttle bus runs every 20 minutes between Terminal 3 and Terminal 1.

Pre-arranged pick-ups Hotels offer pre-arranged airport pick-up, but you'll pay extra to cover the airport parking fee (up to ₹140) and ₹80 charge to enter the arrivals hall. To avoid the entry fee, drivers may wait outside Gates 4 to 6.

Metro The Airport Express line (www.delhimetrorail.com) runs every 10 to 15 minutes from 4.45am to 11.30pm, completing the journey from Terminal 3 to New Delhi train station in around 40 minutes (₹80 to ₹60); there are plans to reduce this journey time. It's usually empty because it's a separate line from the rest of the metro. You can buy a token for the other lines at the Airport station; check with customer services.

Bus Air-conditioned buses run from outside Terminal 3 to Kashmere Gate ISBT every 20 minutes, via the Red Fort, LNJP Hospital, New Delhi Station Gate 2, Connaught Place, Parliament St and Ashoka Rd (₹75).

Taxi In front of the arrivals buildings at Terminal 3 and Terminal 1 are **Delhi Traffic Police Prepaid Taxi Counters** (☑ 23010101; www.delhitrafficpolice.nic.in) offering fixed-price taxi services. You'll pay about ₹350 to New or Old Delhi, and ₹450 to the southern suburbs, plus a 25% surcharge between 11pm and 5am. Travellers have reported difficulty in persuading drivers to go to their intended destination. Insist that the driver takes you to your chosen destination and only surrender your voucher when you arrive.

You can also book a prepaid taxi at the Megacabs (p76) counter outside the arrivals building at both the international and domestic terminals. It costs ₹600 to ₹700 to the centre, but you get a cleaner car with air-con.

AUTORICKSHAW & TAXI

Local taxis (recognisable by their black and yellow livery) and autorickshaws have meters but these are effectively ornamental as most drivers refuse to use them. Delhi Traffic Police runs a network of prepaid autorickshaw booths, where you can pay a fixed fare, including 24-hour stands at the New Delhi, Old Delhi and Nizamuddin train stations; elsewhere, you'll need to negotiate a fare before you set off.

Fares are invariably elevated for foreigners so haggle hard, and if the fare sounds too outrageous, find another cab. For an autorickshaw ride from Connaught Place, fares should be around ₹40 to Paharganj, ₹60 to the Red Fort, ₹70 to Humayun's Tomb and ₹100 to Hauz Khas. However, it may be a struggle to get these prices. Visit www.taxiautofare.com for suggested fares for these and other journeys. To report overcharging, harassment or other problems take the license number and call the Auto Complaint Line on ☑ 42400400/25844444.

Taxis typically charge twice the autorickshaw fare. Note that fares vary as fuel prices go up and down. From 11pm to 5am there's a 25% surcharge for autorickshaws and taxis. The government has proposed to install microchips to track local taxis to make them safer.

CAR

Numerous operators will rent a car with driver, or you can negotiate directly with taxi drivers at taxi stands around the city. Note that some taxis can only operate inside the city limits, or in certain surrounding states. For a day of local sightseeing, there is normally an eight-hour, 80km limit – anything over this costs extra.

Kumar Tourist Taxi Service (Map p42; ☑ 23415930; www.kumarindiatours.com; 14/1 K-Block, Connaught Place; ⊙ 9am-9pm; Ⓜ Rajiv Chowk) Rates are among Delhi's lowest – a day of Delhi sightseeing costs from ₹1200 (the eight hours and 80km limit applies).

Metropole Tourist Service (Map p46; ☑ 24310313; www.metrovista.co.in; 224 Defence Colony Flyover Market; ⊙ 7am-7pm; Ⓜ Jangpura) Under the Defence Flyover Bridge (on the Jangpura side).

BICYCLE

DelhiByCycle (p54) offers cycle tours but bike hire has never taken off in traffic-snarled Delhi.

Jhandewalan Cycle Market (Map p38) To buy your own bike, head to the Jhandewalan Cycle Market, near Videocon Tower at Jhandewalan.

BUS

With the arrival of the metro, travellers rarely use Delhi's public buses, but the red air-con buses are comfortable and there are several useful routes, including the Airport Express bus (₹75) and bus GL-23, which connects the Kashmere Gate and Anand Vihar bus stations. Fares usually range from ₹15 to ₹25.

CYCLE-RICKSHAW

Cycle-rickshaws are useful for navigating Old Delhi and the suburbs, but are banned from many parts of New Delhi, including Connaught Place. Negotiate a fare before you set off – expect to pay around ₹5 to ₹10 per kilometre.

METRO

Delhi's magnificent **metro** (☑23417910; www. delhimetrorail.com) is fast and efficient, with signs and arrival/departure announcements in Hindi and English. Trains run from around 6am to 11pm and the first carriage in the direction of travel is reserved for women only. Note that trains can get insanely busy at peak commuting times (around 9am to 10am and 5pm to 6pm) – avoid travelling with luggage during rush hour if at all possible (however, the Airport Express is always empty, as it's not directly connected to the other lines).

Tokens (₹8 to ₹39) are sold at metro stations. There are also one-/three-day (₹150/300; ₹50 refundable when you return it) 'tourist cards' for unlimited short-distance travel, and a Smart Card (₹100; ₹50 refundable), which can be recharged for amounts from ₹200 to ₹1000 – making fares 10% cheaper than paying by token.

Because of security concerns, all bags are X-rayed and passengers must pass through an airport-style scanner.

MOTORCYCLE

Karol Bagh market is the place to go to buy or rent a motorcycle.

Lalli Motorbike Exports (Map p38; ☑28750869; www.lallisingh.com; 1740-A/55 Hari Singh Nalwa St, Abdul Aziz Rd; Ⓜ Karol Bagh) Run by the knowledgable Lalli Singh, this place sells and rents out Enfields and parts, and buyers get a crash course in running and maintaining these lovable but temperamental machines.

RADIOCAB

You'll need a local mobile number to order a radiocab, or ask a shop or hotel to assist. These air-conditioned cars are clean, efficient and use reliable meters, charging ₹20 at flagfall then ₹20 per kilometre.

Other telephone taxi services exist, such as car-sharing service Uber, which was banned in 2014 following an assault by one of its drivers but subsequently restarted.

Easycabs (☑43434343; www.easycabs.com)
Megacabs (☑41414141; www.megacabs.com) You can book a prepaid taxi at the Megacabs counter outside the arrivals building at both the international and domestic airport terminals. It costs ₹600 to ₹700 to the centre, but you get a cleaner car with air-con.
Quickcabs (☑45333333; www.quickcabs.in)

Greater Delhi

★**Qutb Minar Complex** HISTORIC SITE
(Map p50; ☑26643856; Indian/foreigner ₹10/250, video ₹25, Decorative Light Show Indian/foreigner ₹20/250, audio guide ₹100; ☺dawn-dusk; Ⓜ Qutab Minar) In a city awash with ancient ruins, the Qutb Minar complex is something special. The first monuments here were erected by the sultans of Mehrauli, and subsequent rulers expanded on their work, hiring the finest craftsmen and artisans to create an exclamation mark in stone to record the triumph of Muslim rule. The **Qutb Festival** of Indian classical music and dance takes place here every November/December. To reach the complex, take the metro to Qutab Minar station, then take an autorickshaw for the 1km to the ruins.

The complex is studded with ruined tombs and monuments. Ala-ud-din's sprawling madrasa (Islamic school) and tomb stand in ruins at the rear of the complex, while Altamish is entombed in a magnificent sandstone and marble mausoleum almost completely covered in Islamic calligraphy.

Bags should be left in the cloakroom. For the most atmosphere, try to visit in the morning before the crowds arrive.

➡ **Qutb Minar**

The Qutb Minar complex is dominated by the spectaclular Qutb Minar, a soaring Afghan-style victory tower and minaret, erected by sultan Qutb-ud-din in 1193 to proclaim his supremacy over the vanquished Hindu rulers of Qila Rai Pithora. Ringed by intricately carved standstone bands bearing verses from the Quran, the tower stands nearly 73m high and tapers from a 15m-diameter base to a mere 2.5m at the top. You can no longer climb the tower for safety reasons, but a webcam allows a view from the top (₹10).

The tower has five distinct storeys with projecting balconies, but Qutb-ud-din only completed the first level before being unfortunately impaled on his saddle while playing polo. His successors completed the job, and kept up the work of restoration and maintenance through the centuries.

➡ Quwwat-ul-Islam Masjid

(Might of Islam Mosque) At the foot of the Qutb Minar stands the first mosque to be built in India, intended to be a physical symbol of the triumph of Islam. An inscription over the east gate states that it was built with materials obtained from demolishing '27 idolatrous temples'. As well as intricate carvings that show a clear fusion of Islamic and pre-Islamic styles, the walls of the mosque are studded with sun disks, *shikharas* and other recognisable pieces of Hindu and Jain masonry, defaced as far as possible.

Altamish, Qutb-ud-din's son-in-law, expanded the original mosque with a cloistered court between 1210 and 1220, and Ala-ud-din added the exquisite marble and sandstone **Alai Darwaza gatehouse** in 1310. Nearby is the dainty tomb of the Turkic saint Imam Zamin, erected in the Lodi era.

➡ Iron Pillar

Standing in the courtyard of the Quwwat-ul-Islam mosque is a 7m-high iron pillar that is of such purity that it hasn't rusted in over 1600 years. This extraordinary pillar vastly predates the surrounding monuments. A six-line Sanskrit inscription indicates that it was initially erected outside a Vishnu temple, possibly in Bihar, in memory of Chandragupta II, who ruled from AD 375 to 413. What the inscription does not tell is how it was made – scientists have never discovered how the iron could be cast using the technology of the time.

➡ Alai Minar

When the Sultan Ala-ud-din made additions to the Qutb Minar complex in the 14th century, he also conceived an ambitious plan to erect a second tower of victory, exactly like the Qutb Minar – but twice as high. Construction got as far as the first level before the sultan died; none of his successors saw fit to bankroll this extravagant piece of showboating. The 27m-high plinth can be seen just north of the Qutb Minar.

★ Mehrauli Archaeological Park   PARK

(Map p50; ☉ dawn-dusk; Ⓜ Qutab Minar) Bordering the Qutb Minar complex, but overlooked by most of the tourist hordes, the Mehrauli Archaeological Park preserves some of the most atmospheric relics of the second city of Delhi.

Scattered around a forest park are the ruins of dozens of tombs, palace buildings and colonial-era follies. You can reach the park by turning right from the metro station onto Anuvrat Marg and walking around 500m; the entrance is via a small lane on your left, marked by a board showing the park regulations.

Entering the park from here, the first monuments you'll see are the time-ravaged tombs of Balban and Quli Khan, his son, which formerly incorporated a mosque. A short walk away is Mehrauli's most impressive structure, the Jamali Khamali mosque, attached to the tomb of the Sufi poet Jamali. Ask the caretaker to open the doors so you can see the intricate incised plaster ceiling decorated with Jamali's verses. To the west is the Rajon ki Baoli, a majestic 16th-century step-well with a monumental flight of steps. If you walk from here towards Mehrauli village, on the edge of the street is Adham Khan's mausoleum, which was once used as a British residence, than later as a police station and post office.

Southwest of the archaeological park is a complex of ruined tombs and summer palaces, constructed in the late Mughal period around the **Haus i Shamsi tank** (off Mehrauli-Gurgaon Rd). An empty space between two of the tombs was intended for the last king of Delhi, Bahadur Shah Zafar, who died in exile in Burma (Myanmar) in 1862.

Tughlaqabad   FORT

(Indian/foreigner ₹5/100, video ₹25; ☉ 8.30am-5.30pm; Ⓜ Tughlaqabad) This mammoth stronghold, the third city of Delhi, was built by sultan Ghiyus-ud-din Tughlaq in the 14th century. For its construction, the king poached workers from the Sufi saint Nizam-ud-din, who issued a curse that Tughlaqabad would be inhabited only by shepherds. This was indeed the case – today goats are as common as human visitors among the crumbling, vegetation-choked, but still magnificent ruins. To reach the fort, take an autorickshaw from the Tughlaqabad metro station (₹80).

The sultan's well-preserved sandstone mausoleum, which once stood in the middle of a lake, is separated from his fallen city by a busy highway.

Agra & the Taj Mahal

Best Places to Eat

➡ Pinch of Spice (p92)

➡ Time2Eat –
Mama Chicken (p93)

➡ Esphahan (p92)

➡ Lakshmi Vilas (p93)

➡ Dasaprakash (p93)

Best Places to Stay

➡ Bansi Homestay (p89)

➡ N Homestay (p89)

➡ Tourists Rest House (p91)

➡ Oberoi Amarvilas (p89)

➡ Saniya Palace Hotel (p87)

Why Go?

Agra's Taj Mahal rises from the dust-beaten earth of Uttar Pradesh as it does in dreams, but even the wildest imaginations leave travellers underprepared for that breath-stealing moment its gates are traversed and this magnificent world wonder comes into focus. Skipping it would be a bit like drinking chai without spoonfuls of sugar: absurd. Simply put, it's the most beautiful building in the world and it's almost impossible to see it without feeling awestruck.

But Agra, with its long and rich history, boasts plenty more besides. For 130 years this was the centre of India's great Mughal empire, and its legacy lives on in beautiful artwork, mouth-watering cuisine and magnificent architecture. The Taj is one of three places here that have been awarded Unesco World Heritage status, with the immense Agra Fort and the eerie ruined city of Fatehpur Sikri making up a superb trio of top-draw sights.

When to Go
Agra

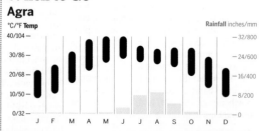

Sep–Oct The best time to visit. Most of the monsoon rains are over and summer temperatures have cooled.

Nov–Feb Daytime temperatures are comfortable but big sights are overcrowded. Evenings are nippy.

Mar–Apr Evening chill is gone but raging-hot midsummer temperatures have yet to materialise.

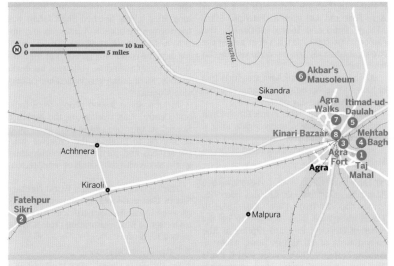

Agra & the Taj Mahal Highlights

❶ Rising before dawn to take in the **Taj Mahal** (p80) minus the crowds, returning later for the cinematic sunset view

❷ Exploring the fascinating abandoned city of **Fatehpur Sikri** (p97)

❸ Gawking at the immensity of the red-sandstone walls that surround **Agra Fort** (p81)

❹ Hiring a rickshaw for the day, taking in a tour of Agra's Mughal gardens, ending at sunset with **Mehtab Bagh** (p86)

❺ Crossing the Yamuna River to **Itimad-ud-Daulah** (p83), an exquisite marble tomb nicknamed the Baby Taj

❻ Hitting the suburbs for **Akbar's Mausoleum** (p83),

the beautiful resting place of the Mughals' greatest emperor

❼ Strolling deeper into ancient Agra on a captivating jaunt with **Agra Walks** (p86)

❽ Battling the throngs at hectic **Kinari Bazaar** (p94), one of India's most mesmerising markets

History

In 1501 Sultan Sikandar Lodi established his capital here, but the city fell into Mughal hands in 1526, when Emperor Babur defeated the last Lodi sultan at Panipat. Agra reached the peak of its magnificence between the mid-16th and mid-17th centuries during the reigns of Akbar, Jehangir and Shah Jahan. During this period the fort, the Taj Mahal and other major mausoleums were built. In 1638 Shah Jahan built a new city in Delhi, and his son Aurangzeb moved the capital there 10 years later.

In 1761 Agra fell to the Jats, a warrior class who looted its monuments, including the Taj Mahal. The Marathas took over in 1770, but were replaced by the British in 1803. Following the First War of Independence of 1857, the British shifted the administration of the province to Allahabad. Deprived of its ad-

ministrative role, Agra developed as a centre for heavy industry, quickly becoming famous for its chemicals industry and air pollution, before the Taj and tourism became a major source of income.

Agra
☑ 0562 / POP 1.7 MILLION

◎ Sights

The entrance fee for Agra's five main sights – the Taj, Agra Fort, Fatehpur Sikri, Akbar's Mausoleum and Itimad-ud-Daulah – is made up of charges from two different bodies, the Archaeological Survey of India (ASI) and the Agra Development Association (ADA). Of the ₹750 ticket for the Taj Mahal, ₹500 is a special ADA ticket, which gives you small savings on the other four sights if visited in the same day. You'll save ₹50 at Agra Fort and ₹10 each at Fatehpur Sikri, Akbar's Tomb and Itimad-ud-Daulah. You can buy this ₹500 ADA ticket at any of the five sights. Just say you intend to visit the Taj later that day.

All the other sights in Agra are either free or have ASI tickets only, which aren't included in the ADA one-day offer.

Admission to all sights is free for children under 15. On Fridays, many sights offer a tax-free discount of ₹10.

See also the illustrated highlight of the Taj Mahal (p84).

★ Taj Mahal
HISTORIC BUILDING

(Map p88; Indian/foreigner ₹20/750, video ₹25; ☺dawn-dusk Sat-Thu) Poet Rabindranath Tagore described it as 'a teardrop on the cheek of eternity', Rudyard Kipling as 'the embodiment of all things pure', while its creator, Emperor Shah Jahan, said it made 'the sun and the moon shed tears from their eyes'. Every year, tourists numbering more than twice the population of Agra pass through its gates to catch a once-in-a-lifetime glimpse of what is widely considered the most beautiful building in the world. Few leave disappointed.

The Taj was built by Shah Jahan as a memorial for his third wife, Mumtaz Mahal, who died giving birth to their 14th child in 1631. The death of Mumtaz left the emperor so heartbroken that his hair is said to have turned grey virtually overnight. Construction of the Taj began the following year and, although the main building is thought to have been built in eight years, the whole

---

ⓘ BEST TIMES TO SEE THE TAJ

The Taj is arguably at its most atmospheric at sunrise. This is certainly the most comfortable time to visit, with far fewer crowds. Sunset is another magical viewing time. You can also view the Taj for five nights around full moon. Entry numbers are limited, though, and tickets must be bought a day in advance from the Archaeological Survey of India office (Map p86; ☎2227261; www.asi.nic.in; 22 The Mall; Indian/foreigner ₹510/750; ☺9.30am-6pm Mon-Fri). See its website for details. Note, this office is known as the Taj Mahal Office by some rickshaw riders.

---

complex was not completed until 1653. Not long after it was finished Shah Jahan was overthrown by his son Aurangzeb and imprisoned in Agra Fort where, for the rest of his days, he could only gaze out at his creation through a window. Following his death in 1666, Shah Jahan was buried here alongside Mumtaz.

In total, some 20,000 people from India and Central Asia worked on the building. Specialists were brought in from as far away as Europe to produce the exquisite marble screens and pietra dura (marble inlay work) made with thousands of semiprecious stones.

The Taj was designated a World Heritage Site in 1983 and looks as immaculate today as when it was first constructed – though it underwent a huge restoration project in the early 20th century.

➡ Entry & Information

Note: the Taj is closed every Friday to anyone not attending prayers at the mosque.

The Taj can be accessed through the west, south and east gates. Tour groups tend to enter through the east and west gates. Independent travellers tend to use the south gate, which is nearest to Taj Ganj, the main area for budget accommodation, and generally has shorter queues than the west gate. The east gate has the shortest queues of the lot, but this is because the ticket office is inconveniently located a 1km walk away at Shilpgram, a dire government-run tourist centre. There are separate queues for men and women at all three gates.

Cameras and videos are permitted but you cannot take photographs inside the mausoleum itself, and the areas in which you can take videos are quite limited.

Do not forget to retrieve your free 500mL-bottle of water and shoe covers (included in Taj ticket price). If you keep your ticket you get small entry-fee reductions when visiting Agra Fort, Fatehpur Sikri, Akbar's Mausoleum or the Itimad-ud-Daulah on the same day. You can also store your luggage for free beside the ticket offices and pick up an audio guide (₹118).

From the south gate, entry to the inner compound is through a very impressive, 30m red-sandstone gateway on the south side of the forecourt, which is inscribed with verses from the Quran.

➡ Inside the Grounds

Once inside, the ornamental gardens are set out along classical Mughal *charbagh* (formal Persian garden) lines – a square quartered by watercourses, with an ornamental marble plinth at its centre. When the fountains are not flowing, the Taj is beautifully reflected in the water.

The Taj Mahal itself stands on a raised marble platform at the northern end of the ornamental gardens, with its back to the Yamuna River. Its raised position means that the backdrop is only sky – a masterstroke of design. Purely decorative 40m-high white minarets grace each corner of the platform. After more than three centuries they are not quite perpendicular, but they may have been designed to lean slightly outwards so that in the event of an earthquake they would fall away from the precious Taj. The red-sandstone mosque to the west is an important gathering place for Agra's Muslims. The identical building to the east, the jawab, was built for symmetry.

The central Taj structure is made of semitranslucent white marble, carved with flowers and inlaid with thousands of semiprecious stones in beautiful patterns. A perfect exercise in symmetry, the four identical faces of the Taj feature impressive vaulted arches embellished with pietra dura scrollwork and quotations from the Quran in a style of calligraphy using inlaid jasper. The whole structure is topped off by four small domes surrounding the famous bulbous central dome.

Directly below the main dome is the Cenotaph of Mumtaz Mahal, an elaborate false tomb surrounded by an exquisite perforated marble screen inlaid with dozens of different types of semiprecious stones. Beside it, offsetting the symmetry of the Taj, is the Cenotaph of Shah Jahan, who was interred here with little ceremony by his usurping son Aurangzeb in 1666. Light is admitted into the central chamber by finely cut marble screens. The real tombs of Mumtaz Mahal and Shah Jahan are in a locked basement room below the main chamber and cannot be viewed.

★Agra Fort   FORT
(Map p86; Indian/foreigner ₹20/300, video ₹25; ⊙dawn-dusk) With the Taj Mahal overshadowing it, one can easily forget that Agra has one of the finest Mughal forts in India. Construction of the massive red-sandstone fort, on the bank of the Yamuna River, was begun by Emperor Akbar in 1565.

TAJ MUSEUM

Within the Taj complex, on the western side of the gardens, is the small but excellent Taj Museum (Map p88; ⊙9am-5pm, closed Fri) FREE, housing a number of original Mughal miniature paintings, including a pair of 17th-century ivory portraits of Emperor Shah Jahan and his beloved wife Mumtaz Mahal. It also has some very well preserved gold and silver coins dating from the same period, plus architectural drawings of the Taj and some nifty celadon plates, said to split into pieces or change colour if the food served on them contains poison.

Further additions were made, particularly by his grandson Shah Jahan, using his favourite building material – white marble. The fort was built primarily as a military structure, but Shah Jahan transformed it into a palace, and later it became his gilded prison for eight years after his son Aurangzeb seized power in 1658.

The ear-shaped fort's colossal double walls rise over 20m in height and measure 2.5km in circumference. The Yamuna River originally flowed along the straight eastern edge of the fort, and the emperors had their own bathing ghats here. It contains a maze of buildings, forming a city within a city, including vast underground sections, though many of the structures were destroyed over the years by Nadir Shah, the Marathas, the Jats and finally the British, who used the fort as a garrison. Even today, much of the fort is used by the military and so is off-limits to the general public.

The Amar Singh Gate to the south is the sole entry point to the fort these days and where you buy your entrance ticket. Its dog-leg design was meant to confuse attackers who made it past the first line of defence – the crocodile-infested moat.

A path leads straight from here up to the large Moti Masjid (Pearl Mosque), which is always closed. To your right, just before you reach Moti Masjid, is the large open Diwan-i-Am (Hall of Public Audiences), which was used by Shah Jahan for domestic government business, and features a throne room where the emperor listened to petitioners. In front of it is the small and rather incongruous grave of John Colvin,

AGRA & THE TAJ MAHAL SIGHTS

TOP TAJ VIEWS

Inside the Taj Grounds

You may have to pay ₹750 for the privilege, but it's only when you're inside the grounds themselves that you can really get up close and personal with the world's most beautiful building. Don't miss inspecting the marble inlay work (pietra dura) inside the *pishtaqs* (large arched recesses) on the four outer walls. And don't forget to bring a small torch with you so that you can shine it on similar pietra dura work inside the dark central chamber of the mausoleum. Note the translucency of both the white marble and the semiprecious stones inlaid into it.

From Mehtab Bagh

Tourists are no longer allowed to wander freely along the riverbank on the opposite side of the Yamuna River, but you can still enjoy a view of the back of the Taj from the 16th-century Mughal park Mehtab Bagh (p86), with the river flowing between you and the mausoleum. A path leading down to the river beside the park offers the same view for free, albeit from a more restricted angle.

Looking Up from the South Bank of the River

This is a great place to be for sunset. Take the path that hugs the outside of the Taj's eastern wall and walk all the way down to the small temple beside the river. You should be able to find boat hands down here willing to row you out onto the water for an even more romantic view. Expect to pay around ₹100 per boat. For safety reasons, it's best not to wander down here on your own for sunset.

From a Rooftop Cafe in Taj Ganj

Perfect for sunrise shots, there are some wonderful photos to be had from the numerous rooftop cafes in Taj Ganj. We think the cafe on Saniya Palace Hotel (p87) is the pick of the bunch, with its plant-filled design and great position, but many of them are good. And all offer the bonus of being able to view the Taj with the added comfort of an early-morning cup of coffee.

From Agra Fort

With a decent zoom lens you can capture some fabulous images of the Taj from Agra Fort, especially if you're willing to get up at the crack of dawn to see the sun rising up from behind it. The best places to shoot it from are probably Musamman Burj and Khas Mahal, the octagonal tower and palace where Shah Jahan was imprisoned for eight years until his death.

a lieutenant-governor of the northwest provinces who died of an illness in the fort during the 1857 First War of Independence (Indian Uprising).

A tiny staircase just to the left of the Diwan-i-Am throne leads up to a large courtyard. To your left, is the tiny but exquisite Nagina Masjid (Gem Mosque), built in 1635 by Shah Jahan for the ladies of the court. Down below was the Ladies' bazaar, where the court ladies bought goods.

On the far side of the large courtyard, along the eastern wall of the fort, is Diwan-i-Khas (Hall of Private Audiences), which was reserved for important dignitaries or foreign representatives. The hall once housed Shah Jahan's legendary Peacock Throne, which was inset with precious stones including the famous Koh-i-noor diamond. The throne was taken to Delhi by Aurangzeb, then to Iran in 1739 by Nadir Shah and dismantled after his assassination in 1747. Overlooking the river and the distant Taj Mahal is Takhti-i-Jehangir, a huge slab of black rock with an inscription around the edge. The throne that stood here was made for Jehangir when he was Prince Salim.

Off to your right from here (as you face the river) is Shish Mahal (Mirror Palace), with walls inlaid with tiny mirrors. At the time of research it had been closed for some time due to restoration, although you could peek through cracks in the doors at the sparkling mirrors inside.

Further along the eastern edge of the fort you'll find Musamman Burj and Khas

Mahal, the wonderful white-marble octagonal tower and palace where Shah Jahan was imprisoned for eight years until his death in 1666, and from where he could gaze out at the Taj Mahal, the tomb of his wife. When he died, Shah Jahan's body was taken from here by boat to the Taj. The now closed Mina Masjid, set back slightly from the eastern edge, was his private mosque.

The large courtyard here is Anguri Bagh, a garden that has been brought back to life in recent years. In the courtyard is an innocuous-looking entrance – now locked – that leads down a flight of stairs into a two-storey labyrinth of underground rooms and passageways where Akbar used to keep his 500-strong harem.

Continuing south, the huge red-sandstone Jehangir's Palace was probably built by Akbar for his son Jehangir. It blends Indian and Central Asian architectural styles, a reminder of the Mughals' Afghani cultural roots. In front of the palace is Hauz-i-Jehangir, a huge bowl carved out of a single block of stone, which was used for bathing. Walking past this brings you back to the main path to Amar Singh Gate.

You can walk here from Taj Ganj, or it's ₹40 in a cycle-rickshaw.

Akbar's Mausoleum   HISTORIC BUILDING
(Indian/foreigner ₹10/110, video ₹25; ☺ dawn-dusk) This outstanding sandstone and marble tomb commemorates the greatest of the Mughal emperors. The huge courtyard is entered through a stunning gateway. It has three-storey minarets at each corner and is built of red sandstone strikingly inlaid with white-marble geometric patterns.

The mausoleum is at Sikandra, 10km northwest of Agra Fort. Catch a bus (₹22, 45 minutes) headed from Bijli Ghar bus stand; they go past the mausoleum.

Itimad-ud-Daulah   HISTORIC BUILDING
(Indian/foreigner ₹10/110, video ₹25; ☺ dawn-dusk) Nicknamed the Baby Taj, the exquisite tomb of Mizra Ghiyas Beg should not be missed. This Persian nobleman was Mumtaz Mahal's grandfather and Emperor Jehangir's *wazir* (chief minister). His daughter Nur Jahan, who married Jehangir, built the tomb between 1622 and 1628 in a style similar to the tomb she built for Jehangir near Lahore in Pakistan.

It doesn't have the same awesome beauty as the Taj, but it's arguably more delicate in appearance thanks to its particularly finely carved *jali* (marble lattice screens). This was the first Mughal structure built completely from marble, the first to make extensive use of pietra dura and the first tomb to be built on the banks of the Yamuna, which until then had been a sequence of beautiful pleasure gardens.

You can combine a trip here with Chini-ka-Rauza, Mehtab Bagh and Ram Bagh, all on the east bank. A cycle-rickshaw covering all four should cost about ₹300 return from the Taj, including waiting time. An autorickshaw should be ₹450.

Chini-ka-Rauza   HISTORIC BUILDING
(☺ dawn-dusk) **FREE** This Persian-style riverside tomb of Afzal Khan, a poet who served as Shah Jahan's chief minister, was built between 1628 and 1639. Rarely visited, it is hidden away down a shady avenue of trees on the east bank of the Yamuna.

(Continued on page 86)

AGRA & THE TAJ MAHAL SIGHTS

TOP AGRA FESTIVALS

Taj Mahotsav (www.tajmahotsav.org; ☺ Feb) This 10-day carnival of culture, cuisine and crafts is Agra's biggest and best party. Held at Shilpgram, the festival features over 400 artisan craft-makers from all over India, as well as a pot-pourri of folk and classical music, dances from various regions and enough regional food to induce a curry coma.

Kailash Fair (☺ Aug/Sep) Held at the Kailash temple, 12km from Agra, this cultural and religious fair honours Lord Shiva, who legendarily appeared here in the form of a stone lingam. It attracts devotees from all over North India.

Ram Barat (☺ Sep) Celebrated before the Hindu festival of Dussehra, Ram Barat is a dramatic recreation of the royal wedding procession of Shri Rama. Expect three days of colourful lights and pounding Hindu rhythms, highlighted by the 12-hour parade itself, featuring caparisoned elephants, horses, more than 125 mobile floats depicting mythological events and 30 marching bands.

Taj Mahal

TIMELINE

1631 Emperor Shah Jahan's beloved third wife, Mumtaz Mahal, dies in Buhanpur while giving birth to their 14th child. Her body is initially interred in Buhanpur itself, where Shah Jahan is fighting a military campaign, but is later moved, in a golden casket, to a small building on the banks of the Yamuna River in Agra.

1632 Construction of a permanent mausoleum for Mumtaz Mahal begins.

1633 Mumtaz Mahal is interred in her final resting place, an underground tomb beneath a marble plinth, on top of which the Taj Mahal will be built.

1640 The white-marble mausoleum is completed.

1653 The rest of the Taj Mahal complex is completed.

1658 Emperor Shah Jahan is overthrown by his son Aurangzeb and imprisoned in Agra Fort.

1666 Shah Jahan dies. His body is transported along the Yamuna River and buried underneath the Taj, alongside the tomb of his wife.

1908 Repeatedly damaged and looted after the fall of the Mughal empire, the Taj receives some long-overdue attention as part of a major restoration project ordered by British viceroy Lord Curzon.

1983 The Taj is awarded Unesco World Heritage Site status.

2002 Having been discoloured by pollution in more recent years, the Taj is spruced up with an ancient recipe known as multani mitti – a blend of soil, cereal, milk and lime once used by Indian women to beautify their skin.

Today More than three million tourists visit the Taj Mahal each year. That's more than twice the current population of Agra.

DANIEL MCCROHAN ©

GO BAREFOOT

Help the environment by entering the mausoleum barefoot instead of using the free disposable shoe covers.

Pishtaqs
These huge arched recesses are set into each side of the Taj. They provide depth to the building while their central, latticed marble screens allow patterned light to illuminate the inside of the mausoleum.

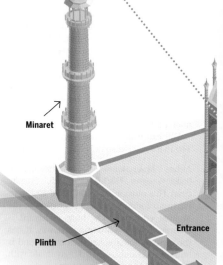

Minaret

Plinth

Entrance

Marble Relief Work
Flowering plants, thought to be representations of paradise, are a common theme among the beautifully decorative panels carved onto the white marble.

DANIEL MCCROHAN ©

BE ENLIGHTENED

Bring a small torch into the mausoleum to fully appreciate the translucency of the white marble and semiprecious stones.

Filigree Screen
This stunning screen was carved out of a single piece of marble. It surrounds both cenotaphs, allowing patterned light to fall onto them through its intricately carved *jali* (latticework).

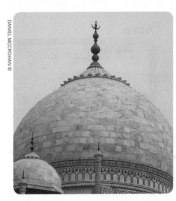

Central Dome
The Taj's famous central dome, topped by a brass finial, represents the vault of heaven, a stark contrast to the material world, which is represented by the square shape of the main structure.

Yamuna River

NORTH →

Pietra Dura
It's believed that 35 different precious and semi-precious stones were used to create the exquisite pietra dura (marble inlay work) found on the inside and outside of the mausoleum walls. Again, floral designs are common.

Calligraphy
The strips of calligraphy surrounding each of the four pishtaqs get larger as they get higher, giving the impression of uniform size when viewed from the ground. There's also calligraphy inside the mausoleum, including on Mumtaz Mahal's cenotaph.

Cenotaphs
The cenotaphs of Mumtaz Mahal and Shah Jahan, decorated with pietra dura inlay work, are actually fake tombs. The real ones are located in an underground vault closed to the public.

Agra

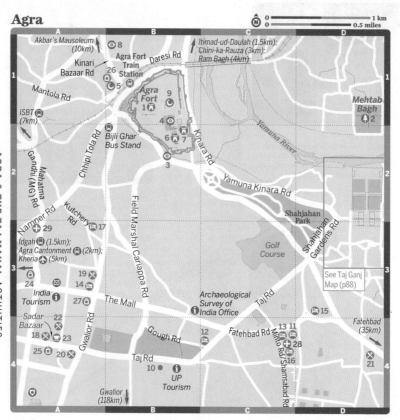

AGRA & THE TAJ MAHAL ACTIVITIES

(Continued from page 83)

★ **Mehtab Bagh**   PARK

(Map p86; Indian/foreigner ₹5/100, video ₹25; ☉ dawn-dusk) This park, originally built by Emperor Babur as the last in a series of 11 parks on the Yamuna's east bank, long before the Taj was conceived, fell into disrepair until it was little more than a huge mound of sand. To protect the Taj from the erosive effects of the sand blown across the river, the park was reconstructed and is now one the best places from which to view the great mausoleum.

The gardens in the Taj are perfectly aligned with the ones here, and the view of the Taj from the fountain directly in front of the entrance gate is a special one.

Jama Masjid   MOSQUE

(Map p86; Jama Masjid Rd) This fine mosque, built in the Kinari Bazaar by Shah Jahan's daughter in 1648, and once connected to

Agra Fort, features striking marble patterning on its domes.

🏃 Activities

Hotels allowing nonguests to use their pools include Yamuna View (p91; ₹500), Howard Plaza (p90; ₹562), Amar (p90; ₹500) and Clarks Shiraz (p91; ₹1000).

☞ Tours

Agra Walks   WALKING TOUR

(☑ 9027711144; www.agrawalks.com; tours ₹1500) Many folks spend but a day in Agra, taking in the Taj and Agra Fort and sailing off into the sunset. If you're interested in digging a little deeper, this excellent walking/cycle-rickshaw combo tour will show you sides of the city most tourists don't see.

The guides are darling and Old Agra highlights include going deeper into Kinari Bazaar and a few off-the-beaten-path temples

Agra

◉ **Top Sights**
1 Agra Fort B1
2 Mehtab Bagh D1

◉ **Sights**
3 Amar Singh Gate B2
4 Diwan-i-Am B1
5 Jama Masjid B1
6 Jehangir's Palace B2
7 Khas Mahal B2
8 Kinari Bazaar B1
9 Moti Masjid B1

⊕ **Activities, Courses & Tours**
10 UP Tourism B4

◉ **Sleeping**
11 Bansi Homestay C4
12 Clarks Shiraz Hotel C4
13 Dasaprakash C4
   Hotel Amar .... (see 13)
14 Hotel Yamuna View A3
15 Howard Plaza D3
16 N Homestay C4
17 Tourists Rest House A3

⊗ **Eating**
18 Brijwasi A4
   Dasaprakash .... (see 13)
19 Dasaprakash A3
20 Lakshmi Vilas A4
21 Pinch of Spice D4
22 Time2Eat – Mama Chicken A4
   Vedic .... (see 19)

◉ **Drinking & Nightlife**
23 Café Coffee Day A4
   Costa Coffee .... (see 11)

◉ **Shopping**
24 Khadi Gramodyog A3
25 Modern Book Depot A4
26 Subhash Bazaar B1
27 Subhash Emporium A3

ⓘ **Information**
28 Amit Jaggi Memorial Hospital C4
   Bag Packer Travel .... (see 17)
29 SR Hospital A3

such as Mankameshwar Mandir and Radha Krishna Mandir. A delectable food tour also debuted in 2014.

Amin Tours   CULTURAL TOURS
(☑9837411144; www.daytourtajmahal.com) If you can't be bothered handling the logistics, look no further than this recommended agency for all-inclusive private Agra day trips from Delhi by car (₹6000) or train (₹6500). One caveat: if they try to take you shopping and you're not interested, politely decline.

UP Tourism   COACH TOURS
(Map p86; ☑2421204; www.up-tourism.com; incl entry fees Indian/foreigner ₹500/2000; ☺6.30am-9.30pm) UP Tourism runs coach tours that leave Agra Cantonment train station at 10.30am Saturday to Thursday, after picking up passengers arriving from Delhi on the Taj Express. The tour includes the Taj Mahal, Agra Fort and Fatehpur Sikri, with a 1¼-hour stop in each place.

Tours return to the station so that day trippers can catch the Taj Express back to Delhi at 6.55pm. Contact either of the UP Tourism offices to book a seat, or just turn up at the train station tourist office at 9.45am to sign up for that day. Tours only depart with 10 people or more.

🛏 Sleeping

The main place for budget accommodation is the bustling area of Taj Ganj, immediately south of the Taj, while there's a high concentration of midrange hotels further south, along Fatehabad Rd. Sadar Bazaar, an area boasting good-quality restaurants, offers another option. Be forewarned: free wi-fi hasn't really caught on in Agra's nicer hotels; expect to pay upwards of ₹500 for 12 hours.

🛏 Taj Ganj Area

Saniya Palace Hotel   HOTEL $
(Map p88; ☑0562-3270199; www.saniyapalace. com; Chowk Kagziyan, Taj South Gate; d ₹400-600, without bathroom ₹200, with AC ₹800-1000; ❄@🖤) Set back from the main strip down an undesirable alleyway, this isn't the sleekest Taj Ganj option, but it tries to imbue character (marble floors and Mughal-style framed carpet wall hangings). The rooms (apart from the bathroomless cheapies) are clean and big enough, although the bathrooms in the non-AC rooms are minuscule.

The real coup is the very pleasant, plant-filled (and recently expanded) rooftop, which trumps its rivals for optimum Taj views.

Taj Ganj

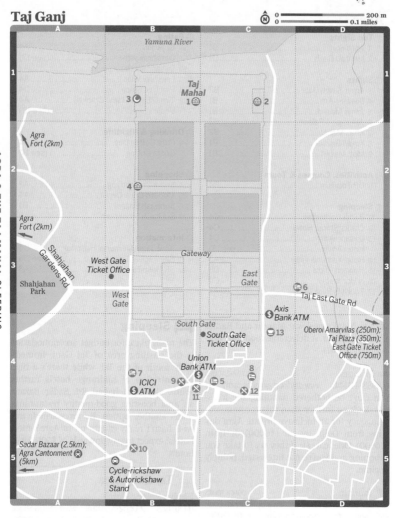

Hotel Kamal HOTEL $

(Map p88; ☑0562-2330126; hotelkamal@hotmail.com; Taj South Gate; d ₹600-900, with AC ₹1800; ✱⊕) The smartest hotel in Taj Ganj proper, Kamal has clean, comfortable rooms with nice touches such as framed photos of the Taj on the walls and rugs on the tiled floors (five in the newer annex are a definitive step-up with welcoming woodwork, extra space and stone-walled showers).

There's a cosy, bamboo-enclosed ground-floor restaurant and an underused rooftop restaurant with a somewhat obscured Taj view.

Hotel Sidhartha HOTEL $

(Map p88; ☑0562-2230901; www.hotelsidhartha.com; Taj West Gate; s/d/tr ₹700/850/960, with AC s ₹900, d ₹1300-1500; ✱@⊕) Of the 21 rooms in this West Gate staple, those on the ground floor are stylish for the price, with marble walls, cable TV and clean bathrooms with hot water (room 111A is the standard to which all future ground-floor rooms will eventually be renovated). Upper-floor rooms are smaller and not as exciting.

Either way, all 21 surround or overlook a small, leafy courtyard overrun by a shade-providing tameshwari plant.

Taj Ganj

Hotel Sheela   HOTEL **$**
(Map p88; ☎0562-2333074; www.hotelsheelaagra.
com; Taj East Gate Rd; s/d with fan ₹500/600, with
AC ₹800/900; ❀🛜) It draws its fair share of
complaints from travellers (cold in winter, in-
different management, questionable hygiene),
but if you're not fussed about looking at the
Taj Mahal 24 hours a day, and don't mind doing a little legwork for an autorickshaw, Sheela
teeters on being an acceptable budget option.

Rooms are no-frills but are set around a
landscaped garden. There are singing birds,
plenty of shade and a restaurant area (better
for atmosphere than food). Book ahead.

Taj Plaza   HOTEL **$$**
(☎0562-2232515; www.hoteltajplaza.com; Shilp-
gram VIP Rd; d ₹1500, with AC ₹2500, Taj-facing
₹3200; ❀@🛜) Depending on demand, this
well-positioned hotel fluctuates between
budget and midrange. You won't be disap-
pointed if you stay here. It has professional
reception and clean rooms with TV, six of
which eye the Taj, and there's a pleasant roof-
top with decent Taj and sunset views.

It's a whole lot closer to the Taj than most
hotels in the same price range.

The Retreat   BOUTIQUE HOTEL **$$$**
(☎0562-3022222; www.theretreat.co.in; Shilpgram
Rd; s/d incl breakfast from ₹5000/6000; ❀@🛜☀)
Everything in this sleek 52-room hotel is done
up boutique-style with Indian sensibilities (lots
of soothing mauve and turquoise throughout)

and modern fixtures abound. There's a small
pool and multicuisine restaurant offering
countrywide specialities such as Goan fish curries and Lahori kebabs. Free wi-fi.

★**Oberoi Amarvilas**   HOTEL **$$$**
(☎0562-2231515; www.oberoihotels.com; Taj East
Gate Rd; d with/without balcony ₹62,960/53,960;
❀@🛜☀) Following Oberoi's iron-clad MO
of Maharaja-level service, exquisite dining
and properties that pack some serious wow,
Agra's best hotel by far oozes style and lux-
ury. Elegant interior design is suffused with
Mughal themes, a composition carried over
into the exterior fountain courtyard and
swimming pool, both of which are set in a
delightful water garden.

All rooms (and even some bathtubs) have
wonderful Taj views.

⚊ **Fatahabad Road Area**

★**Bansi Homestay**   HOMESTAY **$$**
(Map p86; ☎0562-2333033; www.bansi-
homestayagra.com; 18 Handicraft Nagar, Fatehabad
Rd; r incl breakfast ₹3500; ❀🛜) 🗲 A retired director of Uttar Pradesh Tourism is your host
at this wonderful upscale homestay tucked
away in a quiet residential neighbourhood
near Fatehabad Rd. The five large rooms
boast huge bathrooms with pressurised solar-
powered rain-style showers and flank pleasant common areas with bespoke furniture
and Krishna paintings.

The immensely pleasurable 2nd-floor garden is a fabulous retreat to watch the world
go by; and the food – notably the homemade
pickles and *aloo paratha* (potato-stuffed
flatbread) – excels along with the hospitality
in general.

★**N Homestay**   HOMESTAY **$$**
(Map p86; ☎9690107860; www.nhomestay.
com; 15 Ajanta Colony, Vibhav Nagar; s/d incl
breakfast ₹1600/1800; ❀@🛜) Matriarch
Naghma and her helpful sons are a riot
at this wonderful homestay. Their beau-
tiful home, tucked away in a residential

SLEEPING PRICE RANGES

Accommodation price ranges for this
chapter are:

$ below ₹1500

$$ ₹1500 to ₹4000

$$$ above ₹4000

neighbourhood 15 minutes' walk from the Taj's western gate, is nothing short of a fabulous place to stay.

The three-storey house features marble floors throughout, and some of the six large and authentically appointed rooms have pleasant balconies (first-come, first-served). Naghma will even cook you dinner (₹350 to ₹400) – and what a cook she is! You'll rarely break through the cultural surface with such ease.

Dasaprakash HOTEL $$

(Map p86; ☑ 0562-4016123; www.dasaprakash-group.com; 18/163A/6 Shamshabad Rd; s/d incl breakfast ₹3220/3760; ✳ 🛜) This friendly and clean retreat offers 28 modern and functional rooms with small desks, flat-screen TVs and nice bathrooms, all of which haven't been around long enough to show signs of deterioration. It all works well as a good-value escape from the diesel and dust, and is located far enough from Fatehabad Rd to offer relative R&R. Free wi-fi.

Howard Plaza HOTEL $$$

(Map p86; ☑ 0562-4048600; www.howardplazaagra.com; Fatehabad Rd; s/d incl breakfast from ₹7890/8990; ✳ @ 🛜 🏊) Standard rooms in this very welcoming hotel are decked out in elegant dark-wood furniture and stylish decorative tiling. New deluxe rooms boast soothing aqua colour schemes – the results of recent renovations that squared away a new sleek marble lobby and coffee shop/restaurant.

The pool is starting to show its age, but there's a small but well-equipped gym and a very pleasant spa offering a whole range of ayurvedic treatments (massages from ₹1799). The breezy open-air rooftop restaurant doubles as one of the few atmospheric bars in town at night (cocktails ₹325) – distant Taj views are on offer from the 4th-floor terrace. Wi-fi is enabled throughout.

Hotel Amar HOTEL $$$

(Map p86; ☑ 0562-2331884; www.hotelamar.com; Fatehabad Rd; s/d incl breakfast from ₹3820/4270; ✳ @ 🛜 🏊) A little worn, the 66 wi-fi-enabled rooms at the friendly Amar come with big TVs and clean bathrooms. The marble-inlay entrance halls and funky mirrored-ceiling hallways drive home a palpable sense of place. There's a great pool area, complete

---

TAJ MAHAL MYTHS

The Taj is a Hindu Temple

The well-publicised theory that the Taj was in fact a Shiva temple built in the 12th century and only later converted into Mumtaz Mahal's famous mausoleum was developed by Purushottam Nagesh Oak. The Mughals had form in this regard, at Somnath and the Qutb Minar in Delhi among other places, but in 2000 India's Supreme Court dismissed his petition to have the sealed basement rooms of the Taj opened to prove his theory. Oak also claims that the Kaaba, Stonehenge and the Papacy all have Hindu origins.

The Black Taj Mahal

The story goes that Shah Jahan planned to build a negative image of the Taj Mahal in black marble on the opposite side of the river as his own mausoleum, and that work began before he was imprisoned by his son Aurangzeb in Agra Fort. Extensive excavations at Mehtab Bagh have found no trace of any such construction.

Craftsmen Mutilations

Legend has it that on completion of the Taj, Shah Jahan ordered that the hands of the project's craftsmen be chopped off, to prevent them from ever building anything as beautiful again. Some even say he went so far as to have their eyes gouged out. Thankfully, no historical evidence supports either story.

Sinking Taj

Some experts believe there is evidence to show that the Taj is slowly tilting towards and sinking into the riverbed due to the changing nature of the soil beside an increasingly dry Yamuna River. The Archaeological Survey of India has dismissed any marginal change in the elevation of the building as statistically insignificant, adding that it has not detected any structural damage at its base in the seven decades since its first scientific study of the Taj was carried out, in 1941.

THE SPA MAHAL

If India's most glorious monument looks particularly glowing on your visit, it could come down to a day at the spa. After years of research, Indian and American scientists have identified the culprit that has caused an ongoing discolouration of the mausoleum – marble-white by birth, but now brownish-yellow due to ageing – and it's the same pollutants responsible for global warming. Dubbed the Atmospheric Brown Cloud, black carbon, light-absorbing brown carbon and dust (the latter no surprise to anyone who has visited Agra) have slowly tarnished the surface of the Taj with years of open-stove cooking with wood and dung, vehicle exhaust, brick-making and trash burning in the vicinity.

In addition to an ongoing project to alleviate the larger issue, the Taj has received a mud-pack facial cleanse for the fourth time in its history. Based on a traditional recipe used by Indian women to restore their own facial radiance, a lime-rich clay mixture is added to pollution-affected areas of the monument overnight and is scrubbed off with nylon brushes the next day. And a massive clean-up to prepare for US president Barack Obama's scheduled visit in 2015 (he skipped the visit due to the death of Saudi Arabian King Abdullah), resulted in two tonnes of trash being removed from the Yamuna River. Voila! The Taj looks brand new.

with a lush green lawn and a 3.5m-tall water slide.

🛏 Sadar Bazaar Area

Tourists Rest House　　　　HOTEL $
(Map p86; ☎0562-2463961; www.dontworrychickencurry.com; 4/62 Kutchery Rd; s/d ₹350/450, with AC from ₹850/1000; ❄@🛜) If you aren't set on sleeping under the nose of the Taj, this centrally located travellers' hub offers better value than most Agra spots and has been under the watchful eye of the same family since 1965 (though you can't tell it is pushing 50 years).

If you can forgo aircon, the newly renovated cheapies are great value – and things only get better from there. All rooms come with free wi-fi, TV, hot water and large windows, and are set around a peaceful plant-filled, palm-shaded courtyard (a real highlight) and a North Indian pure veg restaurant. The bend-over-backwards owners speak English and French. They couldn't be more helpful, right down to occasionally carting you off somewhere in their hotel rickshaw. Phone ahead for a free station pick-up; otherwise, it's ₹40 in a cycle-rickshaw from the train station. Damn fine masala chai, too.

Clarks Shiraz Hotel　　　　HOTEL $$$
(Map p86; ☎0562-2226121; www.hotelclarksshiraz.com; 54 Taj Rd; s/d incl breakfast from ₹8430/8990; ❄@🛜🏊) Agra's original five-star hotel, opened in 1961, has done well to keep up with the hotel Jones's. The standard doubles are nothing special for this price range, but marble-floored deluxe versions are a pleasant step up and all bathrooms are retiled and spotless.

There are three very good restaurants, two bars (three in season), a gym, a shaded garden and pool area (one of Agra's best) and ayurvedic massages. Some rooms have distant Taj views.

Hotel Yamuna View　　　　HOTEL $$$
(Map p86; ☎0562-3293777; www.hotelyamunaviewagra.com; 6B The Mall; s/d from ₹6183/6745; ❄@🛜🏊) A veteran Marriott manager runs a tight ship in this good-value spot in a quiet part of Sadar Bazaar, where spacious rooms with gleaming bathrooms and marble art tables are worth shelling out a few extra rupees for. There's hardly a need to upgrade to deluxe – they're not noticeably better than standard rooms.

There's a great garden pool, a sleek cocktail bar, a plush Chinese restaurant (with a real Chinese chef – good for an Indian food sabbatical) and free wi-fi (lobby only).

🍴 Eating

Dalmoth is Agra's famous version of *namkin* (spicy nibbles). *Peitha* is a square sweet made from pumpkin and glucose that is flavoured with rosewater, coconut or saffron. You can buy it in shops all over Agra. From October to March look out for *gajak,* a slightly spicy sesame-seed biscuit strip.

✗ Taj Ganj Area

This lively area directly south of the Taj has plenty of budget rooftop restaurants, where menus appear to be carbon copies of one another. None are licensed but most will find you a beer if you are discreet.

Shankar Ji Restaurant   DHABA $

(Map p88; mains ₹35-100; ⊘7am-10pm) Shankar Ji is a *dhaba* (snack bar) perfect for when you're bored of the multicuisine foreigner-friendly tourist restaurants, and want something more down to earth and authentic. As basic as any *dhaba*, but it's all smiles (the cook is a real character), has an English menu and dishes out the *dhaba* experience without taking a toll on your gut.

It's near the autorickshaw stand.

Shankara Vegis   INDIAN $

(Map p88; Chowk Kaghzi; meals ₹60-120; ⊘8am-10.30pm; 🛜) Most restaurants in Taj Ganj ooze a distinctly average air of mediocrity. Shankara Vegis is different. This cosy old-timer, with its red tablecloths and straw-lined walls, stands out not only for its decor, but for great vegetarian thalis (₹110 to ₹150) and, most pleasantly, the genuinely friendly, nonpushy ethos of its hands-on owners.

Joney's Place   MULTICUISINE $

(Map p88; Kutta Park, Taj Ganj; mains ₹30-110; ⊘5am-10.30pm) This pocket-sized institution whipped up its first creamy lassi in 1978 and continues to please despite cooking its meals in what must be Agra's smallest kitchen. The cheese and tomato 'jayfelles' (toasted sandwich), the banana lassi and the *malai* kofta all come recommended, but it's more about crack-of-dawn sustenance than culinary dazzle.

Yash Cafe   MULTICUISINE $

(Map p88; 3/137 Chowk Kagziyan; mains ₹60-300; ⊘7am-11pm; 🛜) This chilled-out 1st-floor cafe has wicker chairs, sports channels on TV, DVDs shown in the evening and a good range of meals, from good-value set breakfasts to thali (₹90), pizza (₹90 to ₹300) and Indian-style French toast (with coconut; we think they made that up). It also offers a shower and storage space (₹50 for both) to day visitors.

Saniya Palace Hotel   MULTICUISINE $$

(Map p88; mains ₹50-200; ⊘6am-11pm; 🛜) With cute tablecloths, dozens of potted plants and a bamboo pergola for shade, this is the most pleasant rooftop restaurant in Taj Ganj. It also has the best rooftop view of the Taj bar none. The kitchen isn't the cleanest in town, but its usual mix of Western dishes and foreigner-friendly Indian dishes usually go down without complaints.

★ Esphahan   NORTH INDIAN $$$

(☏2231515; Oberoi Amarvilas Hotel; Taj East Gate Rd; mains ₹1125-2250; ⊘dinner 6.30pm & 9pm) There are only two sittings each evening at Agra's finest **restaurant** (⊘6.30pm and 9.30pm) so booking a table is essential. The exquisite menu is chock-full of unique delicacies and rarely seen regional heritage dishes. Anything that comes out of the succulent North Indian tandoor is a showstopper (especially the *bharwan aloo,* a potato kebab stuffed with nuts, spices, mint and coriander). Melt-in-your-mouth dishes such as *aloobukhara maaz* (a Mughlai lamb kebab stuffed with prunes) and *safri gosht* (braised lamb with pickled onions, dried tomatoes and spiced pickle) redefine lamb as most know it. It's all set to a romantic background soundtrack of a live santoor player.

✗ Fatehabad Road

Dasaprakash   INDIAN $$

(Map p86; www.dasaprakashgroup.com; 18/163A /6 Shamshabad Rd; thali ₹190-270, mains ₹170-350; ⊘7am-11pm) The Vibhav Nagar branch of this perennial South Indian upper-scale staple ups the ante with a North Indian tandoor. You get the pure veg love of other Dasaprakash branches plus North Indian options such as veg tandoori kebabs, available from noon (that tandoor needs a few hours to heat up). It's inside the hotel of the same name.

Vedic   NORTH INDIAN $$

(Map p86; www.vedicrestaurant.com; 1 Gwalior Rd; meals ₹150-275; ⊘10am-11pm) Modern decor meets traditional ambience at this North Indian veg hot-spot, with paneer (unfermented cheese) dishes featuring highly. The paneer tikka masala and Navaratan korma are particularly good. There's also a range of delicious vegetarian kebabs.

★ Pinch of Spice   NORTH INDIAN $$$

(Map p86; www.pinchofspice.in; Opp ITC Mughal Hotel, Fatehabad Rd; mains ₹280-410; ⊘noon-11.30pm) This modern North Indian superstar at the beginning of Fatehabad Rd is the best spot outside five-star hotels to indulge yourself in rich curries and succulent tandoori kebabs. The *murg boti masala* (chicken tikka swimming in a rich and spicy country gravy) and the *paneer lababdar* (fresh cheese cubes in a spicy red gravy with sauteed onions) are outstanding.

Sadar Bazaar Area

This area offers better-quality restaurants and makes a nice change from the please-all, multicuisine offerings in Taj Ganj.

⭐ **Time2Eat – Mama Chicken** DHABA $
(Map p86; ☑8899199999; Stall No 2, Sadar Bazaar; items ₹30-200; ☺2-10pm) This superstar *dhaba* is a must: duelling veg and nonveg glorified street stalls employing 24 cooks during the rush, each of whom is manning outdoor tandoors or other traditional cookware. They whip up outrageously good *kati* rolls (flatbread wrap; try chicken tikka or paneer tikka), whole chickens numerous ways, curries and chow meins for a standing-room-only crowd hell bent on sustenance. Bright lights, obnoxious signage and funky Indian tunes round out the festive atmosphere – a sure-fire Agra must.

Lakshmi Vilas SOUTH INDIAN $
(Map p86; 50A Taj Rd; meals ₹50-110; ☺8.30am-10.30pm) This no-nonsense, plainly decorated, nonsmoking restaurant is *the* place in Agra to come for affordable South Indian fare. The thali (₹135), served noon to 3.30pm and 7pm to 10.30pm, is good though it comes across as relatively expensive.

Brijwasi SWEETS $
(Map p86; www.brijwasisweethouse.com; Sadar Bazaar; sweets from ₹320 per kg, meals ₹80-150; ☺7am-11pm) Sugar-coma-inducing selection of traditional Indian sweets, nuts and biscuits on the ground floor, with a decent-value Indian restaurant upstairs. It's most famous for its *peda* milk sweets.

⭐ **Dasaprakash** SOUTH INDIAN $$
(Map p86; www.dasaprakashgroup.com; Meher Theater Complex, Gwailor Rd; meals ₹100-300; ☺noon-10.45pm) Fabulously tasty and religiously clean, Dasaprakash whips up consistently great South Indian vegetarian food, including spectacular thalis (₹190 to ₹270), dosas (large savoury crepes) and a few token Continental dishes. The ice-cream desserts (₹80 to ₹210) are another speciality.

Comfortable booth seating and wood-lattice screens make for intimate dining.

🍷 Drinking & Nightlife

A night out in Agra tends to revolve around sitting at a rooftop restaurant with a couple of bottles of beer. None of the restaurants in Taj Ganj are licensed, but they can find alcohol for you if you ask nicely, and don't mind if you bring your own drinks, as long as you're discreet. You can catch live Indian classical music and *ghazal*s (Urdu love songs) at restaurants in several of Agra's top-end hotels, most of which also have bars, albeit of the rather soulless variety.

Café Coffee Day CAFE
(Map p88; www.cafecoffeeday.com; 21/101 Taj East Gate; coffee ₹65-140; ☺6.30am-8pm) This AC-cooled branch of the popular cafe chain is the closest place to the Taj selling proper coffee. There's another branch at **Sadar Bazaar** (Map p86; coffee ₹65-140; ☺9am-11pm).

Costa Coffee CAFE
(Map p86; www.costacoffee.com; 8 Handicraft Nagar, Fatehabad Rd; coffee ₹90-240; ☺8am-11pm; 🛜) Agra's only outlet of this UK coffee chain offers a cool and clean caffeine fix off Fatehabad Rd – and wi-fi.

Amarvilas Bar BAR
(Oberoi Amar Vilas Hotel; Taj East Gate Rd; ☺noon-midnight) For a beer (₹375) or cocktail (₹575) in sheer opulence, look no further than the bar at Agra's best hotel. A terrace opens out to views of the Taj. Nonguests can wander onto the terrace, but staff can be funny about it.

Shopping

Agra is well known for its marble items inlaid with coloured stones, similar to the pietra dura work on the Taj. Sadar Bazaar, the old town and the area around the Taj are full of emporiums. Taj Mahal models are all made of alabaster rather than marble. Very cheap ones are made of soapstone, which scratches easily.

Other popular buys include rugs, leather and gemstones, though the latter are imported from Rajasthan and are cheaper in Jaipur.

Be sure to wander the narrow streets behind the Jama Masjid where the crazy maze of overcrowded lanes bursting with colourful

ℹ STAYING AHEAD OF THE SCAMS

As well as the usual commission rackets and ever-present gem-import scam, some specific methods to relieve Agra tourists of their hard-earned cash include the following.

Rickshaws

When taking an auto- or cycle-rickshaw to the Taj, make sure you are clear which gate you want to go to when negotiating the price. Otherwise, almost without fail, riders will take you to the roundabout at the south end of Shahjahan Gardens Rd – where expensive tongas (horse-drawn carriages) or camels wait to take tour groups to the west gate – and claim that's where they thought you meant. Only nonpolluting autos can go within a 500m radius of the Taj because of pollution rules, but they can get a lot closer than this.

Fake Marble

Lots of 'marble' souvenirs are actually alabaster, or even just soapstone. So you may be paying marble prices for lower quality stones. The mini Taj Mahals are always alabaster because they are too intricate to carve quickly in marble.

markets is known collectively as **Kinari Bazaar** (Map p86; ⏱11am-9pm, closed Tue).

Subhash Emporium   HANDICRAFTS
(Map p86; www.subhashemporium.com; 18/1 Gwalior Rd; ⏱9am-7pm) This expensive but honest marble-carving shop has been knocking up quality pieces for more than 35 years. Its prices are fairer than others in town, considering their experience.

Subhash Bazaar   MARKET
(Map p86; ⏱8am-8pm summer, 9am-8pm winter) Skirts the northern edge of Agra's Jama Masjid and is particularly good for silks and saris.

Khadi Gramodyog   CLOTHING
(Map p86; MG Rd; ⏱11am-7pm, closed Tue) Stocks simple, good-quality men's Indian clothing made from the homespun *khadi* fabric famously recommended by Mahatma Gandhi. No English sign: on Mahatma Gandhi (MG) Rd, look for the *khadi* logo of hands clasped around a mud hut.

Modern Book Depot   BOOKS
(Map p86; Sadar Bazaar; ⏱10.30am-9.30pm, closed Tue) Great selection of novels, plus Lonely Planet guides, at this friendly 60-year-old establishment.

ℹ Information

Agra is more wired than most places, even in restaurants. Taj Ganj is riddled with internet cafes, most charging from ₹40 per hour.

EMERGENCY

Tourist Police (✆0562-2421204; Agra Cantonment Train Station; ⏱6.30am-9.30pm) The guys in sky-blue uniforms are based on Fate-

habad Rd, but have an office here in the Tourist Facilitation Centre. Officers also hang around the East Gate ticket office and the UP Tourism office on Taj Rd, as well as at major sites.

MEDICAL SERVICES

Amit Jaggi Memorial Hospital (Map p86; ✆9690107860; www.ajmh.in; Vibhav Nagar, off Minto Rd) If you're sick, Dr Jaggi, who runs this private clinic, is the man to see. He accepts most health-insurance plans from abroad; otherwise a visit runs ₹1000 (day) or ₹2000 (night). He'll even do house calls.

SR Hospital (Map p86; ✆0562-4025200; Laurie's Complex, Namner Rd) Agra's best private hospital.

MONEY

ATMs are everywhere. There are four close to the Taj, one near each gate (though the East Gate Axis Bank ATM is often on the fritz) and another next to the East Gate ticket office complex. If you need to change money and are worried about being swindled in Taj Ganj, there is a government-sanctioned money-changer at the East Gate ticket office complex as well.

POST

India Post (Map p86; www.indiapost.gov.in; The Mall; ⏱10am-5pm Mon-Fri, to 4pm Sat) Agra's historic GPO (General Post Office) dates to 1913 and includes a handy 'facilitation office' for foreigners.

TOURIST INFORMATION

India Tourism (Map p86; ✆0562-2226378; www.incredibleindia.org; 191 The Mall; ⏱9am-5.30pm Mon-Fri, to 2pm Sat) Very helpful branch; has brochures on local and India-wide attractions and can arrange guides (half-/full day ₹1035/1311).

Tourist Facilitation Centre (Taj East Gate; ⊙9.30am-5pm, closed Fri) This helpful tourist office is part of the East Gate ticket office complex at Shilpgram.

UP Tourism (www.up-tourism.com; ⊙6.30am-9.30pm) The friendly train-station branch inside the Tourist Facilitation Centre offers helpful advice most hours of important train arrivals. This branch, which doubles as the Tourism Police, and the one on Taj Rd (Map p86; ☑0562-2226431; 64 Taj Rd; ⊙10am-5pm Mon-Sat) can arrange guides (half-/full day ₹1035/1310).

TRAVEL AGENCIES

Bag Packer Travel (Map p86; ☑9997113228; www.bagpackertravels.com; 4/62 Kutchery Rd; ⊙9am-9pm) An honest agency for all your travel and transport needs, run by the friendly Anil at Tourists Rest House (p91). English and French spoken.

① Getting There & Away

AIR

Commercial flights to Agra's Kheria Airport began again in late 2012 after a long absence. **Air India** (www.airindia.com) now flies to Varanasi (2.05pm, from ₹4000) via Khajuraho (from ₹3000) Monday, Wednesday and Saturday, and to Mumbai (12.30pm, from ₹1500) via Gwailor (from ₹3200) on Monday and Wednesday. At time of research there was no return flight via Khajuraho.

To access the airport, part of Indian Air Force territory, your name must be on the list of those with booked flights that day. Tickets must be purchased online or by phone.

BUS

The opening of the tolled 165km Yamuna Expressway in 2012 cut drive time from Agra to Noida, a southeastern suburb of Delhi, by 30%. Some luxury coaches now use this route and reach central Delhi faster.

Some services from **Idgah Bus Stand** (☑0562-2420324; off National Hwy 2, near Sikandra):

Bharatpur ₹62, 1½ hours, every 30 minutes, 6am to 6.30pm

Delhi non-AC (₹171, 4½ hours, every 30 minutes, 5am to 11.30pm

Fatehpur Sikri ₹40, one hour, every 30 minutes, 6am to 6.30pm

Gwalior ₹115, three hours, hourly, 5.30am to 6.30pm

Jaipur ₹228, six hours, hourly, 6am to 6.30pm

Jhansi ₹200, six hours, noon, 2.15pm, 8.30pm

A block east of Idgah near Hotel Sakura, the **Rajashstan State Road Transport Corp** (RTDC; ☑0562-2420228; www.rsrtc.rajasthan.gov.in) runs more comfortable coaches to Jaipur throughout the day. Services include non-AC (₹256, 5½ hours, 7.30am, 10am, 1pm and 11.59pm), AC (₹440, five hours, 6.30am and 8.30am) and luxury Volvo (₹530, 4½ hours, 11.30am and 2.30pm).

From **ISBT Bus Stand** (☑0562-2603536), luxury Volvo coaches leave for Delhi (₹557, four hours, 7am, 9.30am, 1pm, 2.30pm, 6.30pm and 7.30pm) and Lucknow (₹906, 7½ hours, 10am and 10pm); as well as standard non-AC services to Allahabad (₹450, nine hours, 4pm) which continue on to Varanasi (₹550, 13 hours, 4pm) and Gorakhpur (₹625, 16 hours, 11.30am, 1.30pm, 2.30pm, 5pm and 10pm). Dehra Dun buses also depart from here (Volvo/AC/non-AC ₹1130/750/375, 2.30pm, 3.30pm, 4.30pm, 5.30pm, 6pm, 8pm, 8.30pm and 9.30pm). If you're shut out of the train to Rishikesh, you'll need to catch the bus to Haridwar (AC/non-AC ₹950/350, 10 hours, 6.30pm, 7.30pm, 8.30pm and 10pm) and switch there.

Bijli Ghar Bus Stand (Map p86; ☑0562-2464557) serves Mathura (₹64, 90 minutes, every 30 minutes, 5am to 11.30pm), Tundla (₹35, one hour, every 30 minutes, 7am to 8pm), from where you can catch the 12382 Poorva Express at 8.15pm to Varanasi if the trains from Agra are sold out.

DELHI–AGRA TRAINS FOR DAY TRIPPERS

ROUTE	TRAIN NO & NAME	FARE (₹)	DURATION (HR)	DEPARTURES
New Delhi–Agra	12002 Shatabdi Exp	505/1000 (A)	2	6am
Agra–New Delhi	12001 Shatabdi Exp	545/1040 (A)	2	9.15pm
Hazrat Nizamuddin–Agra	12280 Taj Exp	100/385 (B)	3	7.05am
Agra–Hazrat Nizamuddin	12279 Taj Exp	100/365 (B)	3	6.55pm

Fares: (A) AC chair/1AC, (B) 2nd-class/AC chair

MORE HANDY TRAINS FROM AGRA

DESTINATION	TRAIN NO & NAME	FARE (₹)	DURATION (HR)	DEPARTURES
Gorakhpur*	19037/19038 Avadh Exp	335/905/1295 (A)	15½	9.50pm
Jaipur*	12036 Shatabdi Exp	650/1215 (C)	3½	5.40pm (except Thu)
Khajuraho	12448 UP SMPRK KRNTI	280/715/1000 (A)	8	11.20pm (except Wed)
Kolkata (Howrah)	13008 UA Toofan Exp	555/1490 (B)	31	12.30pm
Lucknow	12180/12179 LJN Intercity	145/510 (D)	6	5.50am
Mumbai (CST)	12138/12137 Punjab Mail	580/1515/2195 (A)	23	8.55am
Varanasi*	14854 Marudhar Exp	350/940/1350 (A)	14	8.30pm (Mon, Thu, Sat)

Fares: (A) sleeper/3AC/2AC, (B) sleeper/3AC only; (C) AC chair/1AC only; (D) 2nd-class/AC chair; *leaves from Agra Fort station

Shared autos (₹10) run between Idgah and Bijli Ghar bus stands. To get to the ISBT, take the aircon public bus from Agra Cantt train station to Dayalbagh (₹22) but get off at Baghwan Talkies (₹16), from where shared autos (₹8) can take you to the ISBT; or catch an autorickshaw from Taj Ganz (₹150).

TRAIN

Most trains leave from Agra Cantonment (Cantt) train station, although some go from Agra Fort station. A few trains, such as Kota PNBE Express, run as slightly different numbers on different days than those listed, but timings remain the same. If you are heading to Jaipur on Thursday, the best option is the 12403/12404 ALD JP Express, departing Agra at 7.15am.

Express trains are well set up for day trippers to/from Delhi but trains run to Delhi all day. If you can't reserve a seat, just buy a 'general ticket' for the next train (about ₹90), find a seat in sleeper class then upgrade when the ticket collector comes along. Most of the time, he won't even make you pay any more. A new semi-express train between Delhi and Agra, the Gatimaan Express, should be up and running by the time you read this. It travels 160km per hour (India's fastest) and a full 30km per hour faster than the Shatabdi Express.

For Orchha, catch one of the many daily trains to Jhansi (sleeper from ₹110, three hours), then take a shared auto to the bus stand (₹10) from where shared autos run all day to Orchha (₹20). An autorickshaw costs ₹200 for same route.

ⓘ Getting Around

AUTORICKSHAW

Agra's green-and-yellow autorickshaws run on CNG (compressed natural gas) and are less environmentally destructive. Just outside Agra Cantt station is the prepaid autorickshaw booth, which gives you a good guide for haggling elsewhere. Usually, trips under three kilometres should not cost more than ₹50. Note, autos aren't allowed to go to Fatehpur Sikri.

Sample prices from Agra Cantt station: Fatehabad Rd ₹150; ISBT bus stand ₹200; Sadar Bazaar ₹70; Sikandra ₹200; Taj Mahal ₹100 (Taj West Gate) and ₹130 (Taj South Gate), Shilpgram (Taj East Gate) ₹150; half-day (four-hour) tour ₹400; full-day (eight-hour) tour ₹600. If you just want to shoot to the Taj and back with waiting time, they will charge ₹250. Prices listed here do not include the ₹5 booking fee, which is extra.

CYCLE-RICKSHAW

Prices from the Taj Mahal's South Gate include: Agra Cantt train station ₹80; Agra Fort ₹40; Bijli Ghar bus stand ₹50; Fatehabad Rd ₹30; Kinari Bazaar ₹100; Sadar Bazaar ₹50; half-day tour ₹400. Tack on another ₹10 to ₹20 if two people are riding.

TAXI

Outside Agra Cantt the prepaid taxi booth gives a good idea of what taxis should cost. Non-AC prices include: Delhi ₹3500; Fatehabad Rd ₹200; Sadar Bazaar ₹100; Taj Mahal ₹200; half-day (four-hour) tour ₹750; full-day (eight-hour) tour ₹1000. Prices do not include the ₹10 booking fee and tolls or parking charges (if applicable).

Around Agra

Fatehpur Sikri

📞 05613 / POP 29,000

This magnificent fortified ancient city, 40km west of Agra, was the short-lived capital of the Mughal empire between 1571 and 1585, during the reign of Emperor Akbar. Akbar visited the village of Sikri to consult the Sufi saint Shaikh Salim Chishti, who predicted the birth of an heir to the Mughal throne. When the prophecy came true, Akbar built his new capital here, including a stunning mosque – still in use today – and three palaces for each of his favourite wives, one a Hindu, one a Muslim and one a Christian (though Hindu villagers in Sikri dispute these claims). The city was an Indo-Islamic masterpiece, but erected in an area that supposedly suffered from water shortages and so was abandoned shortly after Akbar's death.

It's easy to visit this World Heritage Site as a day trip from Agra, but there are some decent places to stay, and the colourful bazaar in the village of Fatehpur, just below the ruins, as well as the small village of Sikri, a few kilometres north, are worth exploring. The red-sandstone palace walls are at their most atmospheric and photogenic at sunset.

The bus stand is at the eastern end of the bazaar. Walking another 1km northeast will bring you to Agra Gate and the junction with the main Agra–Jaipur road, from where you can catch buses.

⊙ Sights

The palace buildings lie beside the Jama Masjid. Both sit on top of a ridge that runs between the small villages of Fatehpur and Sikri. For more detail, see the illustrated highlight (p98).

Jama Masjid   MOSQUE

This beautiful, immense mosque was completed in 1571 and contains elements of Persian and Indian design. The main entrance, at the top of a flight of stone steps, is through the spectacular 54m-high Buland Darwaza (Victory Gate), built to commemorate Akbar's military victory in Gujarat.

Inside the courtyard of the mosque is the stunning white-marble tomb of Sufi saint Shaikh Salim Chishti, which was completed in 1581 and is entered through an original door made of ebony. Inside it are brightly coloured flower murals, while the sandalwood canopy is decorated with mother-of-pearl shell. Just as Akbar came to the saint four centuries ago hoping for a son, childless women visit his tomb today and tie a thread to the *jali* (carved lattice screens), which are among the finest in India. To the right of the tomb lie the gravestones of family members of Shaikh Salim Chishti and nearby is the entrance to an underground tunnel (barred by a locked gate) that reputedly goes all the way to Agra Fort. Behind the entrance to the tunnel, on the far wall, are three holes, part of the ancient ventilation system. You can still feel the rush of cool air forcing its way through them. Just east of Shaikh Salim Chishti's tomb is the red-sandstone tomb of Islam Khan, the final resting place of Shaikh Salim Chishti's grandson and one-time governor of Bengal.

On the east wall of the courtyard is a smaller entrance to the mosque – the Shahi Darwaza (King's Gate), which leads to the palace complex.

Palaces & Pavilions   PALACES

(Indian/foreigner ₹20/260, video ₹25; ⊙dawn-dusk) The main sight at Fatehpur Sikri is the stunning imperial complex of pavilions and palaces spread among a large abandoned 'city' peppered with Mughal masterpieces: courtyards, intricate carvings, servants quarters, vast gateways and ornamental pools.

A large courtyard dominates the northeast entrance at Diwan-i-Am (Hall of Public Audiences). Now a pristinely manicured garden, this is where Akbar presided over the courts from the middle seat of the five equal seatings along the western wall, flanked by his advisors. It was built to utilise an echo sound system, so Akbar could hear anything at any time from anywhere in the open space. Justice was dealt with swiftly if legends are to be believed, with public executions said to have been carried out here by elephants trampling to death convicted criminals.

The Diwan-i-Khas (Hall of Private Audiences), found at the northern end of the Pachisi Courtyard, looks nothing special from the outside, but the interior is dominated by a magnificently carved stone central column. This pillar flares to create a flat-topped plinth linked to the four corners of the room by narrow stone bridges. From this plinth Akbar is believed to have debated with scholars and ministers who stood at the ends of the four bridges.

(Continued on page 100)

AGRA & THE TAJ MAHAL FATEHPUR SIKRI

Fatehpur Sikri

A WALKING TOUR OF FATEHPUR SIKRI

You can enter this fortified ancient city from two entrances, but the northeast entrance at Diwan-i-Am (Hall of Public Audiences) offers the most logical approach to this remarkable Unesco World Heritage site. This large courtyard (now a garden) is where Emperor Akbar presided over the trials of accused criminals. Once through the ticket gate, you are in the northern end of the **Pachisi Courtyard** ❶. The first building you see is **Diwan-i-Khas** ❷ (Hall of Private Audiences), the interior of which is dominated by a magnificently carved central stone column. Pitch south and enter **Rumi Sultana** ❸, a small but elegant palace built for Akbar's Turkish Muslim wife. It's hard to miss the **Ornamental Pool** ❹ nearby – its southwest corner provides Fatehpur Sikri's most photogenic angle, perfectly framing its most striking building, the five-storey Panch Mahal, one of the gateways to the Imperial Harem Complex, where the **Lower Haramsara** ❺ once housed more than 200 female servants. Wander around the Palace of Jodh Bai and take notice of the towering ode to an elephant, the 21m-high **Hiran Minar** ❻, in the distance to the northwest. Leave the palaces and pavilions area via Shahi Darwaza (King's Gate), which spills into India's second-largest mosque courtyard at **Jama Masjid** ❼. Inside this immense and gorgeous mosque is the sacred **Tomb of Shaikh Salim Chishti** ❽. Exit through the spectacular **Buland Darwaza** ❾ (Victory Gate), one of the world's most magnificent gateways.

Buland Darwaza
Most tours end with an exit through Jama Masjid's Victory Gate. Walk out and take a look behind you: Behold! The magnificent 15-storey sandstone gate, 54m high, is a menacing monolith to Akbar's reign.

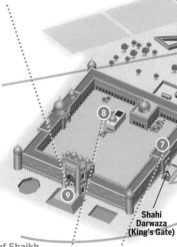

Shahi Darwaza (King's Gate)

Tomb of Shaikh Salim Chishti
Each knot in the strings tied to the 56 carved white marble designs of the interior walls of Shaikh Salim Chishti's tomb represents one wish of a maximum three.

Jama Masjid
The elaborate marble inlay work at the Badshahi Gate and throughout the Jama Masjid complex is said to have inspired similar work 82 years later at the Taj Mahal in Agra.

Hiran Minar

This bizarre, seldom-visited tower off the north-west corner of Fatehpur Sikri is decorated with hundreds of stone representations of elephant tusks. It is said to be the place where Minar, Akbar's favourite execution elephant, died.

Pachisi Courtyard

Under your feet just past Rumi Sultana is the Pachisi Courtyard where Akbar is said to have played the game *pachisi* (an ancient version of ludo) using slave girls in colourful dress as pieces.

Diwan-i-Khas

Emperor Akbar modified the central stone column inside Diwan-i-Khas to call attention to a new religion he called Din-i-Ilahi (God is One). The intricately carved column features a fusion of Hindu, Muslim, Christian and Buddhist imagery.

Panch Mahal

Diwan-i-Am (Hall of Public Audiences)

Lower Haramsara

Akbar reportedly kept more than 5000 concubines, but the 200 or so female servants housed in the Lower Haramsara were strictly business. Knots were tied to these sandstone rings to support partitions between their individual quarters.

Ornamental Pool

Tansen, said to be the most gifted Indian vocalist of all time and one of Akbar's treasured nine *Navaratnas* (Gems), would be showered with coins during performances from the central platform of the Ornamental Pool.

Rumi Sultana

Don't miss the headless creatures carved into Rumi Sultana's palace interiors: a lion, deer, an eagle and a few peacocks were beheaded by jewel thieves who swiped the precious jewels that originally formed their heads.

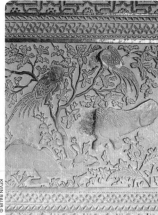

(Continued from page 97)

Next to Diwan-i-Khas is the **Treasury**, which houses secret stone safes in some corners (one has been left with its stone lid open for visitors to see). Sea monsters carved on the ceiling struts were there to protect the fabulous wealth once stored here. The so-called **Astrologer's Kiosk** in front has roof supports carved in a serpentine Jain style.

Just south of the Astrologer's Kiosk is **Pachisi Courtyard**, named after the ancient game known in India today as ludo. The large, plus-shaped game board is visible surrounding the block in the middle of the courtyard. In the southeast corner is the most intricately carved structure in the whole complex, the tiny but elegant **Rumi Sultana**, which was said to be the palace built for Akbar's Turkish Muslim wife. Other theories say it was used by Akbar himself as a palace powder room or R&R room during court sessions. On one corner of the **Ladies Garden** just west of Pachisi is the impressive **Panch Mahal**, a pavilion whose five storeys decrease in size until the top consists of only a tiny kiosk. The lower floor has 84 different columns; in total there are 176 columns.

Continuing anticlockwise will bring you to the **Ornamental Pool**. Here, singers and musicians would perform on the platform above the water while Akbar watched from the pavilion in his private quarters, known as **Daulat Khana** (Abode of Fortune). Behind the pavilion is the **Khwabgah** (Dream House), a sleeping area with a huge stone bunk bed. Nowadays the only ones sleeping here are bats, hanging from the ceiling. The small room in the far corner is full of them.

Heading west from the Ornamental Pool beholds the **Palace of Jodh Bai**, and the one-time home of Akbar's Hindu wife, said to be his favourite. Set around an enormous courtyard, it blends traditional Indian columns, Islamic cupolas and turquoise-blue Persian roof tiles. Just outside, to the left of Jodh Bai's former kitchen, is the **Palace of the Christian Wife**. This was used by Akbar's Goan wife Mariam, who gave birth to Jehangir here in 1569. Some believe Akbar never had a Christian wife and that Mariam was short for Mariam-Ut-Zamani, a title he gave to Jodh Bai meaning 'Beautiful like a Rose', or 'Most Beautiful Woman on Earth'. Like many of the buildings in the palace complex, it contains elements of different religions, as befitted Akbar's tolerant religious beliefs. The domed ceiling is Islamic in style, while remnants of a wall painting of the Hindu god Shiva can also be found.

Walking past the Palace of the Christian Wife once more will take you west to **Birbal Bhavan**, ornately carved inside and out, and thought to have been the living quarters of one of Akbar's most senior ministers. The **Lower Haramsara**, just to the south, housed Akbar's large inventory of live-in female servants.

Plenty of ruins are scattered behind the whole complex, including the **Caravanserai**, a vast courtyard surrounded by rooms where visiting merchants stayed. Badly defaced carvings of elephants still guard **Hathi Pol** (Elephant Gate), while the remains of the small **Stonecutters' Mosque** and a **hammam** (bath) are also a short stroll away. Other unnamed ruins can be explored north of what is known as the **Mint** but is thought to have in fact been stables, including some in the interesting village of Sikri to the north.

Archaeological Museum　　　　　MUSEUM
(⊙9am-5pm, closed Fri) **FREE** Inaugurated in 2014 inside Akbar's former Treasury house, this museum about 100m from Diwan-i-Am showcases pre-Mughal artefacts excavated over many years at Fatehpur Sikri. Well-presented highlights include a few remarkably preserved sandstone Jain *tirthankars* (the 24 holy Jain supreme beings) dating between 982 and 1034.

👉 Tours

Official Archaeological Society of India guides can be hired from the ticket office for ₹250 (English), but they aren't always the most knowledgeable (some are guides thanks to birthright rather than qualifications). Official UP Tourism guides have gone through more rigorous training and can be hired for ₹750. Our favourite is **Pankaj Bhatnagar** (✆8126995552; www.tajinvitation.com).

🛏 Sleeping & Eating

Fatehpur Sikri's culinary speciality is *khataie,* the biscuits you can see piled high in the bazaar.

Hotel Goverdhan　　　　　　　HOTEL **$**
(✆05613-282643; www.hotelfatehpursikriviews.com; Agra Rd; s/d/tr ₹500/800/900, with AC ₹1000/1250/1400; ❋@🖃) There are a variety

of rooms at this old-time favourite (check them out before you book), all of which surround a very well-kept garden. There's a communal balcony and terrace seating, free wi-fi, new beds in every room, air-coolers in the non-AC rooms and CCTV. The restaurant does decent work as well (meals ₹50 to ₹180).

Hotel Ajay Palace   GUESTHOUSE $
(📞 9548801213; Agra Rd; s/d ₹200/300, d with air-cooler ₹400) This friendly family guest-house isn't pretty but offers a few very simple and cheap double rooms with marble floors and sit-down flush toilets. It's also a very popular lunch stop (mains ₹50 to ₹140). Sit on the rooftop at the large, elongated marble table and enjoy a view of the village streets with the Jama Masjid towering above.

Note it is not 'Ajay Restaurant By Near Palace' at the bus stand – it's 50m further along the road.

ℹ Information

DANGERS & ANNOYANCES
Take no notice of anyone who gets on the Fateh-pur Sikri–Agra bus before the final stop at Idgah Bus Stand, telling you that you have arrived at the city centre or the Taj Mahal. You haven't. You're still a long autorickshaw ride away, and the man trying to tease you off the bus is, sur-prise surprise, an autorickshaw driver.

ℹ Getting There & Around

Tours and taxis all arrive at the Gulistan Tourist Complex parking lot, from which shuttle buses (₹10) depart for Fatehpur Sikri's Diwan-i-Am entrance (right side of the street) and Jodh Bai entrance (left side of the street). Note that if you have hired an unauthorised guide, you will not be allowed to enter at Diwan-i-Am.

Buses run to Agra's Idgah Bus Stand every half-hour (₹40) from 5.30am to 6.30pm. If you miss those, walk out through Agra Gate and another 350m to Bypass Crossing Stop on the main road and wave down a Jaipur–Agra bus. They run every 30 minutes or so, day and night.

For Bharatpur (₹25, 40 minutes) or Jaipur (₹190, 4½ hours), wave down a westbound bus from Bypass Crossing Stop.

Regular trains for Agra Fort Station leave Fate-hpur Sikri at 4.49am (59811 Haldighati Pass) and 8.16pm (19037 Avadh Express), but there are simpler passenger trains at 10.17am and 3.55pm as well as four other trains that fly through at various times. Just buy a 'general' ticket at the station and pile in (₹20, one to two hours).

Rajasthan

Best Forts & Palaces

➜ Jaisalmer (p181)
➜ Jodhpur (p171)
➜ Bundi (p140)
➜ Chittorgarh (p145)
➜ Udaipur (p149)

Best off the Beaten Track

➜ Keoladeo Ghana National Park (p124)
➜ Nawalgarh (p165)
➜ Osian (p179)
➜ Shekhawati (p165)
➜ Kumbhalgarh (p159)

Why Go?

It is said there is more history in Rajasthan than in the rest of India put together. Welcome to the Land of the Kings – a fabled realm of maharajas, majestic forts and lavish palaces. India is littered with splendid ruined bastions, but nowhere will you find fortresses quite as magnificent as those in Rajasthan, rising up imperiously from the desert landscape like fairy-tale mirages from a bygone era.

As enchanting as they are, though, there is more to this most royal of regions than its architectural wonders. This is also a land of sand dunes and jungle, of camel trains and wild tigers, of glittering jewels, vivid colours and vibrant culture. There are enough festivals here to fill a calendar (and an artist's palette), while the shopping and cuisine are nothing short of spectacular. In truth, Rajasthan just about has it all – it is the must-see state of this must-see country, brimming with startling, thought-provoking and, ultimately, unforgettable attractions.

When to Go
Jaipur

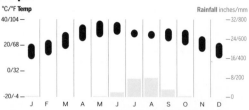

Oct Ranthamb-hore and Sariska National Parks reopen for tiger safaris.

Oct & Nov Don't miss the frenzy of Pushkar's famous Camel Festival.

Mar Jaipur's famous Elephant Festival precedes the typically boisterous Holi celebrations

History

Rajasthan is home to the Rajputs, warrior clans who claim to originate from the sun, moon and fire, and who have controlled this part of India for more than 1000 years. While they forged marriages of convenience and temporary alliances, pride and independence were always paramount; consequently,much of their energy was spent squabbling among themselves. The resultant weakness eventually led to the Rajputs becoming vassals of the Mughal empire.

Nevertheless, the Rajputs' bravery and sense of honour were unparalleled. Rajput warriors would fight against all odds and, when no hope was left, chivalry demanded *jauhar* (ritual mass suicide). The men donned saffron robes and rode out to face the enemy (and certain death), while the women and children perished in the flames of a funeral pyre. It's not surprising that Mughal emperors had such difficulty controlling this part of their empire.

With the Mughal empire declining, the Rajputs gradually clawed back independence – at least until the British arrived. As the British Raj inexorably expanded, most Rajput states allied with the British, which allowed them to continue as independent states, subject to certain political and economic constraints.

These alliances proved to be the beginning of the end for the Rajput rulers. Consumption took over from chivalry so that, by the early 20th century, many of the maharajas spent much of their time travelling the world with scores of retainers, playing polo and occupying entire floors of expensive hotels. While it suited the British to indulge them, the maharajas' profligacy was economically and socially detrimental. When India gained its independence, Rajasthan had one of the subcontinent's lowest rates of life expectancy and literacy.

At Independence, India's ruling Congress Party was forced to make a deal with the nominally independent Rajput states to secure their agreement to join the new India. The rulers were allowed to keep their titles and their property holdings, and they were paid an annual stipend commensurate with their status. It couldn't last forever, though, and in the early 1970s Indira Gandhi abolished the titles and the stipends, and severely sequestered rulers' property rights.

In their absence Rajasthan has made some headway, but the state remains poor. The strength of tradition means that women have a particularly tough time in rural areas. Literacy stood at 67% in 2011 (males 81%, females 53% – a massive rise from 18% in 1961 and 39% in 1991), the third-lowest in India, while the gender gap remains India's widest.

EASTERN RAJASTHAN

Jaipur

☎ 0141 / POP 3.07 MILLION / AREA 65 SQ KM

Jaipur, Rajasthan's capital, is an enthralling historical city and the gateway to India's most flamboyant state.

The city's colourful, chaotic streets ebb and flow with a heady brew of old and new. Careering buses dodge dawdling camels, leisurely cycle-rickshaws frustrate swarms of motorbikes, and everywhere buzzing autorickshaws watch for easy prey. In the midst of this mayhem, the splendours of Jaipur's majestic past are islands of relative calm, evoking a different pace and another world. At the city's heart, the City Palace continues to house the former royal family; the Jantar Mantar (the royal observatory) maintains a heavenly aspect; and the honeycomb Hawa Mahal gazes on the bazaar below. And just out of sight, in the arid hill country surrounding the city, is the fairy-tale grandeur of Amber Fort, Jaipur's star attraction.

History

Jaipur is named after its founder, the great warrior-astronomer Jai Singh II (1688–1744), who came to power at age 11 after the death of his father, Maharaja Bishan Singh. Jai Singh could trace his lineage back to the Rajput clan of Kachhwahas, who consolidated their power in the 12th century. Their capital was at Amber (pronounced 'am-er'), about 11km northeast of present-day Jaipur, where they built the impressive Amber Fort.

Rajasthan Highlights

1 Explore the sandstone alleys of the magical fort at **Jaisalmer** (p180), then ride your camel into the desert dunes

2 Make a lakeside pilgrimage to **Pushkar** (p133), Rajasthan's holiest town

3 Search for tigers in the forests and fortresses of **Ranthambhore National Park** (p138)

4 Take in the views of the Blue City from the imposing ramparts of **Mehrangarh** (p171), Jodhpur's mighty fortress

5 Look for royalty in the grand City Palace in **Udaipur** (p148), before enjoying a romantic sunset over gorgeous Lake Pichola

6 Shop till you drop in the bazaars of Jaipur, the **Pink City** (p107), and explore its marvellous Amber Fort

7 Get away from the tourist hustle in the ancient fort-town of **Bundi** (p140)

8 Uncover the architectural gems of **Shekhawati** (p165), with its many brightly-frescoed *havelis* (ornate traditional buildings)

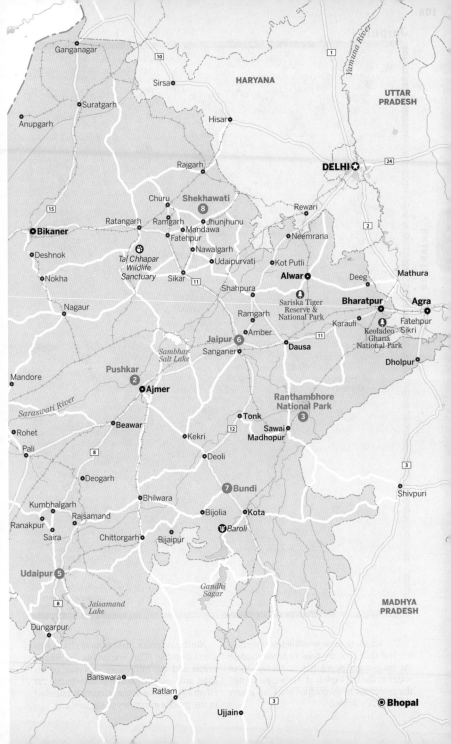

Jaipur

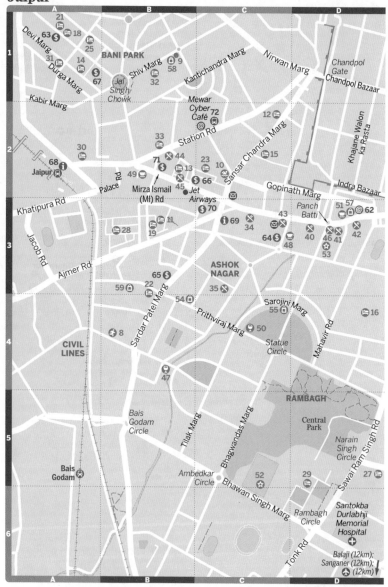

The kingdom grew wealthier and wealthier, and this, plus the need to accommodate the burgeoning population and a paucity of water at the old capital at Amber, prompted the maharaja to commence work on a new city in 1727 – Jaipur.

Northern India's first planned city, it was a collaborative effort combining Jai Singh's vision and the impressive expertise of his chief architect, Vidyadhar Bhattacharya. Jai Singh's grounding in the sciences is reflected in the precise symmetry of the new city.

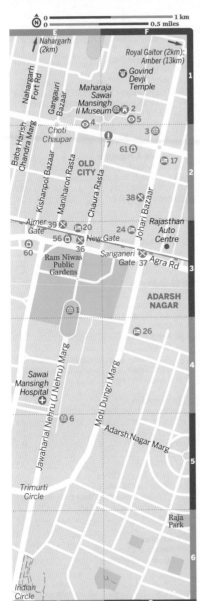

In 1876 Maharaja Ram Singh had the entire Old City painted pink (traditionally the colour of hospitality) to welcome the Prince of Wales (later King Edward VII). Today all residents of the Old City are compelled by law to preserve the pink facade.

◉ Sights

Consider buying a **composite ticket** (Indian/foreigner ₹100/400), which allows you entry into Amber Fort, Central Museum, Jantar Mantar, Hawa Mahal and Nahargarh, and is valid for two days from the time of purchase. It's available for purchase at all of the sights listed.

◉ Old City (Pink City)

The Old City (often referred to as the Pink City) is partially encircled by a crenellated wall punctuated at intervals by grand gateways. The major gates are Chandpol (*pol* means 'gate'), Ajmer Gate and Sanganeri Gate.

Avenues divide the Pink City into neat rectangles, each specialising in certain crafts, as ordained in the Shilpa Shastra (ancient Hindu texts). The main bazaars in the Old City include Johari Bazaar, Tripolia Bazaar, Bapu Bazaar and Chandpol Bazaar.

City Palace   PALACE
(Indian/foreigner incl camera ₹100/400, video camera ₹200, audio guide free, guide from ₹300, Royal Grandeur tour ₹2500; ⊙9.30am-5pm) A complex of courtyards, gardens and buildings, the impressive City Palace is right in the centre of the Old City. The outer wall was built by Jai Singh, but within it the palace has been enlarged and adapted over the centuries. There are palace buildings from different eras, some dating from the early 20th century. Despite the gradual development, the whole is a striking blend of Rajasthani and Mughal architecture.

The price of admission includes entry to Jaigarh, a long climb above Amber Fort. This is valid for two days.

➡ Mubarak Mahal

Entering through Virendra Pol, you'll see the Mubarak Mahal (Welcome Palace), built in the late 19th century for Maharaja Madho Singh II as a reception centre for visiting dignitaries. Its multi-arched and colonnaded construction was cooked up in an Islamic, Rajput and European stylistic stew by the architect Sir Swinton Jacob. It now forms part of the **Maharaja Sawai Mansingh II Museum** containing a collection of royal costumes and superb shawls, including Kashmiri *pashmina*. One remarkable exhibit is Sawai Madho Singh I's capacious clothing. It's said he was a cuddly 2m tall, 1.2m wide and 250kg.

RAJASTHAN JAIPUR

Jaipur

➡ **Diwan-i-Khas (Sarvatobhadra)**

Set between the Armoury and the Diwan-i-Am art gallery is an open courtyard known in Sanskrit as Sarvatobhadra. At its centre is a pink-and-white, marble-paved gallery that was used as the Diwan-i-Khas (Hall of Private Audience), where the maharajas would consult their ministers. Here you can see two enormous silver vessels, 1.6m tall and reputedly the largest silver objects in the world; Maharaja Madho Singh II, as a devout Hindu, used these vessels to take holy Ganges water to England for Edward VII's coronation in 1902.

➡ **Diwan-i-Am**

Within the lavish Diwan-i-Am (Hall of Public Audience) is this art gallery. Exhibits include a copy of the entire Bhagavad Gita

RAJASTHAN JAIPUR

(scripture) handwritten in tiny script, and miniature copies of other holy Hindu scriptures, which were small enough to be easily hidden in the event that zealot Mughal armies tried to destroy the sacred texts.

➡ The Armoury

The Anand Mahal Sileg Khana – the Maharani's Palace – houses the Armoury, which has one of the best collections of weapons in the country. Many of the ceremonial weapons are elegantly engraved and inlaid belying their grisly purpose.

➡ Pitam Niwas Chowk & Chandra Mahal

Located towards the palace's inner courtyard is Pitam Niwas Chowk. Here four glorious gates represent the seasons – the **Peacock Gate** depicts autumn, the **Lotus Gate**, signifying summer, the **Green Gate**, representing spring, and finally winter embodied by the **Rose Gate**.

Beyond this *chowk* (square) is the private Chandra Mahal, which is still the residence of the descendants of the royal family and where you can take a 45-minute **Royal Grandeur guided tour** of select areas.

Jantar Mantar   HISTORIC SITE
(Indian/foreigner ₹40/200, guide ₹200, audio guide ₹150; ☉9am-4.30pm) Adjacent to the City Palace is Jantar Mantar, an observatory begun by Jai Singh in 1728 that resembles a collection of giant bizarre sculptures. Built for measuring the heavens, the name is derived from the Sanskrit *yanta mantr*,

meaning 'instrument of calculation,' and in 2010 it was added to India's list of Unesco World Heritage Sites. Paying for a local guide is highly recommended if you wish to learn how each fascinating instrument works.

Jai Singh liked astronomy even more than he liked war and town planning. Before constructing the observatory he sent scholars abroad to study foreign constructs. He built five observatories in total, and this is the largest and best preserved (it was restored in 1901). Others are in Delhi, Varanasi and Ujjain. No traces of the fifth, the Mathura observatory, remain.

Hawa Mahal   HISTORIC BUILDING
(Johari Bazaar; Indian/foreigner incl camera ₹10/50, guide ₹200, audio guide Hindi/English ₹80/110; ☉9am-5pm) Jaipur's most distinctive landmark, the Hawa Mahal is an extraordinary, fairy-tale, pink sandstone, delicately honeycombed hive that rises a dizzying five storeys. It was constructed in 1799 by Maharaja Sawai Pratap Singh to enable ladies of the royal household to watch the life and processions of the city. The top offers stunning views over Jantar Mantar and the City Palace one way, and over Siredeori Bazaar the other.

There's a small **museum** (Saturday to Thursday), with miniature paintings and some rich relics, such as ceremonial armour, which help evoke the royal past.

RAJASTHAN JAIPUR

TOP STATE FESTIVALS

➡ **Desert Festival** (p180; Feb; Jaisalmer) A chance for moustache twirlers to compete in the Mr Desert contest.

➡ **Elephant Festival** (Mar; Jaipur) Parades, polo and human-versus-elephant tugs of war.

➡ **Gangaur** (Mar/Apr; statewide) A festival honouring Shiva and Parvati's love, celebrated with fervour in Jaipur.

➡ **Mewar Festival** (p153; Mar/Apr; Udaipur) Udaipur's version of Gangaur, with free cultural events and a colourful procession down to the lake.

➡ **Teej** (Aug; Jaipur and Bundi) Honours the arrival of the monsoon, and Shiva and Parvati's marriage.

➡ **Dussehra Mela** (p144; Oct; Kota) Commemorates Rama's victory over Ravana (the demon king of Lanka). It's a spectacular time to visit Kota – the huge fair features 22m-tall firecracker-stuffed effigies.

➡ **Marwar Festival** (p173; Oct; Jodhpur and Osian) Celebrates Rajasthani heroes through music and dance; one day is held in Jodhpur, the other in Osian.

➡ **Pushkar Camel Fair** (p136; Oct/Nov; Pushkar) The most famous festival in the statep; a massive congregation of camels, horses and cattle, pilgrims and tourists.

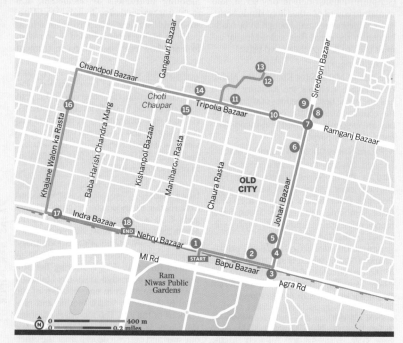

🏃 Walking Tour
Pink City

START NEW GATE
FINISH AJMER GATE
DISTANCE 4.5KM
DURATION THREE TO FIVE HOURS

Entering the old city from ① **New Gate**, turn into ② **Bapu Bazaar**, inside the city wall. Brightly coloured bolts of fabric, *jootis* (traditional shoes) and aromatic perfumes make the street a favourite destination for Jaipur's women. At the end of Bapu Bazaar you'll come to ③ **Sanganeri Gate**. Turn left into ④ **Johari Bazaar**, the jewellery market, where you will find jewellers, goldsmiths and artisans doing highly glazed *meenakari* (enamelling).

Continuing north you'll pass the famous ⑤ **LMB Hotel**, and the ⑥ **Jama Masjid**, with its tall minarets, and the bustling ⑦ **Badi Chaupar**. Be very careful crossing the road here. To the north is ⑧ **Siredeori Bazaar**, also known as Hawa Mahal Bazaar. The name is derived from the spectacular ⑨ **Hawa Mahal** (p109), a short distance to the north. Turning left on ⑩ **Tripolia Bazaar**,

you will see a lane leading to the entrance of Hawa Mahal. A few hundred metres west is the ⑪ **Tripolia Gate** (p149). This is the main entrance to the ⑫ **Jantar Mantar** and ⑬ **City Palace**, but only the maharaja's family may enter here. The public entrance is via the less ostentatious Atishpol (Stable Gate), a little further along.

After visiting the City Palace complex, head back to Tripolia Bazaar and resume your walk west past ⑭ **Iswari Minar Swarga Sal** (p112), which is well worth the climb for the view. Cross the bazaar at the minaret and head west. The next lane on the left is ⑮ **Maniharon ka Rasta**, the best place to buy colourful lac (resin) bangles.

Back on Tripolia Bazaar, continue west to cross Choti Chaupar to Chandpol Bazaar until you reach a traffic light. Turn left into ⑯ **Khajane Walon ka Rasta**, where you'll find marble and stoneware carvers at work. Continue south until you reach a broad road, ⑰ **Indra Bazaar**, just inside the city wall. Follow the road east towards ⑱ **Ajmer Gate**, which marks the end of this tour.

Claustrophobics should be aware that the narrow corridors can get extremely cramped and crowded inside the Hawa Mahal.

Entry is from the back of the complex. To get here, return to the intersection on your left as you face the Hawa Mahal, turn right and then take the first right again through an archway.

◉ New City

By the mid-19th century it became obvious that the well-planned city was bursting at the seams. During the reign of Maharaja Ram Singh (1835–80) the seams ruptured and the city burst out beyond its walls. Civic facilities, such as a postal system and piped water, were introduced. This period gave rise to a part of town very different from the bazaars of the Old City, with wide boulevards, landscaped grounds and grand European-influenced buildings.

Central Museum   MUSEUM
(Albert Hall; J Nehru Marg; Indian/foreigner ₹20/150, audio guide Hindi/English ₹90/124; ⊘9.30am-5pm) This museum is housed in the spectacularly florid Albert Hall, south of the Old City. It was designed by Sir Swinton Jacob, and combines elements of English and North Indian architecture, as well as huge friezes celebrating the world's great cultures. It was known as the pride of the new Jaipur when it opened in 1887. The grand old building hosts an eclectic array of tribal dress, dioramas, sculptures, miniature paintings, carpets, musical instruments and even an Egyptian mummy.

SRC Museum of Indology   MUSEUM
(24 Gangwell Park, Prachyavidya Path; Indian/foreigner incl guide ₹40/100; ⊘8am-6pm) This ramshackle, dusty treasure trove is an extraordinary private collection. It contains folk-art objects and other pieces – there's everything from a manuscript written by Aurangzeb and a 200-year-old mirrorwork swing from Bikaner to a glass bed. The museum is signposted off J Nehru Rd.

◉ City Edge

Nahargarh   FORT
(Tiger Fort; Indian/foreigner ₹10/30; ⊘10am-5pm) Built in 1734 and extended in 1868, this sturdy fort overlooks the city from a sheer ridge to the north. The story goes that the fort was named after Nahar Singh, a dead prince whose restless spirit was disrupting construction. Whatever was built in the day crumbled in the night. The prince agreed to leave on condition that the fort was named for him. The views are glorious here and it's a great sunset spot; there's a restaurant that's perfect for a beer.

Royal Gaitor   HISTORIC SITE
(Gatore ki Chhatryan; Indian/foreigner ₹20/30; ⊘9am-5pm) The royal cenotaphs, just outside the city walls, beneath Nahargarh, are an appropriately restful place to visit and feel remarkably undiscovered. The stone monuments are beautifully and intricately carved. Maharajas Pratap Singh, Madho Singh II and Jai Singh II, among others, are honoured here. Jai Singh II has the most impressive marble cenotaph, with a dome supported by 20 carved pillars.

Jal Mahal   HISTORIC BUILDING
(Water Palace; ⊘closed to public) Near the cenotaphs of the maharanis of Jaipur, and beautifully situated in the watery expanse of Man Sagar, is the beautiful Jal Mahal. It was built in 1799 by Madho Singh as a summer resort for the royal family, which they used to base duck-hunting parties. It's accessed via a causeway at the rear, and is currently undergoing restoration for tourism under the auspices of the Jal Tarang (www.jaltarang.in) project.

🏃 Activities

Several hotels will let you use their pool for a daily fee. Try the pools at the **Raj Mahal Palace** (Sadar Patel Marg; admission ₹270), the **Mansingh Hotel** (Sansar Chandra Marg; admission ₹225) and the **Narain Niwas Palace Hotel** (nonguests ₹200).

Yog Sadhna Ashram   YOGA
(☑9314011884; http://yogsadhnaindia.org; Bapu Nagar; ⊘Wed-Mon) Classes take place among trees off University Rd (near Rajasthan University) and incorporate breathing exercises, yoga asanas (postures) and exercise. Most of the classes are in Hindi, but some English is spoken in the 7.30am to 9.30am class. You can visit for individual classes, or register for longer courses (free).

Kerala Ayurveda Kendra   AYURVEDA
(☑5106743; www.keralaayurvedakendra.com; F-34, Jamnalal Bajaj Marg, Azad Marg; ⊘8am-noon & 4-8pm) Is Jaipur making your nerves jangle? Get help through ayurvedic massage and therapy. Treatments include *sirodhara* (₹1500), where medicated oil is steadily streamed over your forehead for 1½ hours to

reduce stress, tone the brain and help with sleep disorders. Massages (male masseur for male clients and female for female clients) cost from ₹500 for 55 minutes. It offers free transport to/from your hotel.

Courses

Jaipur Cooking Classes COOKING
(☑9928097288; www.jaipurcookingclasses.com; 33 Gyan Vihar, Nirman Nagar, near Ajmer Rd; class ₹1800-3700) Popular cooking classes with chef Lokesh Mathur, who boasts over 25 years experience working in the restaurant and hotel business. Classes cover both classic dishes and Rajasthani menus and can be veg or nonveg. After a three-hour lesson, you sit down for a lunch or dinner of what you've prepared. Lokesh's kitchen is outside the western outskirts of Jaipur.

Sakshi BLOCK PRINTING
(☑2731862; www.handblockprintedproducts. com; Laxmi Colony, Sanganer Village; half-/ full-day course per person ₹1500/2500) Basic block-printing or blue-pottery courses (eight hours per day) are available in Sanganer village, around 16km south of Jaipur. You can also do two- to three-month courses. Costs depend on the number of students; contact Sakshi for more details.

Tours

RTDC SIGHTSEEING
(☑2200778; tours@rtdc.in; RTDC Tourist Office, Platform 1, Jaipur Train Station; half-/full-day tour ₹300/350; ☉8am-6.30pm Mon-Sat) Full-day tours (9am to 6pm) take in all the major sights of Jaipur (including Amber Fort), with a lunch break at Nahargarh. The lunch break can be as late as 3pm, so have a big breakfast. Rushed half-day tours still

squeeze in Amber (8am to 1pm, 11.30am to 4.30pm, and 1.30pm to 6.30pm) – some travellers recommend these, as you avoid the long lunch break. The tour price doesn't include admission charges.

Departing at 6.30pm, the **Pink City by Night tour** (₹450) explores several well-known sights, and dinner at Nahargarh.

Tours depart from Jaipur train station; the company also picks up and takes bookings from the RTDC Hotel Teej, RTDC Hotel Gangaur and the tourist office at the main bus station.

Cyclin' Jaipur CYCLING
(☑28060965; www.cyclinjaipur.com; 4hr tour ₹1800; ☉tour 6.30am) Get up early to beat the traffic for a tour of the Pink City by bike, exploring the hidden lanes, temples, markets and food stalls of Jaipur. It's a unique and fun way to learn about the workings and culture of the city. Breakfast and refreshments during the tour are included, and helmets are provided on demand. Tours start at Karnot Mahal, on Ramganj Chaupar in the Old City.

Sleeping

Prepare yourself to be besieged by autorickshaw and taxi drivers when you arrive by train or bus. If you refuse to go to their choice of hotel, many will either snub you or double the fare. To avoid this annoyance, go straight to the prepaid autorickshaw and taxi stands at the bus and train stations. Even better, many hotels will pick you up if you ring ahead.

From May to September, most midrange and top-end hotels offer bargain rates, dropping prices by 25% to 50%.

DON'T MISS

HEAVEN-PIERCING MINARET

Piercing the skyline near the City Palace is the unusual **Iswari Minar Swarga Sal** (Heaven-Piercing Minaret; admission ₹20; ☉9am-4.30pm), just west of Tripolia Gate. The minaret was erected by Jai Singh's son Iswari, who later ignominiously killed himself by snakebite (in the Chandra Mahal) rather than face the advancing Maratha army – 21 wives and concubines then did the necessary noble thing and committed *jauhar* (ritual mass suicide by immolation) on his funeral pyre. You can spiral to the top of the minaret for excellent views over the Old City. The entrance is around the back of the row of shops fronting Chandpol Bazaar – take the alley 50m west of the minaret along Chandpol Bazaar or go via the Atishpol entrance to the City Palace compound, 150m east of the minaret.

🛏 Around MI Road

★ Hotel Pearl Palace HOTEL $

(☎ 2373700, 9414066311; www.hotelpearlpalace. com; Hathroi Fort, Hari Kishan Somani Marg; dm ₹200, r ₹400-1400; 图@🛜) The delightful Pearl Palace continues to raise the bar for budget digs. There's quite a range of rooms to choose from – small, large, shared bathroom, private bathroom, some with balconies, some with AC or fan cooling, and all are spotless. Services include free pick-up, moneychanging and travel arrangements, and the hotel boasts the excellent Peacock Rooftop Restaurant (p116). Advance booking is highly recommended.

Tony Guest House GUESTHOUSE $

(☎ 9928871717; www.facebook.com/tonyguesthousejaipur; 11 Station Road; dm ₹150, s ₹250, d ₹500, without bathroom ₹250-420; ☻@🛜) A friendly choice on a busy road for backpackers on a tight budget, Tony's is well set up for travellers with a rooftop garden, honest travel advice, internet and free-flowing chai. Rooms are extremely basic, some with plywood partition walls, and only one has a private bathroom, although it's with a cold-water shower. The common shower is hot.

Jwala Niketan GUESTHOUSE $

(☎ 5108303; jwalaniketan@live.com; C6, Lal ji Ka Bag, Motilal Atal Marg; s ₹200-500, d ₹400-580, s/d with AC ₹1000/1200; 图) This quiet yet centrally located guesthouse has a range of good-value, clean but very basic pastel-toned rooms. The host family lives on the premises and the atmosphere is decidedly noncommercial – almost monastic – though rooms do have TVs. There is no restaurant, but meals can be delivered to your room from the nearby cheap and multicuisine Mohan restaurant (p117) or you can sample the family's vegetarian fare.

★ Atithi Guest House GUESTHOUSE $$

(☎ 2378679; www.atithijaipur.com; 1 Park House Scheme Rd; s/d ₹1000/1400; 图@🛜) This nicely presented modern guesthouse, well situated between MI and Station Rds, offers strikingly clean, simple rooms dotted around a quiet courtyard. It's central but peaceful, and the service is friendly and helpful. Meals are available (the thali is particularly recommended) and you can have a drink on the very pleasant rooftop terrace.

Hotel Arya Niwas HOTEL $$

(☎ 4073456; www.aryaniwas.com; Sansar Chandra Marg; r from ₹1200, s/d with AC from ₹1500/1650; 图@🛜) Just off Sansar Chandra Marg, behind a high-rise tower, this very popular travellers' haunt has a travel desk, bookshop and yoga lessons. For a hotel of 92 rooms it is very well run, though its size means it's not as personal as smaller guesthouses. The spotless rooms vary in layout and size so check out a few.

For relaxing, there's an extensive terrace facing a soothing expanse of lawn. The self-service vegetarian restaurant doesn't serve beer (so BYO).

Pearl Palace Heritage HOTEL $$

(☎ 9414066311, 2375242; www.pearlpalaceheritage.com; Lane 2, 54 Gopal Bari; s/d ₹2400/2800; 图🛜図) The second hotel for the successful Pearl Palace team is a midrange hotel with several special characteristics and great attention to detail. Stone carvings adorn the halls and each room re-creates an individual cultural theme such as a village hut, a sandstone fort, or a mirror-lined palace boudoir. Modern luxuries and facilities have been carefully integrated into the traditional designs.

Karni Niwas GUESTHOUSE $$

(☎ 2365433; www.hotelkarniniwas.com; C5, Motilal Atal Marg; r ₹1000, with AC ₹1500; 图@🛜) This friendly hotel has clean, cool and comfortable rooms, often with balconies. There's no restaurant, but there are relaxing plant-decked terraces to enjoy room service on. And being so central, restaurants aren't far away. The owner shuns commissions for rickshaw drivers; free pick-up from the train or bus station is available.

All Seasons Homestay HOMESTAY $$

(☎ 9460387055; www.allseasonshomestayjaipur. com; 63 Hathroi Fort; s ₹1300-1900, d ₹1400-2000; 图🛜) Ranjana and her husband Dinesh run this welcoming homestay in their lovely bungalow on a quiet back street behind deserted Hathroi Fort. There are only four guest rooms, but each is lovingly cared for and two have small kitchens. There's a pleasant lawn and home-cooked meals. Advance booking is recommended.

RTDC Hotel Swagatam HOTEL $$

(☎ 2200595; Station Rd; s/d incl breakfast ₹900/1300, with AC ₹1400/1700; 图) One of the closest digs to the train station (100m down a quite inauspicious lane), this government-run hotel has helpful, friendly management and a neatly clipped lawn. Rooms are well worn, but spacious, clean and acceptable.

Karan's Guest House   GUESTHOUSE **$$**
(☑ 9828284433; www.karans.info; D-76 Shiv Heera Path; s/d ₹1300/1500; ❄️🛜) A sweet family-run guesthouse in a quiet residential part of town, but not too far from all the restaurants on MI Rd. Rooms are very spacious and homely and come with AC, TV and hot-water showers. There's a handy rickshaw stand at the end of the road.

Alsisar Haveli   HERITAGE HOTEL **$$$**
(☑ 2368290; www.alsisar.com; Sansar Chandra Marg; r from ₹7700; ❄️@🛜🏊) A genuine heritage hotel that has emerged from a gracious 19th-century mansion. Alsisar Haveli is set in beautiful green gardens, and boasts a lovely swimming pool and grand dining room. Its bedrooms don't disappoint either, with elegant Rajput arches and antique furnishings. This is a winning choice, though a little impersonal, perhaps because it hosts many tour groups.

🛏 Bani Park

The Bani Park area is relatively peaceful (away from the main roads), about 2km west of the old city (northwest of MI Rd).

Hotel Anuraag Villa   HOTEL **$$**
(☑ 2201679; www.anuraagvilla.com; D249 Devi Marg; r ₹790-990, with AC ₹1650-2050; ❄️@🛜) This quiet and comfortable option has no-fuss, spacious rooms and an extensive lawn where you can find some quiet respite from the hassles of sightseeing. It has a recommended restaurant with its kitchen on view, and efficient, helpful staff.

Tara Niwas   GUESTHOUSE **$$**
(☑ 2203762; www.aryaniwas.com; B-22-B Shiv Marg, Bani Park; s/d from ₹1150/1600, per month from ₹22,000/28,000; ❄️@🛜) Run by the people behind Hotel Arya Niwas, Tara Niwas offers well-furnished apartments suitable for longer stays. Some rooms have attached kitchenettes, and there's also a cafe and dining room and a business centre.

Shahpura House   HERITAGE HOTEL **$$**
(☑ 2203069; www.shahpura.com; D257 Devi Marg; s/d from ₹4000/5000, ste from ₹5000; ❄️@🛜🏊) Elaborately built and decorated in traditional style, this heritage hotel offers immaculate rooms, some with balconies,

featuring murals, coloured-glass lamps, flat-screen TVs, and even ceilings covered in small mirrors (in the suites). This rambling palace boasts a durbar hall (royal reception hall) with huge chandelier and a cosy cocktail bar.

There's an inviting swimming pool and an elegant rooftop terrace that stages cultural shows.

Madhuban   HOTEL **$$**
(☑ 2200033; www.madhuban.net; D237 Behari Marg; r ₹2400/2900; ❄️@🛜🏊) Madhuban has cute and cosy rooms with attractive wood furniture, and although they are small for the price, this is a comfortable stay. The pool is tiny (OK for a quick plunge), but the restaurant is good, and you can sometimes eat out on the lawn.

Jas Vilas   GUESTHOUSE **$$$**
(☑ 2204638; www.jasvilas.com; C9 Sawai Jai Singh Hwy; s/d ₹4440/5080; ❄️@🛜🏊) This small but impressive hotel was built in 1950 and is still run by the same charming family. It offers 11 spacious rooms, most of which face the large sparkling pool set in a romantic courtyard. Three garden-facing rooms are wheelchair accessible. In addition to the relaxing courtyard and lawn, there is a cosy dining room and helpful management.

Hotel Meghniwas   GUESTHOUSE **$$$**
(☑ 4060100; www.meghniwas.com; C9 Sawai Jai Singh Hwy; s/d ₹4000/4500; ❄️@🛜🏊) In a building erected by Brigadier Singh in 1950 and run by his gracious descendants, this very welcoming hotel has comfortable and spotless rooms, with traditional carved-wood furniture and leafy outlooks. The standard rooms are good, but the suite does not measure up to expectations. There's a first-rate restaurant and an inviting pool set in a pleasant lawn area.

🛏 Old City

Hotel Kailash   HOTEL **$**
(☑ 2577372; Johari Bazaar; r without/with bathroom ₹300/500) One of the few budget digs within the Old City, Kailash is right in the thick of it. But it's nothing fancy. Enter through a narrow stairway to the under-sized rooms, which are basic and stuffy despite the central air-cooling. The cheapest rooms are windowless cells and the shared bathrooms can be challenging, while the bigger doubles with attached bath are adequate. Rooms at the back are quieter.

Hotel Sweet Dreams HOTEL $
(☑2314409; www.hotelsweetdreamjaipur.in; Nehru Bazaar; s/d ₹800/1000, with AC from ₹1400/1600; ❋) A decent but basic budget choice in the Old City, if you ignore the rickety elevator that takes you upstairs. The rooms are pretty much identical (with balconies), with increasing amenities the higher up the price scale you go: adding air-cooling, hot water and finally AC. There's a bar and rooftop terrace restaurant.

LMB Hotel HOTEL $$
(☑2565844; www.hotellmb.com; Johari Bazaar; s/d from ₹2325/2525; ❋) Situated above the renowned vegetarian restaurant (p117) of the same name, this hotel offers a prime vantage point from where you can check out the mayhem of the Old City bazaars. Rooms are generally large, bright and clean, though possibly overpriced. Check out a few (including the plumbing) before settling in.

Rambagh Environs

Hotel Diggi Palace HERITAGE HOTEL $$
(☑2373091; www.hoteldiggipalace.com; off Sawai Ram Singh Rd; s/d incl breakfast from ₹4000/5000; ❋@) About 1km south of Ajmer Gate, this former splendid residence of the *thakur* (nobleman) of Diggi is surrounded by vast shaded lawns. The more expensive rooms at this former budget hotel are substantially better than the cheaper options. There's free pick-up from the bus and train stations.

Management prides itself on using organic produce from the hotel's own gardens and farms in the restaurant.

Nana-ki-Haveli HERITAGE HOTEL $$
(☑2615502; www.nanakihaveli.com; Fateh Tiba; r ₹1800-3000; ❋@) Tucked away off Moti Dungri Marg is this tranquil place with attractive, comfortable rooms decorated with traditional flourishes (discreet wall paintings, wooden furniture). It's hosted by a lovely family and is a good choice for solo female travellers. It's fronted by a relaxing lawn and offers home-style cooking and discounted rooms in summer.

Rambagh Palace HERITAGE HOTEL $$$
(☑2211919; www.tajhotels.com; Bhawan Singh Marg; r from ₹38,500; ❋@☎☒) This splendid palace was once the Jaipur pad of Maharaja Man Singh II and, until recently, his glamorous wife Gayatri Devi. Veiled in 19 hectares of gardens, the hotel – now run by the luxury Taj Group brand – has fantastic views across

the immaculate lawns. More expensive rooms are naturally the most sumptuous.

Nonguests can join in the magnificence by dining in the lavish restaurants or drinking tea on the gracious verandah. At least treat yourself to a drink at the spiffing Polo Bar (p117).

Narain Niwas Palace Hotel HERITAGE HOTEL $$$
(☑2561291; www.hotelnarainniwas.com; Narain Singh Rd; s/d incl breakfast from ₹5610/7670; ❋@☎☒) In Kanota Bagh, just south of the city, this genuine heritage hotel has wonderful ramshackle splendour. There's a lavish dining room with liveried staff, an old-fashioned verandah on which to drink tea, and antiques galore. The high-ceilinged rooms vary in atmosphere and the bathrooms also vary greatly – inspect before committing.

Out back you'll find a large secluded pool (nonguests ₹150), heavenly spa and sprawling gardens complete with peacocks.

✕ Eating

✕ Around MI Road

Old Takeaway The Kebab Shop KEBABS $
(151 MI Rd; kebabs ₹90-180; ☉6-11pm) One of a few similarly named roadside kebab shops on this stretch of MI Road, this one (next to the mosque) is the original (so we're told) and the best (we agree). It knocks up outstanding tandoori kebabs, including *paneer sheesh,* mutton *sheesh* and tandoori chicken. Like the sign says: a house of delicious nonveg corner.

Indian Coffee House CAFE $
(MI Rd; coffee ₹11-15, snacks from ₹40; ☉8am-9.30pm) Set back from the street, down an easily missed alley, this traditional coffee house (a venerable co-op owned institution) offers a very pleasant cup of filtered coffee in very relaxed surroundings. Aficionados of Indian Coffee Houses will not be disappointed by the fan-cooled ambience. Inexpensive samosas, *pakoras* (deep-fried battered vegetables) and dosas grace the snack menu.

Rawat Kachori SWEETS $
(Station Rd; kachori ₹20, lassi ₹25; ☉6am-10pm) For great Indian sweets (₹10 each or ₹120 to ₹300 per kg) and famous *kachori* (potato masala in fried pastry case), head to this exceedingly popular place. A delicious milk crown (fluffy dough with cream) should fill you up for the afternoon.

RAJASTHAN JAIPUR

Sankalp/Sam's Pizza SOUTH INDIAN, PIZZA **$$**
(MI Rd; pizzas ₹130-385, mains from ₹170; ⊙11am-11pm) This clean and modern Western-style fast-food restaurant has a bit of a split personality. Waiters are dressed the part to serve up good vegetarian pizzas and offerings from the salad bar, but can also hand you a menu full of South Indian treats. Dosas or deep-pan pizzas? You decide, it's good both ways, and the service is quick.

Anokhi Café ORGANIC **$$**
(2nd fl, KK Square, C-11, Prithviraj Marg; mains from ₹230; ⊙10am-7.30pm; 🐾🍴) A relaxing cafe with a quietly fashionable coffee-shop vibe about it, Anokhi is the perfect place if you're craving a crunchy, well-dressed salad, quiche, or thickly filled sandwich – or just a respite from the hustle with a latte or an iced tea. The delicious organic loaves are made to order and can be purchased separately.

Moti Mahal Delux NORTH INDIAN **$$**
(☑4017733; MI Rd; mains ₹170-430; ⊙11am-11pm) The famous Delhi restaurant now has franchises all over India delivering its world-famous butter chicken to the masses. The tantalising menu features a vast range of veg and nonveg, including some succulent tandoori dishes. Snuggle into a booth and enjoy the ambience, spicy food and a delicious *pista kulfi* (pistachio-flavoured sweet similar to ice cream) for dessert. Beer and wine available.

Peacock Rooftop Restaurant MULTICUISINE **$$**
(☑2373700; Hotel Pearl Palace, Hari Kishan Somani Marg; mains ₹80-260; ⊙7am-11pm) This multilevel rooftop restaurant at the Hotel Pearl Palace gets rave reviews for its excellent, inexpensive cuisine (Indian, Chinese and continental) and relaxed ambience. The mouth-watering food, attentive service, whimsical furnishings and romantic view towards Hathroi Fort make it a first-rate restaurant. There are great value thalis, and alcohol is served.

Surya Mahal SOUTH INDIAN **$$**
(☑2362811; MI Rd; mains ₹90-170; ⊙8am-11pm) This popular option near Panch Batti specialises in South Indian vegetarian food; try the delicious *masala dosa* and the tasty *dhal makhani* (black lentils and red kidney beans). There are also Chinese and Italian dishes, and good ice creams, sundaes and cool drinks.

Handi Restaurant NORTH INDIAN **$$**
(MI Rd; mains ₹140-300; ⊙noon-3.30pm & 6-11pm) Handi has been satisfying customers for years, with scrumptious tandoori and barbecued dishes and rich Mughlai curries. In the evenings it sets up a smoky kebab stall at the entrance to the restaurant. Good vegetarian items are also available. No beer.

It's opposite the main post office, tucked at the back of the Maya Mansions.

Natraj VEGETARIAN **$$**
(☑2375804; MI Rd; mains ₹150-250; ⊙9am-11pm) Not far from Panch Batti is this classy vegetarian place, which has an extensive menu featuring North Indian, continental and Chinese cuisine. Diners are blown away by the potato-encased 'vegetable bomb' curry. There's a good selection of thalis and South Indian food – the *paper masala dosa* is delicious – as well as Indian sweets.

Four Seasons VEGETARIAN **$$**
(☑2373700; D43A Subhas Marg; mains ₹100-210; ⊙noon-3.30pm & 6.30-11pm) Four Seasons is one of Jaipur's best vegetarian restaurants. It's a vastly popular place on two levels, with a glass wall to the kitchens. There's a great range of dishes on offer, including tasty Rajasthani specialities, dosas and a selection of pizzas. No alcohol.

Copper Chimney INDIAN **$$**
(☑2372275; Maya Mansions, MI Rd; mains ₹150-400; ⊙noon-3.30pm & 6.30-11pm) Copper Chimney is casual, almost elegant and definitely welcoming, with the requisite waiter army and a fridge of cold beer. It offers excellent veg and nonveg Indian cuisine, including aromatic Rajasthani specials. Continental and Chinese food is also on offer, as is a small selection of Indian wine, but the curry-and-beer combos are hard to beat.

Niro's INDIAN **$$$**
(☑2374493; MI Rd; mains ₹200-500; ⊙10am-11pm) Established in 1949, Niro's is a long-standing favourite on MI Rd that continues to shine. Escape the chaos of the street by ducking into its cool, clean, mirror-ceiling sanctum to savour veg and nonveg Indian cuisine. Classic Chinese and Continental food are available but the Indian menu is definitely the pick. Alcohol served.

Little Italy ITALIAN **$$$**
(☑4022444; 3rd fl, KK Square, Prithviraj Marg; mains ₹300-500; ⊙noon-11pm) Easily the best Italian restaurant in town, Little Italy is part

of a small national chain that offers excellent vegetarian pasta, risotto and wood-fired pizzas in cool, contemporary surroundings. The menu is extensive and includes some Mexican items and first-rate Italian desserts. There's a lounge bar attached so you can accompany your vegetarian dining with wine or beer.

✗ Old City

Mohan   VEGETARIAN $
(144-5 Nehru Bazaar; mains ₹25-90; ☺9am-10pm) Tiny Mohan is easy to miss: it's a few steps down from the footpath on the corner of the street. It's basic, cheap and a bit grubby, but the thalis, curries (half and full plate) and snacks are freshly cooked and very popular.

Ganesh Restaurant   VEGETARIAN $
(Nehru Bazaar; mains ₹60-120; ☺9am-11.30pm) This pocket-sized outdoor restaurant is in a fantastic location on the top of the Old City wall near New Gate. The cook is in a pit on one side of the wall, so you can check out your pure vegetarian food being cooked. If you're looking for a local eatery with fresh tasty food such as paneer butter masala, you'll love it.

There's an easy-to-miss signpost, but no doubt a stallholder will show you the narrow stairway.

LMB   VEGETARIAN $$
(☏2560845; Johari Bazaar; mains ₹180-340; ☺8am-11pm; ❄) Laxmi Misthan Bhandar, LMB to you and me, is a *sattvik* (pure vegetarian) restaurant in the Old City that's been going strong since 1954. A welcoming AC refuge from frenzied Johari Bazaar, LMB is also an institution with its singular decor, attentive waiters and extensive sweet counter.

Popular with both local and international tourists, try the Rajasthan thali (₹450 and big enough to share) followed by the signature *kulfa* (a fusion of *kulfi* and *falooda* with dry fruits and saffron).

♟ Drinking

Many bars around town tend to be oppressive, all-male affairs; most upper-end hotel bars are good for casual drinking.

★Lassiwala   CAFE
(MI Rd; small/jumbo lassi ₹18/36; ☺7.30am till sold out) This famous, much-imitated institution is a simple place that whips up fabulous, creamy lassis in clay cups. Get here early to avoid disappointment! Will the real Lassiwala please stand up? It's the one that says 'Shop 312' and 'Since 1944', directly next to the alleyway. Imitators spread to the right as you face it.

Henry's the Pub   BAR
(Park Prime Hotel, C-59, Prithviraj Marg; ☺noon-11.45pm) With coloured glass, dark wood and studded leather, this English pub wannabe has local Golden Peacock on tap and a small selection of international beer. You will also find Australian wine and a full array of Indian spirits. Food is also available.

Polo Bar   BAR
(Rambagh Palace Hotel, Bhawan Singh Marg; ☺noon-midnight) A spiffing watering hole adorned with polo memorabilia and arched, scalloped windows framing the neatly clipped lawns. A bottle of beer costs from ₹300 according to the label, with cocktails around ₹450.

Café Coffee Day   CAFE
(Country Inn Hotel, MI Rd; coffee ₹60-90; ☺10am-10pm) The franchise that successfully delivers espresso to coffee addicts, as well as the occasional iced concoction and muffin, has several branches in Jaipur. In addition to this one, sniff out the brews at Paris Point on Sawai Jai Singh Hwy (aka Collectorate Rd), and near the exit point at Amber Fort.

Brewberry's   CAFE
(G-2, Fortune Heights; coffee from ₹40; ☺8am-midnight; ☏) Modern wi-fi-enabled cafe with fresh coffee and a good mix of Indian and Western food and snacks. Has some patio seating. It's located opposite HDFC Bank.

100% Rock   BAR
(Hotel Shikha, Yudhishthir Marg, C-Scheme; beer from ₹160; ☺10am-11.30pm) Attached to, but separate from, Hotel Shikha, this is the closest thing there is to a beer garden in Jaipur, with plenty of outdoor seating as well as AC-cooled side rooms and a clubby main room with a small dance floor. Two-for-one beer offers are common, making this popular with local youngsters.

☆ Entertainment

Jaipur isn't a big late-night party town, although many of its hotels put on some sort of evening music, dance or puppet show. English-language films are occasionally screened at some cinemas in Jaipur – check the cinemas and local press for details.

Raj Mandir Cinema CINEMA

(☑ 2379372; www.therajmandir.com; Baghwandas Marg; tickets ₹60-150; ☺ reservations 10am-6pm, screenings 12.30pm, 3.30pm, 6.30pm & 9.30pm) Just off MI Rd, Raj Mandir is *the* place to go to see a Hindi film in India. This opulent cinema looks like a huge pink cream cake, with a meringue auditorium and a foyer somewhere between a temple and Disneyland. Bookings can be made one hour to seven days in advance at windows 9 and 10 – this is your best chance of securing a seat, but forget it in the early days of a new release.

Alternatively, sharpen your elbows and join the queue when the current booking office opens 45 minutes before curtain up. Avoid the cheapest tickets, which seat you very close to the screen.

Chokhi Dhani THEME PARK

(☑ 2225001; Tonk Rd; adult/child ₹450/350, incl Rajasthani thali ₹650/400; ☺ 6-11pm) Chokhi Dhani, meaning 'special village,' is a mock Rajasthani village 20km south of Jaipur, and is a fun place to take the kids. There are open-air restaurants, where you can enjoy a tasty Rajasthani thali, and there's a bevy of traditional entertainment – dancers, acrobats, snack stalls – as well as adventure park–like activities for kids to swing on, slide down and hide in. A return taxi from Jaipur, including waiting time, will cost about ₹700.

Polo Ground SPORTS

(☑ ticket info 2385380; Ambedkar Circle, Bhawan Singh Marg) Maharaja Man Singh II indulged his passion for polo by building an enormous polo ground next to Rambagh Palace, which is still a polo-match hub today. A ticket to a match also gets you into the lounge, which is adorned with historic photos and memorabilia. The polo season extends over winter, with the most important matches played during January and March. Contact the Rajasthan Polo Club for info about tickets.

During Jaipur's Elephant Festival in March you can watch elephant polo matches at the Chaughan Stadium in the Old City. Contact the RTDC tourist office for details.

🛍 Shopping

Jaipur is a shopper's paradise. Commercial buyers come here from all over the world to stock up on the amazing range of jewellery, gems, artefacts and crafts that come from all over Rajasthan. You'll have to bargain hard – shops have seen too many cash-rich, time-poor tourists, particularly around major tourist centres, such as the City Palace and Hawa Mahal.

Most of the larger shops can pack and send your parcels home for you – although it may be slightly cheaper if you do it yourself.

The city is still loosely divided into traditional artisans' quarters. Bapu Bazaar is lined with saris and fabrics, and is a good place to buy trinkets. Johari Bazaar and Siredeori Bazaar are where many jewellery shops are concentrated, selling gold, silver and *meenakari* (highly glazed enamel), a Jaipur speciality. You may also find better deals for fabrics with the cotton merchants of Johari Bazaar.

Kishanpol Bazaar is famous for textiles, particularly *bandhani* (tie-dye). Nehru Bazaar also sells fabric, as well as jootis, trinkets and perfume. MI Rd is another good place to buy jootis. The best place for bangles is Maniharon ka Rasta, near the Shree Sanjay Sharma Museum.

Plenty of factories and showrooms are strung along the length of Amber Rd, between Zorawar Singh Gate and the Holiday Inn, to catch the tourist traffic. Here you'll find huge emporiums selling block prints, blue pottery, carpets and antiques; but these shops are used to busloads swinging in to blow their cash, so you'll need to wear your bargaining hat.

Rickshaw-wallahs, hotels and travel agents will be getting a hefty cut from any shop they steer you towards. Many unwary visitors get talked into buying things for resale at inflated prices, especially gems. Beware of these get-rich-quick scams.

Kripal Kumbh HANDICRAFTS

(☑ 2201127; http://kripalkumbh.com; B18A Shiv Marg, Bani Park; ☺ 9.30am-6pm Mon-Sat) This tiny showroom in a private home is a great place to buy Jaipur's famous blue pottery produced by the late Mr Kripal Singh, his family and his students. Most pieces cost between ₹250 and ₹500. Free courses (☑ 2201127; B18A Shiv Marg, Bani Park) are also available.

Khadi Ghar CLOTHING, HANDICRAFTS

(MI Rd; ☺ 10am-7.30pm Mon-Sat) The best of a handful of *khadi* (homespun cloth) shops in Jaipur, this branch sells good quality ready-made clothing from the homespun *khadi* fabric, famously endorsed by Gandhi, as well

SHOPPING FOR GEMS

Jaipur is famous for precious and semiprecious stones. There are many shops offering bargain prices, but you do need to know your gems. The main gem-dealing area is around the Muslim area of Pahar Ganj, in the southeast of the old city. Here you can see stones being cut and polished in workshops tucked off narrow backstreets.

There is a **gem-testing laboratory** (☎0141-2568221; www.gtljaipur.info; Rajasthan Chamber Bhawan, MI Rd; ☺10am-4pm Mon-Sat) in the Rajasthan Chamber Bhawan on MI Rd. Deposit your gems between 10am and 4pm, then return the following day between 4pm and 5pm to pick up an authenticity certificate. The service costs ₹1000 per stone, ₹1600 for same-day service, if deposited before 1pm.

A warning: one of the oldest scams in India is the gem scam, where tourists are fooled into thinking they can buy gems to sell at a profit elsewhere. Don't be taken in – the gems you buy will be worth only a fraction of what you pay. Often the scams involve showing you real stones and then packing up worthless glass beads to give you in their place. These scams can be elaborate productions and can begin when touts strike up conversations in excellent English while you're waiting for a bus or eating in a restaurant, until you develop a friendly relationship with them. It might be several hours (or even days if they know where you hang out and can arrange to see you again) before any mention is made of reselling items. Be wary, and never let greed cloud your judgment.

as a small selection of handicrafts. Prices are fixed and pressure to buy is minimal.

Rajasthali   HANDICRAFTS
(MI Rd; ☺11am-7.30pm Mon-Sat) This state emporium, opposite Ajmer Gate, is packed with quality Rajasthani artefacts and crafts, including enamelwork, embroidery, pottery, woodwork, jewellery, puppets, block-printed sheets, miniatures, brassware, mirrorwork and more. The best reason to visit is to scout out prices before launching into the bazaar. Items can be cheaper at the markets, after haggling, and you'll find more choice.

★**Mojari**   CLOTHING
(Shiv Heera Marg; ☺10am-6.30pm Mon-Sat) Named after the traditional decorated shoes of Rajasthan, Mojari is a UN-supported project that helps rural leatherworkers, traditionally among the poorest members of society. A wide variety of footwear is available (₹500 to ₹750), including embroidered, appliquéd and open-toed shoes, mules and sandals. There's a particularly good choice for women, plus a small selection of handmade leather bags and purses.

Silver Shop   JEWELLERY
(Hotel Pearl Palace, Hari Kishan Somani Marg; ☺6-10pm) A trusted jewellery shop backed by the hotel management that hosts the store. A money-back guarantee is offered on all items. Find it under the peacock canopy in the hotel's Peacock Rooftop Restaurant.

Anokhi   CLOTHING, TEXTILES
(www.anokhi.com; 2nd fl, KK Square, C-11, Prithviraj Marg; ☺9.30am-8pm Mon-Sat, 11am-7pm Sun) Anokhi is a classy, upmarket boutique that's well worth visiting – there's a wonderful little cafe on the premises and an excellent bookshop in the same building. Anokhi sells stunning high-quality textiles, such as block-printed fabrics, tablecloths, bed covers, cosmetic bags and scarves, as well as a range of well-designed, beautifully made clothing that combines Indian and Western influences.

Fabindia   CLOTHING
(☎0141 5115991; www.fabindia.com; Sarojini Marg; ☺11am-9pm) A great place to coordinate colours with reams of rich fabrics plus furniture and home accessories. You can also find certified-organic garments, beauty products and condiments. Located opposite Central Park, gate number 4.

ⓘ Information

INTERNET ACCESS

Internet cafes are thin on the ground, but almost all hotels and guesthouses provide wi-fi and/or internet access.

Dhoom Cyber Café (MI Rd; per hr ₹30; ☺8.30am-8.30pm) Enter through an arch into a quiet courtyard just off the main drag.

Mewar Cyber Café (Station Rd; per hr ₹25; ☺7am-11pm) Near the main bus station.

MEDIA

Jaipur Vision and *Jaipur City Guide* are two useful, inexpensive booklets available at bookshops and in some hotel lobbies (where they are free). They feature up-to-date listings, maps, local adverts and features.

MEDICAL SERVICES

Most hotels can arrange a doctor on site.

Santokba Durlabhji Memorial Hospital (SDMH; ☑ 2566251; www.sdmh.in; Bhawan Singh Marg) Private hospital, with 24-hour emergency department, helpful staff and clear bilingual signage. Consultancy fee ₹400.

Sawai Mansingh Hospital (SMS Hospital; ☑ 2518222, 2518597; Sawai Ram Singh Rd) State-run but part of Soni Hospitals group (www.sonihospitals.com). Before 3pm, outpatients go to the CT & MRI Centre. After 3pm, go to the adjacent Emergency Department.

MONEY

There are plenty of places to change money, including numerous hotels and masses of ATMs, most of which accept foreign cards.

Thomas Cook (☑ 2360940; Jaipur Towers, MI Rd; ⊗ 9.30am-6pm)

POST

DHL Express (☑ 2361159; www.dhl.co.in; G8, Geeta Enclave, Vinobha Marg; ⊗ 10am-8pm) Look for the sub-branch on MI Rd then walk down the lane beside it to find DHL Express. For parcels, the first kilo is expensive, but each 500g thereafter is cheap. All packaging is included in the price. Credit cards and cash are accepted.

Main Post Office (☑ 2368740; MI Rd; ⊗ 8am-7.45pm Mon-Fri, 10am-5.45pm Sat) A cost-effective and efficient institution, though the back-and-forth can infuriate. Parcel-packing-wallahs in the foyer must first pack, stitch and wax seal your parcel for a fee (₹50 to ₹100 per small package) before sending.

TOURIST INFORMATION

The Tourism Assistance Force (police) are stationed at the railway and bus stations, the airport and at Jaipur's major tourist sights.

RTDC Tourist Office (www.rajasthantourism. gov.in) Main branch (☑ 5155137; www.rajasthan-tourism.gov.in; Room 21, former RTDC Tourist Hotel, MI Rd; ⊗ 9.30am-6pm Mon-Fri); Airport (☑ 2722647; Airport); Amber Fort (☑ 2530264; Amber Fort); Jaipur train station (☑ 2200778; Jaipur Train Station, Platform 1; ⊗ 24hr); main bus station (☑ 5064102; Main Bus Station, Platform 3; ⊗ 10am-5pm Mon-Fri) Has maps and brochures on Jaipur and Rajasthan.

ⓘ Getting There & Away

AIR

It's possible to arrange flights to Europe, the USA and other places, such as Dubai, all via Delhi. It's best to compare ticket prices from travel agencies with what the airlines supply directly and through their websites – the latter is where you will usually find the best price.

Offices of domestic airlines:

Air India (☑ 2743500, airport 2721333; www. airindia.com; Tonk Rd, Nehru Place) Daily flights to Delhi and Mumbai.

MAIN BUSES FROM JAIPUR

DESTINATION	FARE (₹)	DURATION (HR)	FREQUENCY
Agra	196, AC 407	5½	11 daily
Ajmer	105, AC 269	2½	13 daily
Bharatpur	139	4½	5 daily
Bikaner	225	8	hourly
Bundi	161	5	5 daily
Chittorgarh	233, AC 584	7	6 daily
Delhi	210, AC 558-782	5½	at least hourly
Jaisalmer	471, AC 1239	15	3 daily
Jhunjhunu	135	5	half-hourly
Jodhpur	263, AC 669	7	every 2 hours
Kota	191	5	hourly
Mt Abu (Abu Road)	371	13	daily
Nawalgarh	105	4	hourly
Pushkar (direct)	116	3	daily (direct)
Sawai Madhopur	110	6	2 daily
Udaipur	315, AC 809	10	6 daily

MAJOR TRAINS FROM JAIPUR

DESTINATION	TRAIN NO & NAME	DEPARTURE TIME	ARRIVAL TIME	FARE (₹)
Agra (Cantonment)	19666 Udaipur-Kurj Exp	6.15am	11am	175/485 (A)
Ahmedabad	12958 Adi Sj Rajdhani	12.25am	9.40am	1190/1635 (B)
Ajmer	Ajmer-Agra Fort Intercity	9.40am	11.50am	90/305 (C)
Bikaner	12307 Howrah-Jodhpur Exp	12.45am	8.15am	265/680 (A)
Delhi (New Delhi)	12016 Ajmer Shatabdi	5.50pm	10.40pm	720/1365 (D)
Delhi (S Rohilla)	12985 Dee Double Decker	6am	10.30am	480/1175 (D)
Jaisalmer	14659 Delhi-Jaisalmer Exp	11.45pm	11.15am	340/910 (A)
Jodhpur	22478 Jaipur-Jodhpur SF Exp	6am	10.30am	495/600 (E)
Sawai Madhopur	12466 Intercity Exp	11.05am	1.15pm	170/305/535 (F)
Udaipur	12965 Jaipur–Udaipur Exp	11pm	6.45am	260/690 (A)

Fares: (A) sleeper/3AC, (B) 3AC/2AC, (C) 2nd-class seat/AC chair, (D) AC chair/1AC, (E) AC chair/3AC, (F) sleeper/AC chair/3AC

IndiGo (☑ 2743500, 5119993; www.goindigo.in; Airport) Flights to Delhi, Mumbai, Ahmedabad, Bengalaru and Hyderabad.

Jet Airways (☑ 5112225; www.jetairways.com; Room 112, Jaipur Tower, MI Rd; ☺ 9.30am-6pm Mon-Sat) Flights to Delhi, Mumbai and Bengalaru.

SpiceJet (☑ 9871803333; www.spicejet.com; Airport) Has one direct daily flight to Delhi.

BUS

Rajasthan State Road Transport Corporation (RSRTC aka Rajasthan Roadways) buses all leave from the **main bus station** (Station Rd), picking up passengers at Narain Singh Circle (you can also buy tickets here). There is a left-luggage office at the main bus station (₹10 per bag for 24 hours), as well as a prepaid autorickshaw stand.

Ordinary buses are known as 'express' buses, but there are also 'deluxe' buses (coaches really, but still called buses; usually with air-con but not always); these vary a lot but are generally much more expensive and comfortable than ordinary express buses. Deluxe buses leave from Platform 3, tucked away in the right-hand corner of the bus station. Unlike ordinary express buses seats on them can be booked in advance from the **reservation office** (☑ 5116032) here.

With the exception of those going to Delhi (half-hourly), deluxe buses are much less frequent than ordinary buses.

CAR

Most hotels and the RTDC tourist office can arrange car and driver hire. Depending on the vehicle, costs are ₹8 to ₹12 per kilometre, with a minimum rental rate equivalent to 250km per day. Expect to pay a ₹150 overnight charge, and note, you will have to pay for the driver to return to Jaipur even if you aren't.

MOTORCYCLE

You can hire, buy or fix a Royal Enfield Bullet (and lesser motorbikes) at **Rajasthan Auto Centre** (☑ 2568074, 9829188064; www.royalenfield-salim.com; Sanganeri Gate, Sanjay Bazaar; ☺ 10am-8pm, to 2pm Sun), the cleanest little motorcycle workshop in India. To hire a 350cc Bullet costs ₹500 per day within Jaipur.

TRAIN

For same-day travel, buy your ticket at the northern end of the train station on Platform 1, window 10 (closed 6am to 6.30am, 2pm to 2.30pm, and 10pm to 10.30pm). The railway inquiries number is ☑ 131.

Station facilities on Platform 1 include an RTDC tourist information bureau, Tourism Assistance Force (police), a cloakroom for left luggage (₹10 per bag per 24 hours), retiring rooms, restaurants and air-conditioned waiting rooms for those with 1st class and 2AC train tickets.

There's a prepaid autorickshaw stand and local taxis at the road entrance to the train station.

RAJASTHAN JAIPUR

➡ Nine daily trains go to Delhi (sleeper ₹285; departs 1am, 2.50am, 4.40am, 5am, 6am, 2.35pm, 4.25pm, 5.50pm and 11.15pm), plus more on selected days. The 6am double-decker does the trip in 4½ hours, others take five to six.

➡ Two daily trains leave for Agra (sleeper ₹175; 4½ hours, 6.15am and 3.20pm).

➡ Three go to Bikaner (sleeper ₹265; 6½ to 7½ hours; 12.50am, 3.25am and 9.15pm).

➡ Seven go to Jodhpur (sleeper ₹240; five to six hours; 12.45am, 2.45am, 6am, 9.25am, 11.10am, 10.15pm and 11.45pm).

➡ Three go to Udaipur (2nd class ₹165; seven to eight hours; 6.45am, 2pm and 11pm).

➡ Six go to Ahmedabad (sleeper ₹370; 2.30am, 4.25am, 5.35am, 8.45am, 8.35pm and 12.25am). The 12.25am is the quickest (nine hours), while the others take 11 to 13 hours.

➡ For Pushkar, 11 daily trains make the trip to Ajmer (2nd class ₹90; two hours), plus many more on selected days so you rarely wait more than an hour.

➡ For Ranthambhore, six daily trains go to Sawai Madhopur (2nd class ₹90; two to three hours; 5.40am, 11.05am, 2pm, 4.50pm, 5.35pm and 11.55pm), plus plenty more on selected days.

➡ Two trains make the daily run to Jaisalmer (sleeper ₹360; 12 hours, 11.10am and 11.45pm).

❶ Getting Around

TO/FROM THE AIRPORT
There are no bus services from the airport, which is 12km southeast of the city. An autorickshaw costs at least ₹250; a taxi upwards of ₹450. There's a prepaid taxi booth inside the terminal.

AUTORICKSHAW
Autorickshaw drivers at the bus and train stations might just be the pushiest in Rajasthan. Use the fixed-rate prepaid autorickshaw stands instead. Keep hold of your docket to give to the driver at the end of the journey. In other cases be prepared to bargain hard – expect to pay at least ₹80 from either station to the Old City.

CYCLE-RICKSHAW
You can do your bit for the environment by flagging down a lean-limbed cycle-rickshaw rider. Though it can be uncomfortable watching someone pedalling hard to transport you, this *is* how they make a living. A short trip costs about ₹40.

TAXI
There are unmetered taxis available, which will require negotiating a fare, or you can try **Mericar** (⊿4188888; www.mericar.in; flagfall incl 2km ₹50, afterwards per km ₹13, 25% night surcharge 10pm-5am). It's a 24-hour service and taxis can be hired for sightseeing for four-/six-/eight-hour blocks costing ₹600/1000/1500.

Around Jaipur

Amber

The formidable, magnificent, honey-hued fort of Amber (pronounced am-er), an ethereal example of Rajput architecture, rises from a rocky mountainside about 11km northeast of Jaipur, and is the city's must-see sight.

Amber, the former capital of Jaipur state, was built by the Kachhwaha Rajputs who hailed from Gwalior, in present day Madhya Pradesh, where they reigned for over 800 years. Construction of the fort, which was begun in 1592 by Maharaja Man Singh, the Rajput commander of Akbar's army, was financed with war booty. It was later extended and completed by the Jai Singhs before they moved to Jaipur on the plains below.

◉ Sights

Amber Fort   FORT
(Indian/foreigner ₹25/200, guide ₹200, audio guide Hindi/other ₹100/150; ⊙8am-6pm, last entry 5.30pm) This magnificent fort is largely made up of a royal palace, built from pale yellow and pink sandstone and white marble, and divided into four main sections, each with its own courtyard. You can trudge up to the fort from the road in about 10 minutes, but riding up on **elephant back** (one-way per 2 passengers ₹900; ⊙7.30am-noon & 3.30-5.30pm) is very popular. A return 4WD to the top and back costs ₹300 for five passengers, including one-hour waiting time.

Animal welfare groups have criticised the keeping of elephants at Amber, as recent government inspections have revealed inadequate housing conditions and abuse of the animals, so you may want to think twice before taking a ride.

Whether you walk or ride an elephant, you will enter Amber Fort through **Suraj Pol** (Sun Gate), which leads to the **Jaleb Chowk** (Main Courtyard), where returning armies would display their war booty to the populace – women could view this area from the veiled windows of the palace. The ticket office is directly across the courtyard from Suraj Pol. If you arrive by car you will enter through **Chand Pol** (Moon Gate) on the opposite side of Jaleb Chowk. Hiring a guide or grabbing an audio guide is highly recommended as there are very few signs and many blind alleys.

From Jaleb Chowk, an imposing stairway leads up to the main palace, but first it's worth taking the steps just to the right, which lead to the small Siladevi Temple, with its gorgeous silver doors featuring repoussé (raised relief) work.

Heading back to the main stairway will take you up to the second courtyard and the Diwan-i-Am (Hall of Public Audience), which has a double row of columns, each topped by a capital in the shape of an elephant, and latticed galleries above.

The maharaja's apartments are located around the third courtyard – you enter through the fabulous Ganesh Pol, decorated with beautiful frescoed arches. The Jai Mandir (Hall of Victory) is noted for its inlaid panels and multimirrored ceiling. Carved marble relief panels around the hall are fascinatingly delicate and quirky, depicting cartoonlike insects and sinuous flowers. Opposite the Jai Mandir is the Sukh Niwas (Hall of Pleasure), with an ivory-inlaid sandalwood door and a channel that once carried cooling water right through the room. From the Jai Mandir you can enjoy fine views from the palace ramparts over picturesque Maota Lake below.

The zenana (secluded women's quarters) surrounds the fourth courtyard. The rooms were designed so that the maharaja could embark on his nocturnal visits to his wives' and concubines' respective chambers without the others knowing, as the chambers are independent but open onto a common corridor.

Jaigarh FORT

(Indian/foreigner ₹35/85, camera/video ₹50/200, car ₹50, Hindi/English guide ₹100/150; ⊙9am-5pm) A scrubby green hill rises above Amber and is topped by the imposing Jaigarh, built in 1726 by Jai Singh. The stern fort, punctuated by whimsical-hatted lookout towers, was never captured and has survived intact through the centuries. It's an uphill walk (about 1km) from Amber and offers great views from the Diwa Burj watchtower. The fort has reservoirs, residential areas, a puppet theatre and the world's largest wheeled cannon, Jaya Vana.

Anokhi Museum of Hand Printing MUSEUM

(Anokhi Haveli, Kheri Gate; child/adult ₹15/30, camera/video ₹50/150; ⊙10.30am-4.30pm Tue-Sat, 11am-4.30pm Sun, closed 1 May-15 Jul) This interesting museum, in a restored *haveli*, documents the art of hand-block printing, from old traditions to contemporary design. You can watch masters carve unbelievably intricate wooden printing blocks and even have a go at printing your own scarf or T-shirt. There's a cafe and gift shop too. From the museum you can walk around the ancient town to the restored Panna Meena Baori (step-well) and Jagat Siromani Temple (known locally as the Meera Temple).

🛏 Sleeping

The decidedly untouristy village of Amber, with its colourful food market and scattering of temples and palace ruins, makes a low-key alternative to hectic Jaipur as a possible place to stay.

★Mosaics Guesthouse GUESTHOUSE $$
(☑8875430000, 2530031; www.mosaicsguesthouse.com; Siyaram Ki Doongri, Amber; s/d incl breakfast ₹3200/3500; 🌐@🅿) Get away from it all at this gorgeous arty place (the French owner is a mosaic artist and will show off his workshop) with four lovely rooms and a rooftop terrace with beautiful fort views. Set-price Franco-Indian meals cost ₹500. It's about 1km past the fort near Kunda Village – head for Siyaram Ki Doongri, where you'll find signs.

ℹ Getting There & Away

There are frequent buses to Amber from near the Hawa Mahal in Jaipur (non-AC/AC ₹14/25, 15 minutes). They drop you opposite where you start your climb up to the entrance of Amber Fort.

The elephant rides and 4WDs start 100m further down the hill from the bus drop-off.

An autorickshaw/taxi will cost at least ₹400/700 for the return trip from Jaipur. RTDC city tours (p112) include Amber Fort.

Sanganer

The village of Sanganer is 12km south of Jaipur and has a ruined palace, a group of Jain temples with fine carvings (to which entry is restricted) and two ruined tripolias (triple gateways). The main reason to visit, however, is to see its handmade paper- and block-printing shops, workshops and factories (mostly found around the main drag, Stadium Rd), where you can see the products being made. You can also walk down towards the riverbank to see the enormous, brightly coloured fabrics drying in the sun as they hang on huge racks.

Salim's Paper (☑2730222; www.handmade-paper.com; Gramodyog Rd, Sanganer; ☺9am-5pm) is the largest handmade paper factory in India, and offers tours. The paper is made from fabric scraps, and often decorated with petals or leaves. The 200 or so employees produce 40,000 sheets a day, which are exported all over the world. There's also a beautiful range of paper products for sale in the showroom.

For block-printed fabrics and blue pottery, there are a number of shops, including Sakshi (☑2731862; Laxmi Colony; ☺shop 8.30am-8.30pm, factory 9am-6pm). You can see the block-printing workshop here, and even try your hand at block printing; it runs courses in block printing and blue pottery. There's a tremendous range of blue pottery and block-printed fabrics for sale.

🛈 Getting There & Away

Local buses leave from the Ajmeri Gate in Jaipur for Sanganer every few minutes (₹12, one hour).

Bharatpur & Keoladeo Ghana National Park

☑05644 / POP 205,200

Bharatpur is famous for its wonderful Unesco–listed Keoladeo Ghana National Park, a wetland and significant bird sanctuary. Apart from the park, Bharatpur has a few historical vestiges, though it wouldn't be worth making the journey for these alone. The town is dusty, noisy and not particularly visitor friendly. Bharatpur hosts the boisterous and colourful Brij Festival just prior to Holi celebrations.

The entrance to Keoladeo Ghana National Park lies 2km to the south of Bharatpur's centre.

🔘 Sights

Lohagarh   FORT
The still-inhabited, 18th-century Lohagarh, Iron Fort, was so named because of its sturdy defences. Despite being somewhat forlorn and derelict it is still impressive, and sits at the centre of town, surrounded by a moat. There's a north entrance, at Austdhatu (Eight-Metal) Gate – apparently the spikes on the gate are made of eight different metals – and a southern entrance, at Lohiya Gate.

Maharaja Suraj Mahl, constructor of the fort and founder of Bharatpur, built two towers, the Jawahar Burj and the Fateh Burj, within the ramparts to commemorate his victories over the Mughals and the British. The fort also contains three much decayed palaces within its precincts.

One of the palaces, which is centred on a tranquil courtyard, houses a seemingly forgotten museum. Upstairs you will find a rather ragtag display of royal artefacts, including weaponry. More impressive is the Jain sculpture gallery, which includes some beautiful 7th- to 10th-century pieces. The most spectacular feature of the museum, however, is the palace's original hammam (bathhouse), which retains some fine carvings and frescoes.

🔘 Keoladeo Ghana National Park

This tremendous bird sanctuary and national park (Indian/foreigner ₹55/400, video ₹400, guide ₹150, bike/mountain-bike rental ₹25/50, binoculars rental ₹100; ☺6am-6pm Apr-Sep, 6.30am-5pm Oct-Mar) has long been recognised as one of the world's most important bird breeding and feeding grounds. In a good monsoon season, over one-third of the park can be submerged, hosting over 360 species within its 29 sq km. The marshland patchwork is a wintering area for aquatic birds, including visitors from Afghanistan, Turkmenistan, China and Siberia. The park is also home to deer, nilgai and boar, which can be readily spotted.

Keoladeo originated as a royal hunting reserve in the 1850s. It continued to supply the maharajas' tables with fresh game until as late as 1965. In 1982 Keoladeo was declared a national park and it was listed as a World Heritage Site in 1985.

Local campaigners have voiced concern in recent years at the increase in forest clearing to make way for small, tourism-related developments, such as the car park to your right as you enter the park. You'll notice that much of the park is no longer tree-shaded. They are also calling for a 2km 'no-construction zone' outside the park boundary. The current limit is 500m.

Visiting the Park

The best time to visit is from October to February, when you'll see many migratory birds.

Admission (₹400; sunrise to sunset) entitles you to one entrance per day. Guides cost ₹150 per hour. One narrow road (no motor-

Bharatpur

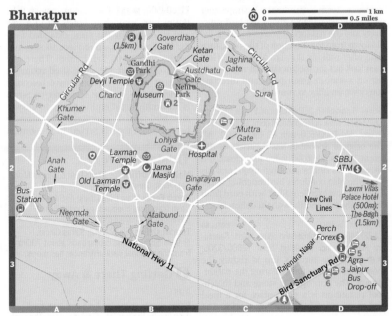

ised vehicles are permitted past checkpoint 2) runs through the park, but a number of tracks and pathways fan out from it and thread their way between the shallow wetlands. Generally speaking, the further away from the main gate you go, the more interesting the scenery, and the more varied the wildlife becomes.

Only the government-authorised cycle-rickshaws (recognisable by the yellow license plate) are allowed beyond checkpoint 2. You don't pay an admission fee for the drivers, but they charge ₹70 per hour. Some are very knowledgeable. However, these cycle-rickshaws can only travel along the park's larger tracks.

An excellent way to see the park is by hiring a bicycle at the park entrance. Having a bike is a wonderfully quiet way to travel, and allows you to avoid bottlenecks and take in the serenity on your own. However, we recommend that lone female travellers who wish to cycle do so with a guide (who will cycle alongside you), as we've had more than one report of lone women being harassed by young men inside the park in recent years.

You get a small map with your entrance ticket, although the park isn't big so it's difficult to get lost.

Bharatpur

🛏 Sleeping & Eating

There are tons of sleeping options near the Keoladeo Ghana National Park (suiting all budgets), either on the stretch of the highway beside Birder's Inn or on the dirt track that the Falcon Guest House is on.

Almost all guesthouses have restaurants and even those without a proper bar can sort you out with a cold beer if you ask.

Shagun Guest House   GUESTHOUSE $
(📱 9828687488; rajeevshagun@hotmail.com; d ₹150, s/d without bathroom ₹150/90) This unusual tree-shaded courtyard guesthouse, in a quiet corner of the old town, is extremely basic, and has only four rooms, but it comes with bags of character. It's run by the affable

Rajeev, a keen environmental campaigner who is knowledgeable about the bird sanctuary and the old fort. If you're entering the old town from the direction of the park, turn right after walking through Mathurara Gate then look out for the guesthouse name written on a wall in green paint and directing you down an alley to your left.

Hotel Spoonbill & Restaurant GUESTHOUSE $
(☑ 223571; www.hotelspoonbill.com; Gori Shankur Colony; s/d ₹500/650, with AC ₹900/1000; ❄) The original Spoonbill has a variety of different rooms, all good value and clean, if a bit worn. It's run by a retired major and his son, who also conducts birdwatching tours. The hotel has excellent food, with curd from the family cow and Rajasthani delicacies..

★ Birder's Inn HOTEL $$
(☑ 227346; www.birdersinn.com; Bird Sanctuary Rd; s/d incl breakfast from ₹2800/3200; ❄@☎❄) The Birder's Inn is rightly the most popular base for exploring the national park. The atmospheric stone and thatch-roof restaurant is a great place for a meal and to compare birdwatching stories. The rooms are airy, spacious, nicely decorated, and are set far back from the road in well-tended gardens. Guides from the hotel are available for Keoladeo.

Hotel Sunbird HOTEL $$
(☑ 225701; www.hotelsunbird.com; Bird Sanctuary Rd; s/d from ₹1800/2200; ❄) A well-run and popular place close to the Keoladeo park entrance. Rooms are clean and comfortable and there's an appealing garden bar and restaurant with a good range of tasty veg and nonveg dishes and cold beer. Packed lunches and guided tours for the park are available.

Falcon Guest House GUESTHOUSE $$
(☑ 223815; falconguesthouse@hotmail.com; Gori Shankur Colony; s/d from ₹600/800, with AC ₹1200-1500; ❄@) The Falcon may well be the pick of a bunch of hotels all in a row and all owned by the same extended family. It's a well-kept, snug place to stay, run by the affable Mrs Rajni Singh. There is a range of comfortable, good-sized rooms at different prices – the best have balconies or views of the sunrise. Husband Tej Singh is an ornithologist and is happy to answer any bird-related questions. Flavoursome home-cooked food is served in the garden restaurant.

ⓘ Information

Main Post Office (◷10am-1pm & 2-5pm Mon-Sat) Near Gandhi Park.
Perch Forex (New Civil Lines; ◷5am-11pm) Cash travellers cheques, get credit-card advances or change money here.
Tourist Office (☑ 222542; Saras Circle; ◷9am-5pm) On the crossroads about 700m from the national park entrance; has maps.

ⓘ Getting There & Away

BUS
Buses running between Agra and Jaipur will drop you by the tourist office or outside the park entrance if you ask.

Buses from Bharatpur bus station include:
Agra (₹57, 1½ hours, every 30 minutes day and night)
Alwar (₹113, four hours, hourly until 8pm)
Deeg (₹28, one hour, hourly until 8pm)
Delhi (₹152 to ₹180, five hours, half-hourly from 6am to 7pm, then hourly until 11pm)
Fatehpur Sikri (₹25, 45 minutes, every 30 minutes day and night)
Jaipur (₹139, 4½ hours, every 30 minutes)

TRAIN
➡ There are eight trains to Delhi (2nd class/sleeper ₹85/170, four hours) leaving throughout the day, plus three other services on selected days.

MAJOR TRAINS FROM BHARATPUR

DESTINATION	TRAIN NO & NAME	DEPARTURE TIME	ARRIVAL TIME	FARE (₹)
Agra (Cantonment)	19666 Udaipur-Kurj Exp	69.10am	11am	140/485 (A)
Delhi (Hazrat Nizamuddin)	12059 Kota-Jan Shatabdi	9.25am	12.30am	110/370 (B)
Jaipur	19665 Kurj-Udaipr Exp	6.57am	10.50am	140/485 (A)
Sawai Madhopur	12904 Golden Temple Mail	10.30am	12.55am	170/535 (A)

Fares: (A) sleeper/3AC, (B) 2nd-class/AC chair

➡ Five daily trains also make the two-hour trip to Agra (2nd class/sleeper ₹110/140; two hours; 4.45am, 6.50am, noon, 5.20pm and 8.15pm), plus once a day to Agra Cantonment (9.10am).

➡ Nine daily trains go to Jaipur (2nd class/sleeper₹100/140; three to four hours) between 6am and 11pm.

➡ For Ranthambhore National Park, nine trains run daily to Sawai Madhopur (2nd class/sleeper ₹120/170; two to three hours) from 1am to 9pm. These trains all continue to Kota (four hours) from where you can catch buses to Bundi.

🛈 Getting Around

An auto- or cycle-rickshaw from the bus station to the main hotel area should cost around ₹30 (add an extra ₹10 from the train station).

Alwar

📞 0144 / POP 266,200

Alwar is perhaps the oldest of the Rajasthani kingdoms, forming part of the Matsya territories of Viratnagar in 1500 BC. It became known again in the 18th century under Pratap Singh, who pushed back the rulers of Jaipur to the south and the Jats of Bharatpur to the east, and who successfully resisted the Marathas. It was one of the first Rajput states to ally itself with the fledgling British empire, although British interference in Alwar's internal affairs meant that this partnership was not always amicable.

Alwar is the nearest town to Sariska Tiger Reserve (p128), and has a ruined fort and a rambling palace with an above-average museum hidden inside it. The town has relatively few tourists so there's a refreshing lack of hassle here.

◉ Sights

Bala Qila   FORT

This imposing fort stands 300m above Alwar, its fortifications hugging the steep hills that line the eastern edge of the city. Predating the time of Pratap Singh, it's one of the few forts in Rajasthan built before the rise of the Mughals, who used it as a base for attacking Ranthambhore. Mughal emperors Babur and Akbar have stayed overnight here, and Prince Salim (later Emperor Jehangir) was exiled in Salim Mahal for three years.

Now in ruins, the fort houses a radio transmitter station and parts can only be visited with permission from the superintendent of police. However, this is easy to get: just ask at the superintendent's office in the City Palace complex. You can walk the very steep couple of kilometres up to the fort entrance or take a 7km rickshaw ride.

City Palace   HISTORIC BUILDING

(Vinay Vilas Mahal) Below Bala Qila sprawls the colourful and convoluted City Palace complex, with massive gates and a tank reflecting a symmetrical series of ghats and pavilions. Today most of the complex is occupied by government offices, overflowing with piles of dusty papers and soiled by pigeons and splatters of *paan* (a mixture of betel nut and leaves for chewing).

Hidden within the City Palace is the excellent **Alwar Museum** (Indian/foreigner ₹5/50; ⊗10am-5pm Tue-Sun).

Alwar Museum's eclectic exhibits evoke the extravagance of the maharajas' lifestyle: stunning weapons, stuffed Scottish pheasants, royal ivory slippers, erotic miniatures, royal vestments, a solid silver table, and stone sculptures, such as an 11th-century sculpture of Vishnu. Somewhat difficult to find in the Kafkaesque tangle of government offices, the museum is on the top floor of the palace, up a ramp from the main courtyard. However, there are plenty of people around to point you in the right direction and from there you can follow the signs.

Cenotaph of Maharaja Bakhtawar Singh   HISTORIC BUILDING

This double-storey edifice, resting on a platform of sandstone, was built in 1815 by Maharaja Vinay Singh, in memory of his father. To gain access to the cenotaph, take the steps to the far left when facing the palace. The cenotaph is also known as the Chhatri of Moosi Rani, after one of the mistresses of Bakhtawar Singh who performed *sati* (self-immolation) on his funeral pyre – after this act she was promoted to wifely status.

🛌 Sleeping & Eating

As not many tourists stop here, Alwar's hotels are mostly aimed at budget business travellers and aren't particularly great value.

Alwar Hotel   GUESTHOUSE $$

(📞2700012; 25-26 Manu Rd; s/d incl breakfast ₹1900/2700; ❇@🛜) Set back from the road in a neatly manicured garden, this well-run hotel has spacious, comfortable rooms. It's easily the best option in town, and staff can be helpful with general information and sightseeing advice. Tours to Sariska Tiger

Reserve can be arranged. The Alwar Hotel also boasts a great multicuisine restaurant, Angeethi.

Hotel Aravali   HOTEL $$
(📞 2332316; reservation.aravali@gmail.com; Nehru Rd; s/d ₹1800/2000, with AC from ₹2100/2400; ❄🛜🍴) One of the town's better choices, this hotel has large, well-furnished rooms and big bathrooms. It has a decent restaurant (mains ₹120 to ₹270) and bar. The pool is open in summer only, and breakfast is only included with the AC rooms. Turn left out of the train station and it's 300m down the road.

RTDC Hotel Meenal   HOTEL $$
(📞 2347352; Topsingh Circle; s/d ₹1400/1400; ❄) A respectable option with bland and tidy rooms typical of the chain. It's located about 1km south of town on the way to Sariska, so it's quiet and leafy, though a long way from the action.

Prem Pavitra Bhojnalaya   INDIAN $
(near Hope Circle; mains ₹50-110; ⏱10.30am-4pm & 6.30-10pm; ❄) Alwar's renowned restaurant has been going since 1957. In the heart of the old town, it serves fresh, tasty pure veg food – try the delicious *aloo parathas* (bread stuffed with spicy potato) and *palak paneer* (unfermented cheese cubes in spinach purée). Servings are big; half-serves available.

You have to pay 10% extra to eat in the air-conditioned section – but it is worth it. Turn right out of the bus station, take the first left (towards Hope Circle) and it's on your left after 100m.

Angeethi   MULTICUISINE $$
(Alwar Hotel, Manu Rd; mains ₹75-200; ⏱Tue-Sun; ❄) Alwar Hotel's restaurant serves first-rate Indian, Continental and Chinese food; the South Indian selection is particularly good. It's slightly gloomy in the restaurant but you can eat in the pleasant gardens.

ℹ Information

ICICI ATM Near the bus stand.

Merharwal's Internet Cyber Zoné (1 Company Bagh Rd; per hr ₹40; ⏱7am-10pm) Opposite Inderlok restaurant.

State Bank of Bikaner & Jaipur (Company Bagh Rd) Changes travellers cheques and major currencies and has an ATM. Near the bus stand.

Tourist Office (📞 2347348; Nehru Rd; ⏱10am-5pm Mon-Sat) Helpful centre offering a map of Alwar and information on Sariska. Near the train station.

ℹ Getting There & Around

A cycle-rickshaw between the bus and train stations costs ₹30. Look out for the shared taxis that ply fixed routes around town (₹10). They come in the form of white minivans and have the word 'Vahini' printed on their side doors. One handy route goes past Hotel Aravali, the tourist office and the train station before continuing on to the bus station and terminating a short walk from Vinay Vilas Mahal (the palace complex).

A return taxi to Sariska Tiger Reserve will cost you around ₹1200.

BUS

Services from Alwar bus station:

Bharatpur (₹113, four hours, every hour from 5am to 8.30pm)

Deeg (₹60, 2½ hours, every hour from 5am to 8.30pm)

Delhi (₹129, four hours, every 20 minutes from 5am to 9pm)

Jaipur (₹120, four hours, half-hourly from 6am to 10.30pm)

Sariska (₹30, one hour, half-hourly from 6am to 10.30pm)

TRAIN

There are around a dozen daily trains to Delhi (3AC/sleeper ₹170/585, three to four hours), leaving throughout the day. Most services go to Old Delhi.

There are 16 daily trains to Jaipur (three to four hours). Prices are almost identical to those for Delhi.

Sariska Tiger Reserve
📞 0144

Enclosed within the dramatic, shadowy folds of the Aravallis, the Sariska Tiger Reserve (Indian/foreigner ₹60/450, vehicle ₹250; ⏱ticket sales 7am-3.30pm Oct-Mar, 6.30am-4pm Apr-Sep, park closes at sunset) is a tangle of remnant semi-deciduous jungle and craggy canyons sheltering streams and lush greenery. It covers 866 sq km (including a core area of 498 sq km), and is home to peacocks, monkeys, majestic sambars, nilgai, chital, wild boars and jackals.

Although Project Tiger has been in charge of the sanctuary since 1979, there has been a dramatic failure in tiger protection. In 2004 there were an estimated 18 tigers in Sariska; however, this was called into question after an investigation by the WWF. That report prompted the federal government to investigate what has happened to the tigers of this reserve.

Sariska is in any case a fascinating sanctuary. Unlike most national parks, it opens year-round, although the best time to spot wildlife is from November to March, and you'll see most wildlife in the evening. During July and August your chances of spotting wildlife are minimal, as the animals move to higher ground, and the park is open primarily for temple pilgrimage rather than wildlife viewing.

Proposals to stop private-car access and to end the free access to pilgrims visiting the Hanuman temple often get press coverage, but to date there has been no further action taken.

◎ Sights

Besides wildlife, Sariska has some fantastic sights within the reserve and around its peripheries, which are well worth seeking out. If you take a longer tour, you can ask to visit one or more of these. A couple of them are also accessible by public bus.

Kankwari Fort   FORT
Deep inside the sanctuary, this imposing small jungle fort, 22km from Sariska, offers amazing views over the plains of the national park, dotted with red mud-brick villages. This is the inaccessible place that Aurangzeb chose to imprison his brother,

Dara Shikoh, Shah Jahan's chosen heir to the Mughal throne, for several years before he was beheaded.

A four- to five-hour **4WD safari** (one to five passengers plus guide) to Kankwari Fort from the Forest Reception Office near the reserve entrance costs ₹1600, plus guide fee (₹150).

Bhangarh   HISTORIC SITE
Around 55km from Sariska, beyond the inner park sanctuary and out in open countryside, is this deserted, well-preserved and notoriously haunted city. Founded in 1631 by Madho Singh, it had 10,000 dwellings, but was suddenly deserted about 300 years ago for reasons that remain mysterious. Bhangarh can be reached by a bus that runs twice daily through the sanctuary (₹35) to nearby Golaka village. Check what time the bus returns, otherwise you risk getting stranded.

☞ Tours

Private cars, including taxis, are limited to sealed roads. The best way to visit the park is by 4WD gypsy (open-topped, six-passenger 4WDs), which can explore off the main tracks. Gypsy safaris start at the park entrance and you'll be quoted ₹1050 for three

RAJASTHAN SARISKA TIGER RESERVE

SARISKA'S TIGER TALE

Sariska Tiger Reserve took centre stage in one of India's most publicised wildlife dramas. In 2005 an Indian journalist broke the news that the tiger population here had been eliminated, a report that was later confirmed officially after an emergency census was carried out.

An inquiry into the crisis recommended fundamental management changes before tigers be reintroduced to the reserve. Extra funding was proposed to cover the relocation of villages within the park as well as increasing the protection force. But action on the recommendations has been slow and incomplete despite extensive media coverage and a high level of concern in India.

Nevertheless, a pair of tigers from Ranthambhore National Park were moved by helicopter to Sariska in 2008. By 2010, five tigers had been transferred. However, in November 2010 the male of the original pair was found dead, having been poisoned by local villagers, who are not supportive of the reintroduction. The underlying problem – the inevitable battle between India's poorest and ever-expanding village populace with the rare and phenomenally valuable wildlife on their doorstep. Plans to relocate and reimburse villagers inside the park have largely failed to come to fruition, and illegal marble mining and clashes between cattle farmers and park staff have remained a problem.

In early 2012 the first cubs were sighted. In recent years Sariska's tiger population was thought to be 13 – made up of seven females, two males and four cubs all born in the park.

Only time will tell if this reintroduction is successful – inbreeding in the small population is an understandably high concern. As things stand, Sariska remains a sad indictment of tiger conservation in India, from the top government officials down to the underpaid forest guards.

hours, or ₹3200 for a full day. Guides are available (₹150 for three hours).

Bookings can be made at the **Forest Reception Office** (☑2841333; Jaipur Rd), directly opposite the Hotel Sariska Palace, which is where buses will drop you off.

🛏 Sleeping & Eating

RTDC Hotel Tiger Den   HOTEL $$
(☑2841342; s/d incl breakfast ₹1900/2500, with AC ₹2400/3000; ☀) Hotel Tiger Den isn't a pretty place – it's an unattractive bloc backed by a rambling garden and the accommodation and meals are drab. On the plus side the rooms have balconies and occupy a pleasant setting close to the reserve entrance. Bring a mosquito net or repellent.

Alwar Bagh   HOTEL $$$
(☑2945151412; www.alwarbagh.com; r from ₹4000; ☀☀) This is a very peaceful option located in the village of Dhawala, between Alwar (14km) and Sariska (19km). The bright heritage-style hotel boasts traditional styling, spotless rooms and romantic tents, an organic orchard, a garden restaurant and a gorgeous swimming pool. Pick-up and drop-off from Alwar can be arranged as well as safaris of Sariska.

Sariska Tiger Heaven   HOTEL $$$
(☑9828225163; www.sariskatigerheaven.com; s/d with full board ₹6000/7500; ☀🛜☀) This isolated place about 3km west of the bus stop at Thanagazi village has free pick-up on offer. Rooms are set in stone-and-tile cottages and have big beds and windowed alcoves. It's a tranquil, if overpriced, place to stay. Staff can arrange 4WDs and guides to the reserve.

❶ Getting There & Away

Sariska is 35km from Alwar, a convenient town from which to approach the reserve. There are frequent (and crowded) buses from Alwar (₹30, one to 1½ hours, at least hourly) and on to Jaipur (₹85). Buses stop in front of the Forest Reception Office.

Ajmer
☑0145 / POP 490,500

Ajmer is a bustling, chaotic city, 13km from the traveller haven of Pushkar. It surrounds the tranquil lake of Ana Sagar, and is itself ringed by the rugged Aravalli hills. Ajmer is Rajasthan's most important site in terms of Islamic history and heritage. It contains one of India's most important Muslim pilgrimage centres – the shrine of Khwaja Muin-ud-din Chishti, who founded India's most important Sufi order. As well as some superb examples of early Muslim architecture, Ajmer is also a significant centre for the Jain religion, possessing an amazing golden Jain temple. However, with Ajmer's combination of high-voltage crowds and traffic, most travellers choose to stay in laid-back Pushkar, and visit on a day trip.

◎ Sights

Dargah of Khwaja
Muin-ud-din Chishti   ISLAMIC SHRINE
(www.dargahajmer.com;   ⊙4am-9pm summer, 5am-9pm winter) This is the tomb of Sufi saint Khwaja Muin-ud-din Chishti, who came to Ajmer from Persia in 1192 and died here in 1236. The tomb gained its significance during the time of the Mughals – many emperors added to the buildings here. Construction of the shrine was completed by Humayun, and the gate was added by the Nizam of Hyderabad. Mughal emperor Akbar used to make the pilgrimage to the dargah from Agra every year.

You have to cover your head in certain parts of the shrine, so remember to take a scarf or cap – there are plenty for sale at the bazaar leading to the dargah, along with floral offerings and delicious toffees.

The main entrance is through **Nizam Gate** (1915). Inside, the green and white mosque, **Akbari Masjid**, was constructed in 1571 and is now an Arabic and Persian school for religious education. The next gate is called the **Nakkarkhana** because it has two large *nakkharas* (drums) fixed above it.

A third gate, **Buland Darwaza** (16th century), leads into the dargah courtyard. Flanking the entrance of the courtyard are the *degs* (large iron cauldrons), one donated by Akbar in 1567, the other by Jehangir in 1631, for offerings for the poor.

Inside this courtyard, the saint's domed tomb is surrounded by a silver platform. Pilgrims believe that the saint's spirit will intercede on their behalf in matters of illness, business or personal problems, so the notes and holy string attached to the railings around are thanks or requests.

Pilgrims and Sufis come from all over the world on the anniversary of the saint's death, the Urs, in the seventh month of the lunar calendar, Jyaistha. Crowds can be suffocating. Bags must be left in the cloakroom (₹10 each, with camera ₹20) outside the main entrance.

Ajmer

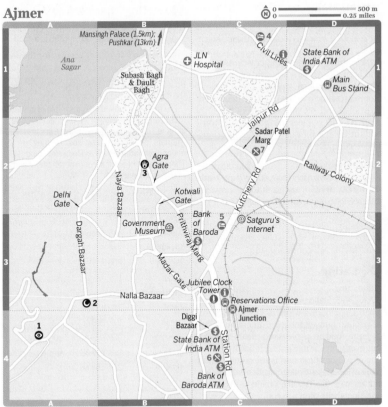

RAJASTHAN AJMER

Adhai-din-ka-Jhonpra
HISTORIC SITE

(Two-and-a-Half-Day Building) Beyond the Dargah of Khwaja Muin-ud-din Chishti, on the town outskirts, are the extraordinary ruins of the Adhai-din-ka-Jhonpra mosque. According to legend, construction in 1153 took only two-and-a-half days. Others say it was named after a festival lasting two-and-a-half days. It was originally built as a Sanskrit college, but in 1198 Mohammed of Ghori seized Ajmer and converted the building into a mosque by adding a seven-arched wall covered with Islamic calligraphy in front of the pillared hall.

Nasiyan (Red) Temple
JAIN TEMPLE

(Prithviraj Marg; admission ₹10; ◷ 8.30am-5.30pm) This marvellous Jain temple, built in 1865, is also known as the Golden Temple, due to its amazing display in the double-storey temple hall. The hall is filled with a huge golden diorama depicting the Jain concept of the ancient world, with 13 continents and oceans, the intricate golden city of Ayodhya, flying peacock and elephant gondolas, and gilded elephants with many tusks. The hall is also decorated with gold, silver and precious stones. It's unlike any other temple in Rajasthan and is worth a visit.

🛏 Sleeping

Haveli Heritage Inn HOTEL **$$**
(📞 2621607; www.haveliheritageinn.com; Kutchery Rd; r ₹900-2875; ❄) Set in a 140-year-old *haveli,* this is a welcoming city-centre oasis and arguably Ajmer's best midrange choice. The high-ceilinged rooms are spacious (some are almost suites), simply decorated, air-cooled and set well back from the busy road. There's a pleasant, grassy courtyard and the hotel is infused with a family atmosphere, complete with home-cooked meals.

Badnor House GUESTHOUSE **$$$**
(📞 2627579; www.badnorhouse.com; d incl breakfast ₹3000; ❄🛜) This guesthouse provides an excellent opportunity to stay with a delightful family and receive down-to-earth hospitality. There are three heritage-style doubles and an older-style, spacious and comfortable self-contained suite.

🍴 Eating

Honeydew MULTICUISINE **$$**
(📞 2622498; Station Rd; mains ₹120-300; ⊙9am-11pm) The Honeydew offers a great selection of veg and nonveg Indian, Chinese and Continental food in a pleasant, clean, relaxed, but overly dim, atmosphere. It has long been one of Ajmer's best, and is the restaurant of choice for Mayo College students having a midterm treat. The ice cream, milkshakes and floats will keep you cool.

Mango Curry/Mango Masala INDIAN, VEGETARIAN **$$**
(📞 01452422100; Sadar Patel Marg; mains ₹100-280; ⊙9am-11pm) With dim, barlike lighting and nursery school decor, this is a popular Ajmer hang out. It's divided in two: Mango Curry is no alcohol and vegetarian, while Mango Masala has plenty of good nonveg options. Pizzas, Chinese, and North and South Indian are available throughout, plus cakes, ice cream and a bakery-deli.

ℹ Information

Bank of Baroda (Prithviraj Marg)
Bank of Baroda ATM (Station Rd)
JLN Hospital (📞 2625500; Daulat Bagh)
Satguru's Internet (60-61 Kutchery Rd; per hr ₹20; ⊙9am-10pm)
State Bank of India ATM (Station Rd)
Tourist Office RTDC Hotel Khadim (📞 2627426; RTDC Hotel Khadim; ⊙9am-6pm Mon-Fri; Ajmer Junction Train Station (Ajmer Junction Train Station; ⊙9am-6pm)

ℹ Getting There & Away

For those passing through en route to Pushkar, haggle hard for a private taxi – ₹350 is a good rate.

BUS

Buses (₹14, 30 minutes) also leave throughout the day from the main bus stand.

The following table shows a sample of government-run buses leaving from the main bus stand in Ajmer. In addition to these, there are less-frequent 'deluxe' coach services running to major destinations such as Delhi and Jaipur. There is a 24-hour cloakroom at the bus stand (₹10 per bag per day).

DESTINATION	FARE (₹)	DURATION (HR)
Agra	297	10
Ahmedabad	455 Sleeper	13
Bharatpur	244	8
Bikaner	206	8
Bundi	135	5
Chittorgarh	146	5
Delhi	311/1051 AC	9
Jaipur	105/269 AC	2½
Jaisalmer	366/969 AC	10
Jodhpur	158/339 AC	6
Udaipur	229/554 AC	8

TRAIN

Ajmer is a busy train junction. To book tickets go to booth 5 at the train station's **reservations office** (⊙8am-8pm Mon-Sat, to 2pm Sun).
➡ Eleven trains run daily to Delhi (2nd class/sleeper ₹170/290, eight hours), mostly to Old Delhi or New Delhi stations, around the clock.
➡ At least two dozen trains leave throughout the day to Jaipur (2nd-class seat/sleeper/AC seat ₹90/170/305; less than three hours) – you won't have to wait for long.
➡ There are four daily trains to Udaipur (sleeper ₹205; five hours; 1.25am, 2.10am, 8.45am, 4.10pm).
➡ Only two direct trains go to Jodhpur (sleeper ₹175, five hours, 1.40pm and 2.25pm), while four go to Agra Fort (sleeper ₹265; 6½ hours; 2.10am, 6.30am, 12.50pm and 3pm).
➡ There are two daily trains to Mumbai (sleeper ₹460; 19 hours; 5.35pm and 11.15pm).
➡ There are three reasonably timed daily trains to Chittorgarh (sleepers ₹140; 3½ hours; 1pm, 7.25pm and 9.05pm).
➡ For Mount Abu, there are 11 daily trains to Abu Road (sleeper ₹205; 11 hours).

MAJOR TRAINS FROM AJMER

DESTINATION	TRAIN NO & NAME	DEPARTURE TIME	ARRIVAL TIME	FARE (₹)
Agra (Fort)	12988 Ajmer-SDAH Exp	12.50pm	6.05pm	265/511 (A)
Delhi (New Delhi)	12016 Ajmer Shatabdi	3.45am	10.40am	865/1690 (B)
Jaipur	12991 Udaipur-Jaipur Exp	11.30am	1.30pm	90/305 (C)
Jodhpur	54802 Ajmer-Jodhpur Fast Passenger	2.25pm	7.55pm	120/485 (D)
Udaipur	09721 Jaipur-Udaipur SF SPL	8.45am	1.45pm	130/470/535 (D)

Fares: (A) sleeper/3AC, (B) AC chair/1AC, (C) 2nd-class seat/AC chair, (D) 2nd-class seat/AC chair/3AC

Pushkar

☎ 0145 / POP 14,800

Pushkar has a magnetism all of its own, and is quite unlike anywhere else in Rajasthan. It's a prominent Hindu pilgrimage town and devout Hindus should visit at least once in their lifetime. The town curls around a holy lake, said to have appeared when Brahma dropped a lotus flower. It also has one of the world's few **Brahma temples**. With 52 bathing ghats and 400 milky-blue temples, the town often hums with *pujas* (prayers) generating an episodic soundtrack of chanting, drums and gongs, and devotional songs.

The result is a muddle of religious and tourist scenes. The main street is one long bazaar, selling everything to tickle a traveller's fancy, from hippy-chic tie-dye to didgeridoos. Despite the commercialism and banana pancakes, the town remains enchantingly small and authentically mystic.

Pushkar is only 11km from Ajmer, separated by Nag Pahar, the Snake Mountain.

◉ Sights

Shiva Temples　　　　　　HINDU TEMPLE
About 8km southwest of the town (past the turn-off to Saraswati Temple) is a collection of Shiva temples near Ajaypal, which make a great trip by motorbike (or bike if you're fit and start early in the day), through barren hills and quiet villages. Be warned: the track is hilly and rocky.

Another Shiva temple is about 8km north of Pushkar, tucked down inside a cave, which would make for a good excursion.

Ghats

Fifty-two bathing ghats surround the lake, where pilgrims bathe in the sacred waters. If you wish to join them, do so with respect. Remember, this is a holy place: remove your shoes and don't smoke or take photographs.

Some ghats have particular importance: Vishnu appeared at **Varah Ghat** in the form of a boar, Brahma bathed at **Brahma Ghat**, and Gandhi's ashes were sprinkled at **Gandhi Ghat**, formerly Gau Ghat.

🏃 Activities

Shannu's Riding School　　HORSE RIDING
(☎ 2772043; www.shannus.weebly.com; Panch Kund Marg; ride/lesson per hr ₹400) French-Canadian and long-time Pushkar resident Marc Dansereau can organise riding lessons and horse safaris on his graceful Marwari steeds. You can stay here too (p136). The ranch is on the southeastern fringes of Pushkar, off the Ajmer Road.

**Government
Homeopathic Hospital**　　AYURVEDIC MASSAGE
(☎ 9413094664; Ajmer Rd; 1hr full-body massage ₹450, steam bath ₹50; ⊙9am-1pm) For a totally noncommercial massage-treatment experience, try the ayurvedic department at the small and basic Government Homeopathic Hospital.

Roshi Hiralal Verma　　REIKI, YOGA
(☎ 9829895906; Ambika Guesthouse, Laxmi Market) Offers reiki, yoga and shiatsu; costs depend on the duration and nature of your session.

Pushkar

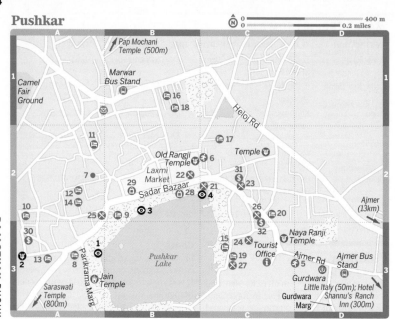

🎓 Courses

Saraswati Music School   MUSIC
(📞 Birju 9828297784, Hemant 9829333548; Mainon ka Chowk) Teaches classical *tabla* (drums), flute, singing and *kathak* (classical dance). For music, contact Birju, who's been playing for around 20 years, and charges from ₹350 for two hours. He often conducts evening performances (7pm to 8pm), and also sells instruments. For dance, contact Hemant.

Cooking Bahar   COOKING
(📞 2773124; www.cookingbahar.com; Mainon ka Chowk; 3hr class ₹1000) Part of the Saraswati Music School family, Deepa conducts cooking classes with three vegetarian courses.

🧭 Tours

Plenty of people in Pushkar offer short camel rides (around ₹200 per hour), which are a good way to explore the starkly beautiful landscape – a mixture of desert and rocky hills – around town. Sunset rides are the most popular. Ask for recommendations at your hotel. For longer camel treks, prices start at around ₹500 per person per day for a group of four. You can head out to Jodhpur (five to six days) or even Jaisalmer (10 to 12 days). Numerous operators line Ajmer Rd, but note, these places are less professional than the operators in Jaisalmer and Bikaner.

🛏 Sleeping

Owing to Pushkar's star status among backpackers, there are more budget than midrange options, though many have a selection of midrange-priced rooms. At the time of the camel fair, prices are up to threefold or more, and it's essential to book several weeks ahead.

⭐ Shyam Krishna Guesthouse   GUESTHOUSE $
(📞 2772461; skguesthouse@yahoo.com; Sadar Bazaar; s/d ₹500/600, without bathroom ₹300/500; 🛜) Housed in a lovely old blue-washed building with lawns and gardens, this guesthouse has ashram austerity and genuinely friendly management. Some of the cheaper rooms are cell-like, though all share the simple, authentic ambience. The outdoor kitchen and garden seating are a good setting for a relaxing meal of hearty vegetarian fare, but watch out for passing troops of monkeys.

Bharatpur Palace   HOTEL $
(📞 2772320; bharatpurpalace_pushkar@yahoo.co.in; Sadar Bazaar; r ₹500-700, without bathroom ₹250-400; ❄) This rambling building occupies one of the best spots in Pushkar, on the upper levels adjacent to Gandhi Ghat. It features aesthetic blue-washed simplicity: bare-bones rooms with unsurpassed views of the holy lake. The rooftop terrace (with

Pushkar

restaurant) has sublime views, but respect for bathing pilgrims is paramount. Room 1 is the most romantic place to wake in: it's surrounded on three sides by the lake. Rooms 9, 12, 13 and 16 are also good.

Alka Guest House GUESTHOUSE $
(☑9782642546, 2773082; Brahm Chowk, Badi Basti; s/d ₹300/400; 🛜) Run by a welcoming but quiet family, Alka has rooms overlooking a large, tree-shaded courtyard. Each is small and basic but neat and tidy, and they come with unusual dressing areas that lend more space. Common bathrooms only, but showers are always hot.

Hotel Everest HOTEL $
(☑2773417; www.pushkarhoteleverest.com; Sadar Bazaar; r ₹200-600, with AC ₹850; ✳@🛜) This welcoming budget hotel is nestled in the quiet laneways north of Sadar Bazaar and is convenient to the mela (fair) ground. It's run by a friendly father-and-son team who can't do too much for their appreciative guests. The rooms are variable in size, colourful and spotless and the beds are comfortable. The roof is a pleasant retreat for meals or just relaxing with a book.

Pushkar Inn's Hotel HOTEL $
(☑2772010; hotelpushkarinns@yahoo.com; r ₹800, without bathroom ₹200, with AC ₹1500; ✳🛜) A charming little hotel comprising a row of clean and bright rooms, backed

by a garden and orchard. The rooms catch the breeze from the lake and that is mostly a positive, though some wafts are less than holy. The best rooms have lake views.

Hotel Paramount Palace HOTEL $
(☑0145-2772428; www.pushkarparamount.com; r ₹200-1000; 🛜) Perched on the highest point in town overlooking an old temple, this welcoming hotel has excellent views of the town and lake (and lots of stairs). The rooms vary widely; the best (106, 108 and 109) have lovely balconies, stained-glass windows and are good value, but the smaller rooms can be dingy. There's a magical rooftop terrace.

Milkman Guesthouse GUESTHOUSE $
(☑2773452; vinodmilkman@hotmail.com; off Heloj Rd; dm/r without bathroom ₹150/300, r ₹500-700; ✳@🛜) Milkman is a cosy guesthouse in a backstreet location with relaxing rooftop retreat featuring the **Ooh-la-la Café** and a lawn with high-altitude tortoises. The rooms are all brightly decorated with paintings. Some of the cheaper rooms are small and doorways are low, though the bright colours, cleanliness and friendly family atmosphere keep this place cheerful.

Hotel White House GUESTHOUSE $
(☑2772147; www.pushkarwhitehouse.com; off Heloj Rd; r ₹250-850, with AC ₹1000-1300; ✳@) This place is indeed white, with spotless rooms. Some are decidedly on the small

side, but the nicest are generous and have balconies to boot. There is good traveller fare and green views from the plant-filled rooftop restaurant. It's efficiently run by a tenacious businesslike mother-and-son team. Yoga is offered.

Hotel Akash   HOTEL $

(☏2772498; filterboy21@yahoo.com; d ₹600, s/d without bathroom ₹300/500) A simple budget place with keen young management and a large tree sprouting up from the courtyard to shade the rooftop terrace. Rooms are basic fan-cooled affairs that open out to a balcony restaurant.

★ Inn Seventh Heaven   HERITAGE HOTEL $$

(☏5105455;   www.inn-seventh-heaven.com; Chotti Basti; r ₹1100-3000; ✻@⊗) You enter this lovingly converted *haveli* through heavy wooden doors and into an incense-perfumed courtyard, centred with a marble fountain and surrounded by tumbling vines. There are just a dozen individually decorated rooms situated on three levels, all with traditionally crafted furniture and comfortable beds. Rooms vary in size, from the downstairs budget rooms to the spacious Asana suite. On the roof you'll find the excellent Sixth Sense restaurant as well as sofas and swing chairs for relaxing with a book. Early booking (two-night minimum, no credit cards) is recommended.

Hotel Shannu's Ranch Inn   GUESTHOUSE $$

(☏2772043; www.shannus.weebly.com; Panch Kund Marg; s/d ₹1000/1500, ste ₹2000) Especially for horse lovers but not exclusively so, this relaxed, family-run hotel is just a short walk from the lake. There is a large garden compound featuring the family home, separate guest accommodation and, of course, the stables housing Marc's beloved Marwari horses (p133). There are usually a couple of friendly dogs wandering around. The large suites easily accommodate a family of five.

Hotel Navaratan Palace   HOTEL $$

(☏2772145; www.pushkarnavaratanpalace.co.in; r ₹750-950, with AC ₹1050; ✻⊠) Located close to the Brahma Temple, this hotel has a lovely enclosed garden with a fabulous pool (₹100 for nonguests), a children's playground and pet tortoises. The rooms are clean, small and crammed with carved wooden furniture.

Hotel Kishan Palace   HOTEL $$

(☏2773056;   www.kishanpalacepushkar.com; Panch Kund Marg; s/d from ₹800/1200, ste ₹4500; ✻@) A welcoming, brightly coloured hotel with abundant potted plants and a range of well-appointed rooms. The blue-domed

---

PUSHKAR CAMEL FAIR

Come the month of Kartika, the eighth lunar month of the Hindu calendar and one of the holiest, Thar camel drivers spruce up their ships of the desert and start the long walk to Pushkar in time for Kartik Purnima (Full Moon). Each year around 200,000 people converge here, bringing with them some 50,000 camels, horses and cattle. The place becomes an extraordinary swirl of colour, sound and movement, thronged with musicians, mystics, tourists, traders, animals, devotees and camera crews.

Trading begins a week before the official fair (a good time to arrive to see the serious business), but by the time the RTDC *mela* (fair) starts, business takes a back seat and the bizarre sidelines (snake charmers, children balancing on poles etc) jostle onto centre stage. Even the cultural program seems peculiar, with events such as a contest for the best moustache, and most beautifully decorated camel. Visitors are encouraged to take part: pick up a program from the RTDC office and see if you fancy taking part in the costumed wedding parade, or join a 'Visitors versus Locals' sports contest such as traditional Rajasthani wrestling.

It's hard to believe, but this seething mass is all just a sideshow. Kartik Purnima is when Hindu pilgrims come to bathe in Pushkar's sacred waters. The religious event builds in tandem with the camel fair in a wild, magical crescendo of incense, chanting and processions to dousing day, the last night of the fair, when thousands of devotees wash away their sins and set candles afloat on the holy lake.

Although fantastical, mystical and a one-off, it must be said that it's also crowded, touristy, noisy (light sleepers should bring earplugs) and occasionally tacky. Those affected by dust and/or animal hair should bring appropriate medication. However, it's a grand epic and is not to be missed if you're anywhere within camel-spitting distance.

It usually takes place in November but dates change according to the lunar calendar.

rooftop terrace is very communal, with guests mingling, munching and watching the satellite TV.

Hotel Pushkar Palace
HERITAGE HOTEL $$$

(📞 2772001; www.hotelpushkarpalace.com; r incl breakfast ₹7000; ❄ @) Once belonging to the maharaja of Kishangarh, the top-end Hotel Pushkar Palace boasts a romantic lakeside setting. The rooms have carved wooden furniture and beds, and the suites look directly out onto the lake: no hotel in Pushkar has better views. A pleasant outdoor dining area overlooks the lake.

✕ Eating

Pushkar has plenty of atmospheric eateries with lake views and menus reflecting backpacker tastes and preferences. Strict vegetarianism, forbidding even eggs, is the order of the day.

Shri Vankatesh
INDIAN $

(Chooti Basti; mains ₹40-90; ⊙ 9am-10pm) Head to this no-nonsense locals favourite and tuck into some dhal, paneer or kofta, before mopping up the sauce with some freshly baked chapatis and washing it all down with some good old-fashioned chai. The thalis (₹70 to ₹130) are excellent value too. There's some upstairs seating overlooking the street.

Falafel Wrap Stalls
MIDDLE EASTERN $

(Sadar Bazaar; wraps ₹60-120; ⊙ 7.30am-10.30pm) Perfect for quelling a sudden attack of the munchies, and a big hit with Israeli travellers, these two adjacent roadside joints knock up a choice selection of filling falafel-and-hummus wraps.

Om Shiva Garden Restaurant
MULTICUISINE $

(📞 5105045; mains ₹70-170; ⊙ 7.30am-late) A traveller stalwart, Om Shiva continues to satisfy with its ₹80 buffet. Wood-fired pizzas and espresso coffee feature on the menu.

Sixth Sense
MULTICUISINE $$

(Inn Seventh Heaven, Chotti Basti; mains ₹80-200; ⊙ 8.30am-4pm & 6-10pm; ☎) This chilled rooftop restaurant is a great place to head to even if you didn't score a room in its popular hotel. The pizza and Indian seasonal vegetables and rice are all serviceable, as are the filter coffee and fresh juice. Its ambience is immediately relaxing and the pulley apparatus that delivers food from the ground-floor kitchen is very cunning.

Save room for the desserts, such as the excellent homemade tarts.

Naryan Café
CAFE $$

(Mahadev Chowk, Sadar Bazaar; juices from ₹80, breakfast from ₹90) Busy any time of day, this is particular popular as a breakfast stop: watch the world go by with a fresh coffee or juice and an enormous bowl of homemade muesli, topped with a mountain of fruit.

Sunset Café
MULTICUISINE $$

(mains ₹75-200; ⊙ 7.30am-midnight; ☎) Right on the eastern ghats, this cafe has sublime lake views. It offers the usual traveller menu, including curries, pizza and pasta, plus there's a German bakery serving reasonable cakes. The lakeside setting is perfect at sunset and gathers a crowd.

Out of the Blue
ITALIAN $$

(Sadar Bazaar; mains ₹100-200; ⊙ 8am-11pm; ☎) Distinctly a deeper shade of blue in this sky-blue town, Out of the Blue is a reliable restaurant. The menu ranges from noodles and *momos* (Tibetan dumplings) to pizza, pasta (those *momos* occasionally masquerade as ravioli) and pancakes. A nice touch is the street-level espresso coffee bar and German bakery.

Honey & Spice
MULTICUISINE $$

(Laxmi Market, off Sadar Bazaar; mains ₹90-340; ⊙ 7.30am-6.45pm) 🖉 Run by a friendly family, this tiny wholefood breakfast and lunch place has delicious South Indian coffee and homemade cakes. Even better are the salads and hearty vegetable stews served with brown rice – delicious, wholesome and a welcome change from frequently oil-rich Indian food.

🛍 Shopping

Pushkar's Sadar Bazaar is lined with enchanting little shops and is a good place to pick up gifts. Many of the vibrant textiles come from the Barmer district south of Jaisalmer. There's plenty of silver and beaded jewellery catering to foreign tastes, and some old tribal pieces, too. As Pushkar is touristy, you'll have to haggle.

Lala International
CLOTHING

(Sadar Bazaar; ⊙ 9.30am-8pm) Brilliantly colourful women's clothing, with modern designs but Indian in theme. Dresses and skirts start from around ₹500. Prices are clearly labelled and fixed.

Khadi Gramodhyog
CLOTHING

(Sadar Bazaar; ⊙ 10am-6pm Mon-Sat) Khadi Gramodhyog, almost hidden on the main drag, is a fixed-price shop selling traditional hand-woven shirts, scarves and shawls.

❶ Information

Foreign-card-friendly ATMs and unofficial moneychangers are dotted around Sadar Bazaar. Internet cafes are sprinkled around the lanes, and tend to charge ₹40 per hour, but most guesthouses and many restaurants and cafes have free wi-fi.

Post Office (off Heloj Rd; ⊘ 9.30am-5pm) Near the Marwar bus stand.

State Bank of Bikaner & Jaipur (SBBJ; Sadar Bazaar; ⊘10am-4pm Mon-Fri, to 12.30pm Sat) Changes travellers cheques and cash. The SBBJ ATM accepts international cards.

Thomas Cook (Sadar Bazaar; ⊘ 9.30am-6.30pm Mon-Sat) Changes cash and travellers cheques and also provides train and flight ticketing.

Tourist Office (☑ 01452772040; Hotel Sarovar; ⊘10am-5pm) Free maps and camel fair programs. Located in the grounds of RTDC Hotel Sarovar.

DANGERS & ANNOYANCES

Beware of anyone peddling flowers to offer as a *puja* (prayer): before you know it you'll be whisked to the ghats in a well-oiled hustle and asked for a personal donation of up to ₹1000. Some priests do genuinely live off the donations of others and this is a tradition that goes back centuries – but walk away if you feel bullied and always agree on a price before taking a red ribbon (a 'Pushkar passport') or flowers.

During the camel fair, Pushkar is besieged by pickpockets working the crowded bazaars. You can avoid the razor gang by not using thin-walled daypacks and by carrying your daypack in front of you. At any time of year, watch out for stray motorbikes in the bazaar.

❶ Getting There & Away

Frequent buses to/from Ajmer (₹14, 30 minutes) stop on the road heading eastwards out of town; other buses leave from the Marwar bus stand to the north. A private taxi to Ajmer costs around ₹300 (note that it's almost always more expensive in the opposite direction). When entering Pushkar by car there is a toll of ₹20 per person.

Local travel agencies sell tickets for private buses – you should shop around. These buses generally leave from Ajmer, but the agencies should provide you with free connecting transport. Check whether your bus is direct as many services from Pushkar aren't. And note, even if they are direct buses they may well stop for some time in Ajmer, meaning it's often quicker to go to Ajmer first and then catch another bus from there.

❶ Getting Around

There are no autorickshaws, but it's a breeze to get around on foot. If you want to explore the surrounding countryside, you could try hiring a scooter (₹250 per day) from one of the many places around town. For something more substantial, try **Shreeram Enfield Gairej** (Ajmer Rd; Enfield hire per day ₹500, deposit ₹50,000). They hire Enfield Bullets for ₹500 per day and sell them from ₹60,000.

Ranthambhore National Park
☑ 07462

This famous **national park**, open from 1 October to 30 June, is the best place to spot wild tigers in Rajasthan. Comprising 1334 sq km of wild jungle scrub hemmed in by rocky ridges, at its centre is the 10th-century Ranthambhore Fort. Scattered around the fort are ancient temples and mosques, hunting pavilions, crocodile-filled lakes and vine-covered *chhatris* (burial tombs). The park was a maharajas' hunting ground until 1970, a curious 15 years after it had become a sanctuary. Tiger numbers are reasonably healthy for a park of Ranthambhore's size (around 48 when surveyed in 2014), but the threat of poaching remains, requiring constant vigilance to protect the big cats.

Seeing a tiger is partly a matter of luck; leave time for two or three safaris to improve your chances. But remember there's plenty of other wildlife to see, including more than 300 species of birds.

It's 10km from Sawai Madhopur (the gateway town for Ranthambhore) to the first gate of the park, and another 3km to the main gate and Ranthambhore Fort. There's a bunch of cheap (and rather grotty) hotels near Sawai Madhopur train station, but the nicest accommodation is stretched out along Ranthambhore Rd, which eventually leads to the park. It's ₹50 to ₹100 for an auto from the train station to Ranthambhore Rd, depending on where you get off. Many hotels, though, will pick you up from the train station for free if you call ahead.

If you want to walk, turn left out of the train station and follow the road up to the overpass (200m). Turn left and cross the bridge over the railway line to reach a roundabout (200m), known as Hammir Circle. Turn right here to reach the Safari Booking Office (1.5km). But turn left to reach the better accommodation options.

✦ Activities

Safaris take place in the early morning and late afternoon, starting between 6am and 7am, and between 2pm and 3pm, depending on the time of year. Each safari lasts for around three hours. The mornings can be exceptionally chilly in the open vehicles, so bring warm clothes.

The best option is to travel by **gypsy** (six-person open-topped 4WD; Indian/foreigner ₹528/927 per person). You have a chance of seeing a tiger from a **canter** (20-seat open-topped truck; Indian/foreigner ₹400/800), but other passengers can be rowdy. Be aware that the rules for booking safaris (and prices) are prone to change. At present, you have to book online through the park's official website (http://rajasthanwildlife.in), which we highly recommend you do, or go in person to the Safari Booking Office, which is inconveniently located 1.5km from Hammir Circle, in the opposite direction to the park from the accommodation on Ranthambhore Rd. You cannot book safaris in person in advance of the day you want to do the safari (you can only do that online). To be sure of getting a seat in a vehicle, start queuing at least an hour (if not two) before the safaris are due to begin – a very early start for morning safaris!

To visit the magical 10th-century **Ranthambhore Fort** (⊘6am-6pm) FREE on the cheap, join the locals who go there to visit the temple dedicated to Ganesh. Shared 4WDs (₹30 to ₹40 per person) leave from the train station for the park entrance – say 'national park' and they'll know what you want. From there, other shared 4WDs (₹20 per person) shuttle to and from the fort, which is inside the park.

🛏 Sleeping

Budget travellers may find the cheapest lodgings in Sawai Madhopur itself, but it isn't a particularly inspiring place to stay. All of the places on Ranthambhore Rd can help with safari bookings, though some are better at this than others. Some hotels may close when the park is closed.

Hotel Aditya Resort   HOTEL **$**
(☑9414728468; www.adityaresort.com; Ranthambhore Rd; r ₹400-700; ❋@☎) This friendly place represents good value for money and is one of the better of the ultra-cheapies in town. There are just six simple, unadorned rooms (get one with an outside window;

only a couple have air-conditioning), and a basic rooftop restaurant. The keen young staff will help with safari bookings.

Hotel Tiger Safari Resort   HOTEL **$$**
(☑221137; www.tigersafariresort.com; Ranthambhore Rd; r ₹1600-2200; ❋@☎☀) A reasonable budget option, with spacious doubles and so-called cottages (larger rooms with bigger bathrooms) facing a garden and small pool. The management is adept at organising safaris, wake-up calls and early breakfasts before the morning safari, although like the other hotels they throw in a chunky commission. There's an expensive restaurant.

Hotel Ankur Resort   HOTEL **$$**
(☑220792; www.hotelankurresort.com; r incl breakfast ₹2000, cottages ₹2500; ❋@☎) Ankur Resort is good at organising safaris, wake-up calls and early breakfasts for tiger spotters. Standard rooms are fairly unadorned but clean and comfortable with TVs. The cottages boast better beds, fridge and settee overlooking the surrounding gardens and pool.

Vatika Resort   HOTEL **$$**
(☑222457; www.ranthambhorevatikaresort.com; Ranthambhore Rd; r ₹1800, incl breakfast/all meals ₹2250/3000; ❋@☎) A lovely little guesthouse with simple but immaculate rooms, each with terrace seating overlooking a beautifully tended, flower-filled garden. It's about 1km beyond the main strip of accommodation on Ranthambhore Rd (although still 5km before the park's main gate) so much quieter than elsewhere. It's 3km from Hammir Circle.

ℹ Information

There's an ATM just by Hammir Circle, as well as others by the train station.

Post Office (Sawai Madhoper) Located 400m northeast of the train station.

Ranthambore Adventure Tours
(☑9414214460; ranthambhoretours@rediff.mail.com; Ranthambhore Rd) Safari agency that gets good reviews.

Safari Booking Office (www.rajasthanwildlife.com) Seats in gypsies and canters can be reserved on the website, though a single gypsy and five canters are also kept for direct booking at the Forest Office. Located 500m from the train station.

Tiger Track Internet (☑222790; Ranthambhore Rd; per hr ₹60; ⊘7am-10.30pm) Near Ankur Resort Hotel, 1.5km from Hammir Circle.

Tourist office (☑220808; Train Station; ⊘9.30am-6pm Mon-Fri) Has maps of Sawai Madhopur, and can offer suggestions on safaris.

ⓘ Getting There & Away

BUS

There are very few direct buses to anywhere of interest so it's always preferable to take the train. Three direct buses leave for Bundi (6am, 6.45am and 2pm; ₹93; five hours) from the Tonk bus stand (take the second left out of the train station and the bus stand is on your right after the petrol station).

TRAIN

➡ Trains run almost hourly to Kota (sleeper ₹100, less than two hours), from where you can catch buses to Bundi.

➡ There are six daily trains to Jaipur (2nd-class seats/sleeper ₹90/170; two hours; 2.05am, 5.55am, 9.40am, 10.40am, 2.35pm and 7.15pm), although plenty of others run on selected days so you rarely have to wait more than an hour.

➡ Ten trains run daily around the clock to Delhi (sleeper/3AC ₹250/635, 5½ to eight hours).

➡ A daily train goes to Agra (Agra Fort station; sleeper ₹200, six hours, 11.15pm).

➡ For Keoladeo Ghana National Park, nine daily trains go to Bharatpur (sleeper/3AC ₹170/535, 2½ hours).

UDAIPUR & SOUTHERN RAJASTHAN

Bundi

☑ 0747 / POP 88,900

A captivating town with narrow lanes of Brahmin-blue houses, lakes, hills, bazaars and a temple at every turn, Bundi is dominated by a fantastical palace of faded parchment cupolas and loggias rising from the hillside above the town. Though an increasingly popular traveller hang-out, Bundi attracts nothing like the tourist crowds of Jaipur or Udaipur, nor are its streets choked with noisy, polluting vehicles or dense throngs of people. Few places in Rajasthan retain so much of the magical atmosphere of centuries past.

Bundi came into its own in the 12th century when a group of Chauhan nobles from Ajmer were pushed south by Mohammed of Ghori. They wrested the Bundi area from the Mina and Bhil tribes, and made Bundi the capital of their kingdom, known as Hadoti.

Bundi was loyal to the Mughals from the late 16th century onwards, but it maintained its independent status until incorporated into the state of Rajasthan after 1947.

⊙ Sights

Bundi has around 60 beautiful *baoris* (step-wells), some right in the town centre. The majesty of many of them is unfortunately diminished by their lack of water today – a result of declining groundwater levels – and by the rubbish that collects in them which noone bothers to clean up. The most impressive, **Raniji-ki-Baori** (Queen's Step-Well), is 46m deep and decorated with sinuous carvings, including the avatars of Lord Vishnu. The **Nagar Sagar Kund** is a pair of matching step-wells just outside the old city's Chogan Gate.

Bundi Palace   PALACE
(Garh Palace; Indian/foreigner ₹20/200, camera/video ₹50/100; ⊘8am-5pm) This extraordinary, partly decaying edifice – described by Rudyard Kipling as 'the work of goblins rather than of men' – almost seems to grow out of the rock of the hillside it stands on. Though large sections are still closed up and left to the bats, the rooms that are open hold a series of fabulous, fading turquoise-and-gold murals that are the palace's chief treasure. The palace was constructed during the reign of Rao Raja Ratan Ji Heruled (Ratan Singh; 1607–31) and added to by his successors.

If you are going up to Taragarh as well as the palace, get tickets for both at the palace entrance. Once inside the palace's **Hathi Pol** (Elephant Gate), climb the stairs to the Ratan Daulat or Diwan-e-Aam (Hall of Public Audience), with a white marble coronation throne. You then pass into the Chhatra Mahal, added by Rao Raja Chhatra Shabji in 1644, with some fine but rather weathered murals. Stairs lead up to the Phool Mahal (1607), whose murals include an immense royal procession, and then the Badal Mahal (Cloud Palace; also 1607), with Bundi's very best murals, including a wonderful Chinese-inspired ceiling, divided into petal shapes and decorated with peacocks and Krishnas.

Taragarh   FORT
(Star Fort; Indian/foreigner ₹20/200, camera/video ₹50/100; ⊘8am-5pm) This ramshackle, partly overgrown 14th-century fort, on the hilltop above Bundi Palace, is a wonderful place to ramble around – but take a stick to battle

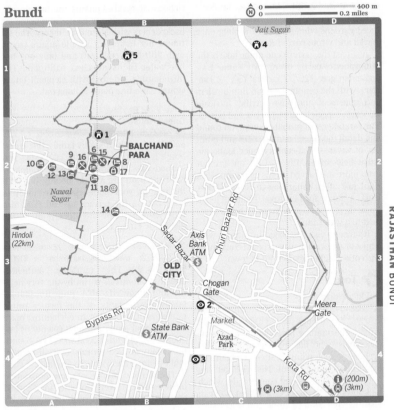

Bundi

Sights

Bundi

◎ Sights
1 Bundi Palace	B2
2 Nagar Sagar Kund	C3
3 Raniji-ki-Baori	C4
4 Sukh Mahal	C1
5 Taragarh	B1

⬡ Sleeping
6 Bundi Vilas	A2
7 Haveli Braj Bhushanjee	A2
8 Haveli Elephant Stable	B2
9 Haveli Katkoun	A2
10 Hotel Bundi Haveli	A2
11 Kasera Heritage View	A2
12 Lake View Paying Guest House	A2
13 Nawal Sagar Palace	A2
14 RN Haveli	B2

⊗ Eating
15 Out of the Blue	B2
16 Rainbow Cafe	A2

⬡ Shopping
17 Yug Art	B2

❶ Information
Front Page Cyber Cafe	(see 8)
18 Roshan Tour & Travel	B2

the overgrown vegetation, help the knees on the steep climb and provide confidence when surrounded by testosterone-charged macaques. To reach it, just continue on the path up behind the Chitrasala.

Jait Sagar
LAKE

Round the far side of the Taragarh hill, about 2km north from the centre of town, this picturesque, 1.5km-long lake is flanked by hills and strewn with pretty lotus flowers during the monsoon and winter months. At its near end, the **Sukh Mahal** (◔10am-5pm) is a small summer palace surrounded by terraced gardens where Rudyard Kipling once stayed and wrote part of *Kim*.

Just past the eastern end of the lake is the atmospheric, partly overgrown **Kshar Bag** (Indian/foreigner ₹20/50, camera ₹50; ◔9am-5pm), with the cenotaphs of 66 Bundi rulers and queens. Some have terrific, intricate carvings, especially of elephants and horses. The caretaker will probably show you round and detail the rulers' names, dates and number of wives – 17th-century ruler Maharaja Satru Sele apparently had 64 queens but even more are carved on his cenotaph. Fork right just after Kshar Bag to reach **Shikar Burj**, a small former royal hunting lodge (once there were tigers, deer and boars here) next to a water tank.

It's nice to visit Jait Sagar by bicycle; with a bike or autorickshaw you could combine it with other sights further out of town.

☞ Tours

Kukki's World
TOUR
(☑9828404527; www.kukkisworld.com; 43 New Colony; half-/full-day tour ₹1000/1600) OP 'Kukki' Sharma is a passionate amateur archaeologist who has discovered around 70 prehistoric rock painting sites in a lifetime's exploring around Bundi. His trips get you out into the villages and countryside, which he knows like the back of his hand. You can visit his collection of finds and select sites from his laptop at his house (about 300m south of the tourist office) beforehand. Vehicle hire is not included in the tour price.

🛏 Sleeping

Most accommodation clusters in the Balchand Para area beneath the palace. Most places will pick you up from the train station or bus stand if you call ahead. Mosquitoes can be a nuisance in places near Nawal Sagar: keep repellent handy.

RN Haveli
GUESTHOUSE $
(☑2443278, 9784486854; rnhavelibundi@yahoo.co.in; Rawle ka Chowk; s/d ₹500/700, without bathroom ₹250/350, with AC ₹800/1000; ❉) This old, slightly rundown house has reasonably well-decorated rooms and a cute garden where you can eat the delicious home cooking. A sound budget choice.

Haveli Elephant Stable
GUESTHOUSE $
(☑9928154064; rajnandini1979@gmail.com; Surang Gate; dm ₹250, r ₹300-600) Once used

to house 15 royal elephants, this basic guesthouse is now a shanty home-from-home for backpackers with a sense of history. The six rooms are extremely simple affairs (some with 20ft-high ceilings!) and only one has hot water in its attached bathroom. The huge garden – dotted with elephant tether stones – is a fine place to hang out.

Lake View Paying Guest House
GUESTHOUSE $
(☑2442326; lakeviewbundi@yahoo.com; r ₹300-600) Overseen by a kindly family, this guesthouse has some rooms with lake views and stained-glass windows. The side rooms by the restaurant are a little gloomy, but with the lake on your doorsteps you're likely to hang out on the terrace instead. The nice little garden restaurant does multicuisine dishes for ₹70 to ₹150.

★Haveli Braj Bhushanjee
HERITAGE HOTEL $$
(☑2442322; www.kiplingsbundi.com; r ₹1200-5000; ❉🖤) This rambling, authentic, 200-year-old *haveli* is run by the very helpful and knowledgeable Braj Bhushanjee family, descendants of the former prime ministers of Bundi. It's an enchanting place with original stone interiors (plenty of low doorways), splendid rooftop views, beautiful, well-preserved murals, and all sorts of other historic and valuable artefacts.

The terrific range of accommodation includes some lovely, recently modernised rooms that are still in traditional style. It's a fascinating living museum where you can really get a feel for Bundi's heritage.

Haveli Katkoun
GUESTHOUSE $$
(☑2444311; www.katkounhavelibundi.com; s from ₹700, d ₹1200-3200; ❉🖤) Just outside the town's western gate, Katkoun is a completely revamped *haveli* with friendly management. It boasts large, spotless rooms offering superb views to either the lake or palace, and has a good rooftop restaurant (mains ₹65 to ₹200).

Kasera Heritage View
GUESTHOUSE $$
(☑2444679; www.kaseraheritageview.com; s/d from ₹600/800; ❉@🖤) A revamped *haveli*, Kasera has an incongruously modern lobby, but offers a range of slightly more authentic rooms. The welcome is friendly, it's all cheerfully decorated, the rooftop restaurant has great views, and discounts of 40% to 50% are frequently offered.

Bundi Vilas
HERITAGE HOTEL $$
(☑5120694; www.bundivilas.com; r incl breakfast ₹4500-5500; ❉@) This 300-year-old *haveli*

up a side alley has been tastefully renovated with Jaisalmer sandstone, earth-toned walls and deft interior design. Sat in the lee of the palace walls, this guesthouse has commanding views of the town from the rooftop terrace (though furniture is kept inside due to the preponderance of visiting monkey).

Hotel Bundi Haveli   HOTEL $$$
(☑ 2447861; www.hotelbundihaveli.com; r ₹2500-4500; ❄ 🛜) The exquisitely renovated Bundi Haveli certainly leads the pack in terms of up-to-date style and sophistication. White walls, stone floors, colour highlights and framed artefacts are coupled with modern plumbing and electricity. Yes, it is very comfortable and relaxed and there's a lovely rooftop dining area boasting palace views and an extensive, mainly Indian menu (mains ₹90 to ₹250).

Nawal Sagar Palace   HERITAGE HOTEL $$$
(☑ 2447050; www.nawalsagarpalace.com; r ₹2000-3000; 🛜) This 300-year-old former royal residence, once home to the ladies of the court, has a beautiful location, with buildings overlooking a grassy lawn (with restaurant seating), which in turn overlooks the lake. Rooms are huge, with some interesting old furniture and artwork; some have balconies with lake views.

🍴 Eating

Guesthouses and hotels provide the main eating options and many of them happily serve nonguests as well as guests. Bundi was once a dry town, so it's not a place for evening revelry; however, a cold beer can usually be arranged.

Out of the Blue   ITALIAN $$
(mains ₹130-220; ☺ 8am-10.30pm; 🛜) Bundi's Out of the Blue was set up by the owners of its namesake in Pushkar (p137), but has since outgrown and outpaced the original. It serves up some of the best Italian pizza and pasta we've had in Rajasthan (the presence of pork products on the nonveg menu adds to the authenticity) as well as the best coffee in town (₹50 to ₹100).

Rainbow Cafe   MULTICUISINE $$
(mains ₹100-260; ☺ 7am-11pm; 🛜) Bohemian ambience with chillout tunes, floor-cushion seating and two types of bhang lassi (a blend of lassi and bhang, a derivative of marijuana). Located on the rooftop of the town's western gate and caged off from marauding macaques with a bamboo trellis.

🛍️ Shopping

Yug Art   ART
(http://www.yugartbundi.com; near Surang Gate; ☺ 10am-7.30pm) Many art shops will offer you Rajasthani miniatures, but Yug Art is the first place that's offered to turn us into one. Provide a photo and you can be pictured on elephant back or in any number of classical scenes. Alternatively, Yug will record your India trip in a unique travel comic – you help with the script and he'll provide the artwork.

ℹ️ Information

There's an Axis Bank ATM on Sadar Bazaar and a State Bank ATM west of Azad Park.
Front Page Cyber Cafe (Balchand Para; per hr ₹40; ☺ 8am-10pm)
Roshan Tour & Travel (☺ 8am-10pm) Internet cafe that also exchanges currency and books train tickets. Located about 300m south of the palace.
Tourist Office (☑ 2443697; Kota Rd; ☺ 9.30am-6pm Mon-Fri) Offers bus and train schedules, free maps and helpful advice.

ℹ️ Getting There & Away

BUS

For Ranthambhore, it's usually quicker to catch a bus to Kota, then hop on a train to Sawai Madhopur.

    Direct services from Bundi bus stand:
Ajmer (₹135, four hours, hourly)
Jaipur (₹161, five hours, hourly)
Kota (₹30, 40 minutes, every 15 minutes)
Pushkar (₹146, 4½ hours, three daily)
Sawai Madhopur (₹104, four to five hours, three daily)
Udaipur (₹215, six hours, three daily)

TRAIN

There are no daily trains to Jaipur, Ajmer or Jodhpur. It's better to take a bus, or to catch a train from Kota or Chittorgarh.
➜ Two trains travel daily to Chittorgarh (sleeper ₹170). The 7.12am takes 3½ hours; the 9.16am takes 2½ hours.
➜ There are three daily trains to Sawai Madhopur (sleeper ₹100; 2½ to five hours; 5.35pm, 5.48pm and 10.35pm); the last train is the fastest.
➜ Two daily trains go to Delhi (Hazrat Nizamuddin). The 5.48pm (sleeper ₹260) takes nearly 12 hours; the 10.35pm (sleeper ₹315) takes just eight.
➜ There's one daily train to Agra (Agra Fort; sleeper ₹150, 12½ hours, 5.35pm).

→ Only one train goes daily to Udaipur, the 12963 Mewar Express (sleeper ₹210, five hours, 2.08am).

ℹ Getting Around

An autorickshaw to the train station costs ₹50 to ₹70 by day and ₹100 to ₹120 by night.

Kota

📞 0744 / POP 703,150

An easy day trip from Bundi, Kota is a gritty industrial, commercial town on the Chamba, Rajasthan's only permanent river. You can take boat trips along the river for some good bird- and crocodile-watching, or explore the city's old palace. It's best experienced as a day trip from Bundi.

◉ Sights & Activities

A lovely hiatus from the city is a Chambal River **boat trip** (10min per person ₹60, 1hr ₹1000, max 6 people; ⊘ 10.30am-dusk). The river upstream of Kota is part of the Darrah National Park and once you escape the city it's beautiful, with lush vegetation and craggy cliffs on either side. It's an opportunity to spot a host of birds, as well as gharials (thin-snouted, fish-eating crocodiles) and muggers (keep-your-limbs-inside-the-boat crocodiles). Boats start from **Chambal Gardens** (Indian/foreigner ₹2/5), 1.5km south of the fort on the river's east bank.

City Palace & Fort   PALACE, FORT
(Indian/foreigner ₹30/200; ⊘ 10am-4.30pm Sat-Thu) The fort and the palace within it make up one of the largest such complexes in Rajasthan. This was the royal residence and centre of power, housing the Kota princedom's treasury, courts, arsenal, armed forces and state offices. Some of its buildings are now used as schools. The City Palace, entered through a gateway topped by rampant elephants, contains the offbeat **Rao Madho Singh Museum** (Indian/foreigner ₹10/100, camera ₹50; ⊘ 10am-4.30pm), where you'll find everything for a respectable Raj existence, from silver furniture to weaponry, as well as perhaps India's most depressingly moth-eaten stuffed trophy animals.

The oldest part of the palace dates from 1624. Downstairs is a durbar (royal audience) hall with beautiful mirrorwork, while the elegant, small-scale apartments upstairs contain exquisite, beautifully preserved paintings, particularly the hunting scenes for which Kota is renowned.

To get here, it's around ₹30 to ₹40 in an autorickshaw from the bus stand, and at least ₹60 from the train station.

✦ Festivals & Events

If you happen to hit Kota in October or November, check whether your visit coincides with the city's huge **Dussehra Mela**, during which massive effigies are built then spectacularly set aflame. Thousands of pilgrims descend on the city in the month of Kartika (October/November) for **Kashavrai Patan**. See the tourist office for festival programs.

ℹ Information

Tourist Office (📞 2327695; RTDC Hotel Chambal; ⊘ 9.30am-6pm Mon-Sat) Has free maps of Kota. Turn left out of the bus stand, right at the second roundabout and it's on your right.

ℹ Getting There & Away

BUS

Services from the main bus stand:

Ajmer (₹165, four to five hours, at least 10 daily)

Bundi (₹30, 40 minutes, every 15 minutes throughout the day)

Chittorgarh (₹135, four hours, half-hourly from 6am)

Jaipur (₹191, five hours, hourly from 5am)

Udaipur (₹241, six to seven hours, at least 10 daily)

TRAIN

Kota is on the main Mumbai–Delhi train route via Sawai Madhopur, so there are plenty of trains to choose from, though departure times aren't always convenient.

→ For Ranthambhore, there are more than two dozen daily trains to Sawai Madhopur (2nd-class seat/sleeper ₹65/140; one to two hours), so you rarely have to wait more than an hour.

→ Trains run almost hourly to Delhi (sleeper ₹270; five to eight hours), mostly to New Delhi or Hazrat Nizamuddin.

→ Six trains run daily to Jaipur (sleeper ₹205; four hours; 2.55am, 7.40am, 8.55am, 12.35pm, 5.20pm and 11.50pm), but there are many others on selected days so you'll rarely have to wait long.

→ Three daily trains go to Chittorgarh (sleeper ₹170; three to four hours; 1.25am, 6.10am and 8.45am).

→ Five fast trains go daily to Mumbai (sleepers ₹465; 14 hours; 7.50am, 2.25pm, 5.30pm, 11.20pm and 11.45pm).

MAJOR TRAINS FROM KOTA

DESTINATION	TRAIN NO & NAME	FARE (₹)	DURATION (HR)	DEPARTURE
Agra	19037/39 Avadh Exp	174/445/601 (A)	7¼	2.50pm
Chittorgarh	59812 Haldighati Pass	170 (B)	4	6.10am
	29020 Dehradun Exp	170/395/650 (C)	3¼	8.45am
Delhi (Nizamuddin)	12903 Golden Temple Mail	270/576/770/1294 (E)	7¼	11.12am
	12964 Mewar Exp	270/576/770/1294 (E)	6½	11.55pm
Jaipur	12181 Dayodaya Exp	205/390/512 (A)	4	7.40am
	12955 Mumbai–Jaipur Exp	205/390/512/852 (E)	4	8.55am
Mumbai	12904 Golden Temple Mail	349/913/1237/2078 (E)	15	2.35pm
Sawai Madhopur	12059 Shatabdi	65/240 (D)	1¼	6am
	12903 Golden Temple Mail	150/280/338/551 (E)	1¼	11.12am
Udaipur	12963 Mewar Exp	179/433/573/955 (E)	6	1.25am

Fares: (A) sleeper/3AC/2AC, (B) sleeper, (C) sleeper/2AC/1AC, (D) 2nd class/AC chair, (E) sleeper/3AC/2AC/1AC

ⓘ Getting Around

Minibuses and shared autorickshaws link the train station and central bus stand (₹6 to ₹10 per person). A private autorickshaw costs around ₹40.

Chittorgarh (Chittor)

☎ 01472 / POP 96,200

Chittorgarh, the fort (garh) at Chittor, is the largest fort complex in India, and a fascinating place to explore. It rises from the plains like a huge rock island, nearly 6km long and surrounded on all sides by 150m-plus cliffs.

Its history epitomises Rajput romanticism, chivalry and tragedy, and it holds a special place in the hearts of many Rajputs. Three times (in 1303, 1535 and 1568) Chittorgarh was under attack from a more powerful enemy; each time, its people chose death before dishonour, performing jauhar. The men donned saffron martyrs' robes and rode out from the fort to certain death, while the women and children immolated themselves on huge funeral pyres. After the last of the three sackings, Rana Udai Singh II fled to Udaipur, where he established a new capital for Mewar. In 1616, Jehangir returned Chittor to the Rajputs. There was no attempt at resettlement, though it was restored in 1905.

◉ Sights

Chittorgarh FORT
(Indian/foreigner ₹5/100, Sound & Light Show ₹75/200; ☺ dawn-dusk, Sound & Light Show dusk)
A zigzag ascent of more than 1km starts at **Padal Pol** and leads through six outer gateways to the main gate on the western side, the **Ram Pol** (the former back entrance). Inside Ram Pol is a still-occupied village that takes up a small northwestern part of the fort – turn right here for the ticket office. The rest of the plateau is deserted except for the wonderful palaces, towers and temples that remain from its heyday, with the addition of a few recent temples. A loop road runs around the plateau, which has a deer park at the southern end.

➡ **Meera & Kumbha Shyam Temples**

Both of these temples southeast of the **Rana Kumbha Palace** (Fort) were built by Rana Kumbha in the ornate Indo-Aryan style, with classic, tall sikharas (spires). The

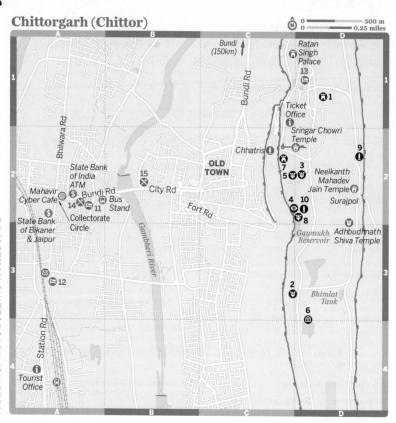

Chittorgarh (Chittor)

◉ **Sights**

1 Chittorgarh D1
2 Kalika Mata Temple C3
3 Kumbha Shyam Temple D2
4 Mahasati C2
5 Meera Temple C2
6 Padmini's Palace D3
7 Rana Kumbha Palace C2
8 Samidheshwar Temple D2
9 Tower of Fame D2
10 Tower of Victory D2

🛏 **Sleeping**

11 Hotel Amber Plaza A2
12 Hotel Pratap Palace A3
13 Padmini Haveli D1

✖ **Eating**

14 Chokhi Dhani Garden
    Family Restaurant A2
15 Saffire Garden
    Restaurant B2

Meera Temple, the smaller of the two, is now associated with the mystic-poetess Meerabai, a 16th-century Mewar royal who was poisoned by her brother-in-law, but survived due to the blessings of Krishna. The **Kumbha Shyam Temple** is dedicated to Vishnu and its carved panels illustrate 15th-century Mewar life.

➜ **Tower of Victory**

The glorious **Tower of Victory** (Jaya Stambha; Fort), symbol of Chittorgarh, was erected by Rana Kumbha in the 1440s, probably to commemorate a victory over Mahmud Khilji of Malwa. Dedicated to Vishnu, it rises 37m in nine exquisitely carved storeys, and you can climb the 157 narrow stairs (the interior is also carved) to the 8th floor, from where there's a good view of the area.

Below the tower, to the southwest, is the **Mahasati** (Fort) area where there are many *sati* stones – this was the royal cremation ground and was also where 13,000 women committed *jauhar* in 1535. The **Samidheshwar Temple** (Fort), built in the 6th century and restored in 1427, is nearby. Notable among its intricate carving is a Trimurti (three-faced) figure of Shiva.

➔ Gaumukh Reservoir

Walk down beyond the Samidheshwar Temple and at the edge of the cliff is a deep tank, the Gaumukh Reservoir, where you can feed the fish. The reservoir takes its name from a spring that feeds the tank from a *gaumukh* (cow's mouth) carved into the cliffside.

➔ Padmini's Palace

Continuing south, you reach the **Kalika Mata Temple**, an 8th-century sun temple damaged during the first sacking of Chittorgarh and then converted to a temple for the goddess Kali in the 14th century. **Padmini's Palace** stands about 250m further south, beside a small lake with a central pavilion. The bronze gates to this pavilion were carried off by Akbar and can now be seen in Agra Fort.

➔ Surajpol & Tower of Fame

Surajpol, on the fort's east side, was the main gate and offers fantastic views across the empty plains. A little further north, the 24m-high **Tower of Fame** (Kirtti Stambha; Fort), dating from 1301, is smaller than the Tower of Victory. Built by a Jain merchant, the tower is dedicated to Adinath, the first Jain *tirthankar* (one of the 24 revered Jain teachers) and is decorated with naked figures of various other *tirthankars*, indicating that it is a monument of the Digambara (sky-clad) order. A narrow stairway leads up the seven storeys to the top. Next door is a 14th-century Jain temple.

🛏 Sleeping & Eating

Hotel Amber Plaza HOTEL **$**
(📷 248862; 32 Kidwai Nagar; r with/without AC ₹900/500; ❄) Down a quietish street near the bus stand, this hotel has quite comfy, medium-sized rooms with bright decorations and a restaurant.

Hotel Pratap Palace HOTEL **$$**
(📷 240099; www.hotelpratappalacechittaurgarh. com; off Maharana Pratap Setu Marg; s/d incl breakfast ₹3820/4400; ❄@🛜) This is Chittorgagh's best option, with a wide range of rooms, a convenient location and travel-savvy staff.

The more expensive rooms have window seats and leafy outlooks. There's a decent garden-side multicuisine restaurant too. It's near the main post office.

Padmini Haveli HERITAGE HOTEL **$$$**
(📷 94141410090, 241251; www.thepadminihaveli. com; Annapoorna Temple Rd, Shah Chowk, Village, Chittorgarh Fort; r incl breakfast ₹4000, ste ₹5000; ❄@🛜) A fantastically set 16th-century palace apparently plucked from the whimsy of Udaipur and dropped into a rural retreat 41km by road east of Chittorgarh. It's a great place to settle down with a good book, compose a fairy-tale fantasy or just laze around. Rooms are romantic and luxurious, and there's a pleasant garden courtyard and an airy restaurant serving Rajasthani food.

Reservations should be made through the website or Hotel Pratap Palace. The owners can arrange transfer from Chittor as well as horse and 4WD safaris, birdwatching, cooking classes, massage and yoga.

Saffire Garden Restaurant MULTICUISINE **$$**
(City Rd; mains ₹100-150; ⏱8am-10pm; ❄) Sit at tables on the small, tree-shaded lawn or inside the air-conditioned room at the back, and tuck into a variety of standard, but tasty enough, Indian and Chinese dishes.

Chokhi Dhani Garden Family Restaurant DHABA **$**
(Bundi Rd; mains ₹50-130; ⏱11am-10pm; ❄) This fan-cooled roadside *dhaba* (snack bar) with extra seating in the back does a good-value selection of vegetarian dishes, including filling thalis and a variety of South Indian dishes.

ℹ Information

You can access an ATM and change money at the **SBBJ** (SBBJ; Bhilwara Rd), and there's an ATM at **SBI** (Bundi Rd).

Mahavir Cyber Cafe (Collectorate Circle; ⏱8am-10pm)

Tourist Office (📷241089; Station Rd; per hr ₹40; ⏱10am-1.30pm & 2-5pm Mon-Sat) Friendly and helpful, with a town map and brochure to give out.

ℹ Getting There & Away

BUS

Services from Chittorgarh:

Ajmer (₹146, four hours, hourly until mid-afternoon)

Jaipur (₹233, seven hours, around every 90 minutes)

Kota (₹135, four hours, half-hourly)

MAJOR TRAINS FROM CHITTORGARH

DESTINATION	TRAIN NO & NAME	DEPARTURE TIME	ARRIVAL TIME	FARE (₹)
Ajmer	12991 Udaipur-Jaipur Exp	8.20am	11.25pm	100/365/505 (A)
Bundi	29019 NMH-Kota Exp	3.45pm	5.45pm	140/690 (B)
Delhi (Nizamuddin)	12964 Mewar Exp	8.50pm	6.35am	370/970 (B)
Jaipur	12991 Udaipur-Jaipur Exp	8.20am	1.30pm	140/505/705 (A)
Sawai Madhopur	29019 NMH-Kota Exp	3.45pm	9.25pm	130/690 (B)
Udaipur	19329 Udaipur City Exp	4.50pm	7.10pm	140/485 (B)

Fares: (A) 2nd-class seat/AC chair/1st-class seat, (B) sleeper/2AC

Udaipur (₹86, 2½ hours, half-hourly)
There are no direct buses to Bundi.

TRAIN

➡ Three trains run daily to Bundi (sleeper ₹100; 2.10pm, 3.45pm and 8.50pm). The first one takes 3½ hours, the others just two hours.

➡ Five daily trains go to Udaipur (sleeper ₹140; two hours; 4.25am, 5.05am, 5.33am, 4.50pm and 9pm).

➡ Three trains make the trip to Jaipur daily (sleeper ₹210; 5½ hours; 8.20am, 12.35am and 2.45am).

➡ In addition to departures at 10.10am and 7.30pm, the trains to Jaipur also make the three-hour trip to Ajmer (sleeper ₹140).

➡ Two fast trains go to Delhi (10 hours, 7.30pm and 8.50pm), arriving at Delih Sarai Rohilla and Hazrat Nizamuddin respectively.

➡ For Ranthambhore, three trains travel daily to Sawai Madhopur (sleeper ₹130; 2.10pm, 3.45pm and 8.50pm). They take nine, six and four hours respectively.

🛈 Getting Around

A full tour of the fort by autorickshaw should cost around ₹400 return. You can arrange this yourself in town. Hotel Pratap Palace (p147) gives 4WD tours of the fort for ₹600.

Udaipur

📞 0294 / POP 389,400

Beside shimmering Lake Pichola, with the ochre and purple ridges of the wooded Aravalli Hills stretching away in every direction, Udaipur has a romantic setting unmatched in Rajasthan and arguably in all of India. Fantastical palaces, temples, *havelis* and countless narrow, crooked, colourful streets add the human counterpoint to the city's natural charms.

Udaipur's tag of 'the most romantic spot on the continent of India' was first applied in 1829 by Colonel James Tod, the East India Company's first Political Agent in the region. Today the romance is wearing ever so slightly thin as Udaipur strains to exploit it for tourist rupees. In the parts of the city nearest the lake, almost every building is a hotel, shop, restaurant, travel agent, or all four rolled into one. Ever-taller hotels compete for the best view, too many mediocre restaurants serve up near-identical menus, and noisy, dirty traffic clogs some of the streets that were made for people and donkeys.

Take a step back from the hustle, however, and Udaipur still has its magic, not just in its marvellous palaces and monuments, but in its matchless setting, the tranquility of boat rides on the lake, the bustle of its ancient bazaars, its lively arts scene, the quaint old-world feel of its better hotels, its endless tempting shops and some lovely countryside to explore on wheels, feet or horseback.

Udaipur was founded in 1568 by Maharana Udai Singh II following the final sacking of Chittorgarh by the Mughal emperor Akbar. Though this new capital of Mewar had a much less vulnerable location than Chittorgarh, Mewar still had to contend with repeated invasions by the Mughals and, later, the Marathas, until British intervention in the early 19th century. This resulted in a treaty that protected Udaipur from invaders while allowing Mewar's rulers to remain effectively all-powerful in internal affairs. The ex-royal family remains influential and in recent decades has been the driving force behind the rise of Udaipur as a tourist destination.

⊙ Sights

Lake Pichola
LAKE

Limpid and large, Lake Pichola reflects the cool grey-blue mountains on its rippling mirror-like surface. It was enlarged by Maharana Udai Singh II, following his foundation of the city, by flooding Picholi village, which gave the lake its name. The lake is now 4km long and 3km wide, but remains shallow and dries up completely during severe droughts. The City Palace complex, including the gardens at its southern end, extends nearly 1km along the lake's eastern shore.

Boat trips (adult/child 10am-2pm ₹400/200, 3-5pm ₹650/350; ⊙10am-5pm) leave roughly hourly from Rameshwar Ghat, within the City Palace complex (note, you have to pay ₹30 to enter). The trips make a stop at Jagmandir Island, where you can stay for as long as you like before taking any boat back. Take your own drinks and snacks, though, as those sold on the island are extortionately expensive. You can also take 30-minute boat rides (₹250 per person) from **Lal Ghat**, throughout the day without the need to enter the City Palace complex: it's worth checking in advance what time the popular sunset departure casts offs.

City Palace
PALACE

(www.eternalmewar.in; adult/child ₹30/15, free if visiting City Palace Museum; ⊙7am-11pm) Surmounted by balconies, towers and cupolas towering over the lake, the imposing City Palace is Rajasthan's largest palace, with a facade 244m long and 30.4m high. Construction was begun in 1599 by Maharana Udai Singh II, the city's founder, and it later became a conglomeration of structures (including 11 separate smaller palaces) built and extended by various maharanas, though it still manages to retain a surprising uniformity of design.

You can enter the complex through **Badi Pol** (Great Gate; 1615) at the northern end, or the **Sheetla Mata Gate** to the south. Tickets for the City Palace Museum are sold at both entrances. Note: you must pay the ₹30 City Palace entrance ticket in order to pass south through **Chandra Chowk Gate**, en route to the Crystal Gallery or Rameshwar Ghat for the Lake Pichola boat rides, even if you have a City Palace Museum ticket.

Inside Badi Pol, eight arches on the left commemorate the eight times maharanas were weighed here and their weight in gold or silver distributed to the lucky locals. You then pass through the three-arched **Tripolia Gate** (1711) into a large courtyard, **Manek Chowk**. Spot the large tiger-catching cage, which worked rather like an oversized mousetrap, and the smaller one for leopards.

City Palace Museum
MUSEUM

(adult/child ₹115/55, camera or video ₹225, ticket plus audio guide ₹225, human guide ₹200; ⊙9.30am-5.30pm, last entry 4.30pm) The main part of the palace is open as the City Palace Museum, with rooms extravagantly

---

DON'T MISS

DURBAR GLITZ

Many palaces in India have a durbar hall (royal reception hall). Usually the grandest room in the place, with a respectable number of chandeliers and gilt overlay, the durbar hall was dressed to impress – it was used by Indian rulers for official occasions, such as state banquets, and to hold meetings.

The restored Durbar Hall (p151) in the City Palace complex is one of India's most impressive, vast and lavish, with some of the country's biggest chandeliers. The walls display royal weapons and striking portraits of former maharanas of Mewar – a most distinguished-looking lot, who come from what is believed to be the oldest ruling dynasty in the world, spanning 76 generations.

The foundation stone of the hall was laid in 1909 by Lord Minto, the viceroy of India, during the reign of Maharana Fateh Singh, and it was originally named Minto Hall. The upper level of this high-ceilinged hall is surrounded by viewing galleries, where ladies of the palace could watch, in veiled seclusion, what was happening below. Nowadays, these are the Crystal Gallery (p150).

The Durbar Hall is included in visits to the Crystal Gallery and you will also see it if you go to the **Gallery Restaurant** (Durbar Hall; Durbar tea ₹325; ⊙9am-6pm). The hall still has the capacity to hold hundreds of people and can even be hired for conferences or social gatherings.

Udaipur

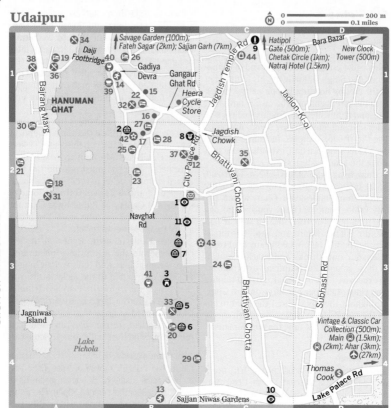

decorated with mirrors, tiles and paintings, and housing a large, varied collection of artefacts. It's entered from **Ganesh Chowk**, which you reach from Manek Chowk.

The City Palace Museum begins with the **Rai Angan** (Royal Courtyard), the very spot where Udai Singh met the sage who told him to build a city here. Rooms along one side contain historical paintings, including several of the Battle of Haldighati (1576), in which Mewar forces under Maharana Pratap, one of the great Rajput heroes, gallantly fought the army of Mughal emperor Akbar to a stalemate.

As you move through the palace, highlights include the **Baadi Mahal** (1699), where a pretty, central garden gives fine views over the city. **Kishan (Krishna) Vilas** has a remarkable collection of miniatures from the time of Maharana Bhim Singh (1778–1828). The story goes that Bhim Singh's daughter Krishna Kumari drank a fatal cup of poison here to solve the dilemma of

rival princely suitors from Jaipur and Jodhpur, who were both threatening to invade Mewar if she didn't marry them. The **Surya Choupad** boasts a huge, ornamental sun (the symbol of the sun-descended Mewar dynasty) and opens into **Mor Chowk** (Peacock Courtyard) with its lovely mosaics of peacocks, the favourite Rajasthani bird.

The southern end of the museum comprises the **Zenana Mahal**, the royal ladies' quarters built in the 17th century. It now contains a long picture gallery with lots of royal hunting scenes (note the comic strip-like progression of the action in each painting). The Zenana Mahal's central courtyard, **Laxmi Chowk**, contains a beautiful white pavilion and a stable of howdahs, palanquins and other people carriers.

Crystal Gallery   GALLERY
(City Palace Complex; adult/child incl audio guide & drink ₹550/350, photography prohibited; ⊙9am-7pm) The Crystal Gallery houses rare crystal

Udaipur

that Maharana Sajjan Singh ordered from F&C Osler & Co in England in 1877. The maharana died before it arrived, and all the items stayed forgotten and packed up in boxes for 110 years. The extraordinary, extravagant collection includes crystal chairs, sofas, tables and even beds. The rather hefty admission fee also includes entry to the grand **Durbar Hall** (City Palace Complex). Tickets are available at the City Palace gates or the Crystal Gallery.

Government Museum   MUSEUM
(⊙10am-5pm Tue-Sun) FREE Entered from Ganesh Chowk, this has a splendid collection of jewel-like miniature paintings of the Mewar school and a turban that belonged to Shah Jahan, creator of the Taj Mahal. Stranger exhibits include a stuffed monkey holding a lamp. There are also regal maharana portraits in profile, documenting Mewar's rulers along with the changing fashions of the moustache.

Jagdish Temple   HINDU TEMPLE
(⊙5.30am-2pm & 4-10pm) Reached by a steep, elephant-flanked flight of steps, 150m north of the City Palace's Badi Pol entrance, this busy Indo-Aryan temple was built by Maharana Jagat Singh in 1651. The wonderfully carved main structure enshrines a black stone image of Vishnu as Jagannath, Lord of the Universe. There's also a brass image of the Garuda (Vishnu's man-bird vehicle) in a shrine facing the main structure.

Bagore-ki-Haveli   HISTORIC BUILDING
(admission ₹30; ⊙10am-5pm) This gracious 18th-century *haveli,* set on the water's edge in the Gangaur Ghat area, was built by a Mewar prime minister and has since been carefully restored. There are 138 rooms set around courtyards, some arranged to evoke the period during which the house was inhabited, while others house cultural displays, including – intriguingly enough – the world's biggest turban.

The *haveli* also houses a gallery featuring a fascinating collection of period photos of Udaipur and a surreal collection of famous monuments carved out of polystyrene.

Sajjan Garh   PALACE
(Monsoon Palace) Perched on top of a distant mountain like a fairy-tale castle, this melancholy, neglected late 19th-century palace was constructed by Maharana Sajjan Singh. Originally an astronomical centre, it became a monsoon palace and hunting lodge. Now government owned, it's in a sadly dilapidated state but visitors stream up here for the marvellous views, particularly at sunset. It's 5km west of the old city as the crow flies, about 9km by the winding road.

At the foot of the hill you enter the 5-sq-km **Sajjan Garh Wildlife Sanctuary** (Indian/foreigner ₹20/160, car ₹60, camera/video free/₹200). A good way to visit is with the daily sunset excursion in a minivan driven by an enterprising taxi driver who picks up tourists at the entrance to Bagore-ki-Haveli at Gangaur Ghat every day at 5pm. The round trip costs ₹200 per person, including waiting time (but not the sanctuary fees). His minivan has 'Monsoon Palace–Sajjangarh Fort' written across the front of it. Alternatively, autorickshaws charge ₹200 including waiting time for a round trip to the sanctuary gate, which they are not allowed to pass. Taxis ferry people the final 4km up to the palace for ₹100 per person.

Vintage & Classic Car Collection   MUSEUM
(Garden Hotel, Lake Palace Rd; adult/child ₹250/150, incl lunch or dinner ₹400/300; ⊙9am-9pm) The maharanas' car collection makes a fascinating diversion, for what it tells about their elite lifestyle and for the vintage vehicles themselves. Housed within the former state garage are 22 splendid vehicles, including a seven-seat 1938 Cadillac, complete with purdah system, the beautiful 1934 Rolls-Royce Phantom used in the Bond film *Octopussy,* and the Cadillac convertible that whisked Queen Elizabeth II to the airport in

1961. The museum is a 10-minute walk east along Lake Palace Rd (bear to the right at the staggered junction).

If you enjoy a vegetarian thali, the combined museum-and-meal ticket is a very good option (lunch 11.30am to 3pm, dinner 7.30pm to 10pm).

🏃 Activities

Bike Tours

Art of Bicycle   CYCLING
(☑8105289167; www.artofbicycletrips.com; 27 Gadiya Devra, inside Chandpol; half-day per person ₹1950) This well-run outfit offers a great way to get out of the city. The Lakecity Loop is a 30km half-day tour that quickly leaves Udaipur behind to have you wheeling through villages, farmland and along the shores of Fateh Sagar and Badi Lakes. Other options include a vehicle-supported trip further afield to Kumbulhgarh and Ranakpur. Bikes are well-maintained and come with helmets.

Horse Riding
The wooded hills, villages and lakes around Udaipur are lovely riding country. You'll saddle up on Rajasthan's celebrated Marwari horses, known for their intelligence, stamina and cute inward-curving ears.

Pratap Country Inn   HORSE RIDING
(☑2583138; www.horseridingindia.in; Jaisamand Rd, Titaradi Village; 2hr rides ₹900, full day ₹2000) Run by the pioneer of horse safaris in Rajasthan, Maharaja Narendra Singh, this inn about 7km south of town organises day or part-day rides and long-distance safaris.

Krishna Ranch   HORSE RIDING
(☑9828059505; www.krishnaranch.com; full-day rides incl lunch ₹1200) Situated in beautiful countryside near Badi village, 7km northwest of Udaipur, and run by the owners of Kumbha Palace guesthouse (p155). Experienced owner-guide Dinesh Jain leads most trips himself, riding local Marwari horses through the surrounding hills. There are also attractive cottages (p152) at the ranch.

HELPING UDAIPUR'S STREET ANIMALS

The spacious **Animal Aid Unlimited** (☑9950531639, 9352511435; www.animalaidunlimited.com; Badi Village) refuge treats around 200 street animals a day (mainly dogs, donkeys and cows) and answers more than 3000 emergency rescue calls a year. The refuge welcomes volunteers and visitors: make contact in advance to fix a time between 9am and 5pm any day. It's in Badi village, 7km northwest of Udaipur. A round trip by autorickshaw, including waiting time, costs around ₹400.

Call Animal Aid Unlimited if you see an injured or ill street animal in Udaipur.

Massage

Ayurvedic Body Care
AYURVEDA, MASSAGE

(☑2413816; www.ayurvedicbodycare.com; 38 Lal Ghat; ⊙10am-8pm) A small and popular old city operation offering ayurvedic massage at reasonable prices, including a 15-minute head or back massage (₹250) and a 45-minute full-body massage (₹750). It also sells ayurvedic products such as oils, moisturisers, shampoos and soaps.

Walking

The horse-riding specialists at Krishna Ranch also offer guided hikes through the same beautiful countryside, passing through small tribal villages en route. Multiday hikes can be arranged too.

Millets of Mewar
WALKING

(☑8890419048; www.milletsofmewar.com; Hanuman Ghat; ₹1000 per person, min 2 people) Health-food specialists Millets of Mewar (p156) organises 2½-hour city tours on which you can meet local artisans who live and work in Udaipur. Tours should be booked a day in advance; they leave from the restaurant at 10am.

₹ Courses

Cooking

Shashi Cooking Classes
COOKING

(☑9929303511; www.shashicookingclasses.blogspot.com; Sunrise Restaurant, 18 Gangaur Ghat Rd; 4hr class ₹1500, max 4 students) Readers rave about Shashi's high-spirited classes, teaching many fundamental Indian dishes.

Sushma's Cooking Classes
COOKING

(☑7665852163; www.cookingclassesinudaipur.com; Hotel Krishna Niwas, 35 Lal Ghat; 2hr class ₹1000) A highly recommended cooking class run by the enthusiastic Sushma. Classes offer up anything from traditional Rajasthani dishes and spice mixes, through bread-making to the all-important method of making the perfect cup of chai.

Music

Prem Musical Instruments
MUSIC

(☑2430599; 28 Gadiya Devra; lessons per hr ₹400; ⊙10.30am-6pm) Rajesh Prajapati (Bablu) is a local musician who gives sitar, tabla and flute lessons. He also sells and repairs instruments and can arrange performances.

Painting

Ashoka Arts
PAINTING

(Hotel Gangaur Palace, Gadiya Devra; lessons per hr ₹200) Learn the basics of classic miniature painting from a local master.

Yoga

Prakash Yoga
YOGA

(☑2524872; inside Chandpol; class by donation; ⊙classes 8am & 7pm) A friendly hatha yoga centre with hour-long classes. The teacher has over 20 years' experience. It's tucked inside Chandpol, near the footbridge, but well-signed.

Tours

Heritage Walks
WALKING

(☑9414164680; www.heritageroyalrajasthan.com; City Palace Rd; tours per person ₹200; ⊙tours 8am & 5pm) If you want to really drill into Udaipur's history, architecture and religious sites, you could do a lot worse than joining one of the twice-daily expert-led tours from Heritage Walks, which will show you the Lal Ghat area that exists beyond the souvenir shops. Tours last two hours.

✺ Festivals & Events

If you're in Udaipur in February or March, you can experience the festival of **Holi** Udaipur-style, when the town comes alive in a riot of colour. Holi is followed in March/April by the procession-heavy **Mewar Festival** – Udaipur's own version of the springtime Gangaur festival.

🛏 Sleeping

Accommodation clusters where most people want to stay – close to the lake, especially on its eastern side, in and near the narrow Lal Ghat. This area is a tangle of streets and lanes (some quiet, some busy and noisy), close to the City Palace and Jagdish Temple. It's Udaipur's tourist epicentre and the streets are strung not just with lodgings but also with tourist-oriented eateries and shops whose owners will be doing their best to tempt you in.

Directly across the water from Lal Ghat, Hanuman Ghat has a slightly more local vibe and often better views, though you're certainly not out of the tourist zone.

🛏 Lal Ghat Area

Many budget and midrange lodgings cluster here, with a particular concentration along the relatively peaceful Lal Ghat.

Nukkad Guest House
GUESTHOUSE $

(☑2411403; nukkad_raju@yahoo.com; 56 Ganesh Ghati; s/d without bathroom ₹100/200, r ₹300-500; ❀☞) Nukkad has simple, fan-cooled, very clean, good-value rooms, plus a sociable, breezy, upstairs restaurant with very good Indian and international dishes. You can join afternoon cooking classes and morning yoga sessions (by donation) without stepping outside the door – just don't stay out past curfew or get caught washing your clothes in your bathroom.

Lal Ghat Guest House
GUESTHOUSE $

(☑ 2525301; www.lalghat.com; 33 Lal Ghat; dm ₹150, r from ₹750, without bathroom ₹250; ✳@🗊) This mellow guesthouse by the lake was one of the first to open in Udaipur, and it's still a sound choice, with an amazing variety of older and newer rooms. Accommodation ranges from a spruce, nonsmoking dorm (with curtained-off beds and lockers under the mattresses) to the best room, which sports a stone wall, big bed, big mirror and AC. Most rooms have lake views and those in the older part of the building generally have more character. There's a small kitchen for self-caterers.

Pratap Bhawan Paying Guest House
GUESTHOUSE $$

(☑ 2560566; 12 Lal Ghat; s ₹1000-1200, d ₹1450-1950; ✳🗊) A curving marble staircase leads up from the wide lobby to large, sparkling-clean rooms with good, big bathrooms and, in many cases, cushioned window seats. A deservedly popular place, even if recent price hikes have spun the place slighltly out of the budget category. The rooftop terrace is nice for sitting out at night.

Poonam Haveli
HOTEL $$

(☑2410303; www.hotelpoonamhaveli.com; 39 Lal Ghat; r ₹1800-2500; ✳@🗊) A fairly modern place decked out in traditional style, friendly Poonam has 16 spacious, spotlessly clean rooms with big beds and spare but tasteful decor, plus pleasant sitting areas. None of the rooms enjoy lake views, but the rooftop restaurant does, and boasts 'real Italian' pizzas among the usual Indian and traveller fare.

Jheel Palace Guest House
GUESTHOUSE $$

(☑2421352; www.jheelguesthouse.com; 56 Gangaur Ghat; r ₹1000-3000; ✳🗊) Right on the lake edge (when the lake is full), Jheel Palace has three nice rooms with little balconies and four-poster beds, and three more ordinary ones. All are AC. Staff are accommodating and hands-off, and there's a good Brahmin pure-veg rooftop restaurant (no beer). Tight budgets will appreciate the basic ₹300 room.

Hotel Gangaur Palace
HERITAGE HOTEL $$

(☑2422303; www.ashokahaveli.com; Gadiya Devra; s ₹400-2000, d ₹500-2500; ✳@🗊) This elaborate, faded *haveli* is set around a stone-pillared courtyard, with a wide assortment of rooms on several floors. It's gradually moving upmarket and rooms range from windowless with flaking paint to bright and recently decorated with lake views. Many have wall paintings and window seats.

The hotel also boasts an in-house palm reader, art shop, art school (p153), the good Cafe Namaste (p156) and a rooftop restaurant serving the same fare as the cafe as well as multicuisine dishes.

★ Jagat Niwas Palace Hotel
HERITAGE HOTEL $$$

(☑2420133; www.jagatniwaspalace.com; 23-25 Lal Ghat; r ₹3250-4250, without lake view ₹1850-2950; ✳@🗊) This leading top-end hotel set in two converted lakeside *havelis* takes the location cake. The lake-view rooms are charming, with carved wooden furniture, cushioned window seats and pretty prints. Rooms without a lake view are almost as comfortable and attractive, and considerably cheaper.

The building is full of character with lots of attractive sitting areas, terraces and courtyards, and it makes the most of its position with a picture-perfect rooftop restaurant

🛏 Hanuman Ghat Area

Dream Heaven
GUESTHOUSE $

(☑2431038; www.dreamheaven.co.in; Hanuman Ghat; r ₹300-1000; ✳@🗊) This popular place to come to a halt is in a higgledy-piggledy building with clean rooms with wall hangings and paintings. Bathrooms are smallish, though some rooms have a decent balcony and/or views. The food at the rooftop restaurant (dishes ₹40 to ₹110), which overlooks the lake and shows Udaipur at its best, is fresh and tasty – the perfect place to chill out on a pile of cushions.

Hibiscus Guest house
GUESTHOUSE $$

(☑9782222299; www.hibiscusudaipur.in; 190 Naga Nagri; r ₹1800-2200; ✳) A friendly, family-run house in a quiet setting back from Hanuman Ghat. The well-sized rooms have pretty Rajasthani decor, and the roof provides nice lake views. The flowers in the charming walled garden might equally have dubbed this place the Frangipani Guest House. Meals are available.

Amet Haveli

HERITAGE HOTEL $$$

(☑2431085; www.amethaveliudaipur.com; Hanuman Ghat; s/d ₹5400/6600; ✳@☎) A 350-year-old heritage building on the lake shore with delightful rooms featuring cushioned window seats and coloured glass with little shutters. They're set around a pretty little courtyard and pond. Splurge on one with a balcony or giant bathtub. One of Udaipur's most romantic restaurants, Ambrai (p156), is part of the hotel.

Udai Kothi

HOTEL $$$

(☑2432810; www.udaikothi.com; Hanuman Ghat; r ₹5500-7000; ✳@☎☲) A bit like a five-storey wedding cake, Udai Kothi is a glittery, modern building with lots of traditional touches – cupolas, interesting art and fabrics, window seats in some rooms, marble bathrooms and carved-wood doors in others, and thoughtful touches such as bowls of floating flowers. Rooms are pretty, individually designed and well equipped.

The apex is the rooftop terrace, where you can dine well at the **restaurant** (Udai Kothi Hotel; mains ₹125-250) and swim in Udaipur's only rooftop pool (nonguests ₹300).

🛏 City Palace

Kumbha Palace

GUESTHOUSE $$

(☑9828059506, 2422702; www.hotelkumbha-palace.com; 104 Bhattiyani Chotta; r ₹550-600, with AC ₹1000; ✳@☎) This excellent place, run by a Dutch-Indian couple, is tucked up a quiet lane off busy Bhattiyani Chotta and backed by a lovely lush lawn. The 10 rooms are simple but comfortable (just one has AC), and the restaurant knows how to satisfy homesick travellers. The owners also run Krishna Ranch, where horse riding and cottage accommodation are available.

Shiv Niwas Palace Hotel   HERITAGE HOTEL $$$

(☑2528016; www.eternalmewar.in; City Palace Complex; r ₹15,000-42,000; ✳@☎☲) This hotel, in the former palace guest quarters, has opulent common areas like its pool courtyard, bar and lawn garden. Some of the suites are truly palatial, filled with fountains and silver, but the standard rooms are poorer value. Go for a suite, or just for a drink (p157), meal (mains ₹500-1000; noon to 3pm and 7pm to 10.30pm), massage or swim in the gorgeous marble pool (nonguests ₹300).

Rates drop dramatically from April to September.

Fateh Prakash
Palace Hotel

HERITAGE HOTEL $$$

(☑2528016; www.hrhhotels.com; City Palace Complex; r ₹15,000, premier ste ₹31,500; ✳@☎) Built in the early 20th century for royal functions (the Durbar Hall is part of it), the Fateh Prakash has luxurious rooms and gorgeous suites, all comprehensively equipped and almost all looking straight out onto Lake Pichola. Views aside, the general ambience is a little less regal than at Shiv Niwas Palace Hotel – although the Sunset Terrace (p157) bar is a great place for an evening drink.

🛏 Other Areas

★Krishna Ranch

COTTAGE $$

(☑9602192902, 3291478; www.krishnaranch.com; s/d incl meals ₹2000/2500) 🍴 This delightful countryside retreat has five cottages set around the grounds of a small farm. Each comes with attached bathroom (with solar heated shower), tasteful decor and farm views. All meals are included and are prepared using organic produce grown on the farm. The ranch is 7km from town, near Badi village, but there's free pick-up from Udaipur.

It's an ideal base for the hikes and horse treks that the management – a Dutch-Indian couple – organises from here, though you don't have to sign up for the treks to stay here.

🍴 Eating

Udaipur has scores of sun-kissed rooftop cafes, many with mesmerising lake views but often with uninspired multicuisine fare. Fortunately there's also a healthy number of places putting a bit more thought into their food.

🍴 Lal Ghat Area

Cafe Edelweiss

CAFE $

(73 Gangaur Ghat Rd; coffee from ₹50, sandwiches from ₹180; ⊙8.30am-8pm; ☎) The Savage Garden restaurant folks run this itsy piece of Europe that appeals to homesick and discerning travellers with superb baked goods and good coffee. Offerings included sticky cinnamon rolls, squidgy blueberry chocolate cake, spinach-and-mushroom quiche or apple strudel, good muesli or eggs for breakfast, and great sandwiches (the unexpected appearance of ham and bacon feels deliciously transgressive).

RAJASTHAN UDAIPUR

Lotus Cafe
MULTICUISINE $

(15 Bhattiyani Chotta; dishes ₹50-210; ⊘9am-10.30pm) This funky little restaurant serves up fabulous chicken dishes (predominantly Indian), plus salads, baked potatoes and plenty of vegetarian fare. It's ideal for meeting other travellers, with a mezzanine to loll about on, and cool background sounds.

Cafe Namaste
CAFE $

(Hotel Gangaur Palace; coffee ₹40-70, breakfasts ₹50-100; ⊘7am-10pm) A European-themed streetside cafe that delivers the goods with scrumptious muffins, apple pies, cinnamon rolls, brownies etc. And to wash it down there's coffee from a shiny silver espresso machine taking pride of place. The noisy street is a minus.

Jagat Niwas Palace Hotel
INDIAN $$

(☑2420133; 23-25 Lal Ghat; mains ₹150-375; ⊘7am-10am, noon-3pm & 6-10pm) A wonderful, classy, rooftop restaurant with superb lake views, delicious Indian cuisine and good service. Choose from an extensive selection of rich curries (tempered for Western tastes) – mutton, chicken, fish and veg – as well as the tandoori classics. There's a cocktail menu and the beer is icy. Book ahead for dinner.

O'Zen Restaurant
MULTICUISINE $$

(City Palace Rd; coffee ₹50-70, mains ₹100-300; ⊘8.30am-11pm; ☎) A swish location on City Palace Rd, this stylish 1st-floor restaurant-cafe does a range of Indian curries plus Italian pizza and pasta. It's bright and modern, does good coffee and beer (₹180), and has views of the street below.

★ Savage Garden
MEDITERRANEAN $$$

(☑2425440; 22 inside Chandpol; mains ₹220-520; ⊘11am-11pm) Tucked away in the backstreets near Chandpol, Savage Garden does a winning line in soups, chicken and homemade pasta dishes. We loved the ravioli with lamb ragu, and the sweet-savoury stuffed chicken breast with nuts, cheese and carrot rice. The setting is a 250-year-old *haveli* with indigo walls and bowls of flowers, and tables in alcoves or a pleasant courtyard. The bar is slick, with red, white and sparkling Indian wines from Nasik, Maharashtra.

✗ Hanuman Ghat Area

Millets of Mewar
INDIAN $

(www.milletsofmewar.com; Hanuman Ghat; mains ₹80-140; ⊘8.30am-10.30pm; ☎) ✏ This place does the healthiest food in town. Local millets are used where possible instead of less environmentally sound wheat and rice. There are vegan options, gluten-free dishes, fresh salads and juices and herbal teas. Also on the menu are multigrain sandwiches and millet pizzas, plus regular curries, Indian street-food snacks, pasta and even pancakes.

The sweet Indian coffee is delicious, and there's ice cream and chocolate pudding to go with the millet cookies on the dessert menu.

Jasmin
MULTICUISINE $

(mains ₹60-90; ⊘8.30am-11pm) Very tasty vegetarian dishes are cooked up in a lovely, quiet, open-air spot looking out on the quaint Daiji Footbridge. There are plenty of Indian options, and some original variations on the usual multicuisine theme including Korean and Israeli dishes. The ambience is super-relaxed and service friendly.

Queen Cafe
INDIAN $

(14 Bajrang Marg; mains ₹60-75; ⊘8am-10pm) This tiny restaurant-cum-family-front-room serves up good home-style Indian vegetarian dishes. Try the pumpkin curry with mint and coconut, and the Kashmir *pulao* (rice dish) with fruit, vegies and coconut. Host Meenu also offers cooking classes and slightly overpriced walking tours, but some diners may find that the hard sell she serves up with the food leaves a slightly bitter taste.

Ambrai
NORTH INDIAN $$$

(☑2431085; www.amethaveliudaipur.com; Amet Haveli; mains ₹250-400; ⊘12.30-3pm & 7.30-10.30pm) The cuisine at this scenic restaurant – set at lake-shore level, looking across to Lal Ghat and the City Palace – does justice to its fabulous position. Highly atmospheric at night, Ambrai feels like a French park, with its wrought-iron furniture, dusty ground and large shady trees, and there's a terrific bar to complement the dining, which is strong on Rajashani dishes.

✗ Other Areas

1559 AD
MULTICUISINE $$$

(☑2433559; PP Singhal Marg; mains ₹200-650; ⊘11am-11pm) Waiters in embroidered-silk waistcoats serve up lovely Indian, Thai and Continental dishes in elegant surroundings at this secluded restaurant near the northwestern side of Fateh Sagar. There are garden tables as well as several different rooms with just a few candlelit tables in each, and Indian classical music in the evenings. Includes a coffee shop with the best coffee we tasted in Udaipur.

Drinking

Most guesthouses have a roof terrace serving up cold Kingfishers with views over the lazy waters of Lake Pichola, but for a real treat try the top-end hotels. Note that you have to pay ₹25 to enter the City Palace complex (p149) if you're not staying in one of its hotels.

Paps Juice JUICE BAR
(inside Chandpol; juices ₹40-100; ☺9am-8pm) This bright-red spot is tiny but very welcoming, and a great place to refuel during the day with a shot of Vitamin C from a wide range of delicious juice mixes. If you want something more substantial, the muesli mix is pretty good too.

Jheel's Ginger Coffee Bar CAFE
(Jheel Palace Guest House, 56 Gangaur Ghat; coffee ₹50-100; ☺8am-8pm; ☎) This small but slick air-con-cooled cafe by the water's edge is on the ground floor of Jheel Palace Guest House. Large windows afford good lake views, and the coffee is excellent. Also does a range of cakes and snacks. Note, you can take your coffee up to the open-air rooftop restaurant if you like, but there's no alcohol served here.

Panera Bar BAR
(Shiv Niwas Palace Hotel; beer from ₹475, shots from ₹250; ☺11.30am-10pm) Sink into plush sofas surrounded by huge mirrors, royal portraits and beautiful paintwork, or sit out by the pool and be served like a maharaja.

Sunset Terrace BAR
(Fateh Prakash Palace Hotel; ☺7am-10.30pm) On a terrace overlooking Lake Pichola, this is perfect for a sunset gin and tonic. It's also a restaurant, with live music performed nightly.

Entertainment

Dharohar DANCE, PUPPETRY
(☑2523858; Bagore-ki-Haveli; Indian/foreigner ₹60/100, camera ₹100; ☺7-8pm) The beautiful Bagore-ki-Haveli (p151) hosts the best (and most convenient) opportunity to see Rajasthani folk dancing, with nightly shows of colourful, energetic Marwari, Bhil and western Rajasthani dances, as well as traditional Rajasthani puppetry.

Mewar Sound & Light Show CULTURAL PROGRAM
(Manek Chowk, City Palace; adult/child ₹100/200; ☺shows 7pm Sep-Feb, 7.30pm Mar-Apr, 8pm May-Aug) Fifteen centuries of intriguing Mewar history are squeezed into one atmospheric hour of commentary and light switching – in English from September to April.

Shopping

Tourist-oriented shops, selling miniature paintings; wood carvings; silver and other jewellery; bangles; traditional shoes; spices; leather-bound, handmade-paper notebooks; ornate knives; camel-bone boxes; and a large variety of textiles, line the streets radiating from Jagdish Chowk. Udaipur is known for its local crafts, particularly its miniature paintings in the Rajput-Mughal style, as well as some interesting contemporary art.

The local market area extends east from the **old clock tower** at the north end of Jagdish Temple Rd, and buzzes loudest in the evening. It's fascinating as much for browsing and soaking up local atmosphere as for buying. Bara Bazar, immediately east of the old clock tower, sells silver and gold, while its narrow side street, Maldas St, specialises in saris and fabrics. A little further east, traditional shoes are sold on Mochiwada. Foodstuffs and spices are mainly found around the new clock tower at the east end of the bazaar area, and at Mandi Market, about 200m north of the tower.

Sadhna CLOTHING
(☑2454655; www.sadhna.org; Jagdish Temple Rd; ☺10am-7pm) ✒ This is the crafts outlet for Seva Mandir, a long-established NGO working with rural and tribal people. The small shop sells attractive fixed-price textiles; profits go to the artisans and towards community development work.

Information

EMERGENCY
Police (☑2414600, 100) There are police posts at Surajpol, Hatipol and Delhi Gate, three of the gates in the old-city wall.

INTERNET ACCESS
You can surf the internet at plenty of places, particularly around Lal Ghat, for ₹30 per hour. Many places double as travel agencies, bookshops, art shops etc.

MEDICAL SERVICES
GBH American Hospital (☑24hr enquiries 2426000, emergency 9352304050; www.gbhamericanhospital.com; Meera Girls College Rd, 101 Kothi Bagh, Bhatt Ji Ki Bari) Modern, reader-recommended private hospital with 24-hour emergency service, about 2km northeast of the old city.

MONEY

There are lots of ATMs, including Axis Bank and State Bank ATMs on City Palace Rd near Jagdish Temple; HDFC, ICICI and State Bank ATMs near the bus stand; and two ATMs outside the train station. Places to change currency and travellers cheques include **Thomas Cook** (Lake Palace Rd; ☺9.30am-6.30pm Mon-Sat).

POST

Main Post Office (Chetak Circle; ☺10am-1pm & 1.30-6pm Mon-Sat) North of the old city.

Post Office (City Palace Rd; ☺10am-4pm Mon-Sat) Tiny post office that sends parcels (including packaging them up) and there are virtually no queues. Beside the City Palace's Badi Pol ticket office.

TOURIST INFORMATION

Small tourist information counters operate erratically at the train station and airport.

Tourist Office (☑2411535; Fateh Memorial Bldg; ☺10am-5pm Mon-Sat) Not situated in the most convenient position, 1.5km east of the Jagdish Temple (though only about 500m from the bus stand), this place dishes out a limited amount of brochures and information.

ℹ Getting There & Away

AIR

➤ **Air India** (☑2410999, airport office 2655453; www.airindia.com; 222/16 Mumal Towers, Saheli Rd) flies to Mumbai daily as well as to Delhi (via Jodhpur) daily.

➤ **Jet Airways** (☑5134000; www.jetairways.com; Airport) flies direct to Delhi twice daily, and Mumbai daily.

➤ SpiceJet (p121) has one direct daily flight to Delhi.

BUS

Private bus tickets can be bought at any one of the many travel agencies lining the road leading from Jagdish Temple to Daiji Footbridge.

The main bus stand is 1.5km east of the City Palace. Turn left at the end of Lake Palace Rd, take the first right then cross the main road at the end, just after passing through the crumbling old Surajpol Gate. It's around ₹40 in an autorickshaw.

If arriving by bus, turn left out of the bus stand, cross the main road, walk through Surajpol Gate then turn left at the end of the road before taking the first right into Lake Palace Rd.

TRAIN

The train station is about 2.5km southeast of the City Palace, and 1km directly south of the main bus stand. An autorickshaw between the train station and Jagdish Chowk should cost around ₹50. There's a prepaid autorickshaw stand at the station, though, so use that when you arrive.

There are no direct trains to Abu Road, Jodhpur or Jaisalmer.

➤ For Pushkar, four daily trains make the journey to Ajmer (sleeper/2nd class ₹480/135, five hours; 6am, 2.15pm, 5.15pm and 10.20pm). The same departures also make the trip to Chittorgarh (2nd class ₹85, two hours).

➤ Trains run daily to Jaipur (sleeper/2nd class ₹260/165, seven hours, 2.15pm and 10.20pm).

➤ Two daily trains run to Delhi (sleeper ₹385, 12 hours, 5.15pm and 6.15pm).

➤ Only one train runs daily to Bundi (sleeper ₹210, 4½ hours, 6.15pm).

➤ Only one daily train runs to Agra (sleeper ₹360, 12½ hours; 10.20pm).

ℹ Getting Around

TO/FROM THE AIRPORT

The airport is 25km east of town. A prepaid taxi to the Lal Ghat area costs ₹400.

BICYCLE & MOTORCYCLE

A cheap and environmentally friendly way to buzz around is by bike; many guesthouses can arrange bicycles to rent, costing around ₹50 per day. Scooters and motorbikes, meanwhile, are great for exploring the surrounding countryside.

RSRTC BUSES FROM UDAIPUR

DESTINATION	FARE (₹)	DURATION (HR)	FREQUENCY
Ahmedabad	196	5	hourly from 5am
Ajmer	233	7	hourly from 6am
Bundi	160	6	4 daily (mornings)
Chittorgarh	86	2½	half-hourly from 6am
Delhi	521	15	4 daily
Jaipur	315	9	hourly
Jodhpur	206	6-8	hourly
Kota	230	7	hourly
Mt Abu (Abu Rd)	133	4	6 daily (mornings)

MAJOR TRAINS FROM UDAIPUR

DESTINATION	TRAIN NO & NAME	DEPARTURE TIME	ARRIVAL TIME	FARE (₹)
Agra (Cantonment)	19666 Udaipur-Kurj Exp	10.20pm	11am	360/970 (A)
Ajmer	Udaipur-Jaipur SF SPL 2.15pm	2.15pm	7.10pm	175/485 (B)
Bundi	12964 Mewar Exp	6.15pm	10.33pm	210/535 (A)
Chittogarh	12982 Chetak Exp	5.15am	7.10pm	170/535 (A)
Delhi (Nizamuddin)	12964 Mewar Exp	6.15pm	6.35am	385/1085 (A)
Jaipur	19666 Udaipur-Kurj Exp	10.20pm	5.45am	260/690 (A)

Fares: (A) sleeper/3AC, (B) 2nd-class seat/AC chair

Heera Cycle Store (☉7.30am-9pm), just off Gangaur Ghat Rd, hires out bicycles/mountain bikes/mopeds/scooters/motorbikes/Bullets for ₹50/100/200/350/350/450 per day (with a deposit of US$50/100/200/300/400/500); you must show your passport and driver's licence.

TAXI

Most hotels, guesthouses and travel agencies (many of which are on the road leading down to the lake from Jagdish Temple) can organise a car and driver to just about anywhere you want. As an example, a return day trip to Ranakpur and Kumbhalgarh will cost you around ₹1800 per vehicle.

Around Udaipur

Kumbhalgarh

☑ 02954

About 80km north of Udaipur, **Kumbhalgarh** (Indian/foreigner ₹5/100, Light & Sound Show ₹200; ☉9am-6pm, Light & Sound Show 6.30pm) is a fantastic, remote fort, fulfilling romantic expectations and vividly summoning up the chivalrous, warlike Rajput era. One of the many forts built by Rana Kumbha (r 1433-68), under whom Mewar reached its greatest extents, the isolated fort is perched 1100m above sea level, with endless views melting into the blue distance. The journey to the fort, along twisting roads through the Aravalli Hills, is a highlight in itself.

Kumbhalgarh was the most important Mewar fort after Chittorgarh, and the rulers, sensibly, used to retreat here in times of danger. Not surprisingly, Kumbhalgarh was only taken once in its entire history. Even then, it took the combined armies of Amber, Marwar and Mughal emperor Akbar to breach its strong defences, and they only managed to hang on to it for two days.

The fort's thick walls stretch about 36km; they're wide enough in some places for eight horses to ride abreast and it's possible to walk right around the circuit (allow two days). They enclose around 360 intact and ruined temples, some of which date back to the Mauryan period in the 2nd century BC, as well as palaces, gardens, step-wells and 700 cannon bunkers. If you are staying here and want to make an early start on your hike around the wall, you can get into the fort before 9am, although no one will be around to sell you a ticket.

There's a **Light & Sound Show** (₹200) at the fort every evening at 6.30pm. The large and rugged Kumbhalgarh Wildlife Sanctuary (p160) can be visited from Kumbhalgarh. Ask at the Aodhi hotel about organising 4WD, horse or walking trips in the sanctuary.

🛏 Sleeping & Eating

Kumbhal Castle HOTEL $$
(☑ 242171; www.thekumbhalcastle.com; Fort Rd; r ₹2900-3500; ❈ ⊠) The modern Kumbhal Castle, 2km from the fort, has plain but pleasant white rooms featuring curly iron beds, bright bedspreads and window seats, shared balconies and good views. The super deluxe rooms are considerably bigger and worth considering for the few hundred extra rupees. There's a good in-house restaurant (lunch/dinner ₹350/400).

Aodhi HOTEL $$$
(☑ 8003722333, 242341; www.eternalmewar.in; Kumbhalgarh; r from ₹7500; ❈ @ 🛜 ⊠) Just under 2km from the fort is this luxurious and blissfully tranquil hotel with an inviting pool, rambling gardens and winter campfires. The spacious rooms, in stone

OFF THE BEATEN TRACK

KUMBHALGARH WILDLIFE SANCTUARY

Ranakpur is a great base for exploring the hilly, densely forested **Kumbhalgarh Wild-life Sanctuary** (Indian/foreigner ₹20/180, 4WD or car ₹150, camera/video free/₹400, guide per day ₹200; ☺ dawn-dusk), which extends over some 600 sq km to the northeast and southwest. It's known for its leopards and wolves, although the chances of spotting ante-lopes, gazelles, deer and possibly sloth bears are higher, especially from March to June. You will certainly see some of the sanctuary's 200-plus bird species.

There are several safari outfits on the road leading up to Kumbhalgarh Fort (don't believe posters suggesting tiger sightings), but some of the best safaris and treks are of-fered (to guests and nonguests) by Shivika Lake Hotel: options include three-hour 4WD safaris (₹850 per person), a three-hour forest and lake walk (₹350), a six-to-seven–hour round-trip walk leading to Parshuram Shiva Temple (₹650), and a one-way hike to Kumbhalgarh (about five hours; ₹850), with a two-person minimum and park fees included.

Note, there is a ticket office for the sanctuary right beside where the bus drops you off for the Jain temples, but the nearest of the sanctuary's four entrances is 2km beyond here, near Shivika Lake Hotel.

buildings, all boast their own palm-thatched terraces, balconies or pavilions, and assorted wildlife and botanical art and photos.

Nonguests can dine in the restaurant, where good standard Indian fare is the pick of the options on offer, or have a drink in the cosy Chowpal Bar. Room rates plummet from April to September.

❶ Getting There & Away

From Udaipur's main bus stand, catch an hourly Ranakpur-bound bus as far as Saira (₹57, 2¼ hours), a tiny crossroads town where you can change for a bus to Kumbhalgarh (₹30, one hour, hourly). That bus, which will be bound for Kelwara, will drop you at the start of the approach road to the fort, leaving you with a pleasant 1.5km walk to the entrance gate.

The last bus back to Saira swings by at 5.30pm (and is always absolutely jam-packed with vil-lagers). The last bus from Saira back to Udaipur leaves at around 8pm.

To get to Ranakpur from Kumbhalgarh, head first to Saira then change for Ranakpur (₹14, 40 minutes, at least hourly).

A day-long round trip in a private car from Udaipur to Kumbhalgarh and Ranakpur will cost around ₹1800 per car.

Ranakpur

☎ 02934

Ranakpur　　　　　　　JAIN TEMPLE
(camera/video ₹100/300; ☺ Jains 6am-7pm, non-Jains noon-5pm) At the foot of a steep wooded escarpment of the Aravalli Hills, Ranakpur is one of India's biggest and most important Jain temple complexes. It's 75km northwest of Udaipur, and 12km west of Kumbhalgarh as the crow flies (but 50km by road, via Saira). **Chaumukha Mandir** (Four-Faced Temple), the main temple, is dedicated to Adinath, the first Jain *tirthankar* (depict-ed in the many Buddha-like images in the temple), and was built in the 15th century in milk-white marble.

An incredible feat of Jain devotion, the Chaumukha Mandir is a complicated series of 29 halls, 80 domes and 1444 individually engraved pillars. The interior is completely covered in knotted, lovingly wrought carv-ing, and has a marvellously calming sense of space and harmony. Shoes, cigarettes, food and all leather articles must be left at the entrance; women who are menstruating are asked not to enter.

Also exquisitely carved and well worth inspecting are two other Jain temples, ded-icated to **Neminath** (22nd *tirthankar*) and **Parasnath** (23rd *tirthankar*), both within the complex, and a nearby **Sun Temple**. About 1km from the main complex is the **Amba Mata Temple**.

Buses from Udaipur and Saira will drop you by the entrance to the temple complex, before continuing past Shivika Lake Hotel (2km), and then going on to Jodhpur.

🛏 Sleeping & Eating

Shivika Lake Hotel　　　GUESTHOUSE $$
(☎ 285078, 9799118573; r ₹600-1200, tent ₹1200; ❄@☎) Two kilometres north of the tem-ple, Shivika is a welcoming, rustic and

family-run hotel that provides free pick-ups and drop-offs at the bus stop near the temple. You can stay in small, cosy rooms amid leafy gardens, or safari-style tents. Two of the tents have prime positions beside beautiful Nalwania Lake, on the edge of the property.

Due to the presence of a few crocodiles, the lake isn't safe for swimming, but there's a swimming pool right beside it and some meals (mains ₹70 to ₹160, thali ₹170, buffet lunch ₹300) are served here too.

Getting There & Away

There are direct buses to Ranakpur from the main bus stands in both Udaipur (₹68, three hours, hourly) and Jodhpur (₹139, four to five hours). You'll be dropped outside the temple complex unless you state otherwise. Return services start drying up at around 7pm.

A day-long round trip in a private car from Udaipur to Ranakpur and Kumbhalgarh costs around ₹1800.

Mt Abu

02974 / POP 22,200 / ELEV 1200M

Rajasthan's only hill station sits among green forests on the state's highest mountain at the southwestern end of the Aravalli Range, close to the Gujarat border. Quite unlike anywhere else in Rajasthan, Mt Abu provides Rajasthanis, Gujaratis and a steady flow of foreign tourists with respite from the scorching temperatures and arid, beige terrain found elsewhere. It's a particular hit with honeymooners and middle-class families from Gujarat.

Mt Abu town sits towards the southwest end of the plateau-like upper part of the mountain, which stretches about 19km from end to end and 6km from east to west. The town is surrounded by the flora- and fauna-rich, 289-sq-km Mt Abu Wildlife Sanctuary, which extends over most of the mountain from an altitude of 300m upwards.

The mountain is of great spiritual importance for both Hindus and Jains and has over 80 temples and shrines, most notably the exquisite Jain temples at Delwara, built between 400 and 1000 years ago.

Try to avoid arriving in Diwali (October or November) or the following two weeks, when prices soar and the place is packed. Mt Abu also gets pretty busy from mid-May to mid-June, before the monsoon. This is when the **Summer Festival** hits town, with music, fireworks and boat races. In the cooler months, you'll find everyone wrapped up in shawls and hats; pack something woolly to avoid winter chills in poorly heated hotel rooms.

Sights & Activities

Nakki Lake   LAKE
Scenic Nakki Lake, the town's focus, is one of Mt Abu's biggest attractions. It's so named because, according to legend, it was scooped out by a god using his *nakh* (nails). Some Hindus thus consider it a holy lake. Another version of its origins is that it was constructed by the British in the 19th century.

It's a pleasant 45-minute stroll around the perimeter – the lake is surrounded by hills, parks and strange rock formations. The best known, **Toad Rock**, looks like a toad about to hop into the lake.

Sunset Point   VIEWPOINT
Sunset Point is a popular place to watch the brilliant setting sun. Hordes stroll out here every evening to catch the end of the day, the food stalls and all the usual jolly hill-station entertainment. To get there, follow Sunset Point road west of the Polo Ground out of town.

**Brahma Kumaris
Peace Hall & Museum**   MUSEUM
The white-clad people you'll see around town are members of the **Brahma Kumaris World Spiritual University** (www.bkwsu. com), a worldwide organisation whose headquarters are here in Mt Abu. The university's **Universal Peace Hall** (Om Shanti Bhawan; ☺8am-6pm), just north of Nakki Lake, where free 30-minute tours are available, includes an introduction to the Brahma Kumaris philosophy (be prepared for a bit of proselytising). The organisation also runs the **World Renewal Spiritual Museum** (☺8am-8pm) **FREE** in the town centre.

Tours

The RSRTC runs full-day (₹100) and half-day (₹45) bus tours of Mt Abu's main sights, leaving from the bus stand at 9.30am and 1pm respectively. Both tours visit Achalgarh, Guru Shikhar and the Delwara Temples and end at Sunset Point. The full-day tour also includes Adhar Devi, the Brahma Kumaris Peace Hall and Honeymoon Point. Admission and camera fees and the ₹20 guide fee are extra. Make reservations at the main bus stand.

Mt Abu

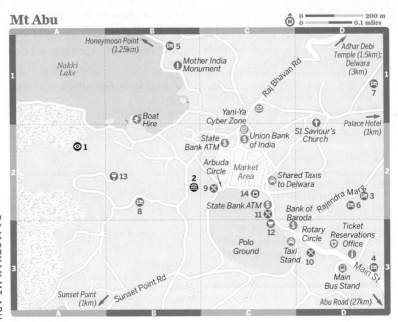

Mt Abu

🛏 Sleeping

Room rates can double (or worse) during the peak seasons – mid-May to mid-June, Diwali and Christmas/New Year – but generous discounts are often available at other times in midrange and top-end places. Book way ahead at Diwali.

Shri Ganesh Hotel HOTEL $
(☑ 237292; lalit_ganesh@yahoo.co.in; dm ₹250, s ₹500, d ₹600-1500; @ 🛜) A fairly central and popular budget spot, Shri Ganesh is well set up for travellers, with an inexpensive cafe and plenty of helpful travel information. Rooms are well used but kept clean. Some have squat toilets and limited hours for hot water. Daily forest **walks** (☑ 237292; lalit_ganesh@yahoo.co.in; 1hr per person ₹500, 4hr ₹1000) and cooking lessons are on offer.

Mushkil Aasan GUESTHOUSE $$
(☑ 235150, 9429409660; ccrrps@yahoo.com; s/d/q ₹1100/1200/1800; 🌀 🛜) A lovely guesthouse nestled in a tranquil vale in the north of town (near Global Hospital), with nine homely decorated rooms and a delightfully planted garden. Home-style Gujarati meals

are available, and check-out is a civilised 24 hours. Rooms next to reception can be noisy.

Hotel Lake Palace
HOTEL $$

(☑237154; http://savshantihotels.com; r incl breakfast ₹2500-2700; ❀ 🛜) Spacious and friendly, Lake Palace has an excellent location, with small lawns overlooking the lake. Rooms are simple, uncluttered, bright and clean. All have AC and some have semiprivate lakeview terrace areas. There are rooftop and garden multicuisine restaurants too, and even an aquarium next door.

Kishangarh House
HERITAGE HOTEL $$$

(☑238092; www.royalkishangarh.com; Rajendra Marg; cottages ₹3500, r ₹4500-6500; ❀🛜) The former summer residence of the maharaja of Kishangarh has been successfully converted into a heritage hotel. The deluxe rooms in the main building are big, with extravagantly high ceilings. The cottage rooms at the back are smaller but cosier. There's a delightful sun-filled drawing room and the lovely terraced gardens are devotedly tended.

Hotel Hilltone
HOTEL $$$

(☑238391; www.hotelhilltone.com; Main St; s/d from ₹4500/5500; P🛜❀) A modern, well-run hotel in spacious grounds, the punningly named Hilltone takes a leaf out of the more famous hospitality brand with stylishly comfortable and modern rooms that punch above the price tag. The inhouse Mulberry Restaurant (p164) serves alcohol and nonveg Indian food – a rarity in Mt Abu.

Connaught House
HERITAGE HOTEL $$$

(☑235439; www.welcomheritagehotels.com; Rajendra Marg; r incl breakfast ₹7400; ❀@) Connaught House is a charming colonial-era bungalow that looks like an English cottage with lots of sepia photographs, dark wood, angled ceilings and a gorgeous shady garden. It's owned by Jodhpur's ruling family. The five rooms in the original 'cottage' have the most character – and big baths. The other five sit in a newer building with good views from their own verandahs.

✖ Eating

Kanak Dining Hall
INDIAN $

(Lake Rd; Gujarati/Punjabi thali ₹60/130; ⏱8.30am-3.30pm & 7-11pm) The excellent all-you-can-eat thalis are contenders for Mt Abu's best meals. There's seating indoors

---

DON'T MISS

DELWARA TEMPLES

Delwara Temples (donations welcome; ⏱Jains 6am-6pm, non-Jains noon-6pm) These Jain temples are Mt Abu's most remarkable attraction and feature some of India's finest temple decoration. They predate the town of Mt Abu by many centuries and were built when this site was just a remote mountain vastness. It's said that the artisans were paid according to the amount of dust they collected, encouraging them to carve ever more intricately. Whatever their inducement, there are two temples here in which the marble work is dizzyingly intense.

The older of the two is the **Vimal Vasahi**, on which work began in 1031 and was financed by a Gujarati chief minister named Vimal. Dedicated to the first *tirthankar,* Adinath, it took 1500 masons and 1200 labourers 14 years to build, and allegedly cost ₹185.3 million. Outside the entrance is the **House of Elephants**, featuring a procession of stone elephants marching to the temple, some of which were damaged long ago by marauding Mughals. Inside, a forest of beautifully carved pillars surrounds the central shrine, which holds an image of Adinath himself.

The **Luna Vasahi Temple** is dedicated to Neminath, the 22nd *tirthankar,* and was built in 1230 by the brothers Tejpal and Vastupal for a mere ₹125.3 million. Like Vimal, the brothers were both Gujarati government ministers. The marble carving here took 2500 workers 15 years to create, and its most notable feature is its intricacy and delicacy, which is so fine that, in places, the marble becomes almost transparent. The many-layered lotus flower that dangles from the centre of the dome is a particularly astonishing piece of work.

As at other Jain temples, leather articles (including belts and shoes) cameras and phones must be left at the entrance, and menstruating women are asked not to enter.

Delwara is about 3km north of Mt Abu town centre: you can walk there in less than an hour, or hop aboard a shared taxi (₹10 per person) from up the street opposite Chacha Cafe. A taxi all to yourself should be ₹100, or ₹200 round-trip with one hour's waiting.

in the busy dining hall or outside under a canopy. It's near the bus stand for the lunch break during the all-day RSRTC tour.

Sankalp   SOUTH INDIAN **$$**
(Hotel Maharaja, Lake Rd; mains ₹90-220; ⊘9am-11pm) A branch of a quality Gujarat-based chain serving up excellent South Indian vegetarian fare. Unusual fillings like pineapple or spinach, cheese and garlic are available for its renowned dosas and *uttapams* (savoury South Indian rice pancake), which come with multiple sauces and condiments. Order *masala papad* (wafer with spicy topping) for a tasty starter.

Mulberry Restaurant   INDIAN **$$**
(Hilltone Hotel, Main St; mains ₹250-320) Mt Abu's Gujarati tourists make veg thalis the order of the day in the town, so if you're craving a bit of nonveg, the smart Mulberry Restaurant at the Hilltone Hotel is the place to go. There are plenty of meaty Indian options on the menu (although the biryanis are a bit bland) and alcohol is often served to wash it down.

Arbuda   INDIAN **$$**
(Arbuda Circle; mains ₹100-150; ⊘7am-10.30pm) This big restaurant is set on a sweeping open terrace filled with chrome chairs. It's very popular for its Gujarati, Punjabi and South Indian food, and does fine Continental breakfasts and fresh juices.

🍷 Drinking

Most of the more upmarket hotels have bars; the prices are predictably high, but the heritage hotels can justify this with their quaint atmospheres.

Polo Bar   BAR
(📞02974-235176; www.royalfamilyjaipur.com; ⊘11.30-3.30pm & 7.30-11pm) The terrace at the Jaipur Hotel, formerly the maharaja of Jaipur's summer palace, is a dreamy place for an evening tipple, with divine views over the hills, lake and the town's twinkling lights. Meals are served (₹135 to ₹300).

Cafe Coffee Day   CAFE
(Rotary Circle; coffee from ₹60; ⊘9am-11pm) A branch of the popular caffeine-supply chain. The tea and cakes aren't bad either.

🛍 Shopping

The street leading down to Nakki Lake is lined with bright little shops mostly flogging all sorts of kitsch curios, and there's more of the same around the market area. **Chacha Museum** (⊘10am-8pm), a larger, fixed-price shop with some crafts and souvenirs, is worth a browse.

ℹ Information

There are State Bank ATMs on Raj Bhavan Rd, opposite Hotel Samrat International and outside the tourist office. There's a Bank of Baroda ATM on Lake Rd.

Main Post Office (Raj Bhavan Rd; ⊘9am-5pm Mon-Sat)

Union Bank of India (Main Market; ⊘10am-3pm Mon-Fri, to 12.30pm Sat) The only bank changing travellers cheques and currency.

Yani-Ya Cyber Zone (Raj Bhavan Rd; internet-per hr ₹40; ⊘9am-10pm)

ℹ Getting There & Away

Access to Mt Abu town is by a dramatic 28km-long road that winds its way up thickly forested hillsides from the town of Abu Road, where the nearest train station is. Some buses from other cities go all the way up to Mt Abu, others only go as far as Abu Road. Buses (₹30, one hour) run between Abu Road and Mt Abu town half-hourly from about 6am to 7pm. A taxi from Abu Road to Mt Abu is ₹300/400 by day/night.

MAJOR TRAINS FROM ABU ROAD

DESTINATION	TRAIN NO & NAME	DEPARTURE TIME	ARRIVAL TIME	FARE (₹)
Ahmedabad	19224 Jammu Tawi-Ahmedabad Exp	10.50am	3pm	140/485 (A)
Delhi (New Delhi)	12957 Swarna J Raj Exp	8.50pm	7.30am	1370/1875 (B)
Jaipur	19707 Aravali Exp	10.10am	6.55pm	260/690 (A)
Jodhpur	19223 Ahmedabad-Jammu Tawi Exp	3.25pm	7.40pm	185/485 (A)
Mumbai	19708 Aravali Exp	4.55pm	6.35am	355/960 (A)

Fares: (A) sleeper/3AC, (B) 3AC/2AC

TREKKING AROUND MT ABU

Getting off the tourist trail and out into the forests and hills of Mt Abu is a revelation. This is a world of isolated shrines and lakes, weird rock formations, fantastic panoramas, nomadic villagers, orchids, wild fruits, plants used in ayurvedic medicine, sloth bears (which are fairly common), wild boars, langurs, 150 bird species and even the occasional leopard.

Mahendra 'Charles' Dan of **Mt Abu Treks** (☑ 9414154854; www.mount-abu-treks.blog spot.com; Hotel Lake Palace; 3-4hr trek per person ₹500, full-day incl lunch ₹1000) arranges tailor-made treks ranging from gentle village visits to longer, wilder expeditions into Mt Abu Wildlife Sanctuary. He's passionate and knowledgeable about the local flora and fauna. Treks include a three- to four-hour trek, a full day including lunch, and an overnight village trek including all meals (₹2000). The sanctuary entrance fee (Indian/foreigner ₹20/160) is not included.

The Shri Ganesh Hotel (p162) also organises good one- or four-hour hikes (₹100/500) hikes starting at 7am or 4pm.

A warning from the locals: it's very unsafe to wander unguided in these hills. Travellers have been mauled by bears, or mugged (and worse) by other people.

BUS

Services from Mt Abu bus stand include:

Ahmedabad (₹138, seven hours, hourly from 6am to 9pm)

Jaipur (seat/sleeper ₹386/411, 11 hours, one daily)

Jodhpur (₹203, six hours, roughly hourly)

Udaipur (₹120, 4½ hours, four daily)

TRAIN

Abu Road station is on the line between Delhi and Mumbai via Ahmedabad. An autorickshaw from Abu Road train station to Abu Road bus stand costs ₹10. Mt Abu has a **railway reservation centre** (☺8am-2pm Mon-Sat), above the tourist office, with quotas on most of the express trains.

Around Mt Abu

Guru Shikhar

At the northeast end of the Mt Abu plateau, 17km from the town, rises 1722m-high Guru Shikhar, Rajasthan's highest point. A winding road goes almost all the way to the summit where you'll find the **Atri Rishi Temple**, complete with a priest and fantastic, huge views. A popular spot, it's a highlight of the RSRTC tour (p161); if you decide to go it alone, a 4WD will cost ₹500 return.

NORTHERN RAJASTHAN (SHEKHAWATI)

Far less visited than other parts of Rajasthan, the Shekhawati region is most famous for its extraordinary painted *havelis* (traditional, ornately decorated residences that enclose one or more courtyards), highlight-ed with dazzling, often whimsical, murals. Part of the region's appeal and mystique is due to these works of art being found in tiny towns, connected to each other by single-track roads that run through lonely, arid countryside. Today it seems curious that such care, attention and money was lavished on these out-of-the-way houses, but from the 14th century onwards Shekhawati's towns were important trading posts on the caravan routes from Gujarati ports.

What makes the artwork on Shekhawati's *havelis* so fascinating is the manner in which their artists combined traditional subjects, such as mythology, religious scenes and images of the family, with contemporary concerns, including brand-new inventions and accounts of current events, many of which these isolated painters rendered straight from their imaginations.

Nawalgarh

☑ 01594 / POP 56,500

Nawalgarh is a small, nontouristy town almost at the very centre of the Shekhawati region, and makes a great base for exploring. It boasts several fine *havelis*, a colourful, mostly pedestrianised bazaar and some excellent accommodation options.

◉ Sights

Dr Ramnath A Podar Haveli Museum MUSEUM

(www.podarhavelimuseum.org; admission ₹100, camera ₹30; ☺8.30am-6.30pm) Built in 1902 on the eastern side of town, and known locally as 'Podar Haveli', this is one of the region's few buildings to have been thoroughly restored. The paintings of this *haveli* are defined in strong colours, and are the most vivid murals in town, although purists point to the fact that they have been simply repainted rather than restored. On the ground floor are several galleries on Rajasthani culture, including costume, turbans, musical instruments and models of Rajasthan's forts.

Morarka Haveli Museum　　　　MUSEUM
(admission ₹50; ⊙ 8am-7pm) This museum has well-presented original paintings, preserved for decades behind doorways blocked with cement. The inner courtyard hosts some gorgeous Ramayana scenes; look out for the slightly incongruous image of Jesus on the top storey, beneath the eaves in the courtyard's southeast corner. Turn left out of Dr Ramnath A Podar Haveli Museum, then take the first right and it's on your right.

Bhagton ki Choti Haveli　　HISTORIC BUILDING
(Bhagat Haveli; admission ₹50) On the western wall of Bhagton ki Choti Haveli is a locomotive and a steamship. Above them, elephant-bodied *gopis* (milkmaids) dance. Adjacent to this, women dance during the Holi festival. Inside you'll find other murals, including one strange picture (in a room on the western side) of a European man with a cane and pipe, and a dog on his shoulder.

To get here, turn left out of Morarka Haveli, take the first right, then left, then first right again and it's on your left.

🏃 Activities & Tours

Ramesh Jangid at **Apani Dhani** and his son Rajesh at **Ramesh Jangid's Tourist Pension** (☑ 224060; www.touristpension.com) are keen to promote sustainable rural tourism. They organise guided hiking trips (two to three days from ₹1900 per person), guided camel-cart rides (half-day ₹1500) to outlying villages, and guided tours by car (full day from ₹800 per person) to other towns in the region. They can also arrange lessons in Hindi, tabla drumming, cooking and local crafts such as *bandhani*.

Roop Niwas Kothi (☑ 222008; www.royalridingholidays.com; 1hr/half-day/full day ₹1000/3000/6000) specialises in high-end horse excursions. Elaborate excursions are available, ranging from one night to a week, including accommodation in luxury tents.

🛏 Sleeping & Eating

DS Bungalow　　　　GUESTHOUSE $
(☑ 9983168916; s ₹350-450, d ₹400-500) Run by a friendly, down-to-earth couple, this simple place with boxy air-cooled rooms is a little out of town on the way to Roop Niwas Kothi. It's backed by a garden with a pleasant outdoor mud-walled restaurant serving decent home cooking. The more energetic can arrange camel tours here.

★ **Apani Dhani**　　　GUESTHOUSE $$
(☑ 222239; www.apanidhani.com; r/cottages with AC ₹1800/2400, with fan ₹1600/2200; ❄ 🛜) 🍃 This award-winning ecotourism venture is a delightfully relaxing place. Rooms with comfortable beds are in cosy mud-hut, thatched-roof bungalows set around a bougainvillea-shaded courtyard. The adjoining organic farm supplies food and there are solar lights, water heaters and compost toilets. It's on the western side of the Jaipur road. Five per cent of the room tariff goes to community projects. Tours around the area, via bicycle, car, camel cart or foot, are available.

Shekhawati Guesthouse　　GUESTHOUSE $$
(☑ 224658; www.shekhawatiguesthouse.com; r ₹600/800, cottage ₹1000-1400; ❄ @ 🛜) This corner of rural loveliness is more like a homestay run by a very friendly couple. There are six rooms in the main building plus five lovely, mud-walled thatched cottages in the garden. The organic garden supplies most of the hotel's produce needs, which can be enjoyed in the lovely outdoor restaurant. It's 4km east of the bus stand (₹60 by taxi). Pick-up from the bus or train station can be arranged, as can cooking lessons.

Ramesh Jangid's Tourist Pension　　GUESTHOUSE $$
(☑ 224060; www.touristpension.com; s/d/tr from ₹800/1050/1350; @ 🛜) 🍃 Near the Maur Hospital, on the western edge of town, this pension is well known, so if you get lost, just ask a local to point you in the right direction. The guesthouse, run by genial Rajesh, Ramesh's son, offers homely, clean accommodation in spacious rooms with big beds. Some rooms have furniture carved by Rajesh's grandfather, and the more expensive rooms also have murals created by visiting artists. Pure veg meals, made with organic ingredients, are available, including a delectable vegetable thali for ₹180. The family also arranges all sorts of tours around Shekhawati.

Shekhawati

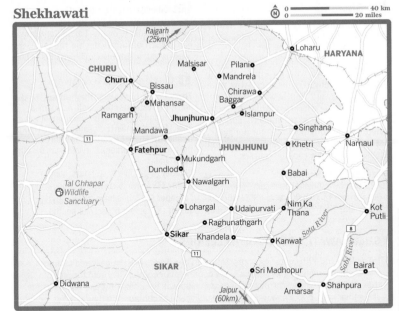

ℹ Getting There & Away

The main bus stand is little more than a dusty car park accessed through a large, yellow double-arched gateway. Services run roughly every hour to Jaipur (₹105, 3½ hours), Jhunjhunu (₹30, one hour) and Mandawa (₹25, 45 minutes). Nawalgarh is on a narrow-gauge train line with slow daily trains running between Jhunjhunu to Jaipur (2nd-class seats only).

Jhunjhunu

☏ 01592 / POP 100,500

Shekhawati's most important commercial centre has a different atmosphere to that of the smaller towns, with lots of traffic, concrete, and hustle and bustle befitting the district capital. It does, though, have some appealing *havelis* and a colourful bazaar.

◎ Sights

Rani Sati Temple   HINDU TEMPLE
(Ram Niwas Bagh; ⊙ 4am-10pm) The enormous, multistorey Rani Sati Temple is notorious for commemorating an act of *sati* by a merchant's wife (after whom the temple is named) in 1595. It's fronted by two courtyards, around which 300 rooms offer shelter to pilgrims. The main hall, in the far courtyard, is made of marble with elaborate silver repoussé work before the inner sanctum. There's a tile-and-mirror mosaic on the ceiling and a relief frieze on one wall depicts the story of Rani Sati.

It's a 10-minute walk north of the private bus stand. Turn left out of the bus stand, take the first left, then keep asking for Rani Sati Mandir.

Modi Havelis   HISTORIC BUILDING
(Nehru Bazaar; admission ₹50) The Modi Havelis face each other and house some of Jhunjhunu's best murals and woodcarving. The *haveli* on the eastern side has a painting of a woman in a blue sari sitting before a gramophone; a frieze depicts a train, alongside which soldiers race on horses. The spaces between the brackets above show the Krishna legends. The *haveli* on the western side has some comical pictures, featuring some remarkable facial expressions and moustaches.

Around the archway, between the inner and outer courtyards, there are some glass-covered portrait miniatures, along with some fine mirror-and-glass tilework. In the second half of the antechamber, Krishna dances with the *gopis* while angels fly overhead. The inner courtyard shows the hierarchy of the universe, with deities in the upper frieze, humans in the middle band, and animal and floral motifs below.

🛏 Sleeping

Hotel Jamuna Resort   HOTEL **$$**
(☏512696; www.hoteljamunaresort.com; near Nath Ka Tilla; r ₹1500-3500; 🅿@🛜🌊) Hotel Jamuna Resort has everything you need. The rooms in the older wing are either vibrantly painted with murals or decorated with traditional mirrorwork (but beware rooms with vanishingly tiny windows), while the rooms in the newer wing are modern and airy. There's an inviting pool (₹50 for nonguests) set in the serene garden and purpose-built kitchens set up for cooking courses.

Hotel Shiv Shekhawati   HOTEL **$$**
(☏232651; www.shivshekhawati.com; Khemi Shakti Rd; s/d from ₹800/1000; 🅿@) Shiv Shekhawati is the best budget option with plain but squeaky-clean rooms. It's 600m from the private bus stand on the eastern edge of town. The affable owner, Laxmi Kant Jangid, is a wealth of knowledge on the villages of Shekhawati and tours can be organised here.

ℹ Getting There & Away

There are two bus stands: the main bus stand and the private bus stand. Both have similar services and prices, but the government-run buses from the main bus stand run much more frequently. Shared autorickshaws run between the two (₹8 per person). Services from the main bus stand:

Bikaner (₹174, five to six hours, hourly)
Delhi (₹183, five to six hours, hourly)
Fatehpur (₹42, one hour, half-hourly)
Jaipur (₹135, four hours, half-hourly)

SHEKHAWATI'S OUTDOOR GALLERIES

In the 18th and 19th centuries, shrewd Marwari merchants lived frugally and far from home while earning money in India's new commercial centres. They sent the bulk of their vast fortunes back to their families in Shekhawati to construct grand *havelis* to show their neighbours how well they were doing and to compensate their families for their long absences. Merchants competed with one another to build ever more grand edifices – homes, temples, step-wells – which were richly decorated, both inside and out, with painted murals.

The artists responsible for these acres of decoration largely belonged to the caste of *kumhars* (potters) and were both the builders and painters of the *havelis*. Known as *chajeras* (masons), many were commissioned from beyond Shekhawati – particularly from Jaipur, where they had been employed decorating the new capital's palaces – and others flooded in from further afield to offer their skills. Soon, there was a cross-pollination of ideas and techniques, with local artists learning from the new arrivals.

The early paintings are strongly influenced by Mughal decoration, with floral arabesques and geometric designs. The Rajput royal courts were the next major influence; scenes from Hindu mythology are prevalent – Krishna is particularly popular.

With the arrival of Europeans, walls were embellished with paintings of the new technological marvels to which the Shekhawati merchants had been exposed to in centres such as Calcutta. Pictures of trains, planes, telephones, gramophones and bicycles featured, often painted directly from the artist's imagination. The British are invariably depicted as soldiers, with dogs or holding bottles of booze.

Haveli walls were frequently painted by the *chajeras* from the ground to the eaves. Often the paintings mix depictions of the gods and their lives with everyday scenes featuring modern inventions, such as trains and aeroplanes, even though these artists themselves had never seen them. Hence, Krishna and Radha are seen in flying motorcars and Europeans can be observed inflating hot-air balloons by blowing into them.

These days most of the *havelis* are still owned by descendants of the original families, but not inhabited by their owners, for whom small-town Rajasthan has lost its charm. Many are occupied by a single *chowkidar* (caretaker), while others may be home to a local family. Though they are pale reflections of the time when they accommodated the large households of the Marwari merchant families, they remain a fascinating testament to the changing times in which they were created. Only a few *havelis* have been restored; many more lie derelict, crumbling slowly away.

For a full rundown on the history, people, towns and buildings of the area, track down a copy of *The Painted Towns of Shekhawati*, by Ilay Cooper, an excellent book which can be picked up at bookshops in the region or Jaipur.

Mandawa (₹20, one hour, half-hourly)
Nawalgarh (₹35, one hour, half-hourly)

The train line to Jaipur via Nawalgarh is narrow gauge, and is not connected to the rest of the rail network. There are slow daily services, but generally it's quicker and more convenient to travel by bus.

Fatehpur

☏ 01571 / POP 78,400

Established in 1451 as a capital for nawabs (Muslim ruling princes), Fatehpur was their stronghold for centuries before it was taken over by the Shekhawati Rajputs in the 18th century. It's a busy little town, with plenty of *havelis*, many in a sad state of disrepair, but with a few notable exceptions.

Sights

Apart from the magnificent Haveli Nadine Le Prince, other sights include the nearby **Jagannath Singhania Haveli**; the **Mahavir Prasad Goenka Haveli** (often locked, but with superb paintings); **Geori Shankar Haveli**, with mirrored mosaics on the antechamber ceiling; and **Harikrishnan Das Saraogi Haveli**, with a colourful facade and iron lacework.

Haveli Nadine Le Prince   HISTORIC BUILDING
(☏233024; www.cultural-centre.com; admission incl guided tour ₹200; ☉9am-6pm) This 1802 *haveli* has been stunningly restored by French artist Nadine Le Prince and is now one of the most exquisite in Shekhawati. Nadine is only here for part of the year, but enlists foreign volunteers to manage the building and conduct the detailed guided tours. There's a cafe of sorts secreted away in a garden courtyard, plus a small gallery. Some of the rooms have been converted into small but beautifully decorated guest rooms (p169).

The *haveli* is around 2km north of the two main bus stands, down a lane off the main road. Turn right out of the bus stands, and the turning will eventually be on your right, or hop into an autorickshaw.

Sleeping & Eating

Haveli Cultural Centre
Guest House & Art Café   BOUTIQUE HOTEL $$
(☏233024; www.cultural-centre.com; Haveli Nadine Le Prince; r from ₹1300; ❄) The beautifully restored Haveli Nadine Le Prince has opened its artist residence rooms to travellers. Several traditional-style rooms over-

look the central courtyard. To just visit the Art Café you'll have to pay to get into the *haveli*, but this is a good option for a light lunch (meals ₹100 to ₹400). It's a cosy place with low tables, next to the garden, as well as Indian snacks.

❶ Getting There & Around

From the private bus stand on the Churu–Sikar road, buses leave for Jhunjhunu (₹28, one hour), Mandawa (₹22, one hour), Churu (₹25, one hour) and Ramgarh (₹16, 45 minutes). From the RSRTC bus stand, which is further south down the same road, buses leave for Jaipur (₹88, 3½ hours, hourly), Delhi (₹184, seven hours, six daily) and Bikaner (₹125, 3½ hours, hourly).

Mandawa

☏ 01592 / POP 20,800

Of all the towns in the Shekhawati region, Mandawa is the one best set up for tourists, with plenty of places to stay and some decent restaurants. It's a little touristy (although this is a relative term compared with other parts of Rajasthan), but this small 18th-century settlement is still a pleasant base for your *haveli* explorations.

There is only one main drag, with narrow lanes fanning off it. The easy-to-find Hotel Mandawa Haveli is halfway along this street and makes a handy point of reference. Most buses drop passengers off on the main drag as well as by the bus stand.

Sights

Binsidhar Newatia Haveli   HISTORIC BUILDING
This 1920s *haveli* on the northern side of the Fatehpur–Jhunjhunu road houses the State Bank of Bikaner & Jaipur. There are fantastically entertaining paintings on the external eastern wall, including a European woman in a chauffeur-driven car, the Wright brothers in flight watched by women in saris, a strongman hauling along a car, and a bird-man flying in a winged device.

Murmuria Haveli   HISTORIC BUILDING
The Murmuria Haveli dates back to the 1930s. From the sandy courtyard out front, you can get a good view of the southern external wall of the adjacent double *haveli*: it features a long frieze depicting a train and a railway crossing. Nehru is depicted on horseback holding the Indian flag. Above the arches on the southern side of the courtyard are two paintings of gondolas on the canals of Venice.

🛏 Sleeping & Eating

There are at least half a dozen *haveli* hotels here, either on or near the main drag. Rooms in them range from ₹1200 to ₹4000. Mandawa is small so wandering around town to find a room is relatively easy.

Hotel Shekhawati　　　　HOTEL $
(☑ 9314698079; www.hotelshekwati.com; r ₹400-1800; ❄@🛜) Near Mukundgarh Rd, the only real budget choice in town is run by a retired bank manager and his son (who's also a registered tourist guide). Bright, comically bawdy murals painted by artistic former guests give the rooms a splash of colour. Tasty meals are served on the peaceful rooftop, and competitively priced camel, horse and 4WD tours can also be arranged.

Hotel Mandawa Haveli　　HERITAGE HOTEL $$
(☑ 223088; www.hotelmandawa.com; s/d from ₹2200/3700; ❄) Close to Sonathia Gate, on the main road, this retreat is set in a glorious, restored 1890s *haveli* with rooms surrounding a painted courtyard. The cheapest rooms are small, so it's worth splashing out on a suite, filled with arches, window seats and countless small windows. There's a rooftop restaurant serving good food; it's especially romantic at dinner time, when the lights of the town twinkle below. A set dinner costs ₹450.

Hotel Castle Mandawa　　HERITAGE HOTEL $$$
(☑ 223124; www.castlemandawa.com; s/d from ₹4500/6000; ❄@🛜🏊) Mandawa's large upmarket hotel in the town's converted fort is a swish and generally comfortable choice. Some rooms are far better appointed than others (the best are the suites in the tower, with four-poster and swing beds), so check a few before you settle in. The gardens and grounds boast restaurants, a coffee shop and cocktail bar, pool and ayurvedic spa.

Monica Rooftop Restaurant　　INDIAN $$
(mains ₹100-300; ⏲8am-9pm) This delightful rooftop restaurant, in between the fort gate and main bazaar, serves tasty meals. It's in a converted *haveli*, but sadly only the facade, rather than the restaurant itself, has frescoes.

Bungli Restaurant　　INDIAN $$
(Goenka Chowk; mains ₹130-300; ⏲5am-10pm) A popular outdoor travellers' eatery near the Bikaner bus stand, Bungli serves piping-hot tandoori and cold beer from a down-at-heel setting. The food is cooked fresh by a chef

who hails from Hotel Castle Mandawa. Early risers can have an Indian breakfast and yoga class for a total of ₹375.

ℹ Getting There & Away

The main bus stand, sometimes called Bikaner bus stand, has frequent services (roughly half-hourly). The main bus stand is at one end of the main drag, on your left as the road bears right. It's a few hundred metres walk left from Hotel Mandawa Haveli.

There is also a separate Nawalgarh bus stand, just off the main drag, with services to Nawalgarh only. Both bus stands are so small they are unrecognisable as bus stands unless a bus is waiting at them. Look for the chai stalls that cluster beside them and you should have the right spot.

Bikaner (₹154, four hours)
Fatehpur (₹22, 30 minutes)
Jhunjhunu (₹20, one hour)
Nawalgarh (₹25, 45 minutes)

WESTERN RAJASTHAN

Jodhpur

☑ 0291 / POP 1,033,900

Mighty Mehrangarh, the muscular fort that towers over the Blue City of Jodhpur, is a magnificent spectacle and an architectural masterpiece. Around Mehrangarh's base, the old city, a jumble of Brahmin-blue cubes, stretches out to the 10km-long, 16th-century city wall. Inside is a tangle of winding, glittering, medieval streets, which never seem to lead where you expect them to, scented by incense, roses and sewers, with shops and bazaars selling everything from trumpets and temple decorations to snuff and saris.

Traditionally, blue signified the home of a Brahmin, but non-Brahmins have got in on the act too. Glowing with a mysterious light, the blue tint is thought to repel insects.

Modern Jodhpur stretches well beyond the city walls, but it's the immediacy and buzz of the old Blue City and the larger-than-life fort that capture travellers' imaginations. This crowded, hectic zone is Jodhpur's main tourist area, and it often seems you can't speak to anyone without them trying to sell you something. Areas of the old city further west, such as Navchokiya, are just as atmospheric, with far less hustling.

History

Driven from their homeland of Kannauj, east of Agra, by Afghans serving Mohammed of Ghori, the Rathore Rajputs fled west around AD 1200 to the region around Pali, 70km southeast of Jodhpur. They prospered to such a degree that in 1381 they managed to oust the Pratiharas of Mandore, 9km north of present-day Jodhpur. In 1459 the Rathore leader Rao Jodha chose a nearby rocky ridge as the site for a new fortress of staggering proportions, Mehrangarh, around which grew Jodha's city: Jodhpur.

Jodhpur lay on the vital trade route between Delhi and Gujarat. The Rathore kingdom grew on the profits of sandalwood, opium, dates and copper, and controlled a large area that became cheerily known as Marwar (the Land of Death), due to its harsh topography and climate. It stretched as far west as what's now the India–Pakistan border area, and bordered with Mewar (Udaipur) in the south, Jaisalmer in the northwest, Bikaner in the north, and Jaipur and Ajmer in the east.

◎ Sights & Activities

★ Mehrangarh   FORT

(www.mehrangarh.org; Indian/foreigner incl audio guide ₹/60/400, camera/video ₹100/250, human guide ₹225; ⊘ 9am-5pm) Rising perpendicular and impregnable from a rocky hill that itself stands 120m above Jodhpur's skyline, Mehrangarh is one of the most magnificent forts in India. The battlements are 6m to 36m high, and as the building materials were chiselled from the rock on which the fort stands, the structure merges with its base. Still run by the Jodhpur royal family, Mehrangarh is packed with history and legend. Mehrangarh's main entrance is at the northeast gate, **Jai Pol**. You don't need a ticket to enter the fort, only the museum section.

It's about a 300m walk up from the old city to the entrance, or you can take a winding 5km autorickshaw ride (around ₹100). The superb audio guide (available in 11 languages) is included with the museum ticket, but bring ID or a credit card as deposit.

Jai Pol was built by Maharaja Man Singh in 1808 following his defeat of invading forces from Jaipur. Past the **museum ticket office** and a small cafe, the 16th-century **Dodh Kangra Pol** was an external gate before Jai Pol was built, and still bears the scars of 1808 cannonball hits. Through here, the main route heads up to the left through the 16th-century **Imritia Pol** and then **Loha Pol**, the fort's original entrance, with iron spikes to deter enemy elephants. Just inside the gate are two sets of small hand prints, the *sati* (self-immolation) marks of royal widows who threw themselves on their maharajas' funeral pyres – the last to do so were Maharaja Man Singh's widows in 1843.

Past Loha Pol you'll find a restaurant and **Suraj Pol**, which gives access to the museum. Once you've visited the museum, continue on from here to the panoramic **ramparts**, which are lined with impressive antique artillery.

Also worth exploring is the right turn from Jai Pol, where a path winds down to the **Chokelao Bagh**, a restored and gorgeously planted 18th-century Rajput garden (you could lose an afternoon here lolling under shady trees reading a book), and the **Fateh Pol** (Victory Gate). You can exit here into the old city quarter of Navchokiya.

➡ Museum

This beautiful network of stone-latticed courtyards and halls, formerly the fort's palace, is a superb example of Rajput architecture, so finely carved that it often looks more like sandalwood than sandstone. The **galleries** around **Shringar Chowk** (Anointment Courtyard) display India's best collection of elephant howdahs and Jodhpur's royal palanquin collection.

One of the two galleries off **Daulat Khana Chowk** displays textiles, paintings, manuscripts, headgear and the curved sword of the Mughal emperor Akbar; the other gallery is the armoury. Upstairs is a fabulous **gallery of miniature paintings** from the sophisticated Marwar school and the beautiful 18th-century **Phul Mahal** (Flower Palace), with 19th-century wall paintings depicting the 36 moods of classical *ragas* as well as royal portraits; the artist took 10 years to create them using a curious concoction of gold leaf, glue and cow's urine.

Takhat Vilas was the bedchamber of Maharaja Takhat Singh (r 1843–73), who had just 30 maharanis and numerous concubines. Its beautiful ceiling is covered with Christmas baubles. You then enter the extensive *zenana*, whose lovely latticed windows (from which the women could watch the goings-on in the courtyards) are said to feature over 250 different designs. Here you'll find the **Cradle Gallery**, exhibiting the elaborate cradles of infant princes, and the 17th-century **Moti Mahal** (Pearl Palace), which was the palace's main durbar hall (royal reception hall) for official meetings and receptions, with gorgeously colourful stained glass.

Jodhpur

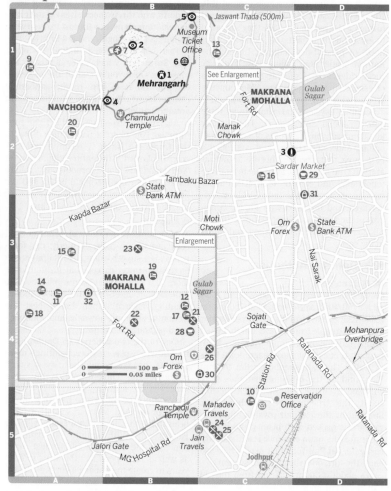

★Rao Jodha Desert Rock Park   PARK
(☏9571271000; www.raojodhapark.com; Mehrangarh; admission ₹50, guide ₹100; ⊙8am-6pm Oct-Mar, 7am-7pm Apr-Sep) This 72-hectare park – and model of intelligent ecotourism – sits in the lee of Mehrangarh. It has been lovingly restored and planted with native species to show the natural diversity of the region. The park is criss-crossed with walking trails that take you up to the city walls, around Devkund Lake, spotting local birds, butterflies and reptiles. For an extra insight into the area's native flora and fauna, take along one of the excellent local guides.

Walks here are the perfect restorative if the Indian hustle has left you in need of breathing space. Visit early in the morning or in the late afternoon for the most pleasant temperatures. The visitors centre is thoughtfully put together, and there's a small cafe too.

Jaswant Thada   HISTORIC BUILDING
(Indian/foreigner ₹15/30, camera/video ₹25/50; ⊙9am-5pm) This milky-white marble memorial to Maharaja Jaswant Singh II, sitting above a small lake 1km northeast of Mehrangarh, is an array of whimsical domes. It's

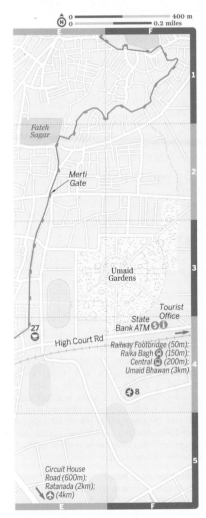

and southern ends. The narrow, winding lanes of the old city spread out in all directions from here. Westward, you plunge into the old city's commercial heart, with crowded alleys and bazaars selling vegetables, spices, sweets, silver and handicrafts.

Umaid Bhawan Palace   PALACE
(museum Indian/foreigner ₹25/60; ⊘ museum 9am-5pm) Take an autorickshaw to this hilltop palace, 3km southeast of the old city. The current royal incumbent, Gaj Singh II, still lives in part of the building. Built in 1929, the 365-room edifice was designed by the British architect Henry Lanchester for Maharaja Umaid Singh. It took more than 3000 workers 15 years to complete, at a cost of around ₹11 million. The building is mortarless, and incorporates 100 wagon-loads of Makrana marble and Burmese teak in the interior. Apparently its construction began as a royal job-creation program during a time of severe drought. Much of the building has been turned into a suitably grand hotel.

Casual visitors are not welcome at either the royal residence or the hotel, but you can visit the **museum**, housed in one side of the building. It includes photos showing the elegant art deco design of the palace interior, plus an eccentric collection of elaborate clocks. Don't miss the maharaja's highly polished classic cars, displayed in front of the museum, by the entrance gate.

Flying Fox   ADVENTURE
(www.flyingfox.asia; tour ₹1800; ⊘ 9am-5pm) This circuit of six zip-lines flies back and forth over walls, bastions and lakes on the northern side of Mehrangarh. A brief training session is given before you start and safety standards are good: awesome is the verdict of most who dare. Flying Fox has a desk near the main ticket office and its starting point is in the Chokelao Bagh. Tours last up to 1½ hours, depending on the group size. Book online for a discount on the walk-up price.

★ Festivals & Events

In September or October Jodhpur hosts the colourful **Marwar Festival**, which includes polo and a camel tattoo. It coincides with the excellent **Rajasthan International Folk Festival** (www.jodhpurriff.org), five days of music concerts by Indian and international artists held at Mehrangarh. This most spectacular of music venues also hosts April's **Jodhpur Flamenco and Gypsy Festival** (http://jfgfestival.com).

a welcome, peaceful spot after the hubbub of the city, and the views across to the fort and over the city are superb. Built in 1899, the cenotaph has some beautiful *jalis* (carved marble lattice screens) and is hung with portraits of Rathore rulers going back to the 13th century. Look out for the memorial to a peacock that flew into a funeral pyre.

Clock Tower   MONUMENT
The century-old clock tower is an old city landmark surrounded by the vibrant sounds, sights and smells of Sardar Market, which is marked by triple gateways at its northern

RAJASTHAN JODHPUR

Jodhpur

🛏 Sleeping

The old city has something like 100 guesthouses, most of which scramble for your custom as soon as you get within breathing distance of Sardar Market.

If a rickshaw rider or friendly local is clamouring to take you to a guesthouse or hotel, it's probably because he is aiming to receive a commission from them. There's a growing anti-commission movement among hoteliers here, but many still pay touts, or your rickshaw/taxi driver an absurd 50% of what you pay for your room. Don't believe drivers or strangers on the street who tell you the place you want has closed, is full, is under repair, is far from the centre etc.

Many lodgings can organise a pick-up from the train station or bus stops, even at night, if you call ahead. Otherwise, for most places in the old city you can avoid nonsense by getting dropped at the clock tower and walking from there.

🛏 Old City (Sardar Market)

Mangal Haveli Guest House   GUESTHOUSE **$**
(☑ 2611001; www.mangalhaveli.com; Killi Khana, Fort Rd; r ₹500-700; ☜) A good budget option between the fort and the clock tower. Rooms are simple but good value for the price; those facing inside are darker but quieter, compared to the airier rooms facing

the busy thoroughfare. It has the obligatory rooftop terrace restaurant.

Hill View Guest House   GUESTHOUSE **$**
(☑ 2441763; Makrana Mohalla; r ₹250-600) Perched just below the fort walls, this is run by a friendly, enthusiastic, no-hassle, Muslim family, who'll make you feel right at home. Rooms are basic, clean and simple, all with bathrooms (but not all with decent windows), and the terrace has a great view over the city. Good, home-cooked veg and nonveg food is on offer.

Kesar Heritage Hotel   GUESTHOUSE **$**
(☑ 09983216625; www.kesarheritage.com; Makrana Mohalla; r ₹700-1200) A popular recent addition to Jodhpur's budget accommodation scene, Kesar plays a good hand with large airy rooms (a few have balconies) and friendly, helpful management, plus a side-street location that puts noisily sputtering rickshaws out of earshot of light sleepers. The rooftop restaurant looks up to Mehrangarh.

Nirvana Hotel   HOTEL **$**
(☑ 5106280; nirwanahome.jod@gmail.com; 1st fl, Tija Mata ka Mandir, Tambaku Bazar; r ₹800-1200; ☀☜) It's not often you get to lay your head down in a converted Hindu temple, but Nirvan Hotel gives you the chance. Rooms run off a lovely courtyard thick with pot plants, and although windows face inside,

your views are instead of original 150-year-old temple frescoes (fixtures and fittings are thankfully newer). Room 11 is the highlight – it's under an original temple dome, and looks straight over the rooftops to Mehrangarh.

Hare Krishna Guest House GUESTHOUSE **$**
(☏ 2635307; www.harekrishnaguesthouse.net; Makrana Mohalla; r ₹600-1200; ☎) An old house that has been extended upwards and squeezes in rooms and stairs wherever possible. The range of rooms is impressive, from the cavelike cheapie to the spacious fort-view rooms. Friendly staff, free wi-fi and, of course, a rooftop restaurant.

Pushp Paying Guest House GUESTHOUSE **$**
(☏ 2648494; sonukash2003@yahoo.co.in; Pipli-ki-Gali, Naya Bass, Manak Chowk; r ₹500-800; ✱ @ ☎) This small family-home-cum-guesthouse has five clean, colourful rooms with windows. It's tucked down the narrowest of alleys, but you get an up-close view of Mehrangarh from the rooftop restaurant, where owner Nikhil rustles up great vegetarian fare (dishes ₹30 to ₹80).

Haveli Inn Pal HERITAGE HOTEL **$$**
(☏ 2612519; www.haveliinnpal.com; Gulab Sagar; r incl breakfast ₹2050-2550; ✱ @ ☎) The smaller, 12-room sibling of Pal Haveli is accessed through the same grand entrance, but is located around to the right in one wing of the grand *haveli*. It's a simpler heritage experience, with comfortable rooms and lake or fort views from the more expensive ones. It also has its own good rooftop restaurant, a mere chapati toss from Indique at Pal Haveli. Free pick-ups from Jodhpur transport terminals are offered, and discounts are often available for single occupancy.

Raas BOUTIQUE HOTEL **$$$**
(☏ 2636455; www.raasjodhpur.com; Tunvarji-ka-Jhalra; r incl breakfast ₹21,000-40,000; ✱ @ ☎ ☋) Developed from a 19th-century city mansion, Jodhpur's first contemporary-style boutique hotel is a splendid retreat of clean, uncluttered style, hidden behind a big castlelike gateway. The red-sandstone-and-terrazzo rooms come with plenty of luxury touches. Most have balconies with great Mehrangarh views – also to be enjoyed from the lovely pool in the neat garden-courtyard.

Pal Haveli HERITAGE HOTEL **$$$**
(☏ 3293328; www.palhaveli.com; Gulab Sagar; r incl breakfast ₹5500-8500; ✱ @ ☎) This stunning *haveli*, the best and most attractive

in the old city, was built by the Thakur of Pal in 1847. There are 21 charming, spacious rooms, mostly large and elaborately decorated in traditional heritage style, surrounding a cool central courtyard. The family still live here and can show you their small museum. Three restaurants serve excellent food and the rooftop Indique (p176) boasts views.

Old City (Navchokiya)

Cosy Guest House GUESTHOUSE **$**
(☏ 9829023390, 2612066; www.cosyguesthouse.com; Chuna Ki Choki, Navchokiya; r ₹400-1550, without bathroom ₹250; @ ☎) A friendly place in an enchanting location, this 500-year-old glowing blue house has several levels of higgledy-piggledy rooftops and a mix of rooms, some monastic, others comfortable. Ask the rickshaw driver for Navchokiya Rd, from where the guesthouse is signposted, or call the genial owner, Mr Joshi.

★ Singhvi's Haveli GUESTHOUSE **$$**
(☏ 2624293; www.singhvihaveli.com; Ramdev-ji-ka-Chowk, Navchokiya; r ₹900-2600; ✱ @ ☎) This red-sandstone, family-run, 500-odd-year-old *haveli* is an understated gem. Run by two friendly brothers, Singhvi's has 13 individual rooms, ranging from the simple to the magnificent Maharani Suite with 10 windows and a fort view. The relaxing vegetarian restaurant is decorated with sari curtains and floor cushions.

Train Station Area

Govind Hotel HOTEL **$$**
(☏ 2622758; www.govindhotel.com; Station Rd; r ₹600-2000; ✱ @ ☎) Well set up for travellers, with helpful management, an internet cafe, and a location convenient to the Jodhpur train station. All rooms are clean and tiled, with fairly smart bathrooms. There's a rooftop restaurant and coffee shop (p176) with excellent espresso and cakes.

✕ Eating

It's convenient to eat in your guesthouse or hotel restaurant (which is usually on the roof, with a fort view), but there are also a number of places well worth going out to.

Jharokha MULTICUISINE **$**
(Hotel Haveli; mains ₹70-170; ⊙ until 11pm) The rooftop terraces of the Hotel Haveli host one of the best veg restaurants in Jodhpur. As

well as the excellent food and views there's nightly entertainment in the form of traditional music and dance. The dishes include Rajasthani specialities and traditional North Indian favourites, as well as pizza, pasta and pancakes for the homesick.

Jhankar Choti Haveli
MULTICUISINE $

(Makrana Mohalla; mains ₹90-150; 8am-10pm;) Stone walls and big cane chairs in a leafy courtyard, prettily painted woodwork and whirring fans set the scene at this semi-open-air travellers' favourite. It serves up good Indian vegetarian dishes plus pizzas, burgers and baked cheese dishes.

Omelette Shops
STREET FOOD $

(omelettes from ₹25; 10am-10pm) On your right and left as you leave Sadar Market through its northern gate, these two omelette stalls compete for the attentions of passing travellers by knocking up seemingly endless numbers and varieties of cheap, delicious omelettes. Both do a decent job, and are run by characters worth spending a few minutes with.

Three tasty, spicy boiled eggs cost ₹15, and a two-egg masala and cheese omelette with four pieces of bread is ₹30.

Nirvana
INDIAN $$

(1st fl, Tija Mata ka Mandir, Tambaku Bazar; mains ₹120-160, regular/special thali ₹160/250; 10.30am-10pm) Sharing premises with a Rama temple, Nirvana has both an indoor cafe, covered in 150-year-old Ramayana wall paintings, and a rooftop eating area with panoramic views. The Indian vegetarian food is among the most delicious you'll find in Rajasthan. The special thali is enormous and easily enough for two. Continental and Indian breakfasts are served in the cafe.

Kalinga Restaurant
INDIAN $$

(off Station Rd; mains ₹130-300; 8am-11pm;) This restaurant near Jodhpur train station is smart and popular. It's in a dimly lit setting and has AC, a well-stocked bar, and tasty veg and nonveg North Indian tandooris and curries. Try the lal maans, a mouthwatering Rajasthani mutton curry.

On the Rocks
INDIAN $$

(5102701; Circuit House Rd; mains ₹115-325; 12.30-3.30pm & 7.30-11pm) This leafy garden restaurant, 2km southeast of the old city, is very popular with locals and tour groups. It has tasty Indian cuisine, including lots of barbecue options and rich and creamy cur-

ries, plus a small playground and a cavelike bar (open 11am to 11pm) with a dance floor (for couples only).

Mid Town
INDIAN $$

(off Station Rd; mains ₹100-150; 7am-10.30pm;) This clean restaurant does great veg food, including some Rajasthani specialities, some particular to Jodhpur, such as *chakki-ka-sagh* (wheat dumpling cooked in rich gravy), *bajara-ki-roti pachkuta* (*bajara* wheat roti with local vegetables) and *kabuli* (vegetables with rice, milk, bread and fruit).

★ Indique
INDIAN $$$

(3293328; Pal Haveli Hotel; mains ₹250-350; 11am-11pm) This candle-lit rooftop restaurant at the Pal Haveli hotel is the perfect place for a romantic dinner, with superb views over the fort, clock tower and Umaid Bhawan. The food covers traditional tandoori, biryanis and North Indian curries, but the Rajasthani *laal maas* (mutton curry) is a delight. Ask the barman to knock you up a gin and tonic before dinner.

Drinking

Try a glass of *makhania* lassi, a thick and filling saffron-flavoured version of that most refreshing of drinks.

Coffee drinkers will enjoy the precious beans and espresso machines at the deliciously air-conditioned **Cafe Sheesh Mahal** (Pal Haveli Hotel; coffee from ₹80; 9am-9pm); the rooftop coffee shop at the **Govind Hotel** (Govind Hotel, Station Rd; 10am-10pm); and, for those who need their dose of double-shot espresso, a branch of **Cafe Coffee Day** (Jaljog Circle, High Court Rd; 10am-11pm).

For other forms of liquid refreshment, pull up a stool at the **Trophy Bar** (Umaid Bhawan Palace, Umaid Bhawan Rd; 11am-3pm & 6-11pm).

Shri Mishrilal Hotel
CAFE

(Sardar Market; lassi ₹30; 8.30am-10pm) Just inside the southern gate of Sardar Market, this place is nothing fancy but whips up the most superb creamy *makhania* lassis. These are the best in town, probably in all of Rajasthan, possibly in all of India.

Shopping

Plenty of Rajasthani handicrafts are available, with shops selling textiles and other wares clustered around Sardar Market and along Nai Sarak (bargain hard).

Jodhpur is famous for antiques, with a concentration of showrooms along Palace

JODHPUR'S JODHPURS

A fashion staple for self-respecting horsey people all around the world, jodhpurs are riding breeches – usually of a pale cream colour – that are loose above the knee and tapered from knee to ankle. It's said that Sir Pratap Singh, a legendary Jodhpur statesman, soldier and horseman, originally designed the breeches for the Jodhpur Lancers. When he led the Jodhpur polo team on a tour to England in 1897, the design caught on in London and then spread around the world.

If you fancy taking home an authentic pair from the city they originated in, head to **Monarch Garments,** (☑ 9352353768; www.monarch-garments.com; A-13 Umaid Bhavan Palace Rd; ☉ 10.30am-8.45pm) opposite the approach road leading up to Umaid Bhawan Palace, where you can buy ready-made jodhpurs or have a pair tailored for you within two days. Prices are polo-club–worthy, starting at around ₹7000.

Rd, 2km southeast of the centre. These warehouse-sized shops are fascinating to wander around, but they're well known to Western antiques dealers, so you'll be hard-pressed to find any bargains. Also remember that the trade in antique architectural fixtures may be contributing to the desecration of India's cultural heritage (beautiful old *havelis* are often ripped apart for their doors and window frames), and restrictions apply to the export of items over 100 years old. However, most showrooms deal in antique reproductions, and can make a piece of antique-style furniture and ship it home for you. The best bets for quality replica antiques are **Ajay Art Emporium** (Palace Rd; ☉ 10am-7pm) or **Rani Handicrafts** (Palace Rd; ☉ 10am-7pm). These shops also have more portable (often less expensive) items than furniture, such as textiles, carvings and silverware.

MV Spices   FOOD & DRINK
(www.mvspices.com; Nai Sarak; ☉ 9am-9pm) The most famous spice shop in Jodhpur (and believe us, there are lots of pretenders!), MV Spices has several small branches around town that are run by the seven daughters of the founder of the original stall. It will cost around ₹80 to ₹100 for 100g bags of spices, and the owners will email you recipes so you can use your spices correctly when you get home.

Sambhali Boutique   CLOTHING, ACCESSORIES
(Makrana Mohalla; ☉ 10am-8pm Mon-Sat, noon-8pm Sun) ✐ This small but interesting shop sells goods made by women who have learned craft skills with the **Sambhali Trust** (☑ 0291-2512385; www.sambhali-trust. org; c/o Durag Niwas Guest House, 1st Old Public Park, Raika Bagh, Jodhpur), which works to empower disadvantaged women and girls. Items include attractive *salwar* trousers,

cute stuffed silk or cloth elephants and horses, bracelets made from pottery beads, silk bags, and block-printed muslin curtains and scarves.

Krishna Book Depot   BOOKS
(Sardar Market; ☉ 10.30am-7.30pm) Upstairs is an Aladdin's Den of new and used books, piled high in no apparent order – great for browsing. Downstairs is handicrafts.

ⓘ Information

There are foreign-card-friendly ATMs dotted around the city, though there are few in the old city, one exception being near Shahi Guest House. Internet cafes, found all around town, especially in the old city, charge around ₹40 per hour.

Main Post Office (Station Rd; ☉ 9am-4pm Mon-Fri, to 3pm Sat, stamp sales only 10am-3pm Sun)

Om Forex (Sardar Market; internet per hr ₹30; ☉ 9am-10pm) Also exchanges currency and travellers cheques.

Police (Sardar Market; ☉ 24hr) Small police post inside the market's northern gate.

Tourist Office (☑ 2545083; High Court Rd; ☉ 9am-6pm Mon-Fri) Offers a free map and willingly answers questions.

ⓘ Getting There & Away

AIR

Jet Airways (☑ 5102222; www.jetairways.com; Residency Rd) and **Indian Airlines** (☑ 2510758; www.indian-airlines.nic.in; Circuit House Rd) fly daily to Delhi and Mumbai.

BUS
Government-Run Buses

Government-run buses leave from **Central Bus Stand** (Raika Bagh), directly opposite Raika Bagh train station. Walk east along High Court

MAJOR TRAINS FROM JODHPUR

DESTINATION	TRAIN NO & NAME	DEPARTURE TIME	ARRIVAL TIME	FARE (₹)
Ajmer	54801 Jodhpur-Ajmer Fast Passenger	7am	12.35pm	175/485
Bikaner	14708 Ranakpur Exp	10am	3.35pm	190/485
Delhi	12462 Mandor Exp	8pm	6.45am	370/485
Jaipur	14854 Marudhar Exp	9.45am	3.30pm	210/555
Jaisalmer	14810 Jodhpur-Jaisalmer Exp	11.45pm	5.25am	205/540
Mumbai	14707 Ranakpur Exp	2.45pm	9.40am	445/1195

Fares: sleeper/3AC

Rd, then turn right under the small tunnel. Services include:

Ajmer (₹158, five hours, hourly until 6.30pm)

Bikaner (₹191, 5½ hours, frequently from 5am to 6pm)

Jaipur (₹259, seven hours, frequently from 5am to midnight)

Jaisalmer (₹208, 5½ hours, six daily)

Mt Abu/Abu Road (₹203, 7½ hours, 14 daily until 9pm)

Osian (₹45, 1½ hours, half-hourly until 10pm)

Rohet (₹36, one hour, every 15 minutes)

Udaipur (₹210, seven hours, 10 daily until 6.30pm)

Private Buses

You can book private buses through your hotel, although it's cheaper to deal directly with the bus operators on the road in front of Jodhpur train station. **Jain Travels** (✆2633831; www. jaintravels.com; ✆7am-11pm) and **Mahadev Travels** (✆2633927; MG Hospital Rd; ✆7am-10pm) are both reliable. Buses leave from bus stands out of town, but the operator should provide you with free transport (usually a shared autorickshaw) from their ticket office. Example services are as follows:

Ajmer (₹220, six hours, at least six daily)

Bikaner (₹200, five hours, at least five daily)

Delhi (seat/sleeper ₹578/788, 12 hours, daily)

Jaipur (seat/sleeper ₹240/368, 7½ hours, five daily)

Jaisalmer (₹240, 5½ hours, hourly)

Mt Abu direct (seat/sleeper ₹250/430, 7½ hours, daily)

Mumbai (seat only ₹1600, 18 hours, at least four daily)

TAXI

You can organise taxis for intercity trips (or longer) through most accommodation places or deal directly with drivers. There's a taxi stand outside Jodhpur train station. A reasonable price is ₹7 to ₹8 per kilometre (for a non-AC car), with a minimum of 250km per day. The driver will charge at least ₹100 for overnight stops and will charge for his return journey.

TRAIN

The computerised **booking office** (Station Rd; ✆8am-8pm Mon-Sat, to 1.45pm Sun) is 300m northeast of Jodhpur train station. Window 786 sells the tourist quota.

➺ Four daily trains make the trip to Jaisalmer (5½ hours; 5.30am, 7.35am, 5.45pm and 11.45pm).

➺ Four daily trains go to Bikaner (5½ hours; 10am, 10.45am, 1.50pm and 8.15pm). The 1.50pm takes more than seven hours.

➺ Eleven daily trains go to Jaipur (five to six hours), departing between 6.10am and midnight.

➺ Four daily trains go to Delhi (11 to 14 hours; 6.25am, 7pm, 8pm and 11pm); the early evening departures are fastest.

➺ Six go to Mumbai (16 to 19 hours; 5.35am, 2.45pm, 6.20pm, 6.45pm, 7.20pm and 11.55pm). Each of these goes via Abu Road, for Mt Abu (4½ hours).

➺ For Pushkar, there are two daily trains to Ajmer (5½ hours, 6.25am and 7am).

There are no direct trains to Udaipur; change at Marwar Junction.

❶ Getting Around

Despite the absurd claims of some autorickshaw drivers, the fare between the clock tower area and the train stations or Central Bus Stand should be about ₹50. **Suncity Cab** (✆6888888) and **Rajasthan Cab** (✆6222222) have reliable fixed-price taxis that can be pre-booked.

The airport is 5km south of the city centre; a taxi/autorickshaw will cost about ₹300/150.

Around Jodhpur

The mainly arid countryside around Jodhpur is dotted with surprising lakes, isolated forts and palaces, and intriguing villages. It's home to a clutch of fine heritage hotels where you can enjoy the slower pace of rural life.

Southern Villages

A number of traditional villages are strung along and off the Pali road southeast of Jodhpur. Most hotels and guesthouses in Jodhpur offer tours to these villages, often called Bishnoi village safaris. The Bishnoi are a Hindu sect who follow the 500-year-old teachings of Guru Jambheshwar, who emphasised the importance of protecting the environment long before it was popular to do so. Many visitors are surprised by the density – and fearlessness – of wildlife such as blackbuck, bluebulls (nilgai), chinkara gazelles and desert fox around the Bishnoi villages. The Bishnoi hold all animal life sacred. The 1730 sacrifice of 363 villagers to protect khejri trees is commemorated in September at Khejadali village, where there is a memorial to the victims fronted by a small grove of khejri trees.

At **Guda Bishnoi**, the locals are traditionally engaged in animal husbandry. There's a small lake (full only after a good monsoon) where migratory birds such as demoiselle cranes, and mammals such as blackbucks and chinkaras, can be seen, particularly at dusk when they come to drink.

The village of **Salawas** is a centre for weaving beautiful *dhurries* (rugs), a craft also practised in many other villages. A co-operative of 42 families runs the **Roopraj Dhurry Udyog** (☑ 0291-2896658; rooprajdurry@sify.com), through which all profits go to the artisans. A 3ft by 5ft *dhurrie* costs a minimum of ₹2800, a price based on two weavers working several hours a day for a month at ₹50 per day each. Other families are involved in block-printing.

Bishnoi village tours from Jodhpur tend to last four hours and cost around ₹800 per person. Those run by Deepak Dhanraj of **Bishnoi Village Safari** (☑ 9829126398; www.bishnoivillagesafari.com) receive good feedback, but many other places offer them.

Rohet

Rohet Garh (☑ 02936-268231; www.rohetgarh.com; Rohet Village; s/d ₹8500/9500, ste ₹12,000; ❋ @ 🛜 ⊠), in Rohet village, 40km south of Jodhpur on the Pali road, is one of the area's most appealing heritage hotels. This 350-year-old, lovingly tended manor has masses of character and a tranquil atmosphere, which obviously helped Bruce Chatwin when he wrote *The Songlines* here, and William Dalrymple when he began *City of*

Djinns in the same room, No 15. Rohet Garh has a gorgeous colonnaded pool, charming green gardens, great food (lunch/dinner ₹750/900) and lovely, individual rooms. It also possesses a stable of fine Marwari horses and organises rides ranging from two-hour evening trots (₹2000) to six-day countryside treks, sleeping in luxury tents. The quirky Om Bana Temple (p180) is a short bus ride from here.

A taxi from Jodhpur will cost around ₹800. There are also frequent buses; once here, turn right out of Rohet's tiny bus stand, take the first right and keep walking for about 1km.

Osian

The ancient Thar Desert town of Osian, 65km north of Jodhpur, was an important trading centre between the 8th and 12th centuries. Known as Upkeshpur, it was dominated by the Jains, whose wealth left a legacy of exquisitely sculpted, well-preserved temples.

The **Mahavira Temple** (Indian/foreigner free/₹10, camera/video ₹50/100; ⊙ 6am-8.30pm) surrounds an image of the 24th *tirthankar*, formed from sand and milk. **Sachiya Mata Temple** (⊙ 6am-7.15pm) is an impressive

---

WORTH A TRIP

THE MOTORBIKE TEMPLE

Om Bana Temple (Motorbike Temple) One of the strangest temples in all India stands 8km south of Rohet beside the Pali road, near Chotila village. The deity at Om Bana Temple is a garland-decked Enfield Bullet motorcycle, known as Bullet Baba. The story goes that local villager Om Bana died at this spot in the 1980s when his motorbike skidded into a tree. The bike was taken to the local police station, but then mysteriously twice made its own way back to the tree, and travellers along the road started seeing visions of Om Bana – inevitably leading to the machine's deification.

Any time of day or night people can be seen at the open-air shrine here, simultaneously praying for safe journeys and making offerings of liquor.

Buses from Jodhpur to Rohet should continue on to Om Bana, but check with the driver. Otherwise, you can hop on almost any passing bus from Rohet (₹10).

---

walled complex where both Hindus and Jains worship.

Prakash Bhanu Sharma, a personable Brahmin priest, has an echoing **guesthouse** (☑ 02922-274331, 9414440479; s/d without bathroom ₹250/300) geared towards pilgrims, opposite the Mahavira Temple. **Safari Camp Osian** (☑ 9928311435; www.safaricamposian.com; tent s/d incl dinner, breakfast & camel ride ₹7000/9000) is a fancier, tented camp option.

Gemar Singh (☑ 9460585154; www.hacra. org; per person per day approx ₹1400, minimum 2 people) arranges popular camel safaris, homestays, camping, desert walks and 4WD trips in the deserts around Osian and the Rajput and Bishnoi villages. The cost is around ₹1400 per person per day (minimum two people). Pick up from Osian bus station, or from Jodhpur, can be arranged.

There are frequent buses from Jodhpur to Osian (₹45, 90 minutes). Trains between Jodhpur and Jaisalmer also stop here. A return taxi from Jodhpur costs about ₹1200.

Jaisalmer

☑ 02992 / POP 89,000

The fort of Jaisalmer is a breathtaking sight: a massive sandcastle rising from the sandy plains like a mirage from a bygone era. No place better evokes exotic camel-train trade routes and desert mystery. Ninety-nine bastions encircle the fort's still-inhabited twisting lanes. Inside are shops swaddled in bright embroideries, a royal palace and numerous businesses looking for your tourist rupee.

Despite the commercialism it's hard not to be enchanted by this desert citadel. Beneath the ramparts, particularly to the north, the narrow streets of the old city conceal magnificent *havelis,* all carved from the same golden-honey sandstone as the fort – hence Jaisalmer's designation as the Golden City.

A city that has come back almost from the dead in the past half-century, Jaisalmer may be remote but it's certainly not forgotten – indeed it's one of Rajasthan's most popular tourist destinations, and few people come here without climbing onto a camel in the surrounding Thar Desert. Competition to get your bum into a camel saddle can be fierce, with some operators adopting unpleasant hard-sell tactics. Generally speaking, though, this is a much more laid-back, hassle-free place to stay than the likes of Jaipur or Jodhpur.

Jaisalmer celebrates its desert culture in January or February each year with the action-packed **Desert Festival** featuring camel races, camel polo, folk music, snake charmers, turban-tying contests and the famous Mr Desert competition. Many events take place at the Sam Sand Dunes.

History

Jaisalmer was founded way back in 1156 by a leader of the Bhati Rajput clan named Jaisal. The Bhatis, who trace their lineage back to Krishna, ruled right through to Independence in 1947.

The city's early centuries were tempestuous, partly because its rulers relied on looting for want of other income, but by the 16th century Jaisalmer was prospering from its strategic position on the camel-train routes between India and Central Asia. It eventually established cordial relations with the Mughal empire. In the mid-17th century Maharawal Sabal Singh expanded the Jaisalmer princedom to its greatest extents by annexing areas that now fall within the administrative districts of Bikaner and Jodhpur.

Under British rule the rise of sea trade (especially through Mumbai) and railways saw Jaisalmer's importance and population decline. Partition in 1947, with the cutting of trade routes to Pakistan, seemingly sealed the city's fate. But the 1965 and 1971 wars between India and Pakistan gave Jaisalmer new strategic importance, and since the 1960s the Indira Gandhi Canal to the north has brought revitalising water to the desert.

Today tourism and the area's many military installations are the pillars of the city's economy.

⊙ Sights

★ Jaisalmer Fort
FORT

Jaisalmer's unique fort is a living urban centre, with about 3000 people residing within its walls. It's honeycombed with narrow, winding lanes, lined with houses and temples – along with a large number of handicraft shops, guesthouses and restaurants. You enter the fort from the east, near Gopa Chowk, and pass through four massive gates on the zigzagging route to the upper part. The final gate opens onto the square that forms the fort's centre, **Dashera Chowk**.

Founded in 1156 by the Rajput ruler Jaisal and reinforced by subsequent rulers, Jaisalmer Fort was the focus of a number of battles between the Bhatis, the Mughals of Delhi and the Rathores of Jodhpur. In recent years, the fabric of the fort has faced increasing conservation problems due to unrestricted water use caused by high tourist numbers.

Fort Palace
PALACE

(Indian/foreigner incl compulsory audio guide ₹50/300, camera/video ₹100/200; ⊙8am-6pm Apr-Oct, 9am-6pm Nov-Mar) Towering over the fort's main square, and partly built on top of the Hawa Pol (the fourth fort gate), is the former rulers' elegant seven-storey palace.

Much of the palace is open to the public – floor upon floor of small rooms provide a fascinating sense of how such buildings were designed for spying on the outside world. The doorways connecting the rooms of the palace are quite low. This isn't a reflection on the stature of the Rajputs, but was a means of forcing people to adopt a humble, stooped position in case the room they were entering contained the maharawal.

The 1½-hour audio-guide tour, available in six languages, is worthwhile, but you must deposit ₹2000 or your passport, driver's licence or credit card.

Highlights of the tour include the mirrored and painted **Rang Mahal** (the bedroom of the 18th-century ruler Mulraj II), a gallery of finely wrought 15th-century sculptures donated to the rulers by the builders of the fort's temples, and the spectacular 360-degree views from the rooftop. One room contains an intriguing display of stamps from the former Rajput states. On the eastern wall of the palace is a sculpted pavilion-style balcony. Here drummers raised the alarm when the fort was under siege. You can also see numerous round rocks piled on top of the battlements, ready to be rolled onto advancing enemies.

The last part of the tour moves from the king's palace (Raja-ka-Mahal) into the queen's palace (Rani-ka-Mahal), which contains an interesting section on Jaisalmer's annual Gangaur processions in spring.

Jain Temples
JAIN TEMPLE

(Indian/foreigner ₹30/200, camera ₹50; ⊙Chandraprabhu 7am-1pm, other temples 11am-1pm) Within the fort walls is a mazelike, interconnecting treasure trove of seven beautiful yellow sandstone Jain temples, dating from the 15th and 16th centuries. Opening times have a habit of changing, so check with the caretakers. The intricate carving rivals that of the marble Jain temples in Ranakpur and Mt Abu, and has an extraordinary quality because of the soft, warm stone. Shoes and all leather items must be removed before entering the temples.

Chandraprabhu is the first temple you come to, and you'll find the ticket stand here. Dedicated to the eighth *tirthankar,* whose symbol is the moon, it was built in 1509 and features fine sculpture in the *mandapa,* whose intensely sculpted pillars form a series of *toranas.* To the right of Chandraprabhu is the tranquil **Rikhabdev temple**, with fine sculptures around the walls, protected by glass cabinets, and pillars beautifully sculpted with *apsaras* and gods.

Behind Chandraprabhu is Parasnath, which you enter through a beautifully carved *torana* culminating in an image of the Jain *tirthankar* at its apex. A door to the south leads to small **Shitalnath**, dedicated to the 10th *tirthankar,* whose image is composed of eight precious metals. A door in the northern wall leads to the enchanting, dim chamber of **Sambhavanth** – in the front courtyard, Jain priests grind sandalwood

RAJASTHAN JAISALMER

Jaisalmer

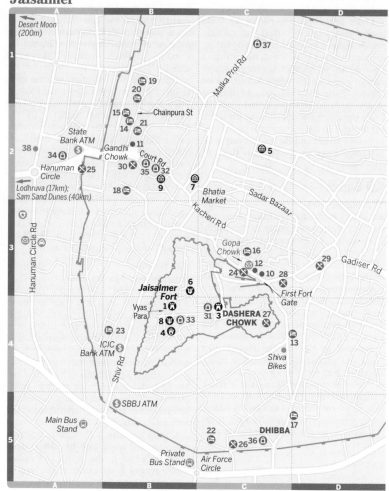

in mortars for devotional use. Steps lead down to the **Gyan Bhandar**, a fascinating, tiny, underground library founded in 1500, which houses priceless ancient illustrated manuscripts. The remaining two temples, **Shantinath** and **Kunthunath**, were built in 1536 and feature plenty of sensual carving. Note, the restrictive visiting times are for non-Jains. The temples are open all day for worshippers.

Laxminarayan Temple   HINDU TEMPLE
The Hindu Laxminarayan Temple, in the centre of the fort, is simpler than the Jain temples here and has a brightly decorated dome. Devotees offer grain, which is distributed before the temple. The inner sanctum has a repoussé silver architrave around its entrance, and a heavily garlanded image enshrined within. There's also a small 16th-century Hindu temple devoted to **Surya**, the sun god, inside the fort.

Havelis
Inside the fort but outside it, too (especially in the streets to the north), Jaisalmer is replete with the fairy-tale architecture of *havelis* – gorgeously carved stone doorways,

most impressive from the outside. The first of the five sections is open as the privately owned **Kothari's Patwa-ki-Haveli Museum** (Indian/foreigner ₹50/150, camera/video ₹50/70), which richly evokes 19th-century life.

Nathmal-ki-Haveli   HISTORIC BUILDING

(donation requested; ⊘ 8am-7pm) This late-19th-century *haveli*, once used as the prime minister's house, is still partly inhabited. It has an extraordinary exterior, dripping with carvings, and the 1st floor has some beautiful paintings using 1.5kg of gold leaf. The left and right wings were the work of two brothers, whose competitive spirits apparently produced this virtuoso work – the two sides are similar, but not identical. Sandstone elephants guard the entrance.

Museums

Desert Cultural Centre
& Museum   MUSEUM

(Gadi Sagar Rd; Indian/foreigner ₹20/50, puppet show ₹30/50, camera/video ₹20/50, combined museum-show ticket ₹70; ⊘ 9am-8pm, puppet shows 6.30pm & 7.30pm) This interesting museum tells the history of Rajasthan's princely states and has exhibits on traditional Rajasthani culture. Features include Rajasthani music (with video), textiles, a *kaavad* mobile temple, and a *phad* scroll painting depicting the story of the Rajasthani folk hero Pabuji, used by travelling singers as they recite Pabuji's epic exploits. It also hosts nightly half-hour **puppet shows** with English commentary. The ticket includes admission to the Jaisalmer Folklore Museum.

Thar Heritage Museum   MUSEUM

(off Court Rd; admission ₹40, camera ₹20) This private museum has an intriguing assortment of Jaisalmer artefacts, from turbans, musical instruments, fossils and kitchen equipment to displays on birth, marriage, death and opium customs. It's brought alive by the guided tour you'll get from its founder, local historian and folklorist LN Khatri. We enjoyed the snakes and ladders game that acts as a teaching guide to Hinduism's spirutal journey. If the door is locked, you'll find Mr Khatri at his shop, Desert Handicrafts Emporium, nearby on Court Rd.

Tours

The tourist office runs sunset tours to the Sam Sand Dunes (₹200 per person, minimum four people). Add ₹100 if you'd like a short camel ride too.

jali screens, balconies and turrets. There are some outstanding examples of incredibly fine sandstone *havelis* built by wealthy merchants and local notables in the 18th to 20th centuries.

Patwa-ki-Haveli   HISTORIC BUILDING

(Indian/foreigner ₹20/50; ⊘ 10am-5pm) The biggest fish in the *haveli* pond is Patwa-ki-Haveli, which towers over a narrow lane, its intricate stonework like honey-coloured lace. Divided into five sections, it was built between 1800 and 1860 by five Jain brothers who made their fortunes in brocade and jewellery. It's

Jaisalmer

⊨ Sleeping

While staying in the fort might appear to be Jaisalmer's most atmospheric choice, tourism has helped exert massive pressure on the fort's infrastructure. As a result, we don't recommend staying inside the fort. Fortunately, there's a wide choice of good places to stay outside the fort.

You'll get massive discounts between April and August, when Jaisalmer is hellishly hot. Some budget hotels are heavily into high-pressure selling of camel safaris and things can turn sour if you don't take up their offers: room rates that sound too good to be true almost always are.

Dylan Cafe & Guesthouse   GUESTHOUSE $
(☑9828561818; dylancafe.guesthouse@yahoo.in; Gandhi Chowk Rd; r ₹200-500, with AC ₹700; @☎) Dirt cheap digs for young backpackers who love to chillout or party or both. Rooms are acceptable, but most of your time will be spent drinking with the young owners on the rooftop. Free wi-fi, fresh coffee and good company.

Hotel Swastika   HOTEL $
(☑252483; swastikahotel@yahoo.com; Chainpura St; dm ₹100, s/d/tr ₹200/300/400, r with AC ₹600; ✻) In this well-run place the only

thing you'll be hassled about is to relax. Rooms are plain, quiet, clean and very good for the price; some have little balconies. There are plenty of restaurants nearby.

Hotel Fort View   HOTEL $
(☑252214; Gopa Chowk; s/d from ₹300/400) A friendly stalwart of the budget scene located close to the fort gate. The cheapest rooms are small and in the back, but clean; those at the front squeak in fort views. There's a popular fort-facing multicuisine restaurant. Watch for the 9am checkout.

Hotel Renuka   HOTEL $
(☑252757; hotelrenuka@rediffmail.com; Chainpura St; r ₹250-650, with AC ₹800; ✻@) Spread over three floors, Renuka has squeaky clean rooms – the best have balconies, bathrooms and AC. It's been warmly accommodating guests since 1988, so management knows its stuff. The roof terrace has great fort views and a good restaurant, and the hotel offers free pick-up from the bus and train stations.

Hotel Tokyo Palace   HOTEL $
(☑255483; www.tokyopalace.net; Dhibba Para; dm ₹200, s ₹400-1500, d ₹600-2000; ✻@☎⊠) Well-run by honest, traveller-friendly management, this new place has clean midrange rooms as well as plenty of budget options,

including separate basement dorms for men and women (bathrooms are the next level up). Wi-fi only extends to some rooms, and although it does have a pool, it's tiny.

Hotel Jaisal Palace HOTEL $

(☑ 252717; www.hoteljaisalpalace.com; s ₹600-1050, d ₹750-1250; ⊛) This is a well-run, good-value hotel, though the rooms tend to be on the small side and characterless. It's near Gandhi Chowk.

Arya Haveli GUESTHOUSE $$

(☑ 9782585337; www.aryahaveli.com; Chainpura St; r ₹900-1800; ⊛ 🖰) Helpful staff at this spruced-up guesthouse add to a stay at Arya Haveli. Rooms are well-appointed and look after; the cheaper ones face an internal courtyard, the best have their own balcony. The top-floor **Blues Cafe** is a nice place to relax to some good music and tasty food.

Desert Moon GUESTHOUSE $$

(☑ 250116, 9414149350; www.desertmoonguesthouse.com; Achalvansi Colony; s ₹600-1000, d ₹1000-1600; ⊛ @ 🖰) On the northwestern edge of town, 1km from Gandhi Chowk, Desert Moon is in a remote-feeling location beneath the Vyas Chhatari sunset point. The guesthouse is run by a friendly Indian-Kiwi couple who offer free pick-up from the train and bus stations. The 11 rooms are cool, clean and comfortable, with polished stone floors, tasteful decorations and sparkling bathrooms. The rooftop vegetarian restaurant has fort and *chhatari* views.

Hotel Pleasant Haveli HOTEL $$

(☑ 253253; www.pleasanthaveli.com; Chainpura St; r ₹2400, ste ₹2950; ⊛ 🖰) This welcoming place has lots of lovely carved stone, a beautiful rooftop (with restaurant) and just a handful of spacious, attractive, colour-themed rooms, all with modern, well-equipped bathrooms and AC. Free pick-ups from transport terminals are available.

Hotel Gorakh Haveli HOTEL $$

(☑ 9982657525; www.hotelgorakhhaveli.com; Dhibba; s/d ₹1000/1500, with AC ₹1500/2500; ⊛) A pleasantly low-key spot south of the fort, Gorakh Haveli is a modern place built with traditional sandstone and some attractive carving. Rooms are comfy and spacious, staff are amiable, and there's a reasonable multicuisine rooftop restaurant (mains ₹60 to ₹120), with fort views, of course.

Shahi Palace HOTEL $$

(☑ 255920; www.shahipalacehotel.com; off Shiv Rd; r ₹600-2500; ⊛ @ 🖰) Shahi Palace is a deservedly popular option. It's a modern building in the traditional style with carved sandstone. It has attractive rooms with raw sandstone walls, colourful embroidery, and carved stone or wooden beds. The cheaper rooms are mostly in two annexes along the street, **Star Haveli** and **Oasis Haveli**. The rooftop restaurant (mains ₹80 to ₹200) is excellent. Indian veg and nonveg dishes are available plus some European fare, cold beer and a superb evening fort view.

Killa Bhawan Lodge HOTEL $$$

(☑ 253833; www.killabhawan.com; r incl breakfast without/with AC ₹3000/3500; ⊛ 🖰) Near Patwa-ki-Haveli, this small hotel is a delight. There are five big and beautifully decorated rooms, a pleasant rooftop restaurant that looks up to the fort, and free tea and coffee all day.

RAJASTHAN JAISALMER

ℹ️ **ARRIVAL IN JAISALMER**

Touts work the buses heading to Jaisalmer from Jodhpur, hoping to steer travellers to guesthouses or hotels in Jaisalmer where they will get a commission. Some may even approach you before the bus leaves Jodhpur; others ride part or all of the way from Jodhpur, or board about an hour before Jaisalmer. On arrival in Jaisalmer, buses can be surrounded by touts baying for your attention. Don't believe anyone who offers to take you 'anywhere you like' for just a few rupees, and do take with a fistful of salt any claims that the hotel you want is 'full', 'closed' or 'no good any more.' Many hotels will offer pick-ups from the bus or train station.

Be very wary of offers of rooms for ₹100 or similar absurd rates. Places offering such prices are almost certainly in the camel-safari hard-sell game and their objective is to get you out of the room and onto a camel as fast as possible. If you don't take up their safari offers, the room price may suddenly increase or you might be told there isn't a room available any more.

Touts are less prevalent on the trains, but the same clamour for your custom ensues outside the station once you have arrived.

JAISALMER CAMEL SAFARIS

Trekking around by camel is the most evocative and fun way to sample Thar Desert life. However, don't expect dune seas – the Thar is mostly arid scrubland sprinkled with villages and wind turbines, with occasional dune areas popping out here and there. You will often come across fields of millet, and children herding flocks of sheep or goats whose neckbells tinkle in the desert silence – a welcome change after the sound of belching camels.

Most trips now include 4WD rides to get you to less frequented areas. The camel riding is then done in two-hour segments: one before lunch, one after. It's hardly camel *trekking*, but it is a lot of fun. A cheaper alternative to arranging things in Jaisalmer is to base yourself in the small village of Khuri, 48km southwest, where similar camel rides are available, but you're already in the desert when you start.

Before You Go

Competition between safari organisers is cut-throat and standards vary. Most hotels and guesthouses are very happy to organise a camel safari for you. While many provide a good service, some may cut corners and take you for the kind of ride you didn't have in mind. A few low-budget hotels in particular exert considerable pressure on guests to take 'their' safari. Others specifically claim 'no safari hassle'.

You can also organise a safari directly with one of the several reputable specialist agencies in Jaisalmer. Since these agencies depend exclusively on safari business it's particularly in their interest to satisfy their clients. It's a good idea to talk to other travellers and ask two or three operators what they're offering.

A one-night safari leaving Jaisalmer in the afternoon and returning the next morning, with a night on some dunes, is the minimum you'll need to get a feel for the experience: you'll probably get 1½ to two hours of riding each day. You can trek for several days or weeks if you wish. The longer you ride, the more you'll gain an understanding of the desert's villages, oases, wildlife and people.

The best-known dunes, at Sam (40km west of Jaisalmer), are always crowded in the evening and visiting them is more of a carnival than a back-to-nature experience. The dunes near Khuri are also quite busy at sunset, but quiet the rest of the time. Operators all sell trips now to 'nontouristy' and 'off the beaten track' areas. Ironically, this has made Khuri quieter again, although Sam still hums with day-tripper activity.

With 4WD transfers included, typical rates are between ₹1100 and ₹1700 per person for an overnight trip (leaving one morning, and returning the next). This should include meals, mineral water and blankets, and sometimes a thin mattress. Check that there will be one camel for each rider. You can pay for greater levels of comfort (eg tents, better food), but *always* get it all down in writing.

You should get a cheaper rate (₹900 to ₹1500 per person) if you leave Jaisalmer in the afternoon and return the following morning. A quick sunset ride in the dunes at Sam costs around ₹550 per person, including 4WD transfer. At the other end of the scale, you can ar-

---

1st Gate HOTEL $$$

(✆ 9462554462; www.1stgate.in; First Fort Gate; r incl breakfast ₹8500; ❄@☎) Italian-designed and super slick, this is Jaisalmer's most sophisticated modern hotel and it is beautiful throughout with a desert-meets-contemporary boutique vibe. The location lends it one of the finest fort views in town, especially from its split-level open-air restaurant-cafe (p188) area. Rooms are immaculate and the food (Italian and Indian) and coffee are both top-notch.

Eating

As well as the many hotel-rooftop eateries, there's a good number of other places to enjoy a tasty meal, often with a view.

Free Tibet TIBETAN $

(Fort; mains ₹120-250; ☉6.30am-10pm) There's multi-multicuisine here, with everything from French baguettes to Mexican tacos, but the speciality is Tibetan, including good noodle soups and *momos* (dumplings). It's near the fort's southeast corner, with good views from the window tables.

range a 20-day trek to Bikaner. Expect to pay between ₹1000 and ₹2000 per person per day for long, multiday trips, depending on the level of support facilities (4WDs, camel carts, etc).

What to Take
A wide-brimmed hat, long trousers, long-sleeved shirt, insect repellent, toilet paper, torch, sunscreen, water bottle (with a strap) and some cash (to tip the camel men, if nothing else) are recommended. It can get cold at night, so if you have a sleeping bag, bring it, even if you're told that blankets will be supplied. Women should consider wearing a sports bra, as a trotting camel is a bumpy ride. During summer, rain is not unheard of, so come prepared.

Which Safari?
There are several options, and recommendations here shouldn't be a substitute for your own research. Whichever agency you go for, insist that all rubbish is carried back to Jaisalmer.

Sahara Travels (☑ 252609; www.saharatravelsjaisalmer.com; Gopa Chowk; ⊙ 6am-8pm) Run by the son of the late LN Bissa (aka Mr Desert), this place is very professional and transparent. Trips are to 'nontouristy' areas only. Prices for an overnight trip (9am to 11am the next day): ₹1500 per person, all inclusive.

Trotters (☑ 9828929974; www.trotterscamelsafarijaisalmer.com; Gopa Chowk; ⊙ 5.30am-7.30pm) This company is transparently run by Del Boy – who else? – with a clear price list showing everything on offer. Does trips to 'nontouristy' areas as well as cheaper jaunts to Sam or Khuri. Overnight trip (8am to 10am the next day): cost ₹1150 to ₹1300 per person, all inclusive.

Thar Desert Tours (☑ 255656; www.tharcamelsafarijaisalmer.com; Gandhi Chowk; ⊙ 8.30am-7.30pm) This well-run operator charges ₹1100 per person per day, adjusting prices depending on trip times. They are slightly pricier than some of the other outfits, but we also receive good feedback about them. Customers pay 80% up front.

In the Desert
Camping out at night, huddling around a tiny fire beneath the stars and listening to the camel drivers' songs is magical.

There's always a long lunch stop during the hottest part of the day. At resting points the camels are unsaddled and hobbled; they'll often have a roll in the sand before limping away to graze on nearby shrubs, while the camel drivers brew chai or prepare food. The whole crew rests in the shade of thorn trees.

Take care of your possessions, particularly on the return journey. Any complaints you do have should be reported in Jaisalmer, either to the **Superintendent of Police** (☑252233), the tourist office (p189), or the intermittently staffed **Tourist Assistance Force** (Gadi Sagar Rd) posts inside the First Fort Gate and on the Gadi Sagar access road.

Camel drivers will expect a tip or gift at the end of the trip; don't neglect to give them one.

Chandan Shree Restaurant　PUNJABI $
(near Hanuman Circle; mains ₹70-190; ⊙ 7am-11pm) An always busy (and rightfully so) dining hall serving up a huge range of tasty, spicy South Indian, Gujarati, Rajasthani, Punjabi and Bengali dishes.

Bhang Shop　CAFE $
(Gopa Chowk; lassi from ₹100) Jaisalmer's infamous lassi shop is a simple, pocket-sized place. The added ingredient is bhang: cannabis buds and leaves mixed into a paste with milk, ghee and spices. It also does a range of bhang-laced cookies. Bhang is legal here, but it doesn't agree with everyone so if you're not used to this sort of thing, go easy or avoid it altogether.

Desert Boy's Dhani　INDIAN $$
(Dhibba; mains ₹100-135; ⊙ 11am-4pm & 7-11pm) A walled-garden restaurant where tables are spread around a large, stone-paved courtyard with a big tree. There's also traditional cushion seating under cover. Rajasthani music and dance is performed from 8pm to 10pm nightly, and it's a very pleasant place to eat excellent, good-value Rajasthani and other Indian veg dishes.

A CASTLE BUILT ON SAND

A decade ago the whole structure of Jaisalmer Fort was in danger of being undermined by water leakage from its antique drainage system. The main problem was material progress in the form of piped water for the fort's inhabitants. Three of the ancient bastions had collapsed and parts of the fort palace were leaning at an alarming rate.

Since then, British-based **Jaisalmer in Jeopardy** (www.jaisalmer-in-jeopardy.org) and several Indian organisations, including the **Indian National Trust for Art & Cultural Heritage** (INTACH; www.intach.org), have raised funds and carried out much-needed conservation works to save the fort. Most important has been the renewal of the fort's drainage system and repaving of the streets, as well as repair works inside the fort palace.

Things have improved, although some conservationists still believe the fort's structure is in danger, and calls remain for the fort's inhabitants, and those who work in the fort, to be forced to leave. The fort's current population has been established since the 1960s; before then, the fort's inhabitants numbered in the few hundreds, made up mostly of royal family and their workers, plus monks and priests connected to the fort's temples. Visitors should be aware of the fort's fragile nature and conserve resources, especially water, as much as possible. Given that the most recent section of wall collapse took place in 2011, we recommend staying in accommodation outside the fort.

Natraj Restaurant MULTICUISINE $$
(mains ₹70-270; ⊙10am-10pm) This is a brilliant place to eat, and the rooftop has a satisfying view of the upper part of the Salim Singh-ki-Haveli next door. The pure veg food is consistently excellent and the service is great. The delicious South India dosas (large savoury crepe) are fantastic value.

Monica Restaurant MULTICUISINE $$
(Amar Sagar Pol; mains ₹100-280) The airy open-air dining room at Monica just about squeezes in a fort view, but if you end up at a non-view table, console yourself with the excellent veg and nonveg options. Meat from the tandoor is particularly well-flavoured and succulent, the thalis well-varied, and the salads fresh and clean.

1st Gate ITALIAN $$$
(📱9462554462; First Fort Gate; mains ₹300-650; ⊙7am-11pm; 🛜) A small but good menu of authentic vegetarian Italian dishes as well as some delicious Indian food served on a split-level, open-air terrace with dramatic fort views. Also does good strong Italian coffee (₹100 to ₹150). A wood-fired oven was being built when we visited.

Saffron MULTICUISINE $$$
(Hotel Nachana Haveli, Gandhi Chowk; mains ₹250-370) On the spacious roof terrace of Hotel Nachana Haveli, the veg and nonveg food here is excellent. The Indian food is hard to beat, though the Italian isn't too bad either. It's a particularly atmospheric place in the evening. Alcohol is served.

🛍 Shopping

Jaisalmer is famous for its stunning embroidery, bedspreads, mirror-word wall hangings, oil lamps, stonework and antiques. Watch out when purchasing silver items: the metal is sometimes adulterated with bronze.

There are several good *khadi* shops where you can find fixed-price tablecloths, rugs, clothes, cushion covers and shawls, with a variety of patterning techniques including tie-dye, block-printing and embroidery. Try **Zila Khadi Gramodan Parishad** (Malka Prol Rd; ⊙10am-6pm Mon-Sat), **Khadi Gramodyog Bhavan** (Dhibba; ⊙10am-6pm Mon-Sat) or **Gandhi Darshan Emporium** (near Hanuman Circle; ⊙11am-7pm Fri-Wed).

Jaisalmer Handloom HANDICRAFTS
(www.jaisalmerhandloom.com; Court Rd; ⊙9am-10pm) This place has a big array of bedspreads, tapestries, clothing (ready-made and custom-made) and other textiles, made by its own workers and others. Staff don't hassle you with too much of a hard sell.

Desert Handicrafts Emporium HANDICRAFTS
(Court Rd; ⊙9.30am-9.30pm) With some unusual jewellery, paintings and all sorts of textiles, this is one of the most original of numerous craft shops around town.

Dharan Book Store BOOKS
(Vyas Para, Fort) Bookshops are 10 to the rupee in Jaisalmer, but this one wins us over with the cubbyhole cafe at the back, where you can browse through your latest purchase or get online while sipping a decent espresso. It's opposite Surya Temple.

Bellissima
HANDICRAFTS

(Dashera Chowk, Fort; ⊙8am-9pm) This small shop near the fort's main square sells beautiful patchworks, embroidery, paintings, bags, rugs, cushion covers and all types of Rajasthani art. Proceeds assist underprivileged women from surrounding villages, including those who have divorced or been widowed.

ℹ Information

INTERNET ACCESS
There are several internet cafes in the fort, but not so many outside it. Typical cost is ₹40 per hour.

MONEY
ATMs include State Bank and SBBJ near Hanuman Circle, SBBJ and ICIC Bank on Shiv Rd, and State Bank outside the train station. There are lots of licensed money changers in and around Gandhi Chowk.

POST
Main Post Office (Hanuman Circle Rd; ⊙10am-5pm Mon-Sat) West of the fort.
Post Office (Gopa Chowk; ⊙10am-5pm Mon-Fri, to 1pm Sat) Just outside the fort gate; sells stamps and you can send postcards.

TOURIST INFORMATION
Tourist Office (✆252406; Gadi Sagar Rd; ⊙9.30am-6pm) Friendly office with a free town map.

ℹ Getting There & Away

BUS
RSRTC buses leave from the main bus stand. One daily air-conditioned coach goes to Delhi (₹2001, 15 to 17 hours, 5pm) via Jodhpur, Ajmer (₹366) and Jaipur (₹467), but it has reclining seats only. There are daily services to Jodhpur (₹208, 5½ hours) throughout the day

A number of private bus companies have ticket offices at **Hanuman Circle**. **Hanuman Travels** (✆9413362367) and **Swagat Travels**

(✆252557) are typical. The buses themselves leave from the private bus stand. Typical services include the following:
Ajmer (₹370, nine hours, two or three daily)
Bikaner (₹210, six hours, three to four daily)
Jaipur (seat/sleeper ₹220/500, 11 hours, two or three daily)
Jodhpur (₹400 to ₹500, five hours, half-hourly from 6am to 10pm)
Udaipur (sleeper ₹650, 12 hours, one or two daily)

TAXI
One-way taxis should cost about ₹1800 to Jodhpur, ₹4000 to Bikaner and ₹6500 to Udaipur. There's a stand on Hanuman Circle Rd.

TRAIN
The **station** (⊙ticket office 8am-8pm Mon-Sat, to 1.45pm Sun) is on the eastern edge of town, just off the Jodhpur road. There's a reserved ticket booth for foreigners.
➡ Three daily trains go to Jodhpur (2nd class ₹205; five to six hours; 1.20am, 6.15am and 5pm).
➡ One train a day runs to Bikaner (six hours, 11.20pm)
➡ One daily train goes to Delhi (18 hours, 5pm) via Jaipur (12 hours).

ℹ Getting Around

AUTORICKSHAW
It costs around ₹40 from the train station to Gandhi Chowk.

CAR & MOTORCYCLE
It's possible to hire taxis or 4WDs from the stand on Hanuman Circle Rd. To Khuri, the Sam Sand Dunes or Lodhruva, expect to pay ₹800 to ₹1000 return, including a wait of about an hour.
Shiva Bikes (First Fort Gate; motorbike per day ₹500-2000; ⊙8am-9pm) is licensed to hire motorbikes (including Royal Enfield Bullets) and scooters for exploring town and nearby sights. Helmets and area maps are included.

RAJASTHAN JAISALMER

MAJOR TRAINS FROM JAISALMER

DESTINATION	TRAIN NO & NAME	DEPARTURE TIME	ARRIVAL TIME	FARE (₹)
Bikaner	22479 Jaisalmer-Bikaner Exp	11.20pm	4.35am	135 (A)
Delhi	14660 Jaisalmer-Delhi Exp	5pm	11.10am	440/1185 (B)
Jaipur	14660 Jaisalmer-Delhi Exp	5pm	4.50am	340/910 (B
Jodhpur	14809 Jaisalmer-Jodhpur Exp	6.15am	12.15pm	205/540 (B)

Fares: (A) sleeper, (B) sleeper/3AC

Around Jaisalmer

Sam Sand Dunes

The silky **Sam Sand Dunes** (admission vehicle/camel ₹50/80), 41km west of Jaisalmer along a good sealed road (maintained by the Indian army), are one of the most popular excursions from the city. The band of dunes is about 2km long and is undeniably one of the most picturesque in the region. Some camel safaris camp here, but many more people just roll in for sunset, to be chased across the sands by dressed-up dancing children and tenacious camel owners offering short rides. Plenty more people stay overnight in one of the couple of dozen tent resorts near the dunes.

All in all the place acquires something of a carnival atmosphere from late afternoon till the next morning, making it somewhere to avoid if you're after a solitary desert sunset experience.

If you're organising your own camel ride on the spot, expect to pay ₹200 to ₹300 for a one-hour sunset ride, but beware the tricks pf some camel men such as demanding more money en route.

Khuri

☑ 03014

The village of Khuri, 48km southwest of Jaisalmer, has quite extensive dune areas attracting their share of sunset visitors, and a lot of mostly smallish 'resorts' offering the same sort of overnight packages as those at Sam. It also has a number of low-key guesthouses where you can stay in tranquility in a traditional-style hut with clay-and-dung walls and thatched roof, and venture out on interesting camel trips in the relatively remote and empty surrounding area. Khuri is within the **Desert National Park**, which stretches over 3162 sq km southwest of Jaisalmer to protect part of the Thar ecosystem, including wildlife such as the desert fox, desert cat, chinkara gazelle, nilgai or bluebull (a large antelope), and some unusual bird life including the endangered great Indian bustard.

Be aware that the commission system is entrenched in Khuri's larger accommodation options. If you just want a quick camel ride on the sand dunes, expect to pay around ₹150 per person.

🛏 Sleeping

⭐ **Badal House** HOMESTAY $
(☑ 8107339097; r or hut per person incl full board ₹450) Here you can stay in a family compound in the centre of the village with a few spotlessly clean, mud-walled, thatch-roofed huts and equally spotless rooms (one with its own squat toilet), and enjoy good home cooking. Former camel driver Badal Singh is a charming, gentle man who charges ₹500 for a camel safari with a night on the dunes. He doesn't pay commission so don't let touts warn you away.

ℹ Getting There & Away

You can catch local buses from Jaisalmer to Khuri (₹32, one hour) from a road just off Gadi Sagar Rd. Walking from Jaisalmer Fort towards the train station, take the second right after the tourist office, then wait by the tree on the left, with the small shrine beside it. Buses pass here at around 10am, 11.30am, 3.30pm and 4pm.

Return buses from Khuri to Jaisalmer leave at 8am, 9am, 10.30am, 11.30am and 2.30pm.

Bikaner

☑ 0151 / POP 647,800

Bikaner is a vibrant, dust-swirling desert town with a fabulous fort and an energising outpost feel. It's less dominated by tourism than many other Rajasthan cities, though it has plenty of hotels and a busy camel-safari scene, which attracts travellers looking to avoid the Jaisalmer hustle.

Around the full moon in January or very late December, Bikaner celebrates its three day **Camel Festival**, with one day of events at the Karni Singh Stadium and two days out at Ladera, 45km northeast of the city.

History

The city was founded in 1488 by Rao Bika, a son of Rao Jodha, Jodhpur's founder, though the two Rathore ruling houses later had a falling out over who had the right to keep the family heirlooms. Bikaner grew quickly as a staging post on the great caravan trade routes from the late 16th century onwards, and flourished under a friendly relationship with the Mughals, but declined as the Mughals did in the 18th century. By the 19th century the area was backward, but managed to turn its fortunes around by hiring out camels to the British during the First Anglo-Afghan War. In 1886 it was the first desert princely state to install electricity.

◉ Sights

Junagarh
FORT

(Indian/foreigner ₹50/300, video ₹100, audio guide ₹50; ⊘10am-5.30pm, last entry 4.30pm) This most impressive fort was constructed between 1589 and 1593 by Raja Rai Singh, ruler of Bikaner and a general in the army of the Mughal emperor Akbar. You enter through the **Karan Prole** gate on the east side and pass through three more gates before the ticket office for the palace museum. An informative audio guide (requiring an identity document as a deposit), is available in English, French, German and Hindi.

Old City
AREA

The old city still has a medieval feel despite the motorbikes and autorickshaws. This labyrinth of narrow, winding streets conceals a number of fine old *havelis,* and a couple of notable Jain temples just inside the southern wall, 1.5km southwest of Bikaner Junction train station. It makes for an interesting wander – we guarantee you'll get lost at least once. The old city is encircled by a 7km-long, 18th-century wall with five entrance gates, the main entrance being the triple-arched Kothe Gate.

Bhandasar Temple
JAIN TEMPLE

(⊘5am-1pm & 5.30-11.30pm) Of Bikaner's two Jain temples, Bhandasar is particularly beautiful, with yellow-stone carving and dizzyingly vibrant paintings. The interior of the temple is stunning. The pillars bear floral arabesques and depictions of the lives of the 24 *tirthankars.* It's said that 40,000kg of ghee was used instead of water in the mortar, which locals insist seeps through the floor on hot days. The priest may ask for a donation for entry, although a trust pays for the temple upkeep.

On the 1st floor of the three-storey temple are beautiful miniatures of the sentries of the gods. There are fine views over the city from the 3rd floor, with the desert stretching to the west. The temple is dedicated to the fifth *tirthankar,* Sumtinath, and was commissioned in 1468 by a wealthy Jain merchant, Bhandasa Oswal. It was completed after his death in 1514.

RAJASTHAN BIKANER

BIKANER SAFARIS

Bikaner offers an excellent alternative to the Jaisalmer camel safari scene. There are fewer people running safaris here, so the hassle factor is quite low. Camel trips tend to be in the areas east and south of the city and focus on the isolated desert villages of the Jat, Bishnoi, Meghwal and Rajput peoples. Interesting wildlife can be spotted here, such as bluebull antelopes (nilgai), chinkara gazelles, desert foxes, spiny-tailed lizards and plenty of birds including (from September to March) the demoiselle crane.

Three days and two nights is a common camel-safari duration, but half-day, one-day and short overnight trips are all also possible. If you're after a serious trip, Jaisalmer is a two-week trek away. The best months to head into the desert are October to February. Avoid mid-April to mid-July, when it's searingly hot.

Typical costs are ₹1400 to ₹2000 per person per day including overnight camping, with tents, mattresses, blankets, meals, mineral water, one camel per person, a camel cart to carry gear (and sometimes tired riders), and a guide, in addition to the camel men.

Many trips start at Raisar, about 8km east of Bikaner, or Deshnok, 30km south. Travelling to the starting point by bus rather than 4WD is one way of cutting costs.

The standout operator in terms of quality, reliability and transparency is Vijay Singh Rathore, aka **Camel Man** (☑2231244, 9829217331; www.camelman.com; Vijay Guest House, Jaipur Rd; half-/full-/multiday trip per person per day from ₹700/1000/1200, 1-day, 1-night per person ₹1600), who operates from Vijay Guest House. Also popular and long-established is **Vino Desert Safari** (☑2270445, 9414139245; www.vinodesertsafari.com; Vino Paying Guest House; 1-day, 1-night per person ₹1800, multiday trek per person ₹1500-2000) run by Vinod Bhojak, of Vino Paying Guest House. **Vinayak Desert Safari** (☑2202634, 9414430948; www.vinayakdesertsafari.com; Vinayak Guest House; half-day 4WD safari per person ₹500, full- or multiday 4WD safari per person ₹900-2000) runs appealing 4WD safaris with zoologist Jitu Solanki. This safari focuses on desert animals and birds including the enormous cinereous vulture, with its 3m wingspan, which visits the area in numbers from November to March.

Bikaner

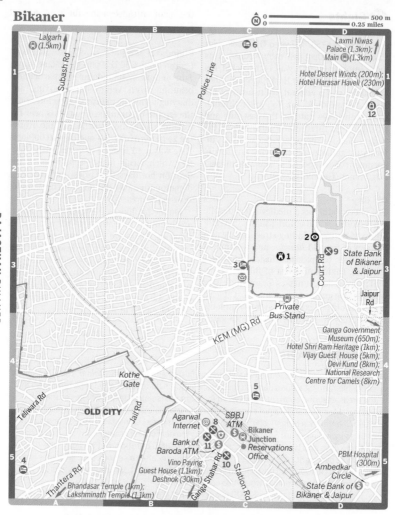

Lakshminath Temple
HINDU TEMPLE

(⊙ 5am-1pm & 7.30-11.30pm) The splendid Hindu Lakshminath Temple, behind Bhandasar Temple, was built during the reign of Rao Lunkaran between 1505 and 1526. Lakshminath was the patron god of the rulers of Bikaner, and during major religious festivals a royal procession headed by the maharaja pays homage here. The elaborate edifice was maintained with tributes received from five villages and several shops, which were granted to the temple by Maharaja Ganga Singh. Photography is prohibited here.

🛏 Sleeping

⭐ Vijay Guest House
GUESTHOUSE $

(☎ 2231244, 9829217331; www.camelman.com; Jaipur Rd; r ₹400-800, with AC ₹1200; ❄) About 4km east of the centre, this is a home away from home with spacious, light-filled rooms, a warm welcome and good home-cooked meals. Owner Vijay is a camel expert and a recommended safari operator (p191). As well as camel trips, it offers 4WD outings to sights around Bikaner, and tours to the owner's house in the untouristy village of Thelasar, Shekhawati.

Bikaner

Vino Paying Guest House GUESTHOUSE $
(⟟ 2270445, 9414139245; www.vinodesertsafari. com; Ganga Shahar; s ₹200-250, d ₹350-400; @🖵) This guesthouse, in a family home 3km south of the main train station, is a cosy choice and the base of a good camel-safari operator (p191). It has six rooms in the house and six in cool adobe huts around the garden, where there's also a plunge pool. It's excellent value, and the family is helpful and welcoming. Home-cooked food is served and cooking classes are on offer. It's opposite Gopeshwar Temple; free pick-ups are offered.

Vinayak Guest House GUESTHOUSE $
(⟟ 2202634, 9414430948; vinayakguesthouse@ gmail.com; r ₹150-400, s without bathroom ₹100; ❄@🛜) This place offers six varied and clean rooms in a quiet family house with a little sandy garden (hot water only by bucket in some rooms). On offer are a free pick-up service, good home-cooked food, cooking lessons, bicycles (₹25 per day), and camel safaris and wildlife trips with Vinayak Desert Safari (p191). It's 500m north of Junagarh.

Hotel Harasar Haveli HOTEL $$
(⟟ 2209891; www.harasar.com; r ₹2000-2500; ❄🛜) At this modern hotel with the frontage of an old sandstone haveli, you'll find unexpectedly grand accommodation. The decor is extravagant: that's not fancy blue-and-gold wallpaper in your room, but exquisitely handpainted floral patterns. Old dark-wood furniture continues the classy character. Service is great, and the in-house restaurant on the terrace serves alcohol. Located opposite Karni Singh Stadium, nearly 1km north of Junargarh.

Hotel Jaswant Bhawan HOTEL $$
(⟟ 2548848, 9001554746; www.hoteljaswantbha-wan.com; Alakh Sagar Rd; s/d ₹800/1000; ❄@) This is a quiet, welcoming place run by descendants of Bikaner prime ministers. It has a small garden and a comfy, old-fashioned sitting room with historic family photos. The air-conditioned rooms are spacious, plain and airy, though some of the paintwork

RAJASTHAN BIKANER

DON'T MISS

THE TEMPLE OF RATS

The extraordinary **Karni Mata Temple** (camera/video ₹20/50; ⊘4am-10pm) at Deshnok, 30km south of Bikaner, is one of India's weirder attractions. Its resident mass of holy rodents is not for the squeamish, but most visitors to Bikaner brave the potential for ankle-nipping and put a half-day trip here on their itinerary. Frequent buses leave from Bikaner's main bus stand. A return autorickshaw from Bikaner with a one-hour wait costs ₹400.

Karni Mata lived in the 14th century and performed many miracles during her lifetime. When her youngest son, Lakhan, drowned, she ordered Yama (the god of death) to bring him back to life. Yama said he was unable to do so, but that Karni Mata, as an incarnation of Durga, could restore Lakhan's life. This she did, decreeing that members of her family would no longer die but would be reincarnated as *kabas* (rats). Around 600 families in Deshnok claim to be descendants of Karni Mata and that they will be reincarnated as *kabas*.

The temple isn't swarming with rats, but there are a lot of them here, especially in nooks and crannies and in areas where priests and pilgrims leave food for them. And yes, you do have to take your shoes off to enter the temple: it's considered highly auspicious to have a *kaba* run across your feet – you may be graced in this manner whether you want it or not.

You can find food and drinks for yourself at the numerous snack stalls outside.

needs attention. Good meals are available. It's a two-minute walk from the main train station, via the station's 'foot over bridge'.

Hotel Kishan Palace HOTEL **$$**
(☑2527762; www.kishanpalaceheritage.com; 8B Gajner Rd; r with fan ₹650, with AC ₹1500; ✳🕱) An old Bikaner house, this hotel was once the home of a colonel of the Bikaner Camel Corps, and is now run by his grandson. Rooms are unfussy but generously sized, and the place is festooned with old photos and military memorabilia – check out grandfather's MBE, and watercolours by the Japanese prisoners of war he once guarded. Get a room at the back away from the main road.

Bhairon Vilas HERITAGE HOTEL **$$$**
(☑2544751, 9928312283; http://hotelbhaironvilas.tripod.com; r from ₹2000; ✳@🕱) This hotel on the western side of Junagarh is run by a former Bikaner prime minister's great-grandson. Rooms are mostly large and are eclectically decorated with antiques, gold-threaded curtains and old family photographs. There's a bar straight out of the Addams Family, a garden restaurant and a boutique specialising in original wedding saris.

Laxmi Niwas Palace HERITAGE HOTEL **$$$**
(☑2202777; www.laxminiwaspalace.com; r ₹10,000-14,000, ste ₹18,000-25,000; ✳@🕱) Located 2km north of the city centre, this pink-sandstone hotel is part of the royal palace, dating from 1902. It has opulent interiors with stone carvings, and is set in large lovely grounds. Rooms are large, elegant and evocative, while the bar and billiards room contain more trophy skins from tigers than are probably still alive in Rajasthan.

Bhanwar Niwas HERITAGE HOTEL **$$$**
(☑2529323; www.bhanwarniwas.com; Rampuria St; r ₹4500; ✳@) This superb hotel has been developed out of the beautiful Rampuria Haveli – a gem in the old city, 300m southwest of the City Kotwali police station. It has 26 all-different, spacious and delightfully decorated rooms, featuring stencil-painted

wallpaper, marble or mosaic floors and antique furnishings. Comfortable common rooms drip with antiques and are arranged around a large courtyard. The *haveli* was completed in 1927 for Seth Bhanwarlal Rampuria, heir to a textile and real-estate fortune. Inside the entrance gate is a stunning blue 1927 Buick.

✗ Eating

Bikaner is noted for its *bhujiya,* a special kind of *namkin* (spicy nibbles), sold in the shops along Station Rd among other places.

Heeralal's MULTICUISINE **$**
(Station Rd; mains ₹50-150; ⊘7.30am-10.30pm) This bright and hugely popular 1st-floor restaurant serves up pretty good veg and nonveg Indian dishes, plus a few Chinese and pizzas (but unfortunately no beer), amid large banks of plastic flowers. The groundfloor fast-food section is less appetising but it has a good sweets counter.

Laxmi Hotel DHABA **$**
(Station Rd; mains ₹50-90, thali ₹60-100; ⊘8am-10pm) A simple place, Laxmi is open to the street and dishes up tasty, fresh vegetarian thalis. You can see the roti being flipped.

★Gallops INDIAN **$$**
(Court Rd; mains ₹200-400; ⊘10am-10pm) This fairly modern cafe and restaurant close to the Junagarh entrance is known as 'Glops' to rickshaw-wallahs. There are snacks such as pizzas, *pakoras* (deep-fried battered vegetables) and sandwiches, and a good range of Indian and Chinese veg and nonveg dishes. You can sit outside or curl up in an armchair in the air-conditioned interior with a cold beer or espresso coffee.

Evergreen INDIAN **$$**
(☑2542061; Station Rd; mains from ₹110; ⊘7am-10.30pm; ✳🍴) Evergreen is a neat and clean restaurant whose delicious air conditioning hits you the moment you walk through the door. Despite the Egyptian heiroglyphic wallpaper, the cuisine leans strongly towards

MAJOR TRAINS FROM BIKANER JUNCTION

DESTINATION	TRAIN NO & NAME	DEPARTURE TIME	ARRIVAL TIME	FARE (₹)
Delhi (S Rohilla)	12456 Bikaner-Dee SF Exp	5pm	7.20am	382/1006
Jodhpur	14887 KLK-BME Exp	11am	4pm	190/278
Jaipur	SGNR Kota SF	11.05pm	5.30am	265/680

Fares: sleeper/3AC

South India, with a few classics like *paneer tikka* and *malai kofta*. Diners sometimes receive their dishes in sequence rather than all together, but the taste is worth the wait.

Palace Garden Restaurant   INDIAN, CHINESE $$$
(Laxmi Niwas Palace; mains ₹250-800; ⊗ 7.30-10pm) This excellent garden restaurant at one of Bikaner's best hotels is a lovely place to eat – at least until the nights become too chilly. The fare spans South Indian, veg and nonveg North Indian, and Chinese, and if you're lucky there will be live music.

🛍 Shopping

Bikaner Miniature Arts   ART
(Fort Rd) The Swami family has been painting miniatures in Bikaner for four generations, and now runs this art school-cum-gallery. The quality of work is astounding, and cheaper than you'll find in some of the bigger tourist centres. Art classes can be arranged.

ⓘ Information

You'll find a **State Bank ATM** (Ambedkar Circle) outside the main train station, and Bank of Baroda ATMs opposite the station and next to the tourist office. There are several internet cafes on Ganga Shahar Rd.

Main Post Office (⊗ 9am-4pm Mon-Fri, to 2pm Sat) Near Bhairon Vilas hotel.

PBM Hospital (✑ 2525312; Hospital Rd) One of Rajasthan's best government hospitals, with 24-hour emergency service.

Tourist Office (✑ 2226701; ⊗ 9.30am-6pm Mon-Fri) This friendly office (near Pooran Singh Circle) can answer most tourism-related questions and provide transport schedules and maps.

ⓘ Getting There & Away

BUS
There's a private bus stand outside the south wall of Junagarh with similar services (albeit slightly more expensive and less frequent) to the government-run services departing from the main bus stand, which is 2km directly north of the fort. An autorickshaw will cost around ₹20.

Services from the main bus stand include:

Ajmer (₹206, six hours, half-hourly until 6pm)
Delhi (₹352, 11 hours, at least four daily) Departs early morning.
Deshnok (₹26, one hour, half-hourly until 5.30pm)
Fatehpur (₹136, 3½ hours, half-hourly until 5.45pm)
Jaipur (₹255, seven hours, hourly until 5.45pm)
Jaisalmer (₹263, 7½ hours, 12pm)

Jhunjhunu (₹173, five hours, 7.30am, 8.30am, and 6.30pm)
Jodhpur (₹191, five hours, half-hourly until 4.30pm)
Pokaran (₹176, five hours, hourly until 2.15pm).

TRAIN
The main train station is Bikaner Junction, which has a **computerised reservations office** (⊗ 8am-10pm Mon-Sat, to 2pm Sun) in a separate building just east of the main station building. The foreigner's window is 2931. A couple of other useful services depart from Lalgarh station in the north of the city (₹50 in an autorickshaw).

➡ For Jaisalmer, an evening train with reserved ticketing runs only on Tuesday (sleeper/3AC ₹240/600, five hours, 6.30pm) from Bikaner Junction. On all other days there is the 22480 Bikaner-Jaisalmer Express (2nd class ₹135, five hours, 10.55pm), with unreservable seats. Turn up no less than 30 minutes before departure.

➡ Five daily trains go to Jodhpur (five hours; 12.45am, 6.30am, 9.30am, 11am and 4pm).

➡ Four daily trains go to Delhi (Delhi Sarai Rohilla; 9.15am, 5pm, 7.45pm and 10.20pm). The trip takes eight to 14 hours depending on the departure: the 9.15am and 10.20pm services are the fastest.

➡ Five daily trains go to Jaipur (6½ hours; 5.20am, 6am, 5.15pm 6.45pm and 11.05pm).

There are no direct trains to Ajmer for Pushkar.

ⓘ Getting Around

An autorickshaw from the train station to Junagarh palace should cost ₹40, but you'll probably be asked for more.

Around Bikaner

National Research Centre on Camels

The **National Research Centre on Camels** (✑ 01512230183; www.nrccamel.res.in; Indian/foreigner ₹20/50, camera ₹30, rides ₹30; ⊗ 2-6pm) is 8km southeast of central Bikaner, beside the Jodhpur–Jaipur Bypass. While here you can visit baby camels, go for a short ride and look around the small museum. There are about 400 camels, of three different breeds. The British Army had a camel corps drawn from Bikaner during WWI. Guides are available for ₹50-plus. The on-site Camel Milk Parlour offers samples to try, as well as lassis. Camel grazing time is 3pm to 6pm and is the best time to come. The round trip, including a half-hour wait at the camel farm, is around ₹150/₹300 for an autorickshaw/taxi.

Understand Rajasthan, Delhi & Agra

Rajasthan, Delhi & Agra Today

India can often seem to be a country pulling in two directions. It's an ancient country drawing great strength from its long-held cultural and religious traditions, while at the same time racing into the 21st century as the world's largest democracy and one of its fastest growing economies. These two factors generate as much tension as much as they do opportunity, but India presses ahead with unbridled energy and a pride in its growing stature on the international stage.

Best on Film

Pather Panchali (1955) Haunting masterpiece from Satyajit Ray.
Fire (1996), **Earth** (1998) & **Water** (2005) Classic trilogy of social observation by Deepa Mehta.
Gandhi (1982) The classic biopic.
Lagaan (2001) Raj-era cricketing epic by Ashutosh Gowariker.

Best in Print

Desert Places Robyn Davidson travels by camel through the Thar Desert.
City of Djinns William Dalrymple's fascinating study of Delhi.
Twilight in Delhi Ahmed Ali's novel paints a revealing picture of pre-Independence Delhi.
Maharanis Lucy Moore's delightful account of the lives and loves of three generations of Indian princesses.
India After Gandhi Ramachandra Guha's history of the world's largest democracy.
The Elephant, the Tiger, and the Cellphone Shashi Tharoor's reflections on life in 21st-century India

A Populated Desert

Covering an area of 342,236 sq km, Rajasthan represents roughly 10% of the Indian landmass. Much of it embraces the vast Thar Desert, which is scattered with rural villages, trade-route towns and rapidly growing cities that were once the capitals of princely states.

The desert supports life because of the monsoon rains that percolate through the sands into the water table to be tapped throughout the year at the ubiquitous wells scattered across the country. In recent years, Rajasthan's life-giving monsoon has become less and less predictable, however, and the scarcity of rain and rapid drop in the water table has affected people's livelihoods as well as the greater environment. Chronic droughts have accelerated migration from the parched agricultural lands to the already overburdened cities. For those who remain on the land, it has become a battle for survival. The Sardar Sarovar Dam, part of the controversial Narmada River Project in Gujarat, finally trickled into deserts around Barmer and Jalore, bringing drinking and irrigation water to millions of people, but for many others the drift to abandon the land for the region's growing cities has proved irresistible.

Tourism State & Hi-Tech City

Around 40% of all visitors to India come to Rajasthan, bringing in foreign revenue and providing much needed employment. Tourism is the most important industry in Rajasthan, funding the conservation of Rajasthan's magnificent heritage and revitalising the region's splendid arts and crafts. The surge in tourism has provided many locals from all walks of life with alternative and promising career options. A large number of young Rajasthanis now earn a living by working in hotels or souvenir shops, driving taxis or by sprucing up their knowledge of history to become tourist guides.

Over in Delhi, the cogs in the Indian economic juggernaut continue to spin, and received a further boost with the election of pro-business prime minister Narendra Modi. Scores of outsourcing firms dot the skylines of Delhi's suburbs, providing employment to hordes of graduates, while the expanding Delhi metro maps the city's future ambitions. Living standards are rising, bringing previously unaffordable luxuries within arm's reach of many of urban India's inhabitants.

Trending Now

Rajasthan's population has more than quadrupled since 1951. There are several contributing factors, such as vastly improved medical facilities and increased availability of medicines, which have led to a big drop in the mortality rate. The local mindset has not always kept pace with these changes, which is why procreation still follows the norm of having 'an heir and a spare' – at least two male offspring. The reluctance to practise contraception is another reason behind the sharp rise in the headcount; government-sponsored family-planning programs are fighting a losing battle on this front.

The economy, whether you are talking about Rajasthan or the entire country, has undeniably made giant strides in recent years; however, the challenges for today's politicians – redistribution of wealth and environmental conservation – remain unresolved. Rajasthan continues to lose its wildlife, fertile soils and vegetation, and India is the fifth-highest carbon emitter in the world, after the EU and ahead of Russia. In a land where juxtaposition of old and new has become a hackneyed slogan, the visitor must still marvel at the scene of ancient cenotaphs of silk-route nobility standing shoulder-to-shoulder with state-of-the-art wind turbines, which are helping to address India's burgeoning energy and pollution crisis.

POPULATION (RAJASTHAN): **68.9 MILLION**

POPULATION (DELHI): **16.7 MILLION**

LIFE EXPECTANCY (WOMEN/MEN): **68/64.5 YEARS**

GDP (PER CAPITA): **US$5411**

NATIONAL GDP GROWTH RATE: **7.5%**

if India were 100 people

30 would be 14 years or younger
65 would be aged between 15 and 64 years
5 would be older than 65 years

belief systems
(% of population)

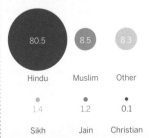

80.5	8.5	8.3
Hindu	Muslim	Other
1.4	1.2	0.1
Sikh	Jain	Christian

population per sq km

DELHI · RAJASTHAN · INDIA

👤 ≈ 200 people

History

A popular Indian saying goes that the state of Rajasthan alone has more history than the rest of the country put together. Given that its name literally translates as 'the land of kings', perhaps the idea holds some truth. Throw in the neighbouring medieval capitals of Delhi and Agra, and you've got a heady cocktail laced with a thousand royal legends, potent enough to work its charm on even the most prosaic of imaginations.

Back Where It All Began

The desert and scrub areas of Rajasthan have been home to humans for several thousand years. Excavations in Kalibangan, near Ganganagar in northern Rajasthan, have unearthed terracotta pottery and jewellery dating back to around 3000 BC – evidence of the region's earliest known settlements. Some of these urban centres were presumably absorbed into the Harappan segment of the Indus Valley civilisation, where they flourished until the settlement was mysteriously abandoned 3700 years ago. The mass exodus, possibly triggered by flooding or a severe climatic change, rendered the region devoid of human settlement for some time, until indigenous tribes such as the Bhils and the Minas moved in to set up their own squabbling small kingdoms, thereby commencing the long history of argumentative neighbours in the region.

But even as the tribes tore away at each other, another civilisation was sprouting in the fertile plains to the east of Rajasthan, between the rivers Yamuna and Ganga (Ganges), out of the seminomadic Indo-European race known as Aryans or 'noblemen'. It was in this civilisation that Hinduism first evolved as a religious tradition and a way of life, along with a complex patriarchal social structure and the tiered caste system that the greater Indian society adheres to even today. By 1000 BC, the province had seen the establishment of at least two prominent kingdoms: the Matsya territory of Viratnagar encompassing Alwar, Bharatpur, Dholpur and Karauli; and Indraprastha, the earliest-known incarnation of Delhi, which was successively built on by several dynasties to come.

Little is known of Rajasthan's development at this time, as the mighty empires that were then strengthening their hold on the subcontinent

TIMELINE	10,000 BC	2600–1700 BC	c 1500 BC
	Stone Age paintings created in the Bhimbetka rock shelters, in what is now Madhya Pradesh; the art continues here for many centuries. Settlements thought to exist across subcontinent.	The heyday of the Indus Valley civilisation; the settlement spans parts of Rajasthan, Gujarat and the Sindh province in Pakistan.	The Indo-Aryan civilisation takes root in the fertile plains of the Indo-Gangetic basin. The settlers speak an early form of Sanskrit, from which several Indian languages later evolve.

largely chose to pass over the state. Alexander the Great, who reached as far as the Punjab on his epic campaign to conquer the 'known world', was forced to return when his troops, homesick and weary after the campaign, convinced him to retreat. The Mauryan empire (323–185 BC) had minimal impact too, largely due to its most renowned emperor, Ashoka, taking to nonviolent ways after he converted to Buddhism. In stark contrast to the atrocities he had inflicted on the eastern Indian kingdom of Kalinga, the only evidence Ashoka left of his reign in Rajasthan were Buddhist caves and stupas (Buddhist shrines) near Jhalawar, rock-cut edicts at Bairat, an ancient Buddhist site near Sariska Tiger Reserve, and a 13m-high pillar he inscribed in Delhi.

The oldest natural relics in Rajasthan are fossilised remains of a 180-million-year-old forest, located at the Akal Wood Fossil Park in the Thar Desert near Jaisalmer.

Marauding Huns & the Advent of Kings

The insulation that Rajasthan enjoyed through its early years came to an abrupt end during the 5th century AD, when armies of fierce Hun warriors rode in from Central Asia to carry out a series of pillaging raids across north India. These raids were to alter the course of the region's history in two major ways. To begin with, they resulted in the disintegration of the Gupta dynasty, which had taken over from the Mauryas as a central power and had reigned over the country from 320 to 550. But more importantly, they triggered a parallel invasion, as the Rajputs finally came to make Rajasthan their home and, in the absence of an overarching monarchy, grew from strength to strength to usher in the golden age of Rajasthan.

Historical evidence suggests that the Rajputs (their name meaning 'children of kings') fled their homelands in Punjab, Haryana, Gujarat and Uttar Pradesh to settle in Rajasthan, primarily to escape the wrath of the White Huns (and later the Arabs) who had begun to storm in from Pakistan and Afghanistan. Once they had arrived in Rajasthan, the Rajputs trampled over the Bhils and Minas, and set up their own small fiefdoms in the face of mounting local chaos. Though they largely belonged to the lower rungs of Hindu society, volatile circumstances demanded that the Rajputs don the role of warriors, if only to fend off further advances by foreign invaders. So in spite of rigid social norms, which didn't allow for any kind of self-promotion, early Rajput clans such as the Gurjara Pratiharas crossed the caste barriers to proclaim themselves Kshatriyas, members of the warrior class, who came second only to the Brahmins (priests) in the caste hierarchy.

To facilitate their smooth transition through social ranks, and to avoid stinging criticism from the Brahmins, these early Rajput clans chose to jettison their worldly ancestry and took to trumpeting a mythological genealogy that supposedly evolved from celestial origins. From the 6th century onward, some of the clans began calling themselves Suryavanshis

Discover the bygone days of Rajasthan's royalty in *A Princess Remembers*, the memoirs of Gayatri Devi, maharani of Jaipur. Cowritten by Santha Rama Rau, it's an enthralling read.

c 1000 BC	c 540 BC	326 BC	323–185 BC
Indraprastha, Delhi's first incarnation, comes into being. Archaeological excavations at the site where the Purana Qila now stands continue even today.	The writing of the Mahabharata begins. The longest epic in the world, it takes nearly 250 years to complete, and mentions settlements such as Indraprastha, Pushkar and Chittorgarh.	Alexander the Great invades India. He defeats Porus in Punjab to enter the subcontinent, but a rebellion keeps him from advancing beyond the Beas River in Himachal Pradesh.	India comes under the rule of the Maurya kings. Founded by Chandragupta Maurya, this Pan-Indian empire is ruled from Pataliputra (Patna), and briefly adopts Buddhism.

THE INDOMITABLE SISODIAS

In a region where invasions and political upheavals were historical norms, the Sisodias of Mewar stood out as an exception, using everything from diplomacy to sheer valour to retain an iron grip over their land. Pillage and blood baths notwithstanding, the dynasty administered its kingdom in southern Rajasthan for 1400 years. Lorded over by 76 monarchs throughout the ages, the Sisodias have one of the longest-serving dynasties in the world.

The lineage of the Sisodia kings can be traced back to a prince named Guhil, born to a Rajput queen in the 6th century AD. Orphaned soon after birth and his kingdom ransacked by Huns, Guhil forged an alliance at age 11 with a Bhil chieftain to establish a dynasty called the Guhilots, and founded the state of Mewar.

In the 12th century the family split, resulting in a breakaway faction that relocated to the town of Sissoda, rechristening themselves Sisodias. They soon took over Chittorgarh, an ancient garrison that remained under their control until it was sacked by Mughal emperor Akbar in 1568. Though it came as a major military setback, the Sisodias lost no time in retreating into the Aravalli Hills, where they put together a new capital called Udaipur. A serenely beautiful city, Udaipur was never lost to the enemy, and remained the capital of Mewar until the kingdom was absorbed into the state of Rajasthan following India's independence.

The Sisodias have been credited with producing some of the most flamboyant kings ever to have reigned in Rajasthan. The family boasts names such as Rana Sanga, who died a valiant death in 1527 while fending off Mughal troops under Babur, and Maharana Pratap (1540–97), who made several daring though unsuccessful attempts to win Chittorgarh back from Akbar during his time in power. Being prolific builders, the Sisodias also gave Mewar some of its finest structures, including the Victory Tower at Chittorgarh, the grand City Palace in Udaipur, the elegant Monsoon Palace atop Sajjangarh Hill and the spectacular Lake Palace, which stands on an island amid the placid waters of Lake Pichola, also in Udaipur.

(Descendants of the Sun), while others chose to be known as Chandravanshis (Descendants of the Moon). A third dynasty, on the other hand, traced their roots to the sacrificial fire that was lit on Mt Abu during the Mauryan era, thereby naming themselves Agnivanshis (Fire-Born).

As the Rajputs slowly consolidated their grip over Rajasthan, they earned a reputation for their chivalry, noble traditions and strict code of conduct, and gave rise to several dynasties that established some of the most renowned princely states of Rajasthan. The largest of these kingdoms, and the third largest in India after Kashmir and Hyderabad, was Marwar. Founded by the Suryavanshi Rathores, who rode in from Uttar Pradesh, it was initially ruled from Mandore, before the seat of power was relocated to the Mehrangarh Fort in nearby Jodhpur. The

1st century AD	320–550	500–600	610
International trade booms: the region's overland trade networks connect with ports linked to maritime routes. Trade to Africa, the Gulf, Socotra, Southeast Asia, China and Rome thrives.	The period of the Gupta dynasty, the second of India's great monarchies after the Mauryas. This era is marked by a creative surge in literature and the arts.	The emergence of the Rajputs in Rajasthan. Stemming from three principal races supposedly of celestial origin, they form 36 separate clans who claim their own kingdoms across the region.	Prophet Mohammed establishes Islam. He soon invites the people of Mecca to adopt the new religion under the command of God, and his call is met with an eager response.

Sisodias migrated from Gujarat to assemble in the folds of the Aravalli Hills to the south, where they formed the state of Mewar encompassing Chittorgarh and Udaipur. The Kachhwahas, from Gwalior in Madhya Pradesh, settled in Jaipur in eastern Rajasthan, their capital nestled in the twin fort complex of Amber and Jaigarh. Meanwhile, a fourth kingdom, called Jaisalmer, was established in the Thar Desert by the Bhattis. Obscured by the dunes, the Bhattis remained more or less entrenched in their kingdom until Jaisalmer was integrated into the state of Rajasthan after Independence.

Over the years, Rajasthan saw the mushrooming of many other smaller dynasties, each of which staked claim to its own patch of territory in the region and ruled with complete autonomy, often refusing to submit to the whims of the bigger kingdoms. The clans were so content with their tiny fiefdoms that they rarely thought of looking beyond their borders to explore and conquer newer territories.

One dynasty was the exception. The Chauhans settled in Ajmer, from where they gradually extended their rule into Haryana and Uttar Pradesh. Within Rajasthan, the Hada offshoot of the Chauhans crossed over to the Hadoti region and captured the cities of Bundi and Kota, while the Deora branch took over the nearby Sirohi area, making way for successive generations to zero in on the provinces of Ranthambhore, Kishangarh and Shekhawati. The most illustrious of the Chauhan kings, Prithviraj III even invaded Delhi – then on one of its temporary wanes – and commissioned the building of a settlement called Qila Rai Pithora, the ramparts of which can still be seen near the Qutb Minar in Mehrauli. One of the few Hindu kings to hold fort in Delhi, Prithviraj Chauhan administered his empire from the twin capitals of Qila Rai Pithora and Ajmer, before his reign was put to an end by Islamic warriors, who galloped in by the thousands to change the face of the region forever.

The concepts of zero and infinity are widely believed to have been devised by eminent Indian mathematicians, such as Aryabhatta and Varahamihira, during the reign of the Guptas.

The Sword of Islam

Some 400 years after Prophet Mohammed had introduced Islam into Arabia, northern India saw the arrival of Muslims. With the banner of Islam fluttering high, invading armies with a proselytising agenda first seized the province of Sindh (in Pakistan), and then moved on to occupy the formerly Buddhist city of Ghazni in neighbouring Afghanistan. It was obvious that India would figure next on the agenda. So at the beginning of the 11th century, zealous Turk warriors, led by the fearsome Sultan Mahmud of Ghazni, stormed into India, razing hundreds of Hindu temples and plundering the region to take away vast amounts of wealth to fill their coffers back home. The Turks made their raids into India almost an annual affair, ransacking the northern part of the country 17 times in as many years. Jolted out of their internal bickering, the Rajput princes

Rajput armies primarily consisted of cavalries. They were known to breed pedigree horses such as the Marwari and Kathiawari for use by their mounted forces.

1024	1192	1206	1303
Mahmud of Ghazni raids India for the last time, ransacking on this occasion the Somnath Temple in Gujarat, where he purportedly smashes the idol with his own hands.	Prithviraj Chauhan loses Delhi to Mohammed of Ghori. The defeat effectively ends Hindu supremacy in the region, exposing Rajasthan and the subcontinent to subsequent Muslim invaders.	Ghori is murdered during a prayer session while returning to Ghazni from a campaign in Lahore. In the absence of an heir, his kingdom is usurped by his generals. The Delhi Sultanate is born.	Ala-ud-din Khilji sacks Chittorgarh with the intention of carrying away the beautiful Sisodia queen Padmini. The queen immolates herself to escape humiliation – the first recorded instance of *sati* in Rajasthan.

organised some hasty defence, but their army was torn to shreds even before they could retaliate. Rajasthan had been incorporated into the Islamic empire.

The 24-spoke wheel, an emblem designed by Ashoka, has been adopted as the central motif on the national flag of India, where it is rendered in blue against a white background.

Delhi, located further east, was initially spared the wrath of these invaders, as the Sultan largely confined his raids to Rajasthan and parts of Gujarat. Trouble, however, came by the name of Mohammed of Ghori, governor of Ghazni, who invaded India in the late 12th century, taking up where his predecessor had left off. He was thwarted on his first campaign by Prithviraj Chauhan, but the resolute Ghori returned a year later to defeat the Rajput king in the Second Battle of Tarain. Having convincingly stamped his victory over the region, Ghori trotted back to Ghazni, leaving Delhi under the governorship of Qutb-ud-din Aibak, a former Turk slave who had risen to command forces in India. When news of Ghori's death arrived in Delhi a decade and a half later, Qutb-ud-din shrugged off competition from rivals to stake a claim to the Indian part of Ghori's empire. He declared himself Sultan of the region, and founded the Mamluk or Slave dynasty, giving Delhi the first of its many Islamic monarchies.

An Age of Treachery & Exploits

The enthronement of Qutb-ud-din Aibak flagged the end of the Sultanate era of Delhi, which lasted for about 350 years. Throughout this period, Delhi was ruled by five different Islamic dynasties, before the first period of Mughal rule in 1526. The Mughals were then briefly expelled by the sixth Delhi sultanate, founded by Sher Shah Suri in 1540, before regaining the upper hand in 1555. The six Delhi sultanates produced a line of 38 rulers, who gradually pushed the boundaries of their kingdoms to conquer new land. The whole of the Gangetic basin soon came under the Sultanates' control, as did Rajasthan and Gujarat – the princely states there had little option but to bow down to their might.

Upon losing Delhi to the Afghans, Prithviraj Chauhan, the last Hindu king, was captured and taken back to Mohammed of Ghori's court in Ghazni, where he was later blinded and killed.

Apart from expanding their empire, the Sultanate kings also significantly urbanised Delhi. The Mamluks created the city of Mehrauli, whose most famous monument is the Qutb Minar. The Khiljis, on their part, seated their capital at Siri. The Tughlaqs constructed the forts of Tughlaqabad and Firoz Shah Kotla, while Sher Shah Suri, the most renowned of the Sur kings, chose to rule from Shergarh, built on the site of the Purana Qila, which he had won from the Mughal emperor Humayun.

Despite the glorious developments, however, the Sultanate era was marked by prolonged phases of political turmoil and administrative tension. Having become the jewel of foreign eyes, Delhi was persistently being attacked from the northwest by Mongol, Persian, Turk and Afghan raiders, who all wanted to set up their own outposts in the city. Within

1321	1345	1398	1469
The Tughlaqs come to power in Delhi. Mohammed bin Tughlaq expands his empire but becomes known for inelegant schemes such as creating forgery-prone currency.	Bahmani Sultanate is established in the Deccan following a revolt against the Tughlaqs of Delhi. The capital is set up at Gulbarga, in today's northern Karnataka, later shifting to Bidar.	Timur the Lame invades Delhi, on the pretext that the Sultans of Delhi are too tolerant with their Hindu subjects. He executes more than 100,000 Hindu captives before the battle for Delhi.	Guru Nanak, founder of the Sikh faith, which has millions of followers within and beyond India to the present day, is born in a village near Lahore (in modern-day Pakistan).

the empire, stability had given way to turncoat politics, conspiracy and internal strife, as deceitful kings contrived bloody assassinations and coups to either remove or upstage their predecessors. Things got murkier with time, until two noblemen who were disgraced by Emperor Ibrahim Lodi decided to get even with the Sultan by inviting Babur, prince of Kabul, to invade Delhi. Ironically, in plotting their revenge, the two men unknowingly paved the way for the most celebrated Islamic dynasty to roll into India.

Enter the Mughals

Babur, whose Turkic-Mongol lineage included great warriors such as Genghis Khan and Timur the Lame, marched into India through Punjab, defeating Ibrahim Lodi in the First Battle of Panipat (1526) to establish the Mughal dynasty in the country. Once he had seized Delhi, Babur focused his attention on Rajasthan, where many princely states, anticipating his moves, had already banded together to form a united front under the Sisodia king Rana Sanga. Taking advantage of the chaos in Delhi, the Rajputs had meanwhile clawed their way back in the power race, and states such as Mewar had become formidable enough to pose a considerable threat to the rulers of Delhi. Babur, however, squared everything by defeating the Rajput alliance in a blood-spattered battle in which several Rajput chiefs, including Rana Sanga, fell to the enemy's wrath. The defeat, which shook the foundations of the Rajput states, also left the Mughals as the undisputed rulers of northern India.

Mughal supremacy was briefly cut back in the mid-16th century by Sher Shah Suri, who defeated Babur's successor Humayun to give Delhi its sixth and final Sultanate. Humayun reclaimed Delhi 14 years later, and was succeeded upon his accidental death by his 13-year-old son Akbar. Known as the greatest of the Mughal emperors, Akbar ruled for a period of 49 years, and, being a master diplomat, used both tact and military force to expand and consolidate the Mughal empire in India. Realising that the Rajputs could not be conquered on the battlefield alone, Akbar arranged a marriage alliance with a princess of the important Kachhwaha clan which held Amber (and later Jaipur), and even chose Rajput warriors to head his armies. Honoured by these gestures, the Kachhwahas, unlike other Rajputs, aligned themselves with the powerful Mughals, as Akbar indirectly succeeded in winning over one of the biggest Rajput states.

Of course, when diplomacy didn't work, Akbar resorted to war; he conquered Ajmer, and later proceeded to take the mighty forts of Chittorgarh and Ranthambhore. Gradually, all the important Rajput states except Mewar had acknowledged Mughal sovereignty to become vassal states. But even as he was well on his way to becoming the supreme ruler

In 1327 the eccentric Tughlaq emperor Mohammed bin Tughlaq reduced Delhi to a ghost town for two years by moving the entire population to a new capital called Daulatabad, more than 1100km away in the Deccan.

Best Rajput Monuments

Amber Fort, Jaipur

Mehrangarh, Jodhpur

Jaisalmer Fort

Chittorgarh, Chittor

Kumbhalgarh

Ranthambhore Fort

1498	1504	1526	1540
Vasco da Gama, a Portuguese voyager, discovers the sea-route from Europe to India. He arrives in Kerala and engages in trade with the local kings.	Agra is founded on the banks of the Yamuna River by Sikandar Lodi. Its glory days begin when Akbar makes it his capital, and the city is briefly called Akbarabad during his reign.	Babur conquers Delhi and stuns Rajasthan by routing its confederate force, gaining a technological edge on the battlefield due to the early introduction of matchlock muskets in his army.	The Sur dynasty briefly captures Delhi from the Mughals – the loss forces the Mughals to temporarily seek help from the Rajputs.

DELHI'S TWILIGHT YEARS

The death of Aurangzeb marked the beginning of Delhi's Twilight Years, a period through which the degenerating Mughal empire was laid to waste by the Marathas and the Persians. The Marathas had risen to prominence between 1646 and 1680 led by the heroic Shivaji, under whom their empire was administered by the *peshwas* (or chief ministers), who later went on to become hereditary rulers. At a time when the Mughals were struggling to hold their empire together, the Marathas supplied them with regiments from the south, gaining their own stranglehold on Delhi at the same time. The new army soon went out of control and began to take possession of the land. Contemporary Mughal rulers, who were both ineffective and cowardly, failed to curb the unruly military behaviour. The resulting confusion was capitalised on by the Persian invader Nadir Shah, who sacked Delhi in 1739 and robbed the city of much of its wealth. Seeing which way the wind was blowing, the Marathas abandoned the Mughals and joined the Persians in pillaging the capital. They soon sucked Delhi dry of all its treasures, and when there was nothing left to rob, the Marathas turned their eyes on Rajasthan. Raids and skirmishes with the Rajputs followed; cities were sacked, lives were lost, and the Marathas began to win large tracts of Rajput land in the state. The absence of a central Indian authority only contributed to the mayhem, so much so that India had to wait till the early 19th century for another invasion to bring the country under a single umbrella once again.

of India, Akbar became more tolerant in many ways. He married a Hindu Rajput princess and encouraged good relations between Hindus and Muslims, giving Rajputs special privileges so that they were embraced within his empire. A monarch with great social insight, he discouraged child marriage, banned *sati* (ritual suicide of a widow on her husband's funeral pyre) and arranged special market days for women. Akbar's reign also saw an unprecedented economic boom in the country, as well as great development in art and architecture.

While the construction of the Qutb Minar in Delhi was started by Qutb-ud-din Aibak in 1193, it was completed during the reign of Firoz Shah, more than 150 years later.

The Last of the Mughal Greats

Jehangir, Akbar's son, was the next Mughal emperor (r 1605–27), and he ruled alongside his adored Persian wife, Nur Jahan, who wielded considerable power and brought Persian influences to the court. Nur Jahan also commissioned the beautiful Itimad-ud-Daulah, the first Mughal structure to be built in marble, in Agra for her parents. The Rajputs maintained cordial relationships with the Mughals through Jehangir's rule, a notable development being that Udai Singh, king of Udaipur, ended Mewar's reservations about the Muslims by befriending Jehangir.

Good times, however, came to an end soon after Jehangir's period in office, as his descendants' greater emphasis on Islam began to rock the

1556	1568	1608	1631
Hemu, a Hindu general in Adil Shah Suri's army, seizes Delhi after Humayun's death. He rules for barely a month before losing to Akbar in the Second Battle of Panipat.	Akbar leads his army to Chittorgarh and wrests it from the Sisodias. Udai Singh, then king of Mewar, survives the onslaught and transfers his capital to the new city of Udaipur.	Granted trading rights by way of a royal charter, the first ships of the British East India Company sail up the Arabian Sea to drop anchor at Surat in Gujarat.	Construction of the Taj Mahal begins after Shah Jahan, devastated by the death of his wife Mumtaz Mahal, vows to build the most beautiful mausoleum in the world in her memory.

relative peace in the region. Upon Jehangir's death, the prince Khurram took over, assuming the title Shah Jahan, which meant 'monarch of the world'. His reign was the pinnacle of Mughal power. Like his predecessors, Shah Jahan was a patron of the arts, and some of the finest examples of Mughal art and architecture were produced during his reign, including the Taj Mahal, an extravagant work of extreme refinement and beauty. Shah Jahan also commenced work on Delhi's seventh incarnation, Shahjahanabad, constructing the Red Fort and the Jama Masjid.

Unfortunately, the emperor harboured high military ambitions, and often bled the country's financial resources to meet his whims. His exhaustion of the state treasury didn't go down well with the Rajputs, and towards the end of Shah Jahan's rule, the Rajputs and the Mughals had become uneasy bedfellows. Things worsened when Aurangzeb became the last great Mughal emperor in 1658, deposing his father who died in imprisonment at Musamman Burj in Agra eight years later. An Islamic hardliner, Aurangzeb quickly made enemies in the region. His zeal saw him devoting all his resources to extending the Mughal empire's boundaries. His government's emphasis on Islam alienated his Hindu subjects. Aurangzeb imposed punitive taxes, banned the building of new temples, destroyed many more, and forbade music and ceremonies at court. Challenges to his power mounted steadily as people reacted against his dour reign. And when he claimed his rights over Jodhpur in 1678, his relations with the Rajputs turned into full-scale war. Before long, there was insurgency on all sides, which only increased as Aurangzeb died in 1707 to leave the empire in the hands of a line of inefficient successors given to bohemian excesses, who had little or no interest in running the state. The Mughal empire was on a one-way journey towards doom.

The British Drop Anchor
The British invaders came by the sea, following the Portuguese explorer Vasco da Gama, who had first discovered the sea route from Europe to India around Africa in 1498. The British East India Company, a London trading firm that wanted a slice of the Indian spice trade (having seen how well the Portuguese were doing), landed in India in the early 1600s. Granted trading rights by Jehangir, the company set up its first trading outpost in Surat in Gujarat, and gradually went about extending its influence across the country, harbouring interests that went beyond mere trade. Extraordinarily enough, this commercial firm ended up nominally ruling India for 250 years.

Sooner or later, all leading European maritime nations came and pitched tent in India. Yet none managed to spread out across the country as efficiently as the British. The early English agents became well assimilated in India, learning Persian and intermarrying with local people,

Known for his religious tolerance, Akbar propounded a cult called Din-i-Ilahi, which incorporated the best elements of the two principal religions of his empire, Hinduism and Islam.

William Dalrymple's *City of Djinns* is a wonderful book that draws upon his personal experiences in Delhi, and chronicles the fascinating history of the city in its many incarnations.

1674	1707	1739	1747
Shivaji establishes the Maratha kingdom, spanning western India and parts of the Deccan and north India. He assumes the supercilious title of Chhatrapati ('Lord of the Universe').	Death of Aurangzeb, the last of the Mughal greats. His demise triggers the gradual collapse of the Mughal empire, as anarchy and rebellion break out across the country.	Nadir Shah plunders Delhi, and carries away with him the Peacock Throne, as well as the Koh-i-noor, a magnificent diamond which eventually becomes the property of the British royalty.	Afghan ruler Ahmad Shah Durrani sweeps across northern India, capturing Lahore and Kashmir, sacking Delhi and dealing another blow to the rapidly contracting Mughal empire.

The Great Mughals

Babur
(r 1526–1530)

Humayun
(r 1530–1556)

Akbar
(r 1556–1605)

Jehangir
(r 1605–1627)

Shah Jahan
(r 1627–1658)

Aurangzeb
(r 1658–1707)

The Doctrine of Lapse, a policy formulated by Lord Dalhousie, enabled the East India Company to annex any princely state if its ruler was either found incompetent or died without a direct heir.

which gave them an edge over other European hopefuls. When the Mughal empire collapsed, they made a calculated political move, filling the power vacuum and taking over the reins of administration through a series of battles and alliances with local rulers. By the early 19th century, India was effectively under British control, and the British government in London had begun to take a more direct role in supervising affairs in India, while leaving the East India Company to deal with day-to-day administrative duties.

Outside British territory, the country was in a shambles. Bandits were on the prowl in the rural areas, and towns and cities had fallen into decay. The Marathas' raids in Rajasthan continued, and though the British at first ignored the feuding parties, they soon spotted an opportunity for expansion and stepped into the fray. They negotiated treaties with the leaders of the main Rajput states, offering them protection from the Marathas in return for political and military support. The trick worked. Weakened by habitual wrangling and ongoing conflicts, the rulers forfeited their independence in exchange for protection, and British residents were installed in the princely states. The British ultimately eliminated the Maratha threat, but, in the process, the Rajputs were effectively reduced to puppets. Delhi's prominence as a national capital dwindled too, as the British chose to rule the country from Calcutta (now Kolkata).

The later British authorities had an elitist notion of their own superiority that was to have a lasting impact on India. The colonisers felt that it was their duty to civilise the nation, unlike the first agents of the East India Company who had seen and recognised the value in India's native culture. During the first half of the 19th century, the British brought about radical social reforms. They introduced education in the English language, which replaced Persian as the language of politics and governance. New roads and canal systems were installed, followed by the foundation of schools and universities modelled on the British system of education. In the later stages, they brought in the postal system, the telegraph and the railways, introductions that remain vital to the Indian administrative system today.

But at the same time, British bureaucracy came with controversial policies. Severe taxes were imposed on landowners and, as raw materials from India were used in British industry, cheap British-produced goods began to flood Indian markets and destroy local livelihoods. Mass anger in the country began to rise, and found expression in the First War of Independence (Indian Uprising) in 1857. Soldiers and peasants took over Delhi for four months and besieged the British Residency in Lucknow for five months before they were finally suppressed by the East India Company's forces. Rajasthan also saw uprisings among the poor and middle classes, but there was little effect in the royal circles as Rajput kings

1756	1757	1857	1858
The rise of the notorious Jat dynasty of Bharatpur in Rajasthan. Under the leadership of Suraj Mahl and his son Jawahar Singh, the Jats join the Marathas and Persians in looting Delhi and Agra.	Breaking out of its business mould, the East India Company registers its first military victory on Indian soil. Siraj-ud-Daulah, nawab of Bengal, is defeated by Robert Clive in the Battle of Plassey.	The short-lived First War of Independence breaks out across India. In the absence of a national leader, the rebels coerce the last Mughal king Bahadur Shah Zafar to proclaim himself emperor of India.	British government assumes control over India – with power officially transferred from the East India Company to the Crown – beginning the period known as the British Raj.

THE FIRST WAR OF INDEPENDENCE: THE INDIAN UPRISING

In 1857, half a century after having established firm control of India, the British suffered a serious setback. To this day, the causes of the Uprising (known at the time as the Indian Mutiny and subsequently labelled by nationalist historians as the War of Independence) are the subject of debate. The key factors included the influx of cheap goods, such as textiles, from Britain which destroyed many livelihoods, the dispossession of territories from many rulers and taxes imposed on landowners.

The incident that's popularly held to have sparked the Uprising, however, took place at an army barracks in Meerut in Uttar Pradesh on 10 May 1857. A rumour leaked out that a new type of bullet was greased with what Hindus claimed was cow fat, while Muslims maintained that it came from pigs; pigs are considered unclean to Muslims, and cows are sacred to Hindus. Since loading a rifle involved biting the end off the waxed cartridge, these rumours provoked considerable unrest.

In Meerut, the situation was handled with a singular lack of judgment. The commanding officer lined up his soldiers and ordered them to bite off the ends of their issued bullets. Those who refused were immediately marched off to prison. The following morning, the soldiers of the garrison rebelled, shot their officers and marched to Delhi. Of the 74 Indian battalions of the Bengal army, seven (one of them Gurkhas) remained loyal, 20 were disarmed and the other 47 mutinied. The soldiers and peasants rallied around the ageing Mughal emperor in Delhi. They held Delhi for some months and besieged the British Residency in Lucknow for five months before they were finally suppressed. The incident left festering scars on both sides.

Almost immediately the East India Company was wound up, and direct control of the country was assumed by the British government, which announced its support for the existing rulers of the princely states, claiming they would not interfere in local matters as long as the states remained loyal to the British.

continued to support the British, and were rewarded for their loyalty after the British government assumed direct control of the country the following year.

Independence, Partition & After

Following a lengthy freedom movement, India finally liberated itself from British domination in 1947. The road to Independence was an extraordinary one, influenced by Mohandas Karamchand Gandhi, later known as the Mahatma (Great Soul), who galvanised the peasants and villagers into a nonviolent resistance that was to spearhead the nationalist movement. A lawyer by qualification, he caused chaos by urging people to refuse to pay taxes and boycott British institutions and products. He campaigned for the Dalits (the lower classes of Hindu society, who he called Harijans or the 'Children of God'), and the rural

In an attempt to prevent partition, Mahatma Gandhi unsuccessfully argued that the leader of the Muslim League, Mohammed Ali Jinnah, should lead a united India.

1869	1885	1906	1911
The birth of Mohandas Karamchand Gandhi in Porbandar (Gujarat) – the man who would later become popularly known as Mahatma Gandhi and affectionately dubbed 'Father of the Nation'.	The Indian National Congress, India's first home-grown political organisation, is set up. It brings educated Indians together and plays a key role in India's freedom struggle.	All-India Muslim League is formed, following an education conference in Dhaka, in response to concerns that a Hindu majority would not recognise Islam or serve Muslim interests.	Architect Edwin Lutyens begins work on New Delhi, the newest manifestation of Delhi, subsequently considered in architectural circles to be one of the finest garden cities ever built.

MEANWHILE IN AGRA

As Delhi's light began to shine again, Agra, sadly, slid further from recognition. Being predominantly a satellite capital, where power occasionally spilt over from Delhi, the city had lost most of its political importance after the Mughals had departed. In the modern context, it made little sense to invest it with any kind of government machinery, so much so that it lost out to Lucknow when it came to selecting a state capital for Uttar Pradesh. Nonetheless, Agra continues to be high up on the tourism map of India, as travellers throng the city to visit its many historic sites and monuments.

Best Mughal Monuments

Taj Mahal, Agra

Fatehpur Sikri

Humayun's Tomb, Delhi

Jama Masjid, Delhi

Agra Fort, Agra

Red Fort, Delhi

poor, capturing public imagination through his approach, example and rhetoric. The freedom struggle gained momentum under him such that the British Labour Party, which came to power in 1945, saw Indian independence as inevitable. The process of the handover of power was initiated, but Hindu–Muslim differences took their toll at this crucial moment, and saw the country being divided on religious lines, with Pakistan being formed to appease the Muslim League, which sought to distance itself from a Hindu-dominated country.

Prior to the change of guard, the British had shifted their capital out of Calcutta (Kolkata) and built the imperial city of New Delhi through the early 1900s, work on which was overseen by architect Edwin Lutyens. Meant to be an expression of British permanence, the city was speckled with grand structures such as the Rashtrapati Bhavan, the Central Vista and hundreds of residential buildings that came to be known as Lutyens Bungalows. After Independence, many of these colonial buildings were used to house the brand-new Indian government, as Delhi was reinstated to its former status as the administrative and political capital of the country.

The long history of insurgency and unrest in India did not end with Independence. In 1962, India had a brief war with China over disputed border territories, and went on to engage in three battles with Pakistan over similar issues. Political assassinations didn't recede into history either. Mahatma Gandhi was slain soon after Independence by a Hindu extremist who hated his inclusive philosophy. Indira Gandhi, India's first woman prime minister (and daughter of Jawaharlal Nehru, India's prime minister at Independence) was gunned down by her Sikh bodyguards in retaliation for her ordering the storming of the Golden Temple, the holiest of Sikh shrines, in 1984. Her son, Rajiv, who succeeded her to the post of prime minister was also assassinated by Tamil terrorists protesting India's stance on Sri Lankan policies. Rajiv's Italian-born widow, Sonia, was the next of the Gandhis to take up the dynastic mantle of power. She

1940	1947	1948	1948–56
The Muslim League adopts its Lahore Resolution, which champions greater Muslim autonomy in India. Subsequent campaigns for a separate Islamic nation are spearheaded by Mohammed Ali Jinnah.	India gains independence on 15 August. Pakistan is formed a day earlier. Thousands of Hindus and Muslims brave communal riots to migrate to their respective nations.	Mahatma Gandhi is assassinated in New Delhi on 30 January by Nathuram Godse. Godse and his co-conspirator Narayan Apte are later tried, convicted and executed.	Rajasthan takes shape, as the princely states form a beeline to sign the Instrument of Accession and give up their territories, which are incorporated into the newly formed Republic of India.

became president of the Congress Party, and in 2004 anointed her son Rahul as chosen successor. However, in Rajasthan as elsewhere across India, the party that has fed on the reputation and charisma of the Nehru-Gandhi dynasty since India's formative years was swept away in a 2014 electoral tidal wave that brought the Bharatiya Janata Party (BJP) into power, led by the dynamic figure of Narendra Modi.

Rajasthan is Born

Ever since they swore allegiance to the British, the Rajput kingdoms subjugated themselves to absolute British rule. Being reduced to redundancy, they also chose to trade in their real power for pomp and extravagance. Consumption took over from chivalry and, by the early 20th century, many of the kings were spending their time travelling the world with scores of retainers, playing polo and occupying entire floors of

MAHARAJA METAMORPHOSIS

The fate of the royal families of Rajasthan since Independence has been mixed. A handful of the region's maharajas have continued their wasteful ways, squandering away their fortunes and reducing themselves to abject poverty. A few zealous ones, who hated to see their positions of power go, have switched to politics and become members of leading political parties in India. Some have skipped politics to climb the rungs of power in other well-known national institutions, such as sports administration bodies or charitable and nonprofit organisations in the country. Only a few have chosen to lead civilian lives, earning a name for themselves as fashion designers, cricketers or entertainers.

The majority of kings, however, have refused to let bygones be bygones, and have cashed in on their heritage by opening ticketed museums for tourists and converting their palaces to lavish hotels. With passing time, the luxury hospitality business has begun to find more and more takers from around the world. The boom in this industry can be traced back to 1971, when Indira Gandhi, then India's Prime Minister, abolished the privileges granted to the Rajasthan princes at the time of accession. Coming as a massive shock to those at the top of the pile, the snipping of the cash cord forced many kings to inadvertently join the long list of heritage hotel owners.

In spite of the abolition, many kings choose to continue using their royal titles for social purposes. While these titles mean little more than status symbols now, they still help garner enormous respect from the public. On the other hand, nothing these days quite evokes the essence of Rajput grandeur like a stay in palatial splendour surrounded by vestiges of the regal age, in places such as the Rambagh Palace (p115; Jaipur) and the Umaid Bhawan Palace (p173; Jodhpur). Not all the royal palaces of Rajasthan are on the tourist circuit, though. Many of them continue to serve as residences for erstwhile royal families, and some of the mansions left out of the tourism pie are crumbling away, ignored and neglected, their decaying interiors home to pigeons and bats.

1952	1971	1984	1998
The first elections are held in Rajasthan, and the state gets its first taste of democracy after centuries of monarchical rule. The Congress is the first party to be elected to office.	The Third Indo-Pakistan War spills into Rajasthan, with the Battle of Longewala fought in the Thar Desert. The conflict concludes with the independence of East Pakistan as Bangladesh.	Prime Minister Indira Gandhi is assassinated by her Sikh bodyguards. Her son Rajiv succeeds her as leader, but is himself murdered in office in 1991.	India faces international condemnation for carrying out nuclear weapons testing. Pakistan shortly follows suit with its own tests.

expensive Western hotels. Many maintained huge fleets of expensive cars, a fine collection of which can be seen in the automobile museum at the Garden Hotel in Udaipur. While it suited the British to indulge them, the maharajas' profligacy was economically and socially detrimental to their subjects, with the exception of a few capable rulers such as Ganga Singh of Bikaner. Remnants of the Raj (the British government in India before 1947) can be spotted all over the region today, from the Mayo College in Ajmer to the colonial villas in Mt Abu, and black-and-white photographs, documenting chummy Anglo-Rajput hunting expeditions, which deck the walls of any self-respecting heritage hotel in the state.

The Proudest Day: India's Long Road to Independence, by Anthony Read and David Fisher, is an engaging account of India's pre-Independence period.

After Independence it became crucial, from a security point of view, for the new Indian union to ensure that the princely states of Rajasthan were integrated into the new nation. Most of these states were located near the vulnerable India–Pakistan border, and it made sense for the government to push for a merger that would minimise possibilities of rebellion in the region. Thus, when the boundaries of the new nation were being chalked out, the ruling Congress Party made a deal with the nominally independent Rajput states to cede power to the republic. To sweeten the deal, the rulers were offered lucrative monetary returns and government stipends, as well as being allowed to retain their titles and property holdings. Having fallen on hard times, the royals couldn't but agree with the government, and their inclination to yield to the Indian dominion gradually brought about the formation of the state of Rajasthan.

To begin with, the state comprised only the southern and southeastern regions of Rajasthan. Mewar was one of the first kingdoms to join the union. Udaipur was initially the state capital, with the maharaja of Udaipur becoming rajpramukh (head of state). The Instrument of Accession was signed in 1949, and Jaipur, Bikaner, Jodhpur and Jaisalmer were then merged, with Jaipur as the state's new capital. Later that year, the United State of Matsya was incorporated into Rajasthan. The state finally burgeoned to its current dimensions in November 1956, with the additions of Ajmer-Merwara, Abu Rd and a tract of Dilwara, originally part of the princely state of Sirohi that had been divided between Gujarat and Rajasthan. Rajasthan is now India's largest state.

2001	2012	2014	2015
A suicide attack on the Indian parliament in New Delhi nearly leads to war with Pakistan, with mass troop mobilisation along the border including in Rajasthan.	The gang-rape and murder of a female medical student in Delhi brings forth protests across the country and internationally, and new anti-rape laws.	Narendra Modi becomes prime minister, as the Hindu-nationalist BJP wins parliamentary elections in a landslide.	The anti-corruption Aam Aadmi Party (AAP) unexpectedly wins state elections in Delhi, overturning the BJP ascendancy.

Rajasthani Way of Life

From the tribal villages of Rajasthan and ancient palaces of the Rajput kings to the modern hustle of Delhi, there are few places in India where traditional and modern life jut up against each other as they do in this region, and in such an exciting and intriguing manner.

Contemporary Life

Indian society as a whole continues to grapple with the competing claims of traditionalism and the effects of globalisation. Cities such as Delhi and Jaipur may have acquired a liberal sheen on the outside, and foreign influences are apparent in the public domain: satellite TV rules the airwaves, mobile phones are nothing short of a necessity, and coffee shops are jam-packed on the weekends. But within the walls of a typical home, life often remains conservative at heart, with family affairs dominated by the man of the house. Gender politics, from sexual relationships outside marriage to the independence of women, are a touchstone issue. The gang-rape and death of a female medical student in Delhi in 2012, and the very public reactions against it, shone a light on some of the fault lines that Indian society is trying to negotiate.

In the region's backyard, the scene is rather stark. Rural Rajasthan remains one of the poorest areas in the country. Being in close proximity to the Thar Desert, the climate here is harsh, and people dwelling in the region's villages are locked in a day-to-day battle for survival, as they have been for ages. Unemployment is rife, which in turn has led to problems such as debt, drug abuse, alcoholism and prostitution. Indigenous tribes have been the worst affected and it isn't uncommon to see members from their communities begging or performing tricks at Delhi's traffic signals in return for loose change.

Rajasthan also lags behind on the education front, its literacy rate being about 8% behind the national average of 74.4%. Introduced in 2001, the nationwide 'education-for-all' program aims to impart elementary education to all Indian children. The project focuses on the education of girls, who have historically been deprived of quality schooling; a particular problem in Rajasthan, where the female literacy rate is just under 50%, compared to two-thirds of men.

Rustom Bharucha's *Rajasthan: An Oral History* is a great book to read your way into the patterns of traditional Rajasthani life.

Marriage & Divorce

Indian marriages were always meant to unite families, not individuals. In rural Rajasthan, this remains much the same today. Unlike in cities, where people now find love through online dating sites, weddings in villages and small towns are still arranged by parents. Those getting married have little say in the proceedings and cross-caste marriages are almost always forbidden. Few move out of their parents' homes after tying the knot; setting up an independent establishment post-marriage is often considered an insult to the elderly.

FIRST IMPRESSIONS

It's not the turbaned maharajas, or the call-centre graduates, or even the stereotypical beggars, for that matter. The first people you run into upon arriving in Rajasthan, Agra or Delhi are a jostling bunch of overly attentive locals, who ambush travellers the moment they step out of the airport or the railway station and swamp them in a sea of unsolicited offers. Great hotels, taxi rides at half-price, above-the-rate currency exchange...the list goes on, interspersed with beaming smiles you would usually only expect from long-lost friends. Famed Indian hospitality at work? This is no reception party; the men are touts out on their daily rounds, trying to wheedle a few bucks off unsuspecting travellers. There's no way you can escape them, though a polite but firm 'no, thank you' often stands you in good stead under such circumstances. It's a welcome each and every newcomer is accorded in India.

It's hard not to get put off by the surprise mobbing, but don't let the incident make you jump to the hasty conclusion that every local is out to hound the daylights out of you. Walk out of the terminal and into the real India, and things suddenly come across as strikingly different. With little stake in your activities, the people you now meet are genuinely warm (even overtly curious), hospitable and sometimes helpful beyond what you'd call mere courtesy. For example, someone might volunteer to show you around a monument expecting absolutely nothing in return. And while it's advisable to always keep your wits about you, going with the flow often helps you understand the Indian psyche better, as well as making your trip to the region all the more memorable.

By and large, marriages in rural areas are initiated by professional matchmakers who strike a suitable match based on family status, caste and compatible horoscopes. Once a marriage is finalised, the bride's family often arranges for dowry to be paid to the groom's parents, as an appreciation of their graciously accepting the bride as a member of their family. These dowries are officially banned, but remain commonplace and can run into hundreds of thousands of rupees, ranging from hard cash to items such as TVs, motorcycles and household furniture. Despite the exact amount of dowry being finalised at the time of betrothal, there have been sporadic cases reported where the groom's family later insists that the girl's parents cough up more, failing which the bride might be subjected to abuse and domestic violence. Stories of newly married girls dying in kitchen 'accidents' are not uncommon. In most cases, they leave the grooms free to remarry and claim another dowry.

Indian law sets the marriageable age of men and women at 21 and 18 respectively, yet child marriages continue to occur in rural Rajasthan. It is estimated that one in every two girls in the state's villages are married off before they turn 15. Divorce, on the other hand, remains forbidden, which complicates things if marriages don't work out. Even if a divorce is obtained, it is difficult for a woman to find another husband; as a divorcee, she is considered less chaste than an unmarried woman. Given the stigma associated with divorce, few people have the courage to walk out on each other, instead preferring to silently endure. Widows also face frequent social stigma. While the practice of *sati* (the ritual self-immolation of a wife on her husband's funeral pyre) has passed into history, many expect widows to remain in mourning for the rest of their lives, and face being ostracised from their families and communities.

Matchmaking has embraced the cyber age, with popular sites including www.shaadi.com, www.bharatmatrimony.com and, more recently, www.secondshaadi.com – for those seeking a partner again.

Women in Rajasthan

Women are seen primarily as mothers in Indian society, and gender equality is a distant aspiration for the majority of Rajasthani women. Being socially disadvantaged, women face many restrictions on their freedoms, and, as keepers of a family's honour, they risk accusations of immorality if they mingle freely with strangers. For a visitor to India, it can be quite disconcerting to walk through a rural village and see women beating a quick retreat into the privacy of their homes, their faces hidden behind folds of their saris. In Indian culture, a woman's beauty is only for her family to appreciate.

Screened from the outside world, most women in rural Rajasthan live a life that revolves around strenuous household tasks and raising children. Where women are permitted to work, this usually involves toiling in the family fields. Even in professional circles, women are generally paid less than their male counterparts. Besides all this, India's patriarchal society rarely recognises women as inheritors of family property, which almost always goes to male heirs. The birth of a girl child is often seen as unlucky, since it not only means an extra mouth to feed, but also a dowry that needs to be given away at the time of marriage. Embryo sex determination, despite being illegal, is practised, and local media occasionally blows the lid off surgical rackets where surgeons charge huge amounts of money to carry out female-foeticide operations.

Progress has been made, however, in the form of development programs run by the central and state governments, as well as nongovernmental organisations (NGOs) and voluntary outfits that have swung into action. Organisations such as the Barefoot College, URMAL Trust and Seva Mandir all run grass-roots programs in Rajasthan – with volunteering opportunities (p255) – devoted to awareness, education, health issues and female empowerment.

In the cities, the scene is much better. Urban women in Delhi and Jaipur have worked their way to social and professional recognition, and feminists are no longer dismissed as fringe extremists. Even so, some of India's first-generation female executives recall a time not very long ago when employers would go into a tizz every time a woman put in a request for maternity leave, as motherhood had been precluded as an occasion that merited time off from work.

Opium was traditionally served to guests at social functions held by several indigenous communities of Rajasthan. Though the sale of opium is now illegal, it continues behind the backs of law-enforcers.

Peoples of Rajasthan

Demographically speaking, much of the region's population still lives in its villages but people are on the move. The cities attract people from all walks of life to creating a high-density, multiethnic population. Religious ghettos can be found in places such as Ajmer and Jaipur, where a fair number of Christian families live; the Ganganagar district, home to a large number of Sikhs; and parts of Alwar and Bharatpur, where the populace is chiefly Muslim. Though most Muslims in Rajasthan belong to the Sunni sect, the state also has a small but affluent community of Shiite Muslims, called the Bohras, living to the southeast.

Tribes & Indigenous Communities

Rajasthan has a large indigenous population, comprising communities that are native to the region and have lived there for centuries. Called

---

HIJRAS – THE THIRD SEX

India's most visible nonheterosexual group is the *hijras*, a caste of transvestites and eunuchs who dress in women's clothing. Some are gay, some are hermaphrodites and some were unfortunate enough to be kidnapped and castrated. Since it has long been traditionally frowned upon to live openly as a gay man in India, *hijras* get around this by becoming, in effect, a third sex of sorts. They work mainly as wandering entertainers at weddings and celebrations of the birth of male children, and also as prostitutes.

Read more about *hijras* in *The Invisibles* by Zia Jaffrey and *Ardhanarishvara the Androgyne* by Alka Pande.

CRICKET

Cricket is a national obsession in India, and Rajasthan is no exception. Nearly everybody claims to understand the game down to its finer points, and can comment on it with endless vigour. Shops down shutters and streets take on a deserted look every time India happens to be playing a test match or a crucial one-day game. The arrival of the Twenty20 format and domestic leagues such as the Indian Premier League (IPL) has only taken the game's popularity a notch further.

Keep your finger on the cricketing pulse at www.espncricinfo.com and www.cricbuzz. com. Cricket tragics will be bowled over by *The Illustrated History of Indian Cricket* by Boria Majumdar and *The States of Indian Cricket* by Ramachandra Guha.

Adivasis (ancient dwellers), most of these ethnic groups have been listed as Scheduled Tribes by the government. The majority of the Adivasis are pagan, though some have either taken to Hindu ways or converted to Christianity over time.

Bhils

The largest of Rajasthan's tribes, the Bhils live to the southeast, spilling over into Madhya Pradesh. They speak their own distinct native language and have a natural talent for archery and warfare. Witchcraft, magic and superstition are deeply rooted in their culture. Polygamy is still practised by those who can afford it, and love marriages are the norm.

Originally a hunter-gatherer community, the Bhils have survived years of exploitation by higher castes to finally take up small-scale agriculture. Some have left their villages to head for the cities. Literacy is still below average and not too many Bhil families have many assets to speak of, but these trends are slowly being reversed. The Baneshwar Fair is a huge Bhil festival, where you can sample the essence of their culture first hand.

Minas

The Minas are the second-largest tribal group in Rajasthan and live around Shekhawati and eastern Rajasthan. The name Mina comes from *meen* (fish), and the tribe claims it evolved from the fish incarnation of Vishnu. Minas once ruled supreme in the Amber region, but their miseries began once they were routed by the Rajputs. To make matters worse, they were outlawed during the British Raj, after their guerrilla tactics earned them the 'criminal-tribe' label. Following Independence, the criminal status was lifted and the Minas subsequently took to agriculture.

Festivities, music and dance form a vital part of Mina culture; they excel in performances such as swordplay and acrobatics. Minas view marriage as a noble institution, and their weddings are accompanied by enthusiastic celebrations. They are also known to be friendly with other tribes and don't mind sharing space with other communities.

For comprehensive information on India's native and tribal communities, check out the website www.tribal.nic.in, maintained by the Ministry of Tribal Affairs under the Government of India.

Bishnois

The Bishnois are the most progressive of Rajasthan's indigenous communities, and even have their presence on the internet (http://bishnoi.org). However, they can't be strictly classified as a tribe. The Bishnois owe their origin to a visionary named Jambho Ji, who in 1485 shunned the Hindu social order to form a casteless faith that took inspiration from nature. Credited as the oldest environmentalist community in India, the Bishnois are animal-lovers and take an active interest in preserving forests and wildlife. Felling of trees and hunting within Bishnoi territory is strictly prohibited.

Sacred India

Hindus comprise nearly 90% of Rajasthan's population. Much of the remaining 10% are Muslims, followed by decreasing numbers of Sikhs, Jains, Christians and Buddhists. In spite of this religious diversity, tolerance levels here are high and incidents of communal violence are rare, at least in comparison to the volatile nature of things in the neighbouring state of Gujarat.

Hinduism & the Caste System

Hinduism is among the world's oldest religious traditions, with its roots going back at least 3000 years. Theoretically, Hinduism is not a religion; it is a way of life, an elaborate convention that has evolved through the centuries, in contrast to many other religions that can trace their origins to a single founder. Despite being founded on a solid religious base, Hinduism doesn't have a specific theology, or even a central religious institution. It also has no provision for conversion; one is always born a Hindu.

Being an extremely diverse religion, Hinduism can't be summed up by a universal definition. Yet, there are a few principal tenets that most Hindu sects tend to go by. Hindus believe that all life originates from a supreme spirit called Brahman, a formless, timeless phenomenon manifested by Brahma, the Hindu lord of creation. Upon being born, all living beings are required to engage in dharma (worldly duties) and samsara (the endless cycle of birth, death and rebirth). It is said that the road to salvation lies through righteous karma (actions that evoke subsequent reactions), which leads to moksha (emancipation), when the soul eventually returns to unite with the supreme spirit.

If that's not complex enough, things are convoluted further by the caste system, which broadly divides Hindus into four distinct classes based on their mythical origins and their occupations. On top of the caste hierarchy are the Brahmins, priests who supposedly originated from Brahma's mouth. Next come the Kshatriyas, the warriors who evolved from the deity's arms – this is the caste that the Rajputs fit into. Vaishyas, tradespeople born from the thighs, are third in the pecking order, below which stand the Shudras. Alternatively called Dalits or Scheduled Castes, the Shudras comprise menial workers such as peasants, janitors or cobblers and are known to stem from Brahma's feet. Caste, by the way, is not changeable.

In Hinduism, the syllable 'Om' is believed to be a primordial sound from which the entire universe takes shape. It is also a sacred symbol, represented by an icon shaped like the number three.

Hindu Sacred Texts & Epics

Hindu sacred texts fall under two categories: those believed to be the word of God (*shruti,* meaning 'hearing') and those produced by people (*smriti,* meaning 'memory').

Introduced in the subcontinent by the Aryans, the Vedas are regarded as *shruti* knowledge and are considered to be the authoritative basis for Hinduism. The oldest works of Sanskrit literature, the Vedas contain mantras that are recited at prayers and religious ceremonies. The Vedas are divided into four Samhitas (compilations); the Rig-Veda, the oldest of the Samhitas, is believed to have been written more than 3000 years ago. Other Vedic works include the Brahmanas, touching on rituals; the

RAJASTHANI FOLK GODS & GODDESSES

Folk deities and deified local heroes abound in Rajasthan. Apart from public gods, families are often known to pay homage to a *kuladevi* (family idol).

Pabuji is one of many local heroes to have attained divine status. Pabuji promised to protect the cows of a woman called Devalde, for which he would receive a mare. He was called upon during his own wedding, and in defending the herd against the villainous Jind Raj Khinchi, was killed, along with all his male relatives. To preserve the family line, Pabuji's sister-in-law cut open her own belly and produced Pabuji's nephew, Nandio, before throwing herself on her husband's funeral pyre.

Professional storytellers called Bhopas pay homage to Pabuji by performing *Pabuji-ka-phad*, reciting poetry alongside *phad* (cloth-scroll) paintings that chronicle the life of the hero. You can attend these performances at places such as Chokhi Dhani or Jaisalmer, if they happen at a time when you're around.

Gogaji was an 11th century warrior and could cure snakebite; today, victims are brought to his shrines by both Hindu and Muslim devotees. Also believed to cure snakebite is Tejaji who, according to tradition, was blessed by a snake, which decreed that anyone honouring Tejaji by wearing a thread in his name would be cured of snake bite.

Goddesses revered by Rajasthanis include incarnations of Devi (the Mother Goddess), such as the fierce Chamunda Mata, an incarnation of Durga, and Karni Mata, worshipped at Deshnok near Bikaner. Women who have committed *sati* (self immolation) on their husband's funeral pyres are also frequently worshipped as goddesses, such as Rani Sati, who has an elaborate temple in her honour in Jhunjhunu, Shekhawati. Barren women pay homage to the god Bhairon, an incarnation of Shiva, at his shrines, which are usually found under khejri trees. In order to be blessed with a child, a woman is required to leave a garment hanging from the branches of the tree. The deified folk hero Ramdev also has an important temple at Ramdevra, near Pokaran in western Rajasthan.

Aranyakas, whose name means the 'wilderness texts', meant for ascetics who have renounced the material world; and the Upanishads, which discuss meditation, philosophy, mysticism and the fate of the soul.

The Puranas comprise a post-Vedic genre that chronicles the history of the universe, royal lineages, philosophy and cosmology. The Sutras, on the other hand, are essentially manuals, and contain useful information on different human activities. Some well-known Sutras are Griha Sutra, dealing with the nuances of domestic life; Nyaya Sutra, detailing the faculty of justice and debate; and Kamasutra, a compendium of love and sexual behaviour. The Shastras are also instructive in nature, but are more technical as they provide information pertaining to specific areas of practice. Vaastu Shastra, for example, is an architect's handbook that elaborates on the art of civic planning, while Artha Shastra focuses heavily on governance, economics and military policies of the state.

The Mahabharata is a 2500-year-old rip-roaring epic that centres on the conflict between two fraternal dynasties, the Pandavas and the Kauravas, overseen by Krishna. Locked in a struggle to inherit the throne of Hastinapura, the Kauravas win the first round of the feud, beating their adversaries in a game of dice and banishing them from the kingdom. The Pandavas return after 13 years and challenge the Kauravas to an epic battle, from which they emerge victorious. Being the longest epic in the world, unabridged versions of the Mahabharata incorporate the Bhagavad Gita, the holy book of the Hindus, which contains the worldly advice given by Krishna to Pandava prince Arjuna before the start of the battle.

Composed around the 2nd or 3rd century BC, the Ramayana tells of Rama, an incarnation of Vishnu, who assumed human form to facilitate the triumph of good over evil. Much like the Mahabharata, the Ramayana revolves around a great war, waged by Rama, his brother Lakshmana and an army of apes led by Hanuman against Ravana, the demon king who had kidnapped Rama's wife Sita and had held her hostage in his kingdom of Lanka (Sri Lanka). After slaying Ravana, Rama returned to his kingdom of Ayodhya, his homecoming forming the basis for the important Hindu festival of Dussehra.

Hindu Gods & Goddesses

According to Hindu scriptures, there are around 330 million deities in the Hindu pantheon. All of them are regarded as a manifestation of Brahman (the supreme spirit), which otherwise has three main representations, known as the Trimurti – the trio of Brahma, Vishnu and Shiva.

Brahman

The One; the ultimate reality – Brahman is formless, eternal and the source of all existence. Brahman is *nirguna* (without attributes), as opposed to all the other gods and goddesses, which are manifestations of Brahman and therefore *saguna* (with attributes).

Brahma

The only active role that Brahma ever played was during the creation of the universe. Since then, he has been immersed in eternal meditation and is therefore regarded as aloof. His vehicle is a swan and he is sometimes shown sitting on a lotus.

Vishnu & Krishna

Being the preserver and sustainer of the universe, Vishnu is associated with 'right action'. He is usually depicted with four arms, holding a lotus, a conch shell, a discus and a mace. His consort is Lakshmi, the goddess of wealth, and his vehicle is Garuda, a creature that's half bird, half beast. Vishnu has 10 incarnations, including Rama, Krishna and Buddha. He is also referred to as Narayan.

Krishna, the popular incarnation of Vishnu, was sent to earth to fight for good and combat evil, and his exploits are documented in the Mahabharata. A shrewd politician, his alliances with *gopis* (milkmaids) and his love for Radha, his paramour, have inspired countless paintings and songs.

Shiva & Parvati

Although he plays the role of the destroyer, Shiva's creative role is symbolised by his representation as the frequently worshipped lingam (phallus). With snakes draped around his neck, he is sometimes shown holding a trident while riding Nandi the bull. With 1008 names, Shiva takes many forms, including Pashupati, champion of the animals, and Nataraja, performer of the *tandava* (cosmic dance of fury). He is also the lord of yoga.

Shiva's consort is the beautiful goddess Parvati, who in her dark side appears as Kali, the fiercest of the gods who demands sacrifices and wears a garland of skulls. Alternatively, she appears as the fair Durga, the demon slayer, who wields supreme power, holds weapons in her 10 hands and rides a tiger or a lion.

Ganesh

The pot-bellied, elephant-headed Ganesh is held in great affection by Indians. He is the god of good fortune, prosperity and the patron of scribes, being credited with writing sections of the Mahabharata. Ganesh is good at removing obstacles, and he's frequently spotted above doorways and in the entrances of Indian homes.

Hanuman

Hanuman is the hero of the Ramayana and is Rajasthan's most popular god. He is the loyal ally of lord Rama, and the images of Rama and his

Shiva is sometimes characterised as the lord of yoga, a Himalaya-dwelling ascetic with matted hair, an ash-smeared body and a third eye symbolising wisdom.

wife Sita are emblazoned upon his heart. He is king of the monkeys and thus assures them refuge in temple complexes across the country.

Islam

Islam was founded in Arabia by the Prophet Mohammed in the 7th century AD. The Arabic term 'Islam' means 'surrender', and believers undertake to surrender to the will of Allah (God), which is revealed in the Quran, the holy book of Islam. A devout Muslim is required to pray five times a day, keep daylong fasts through the month of Ramadan, and make a pilgrimage to the holy city of Mecca in Saudi Arabia, if possible.

Islam is monotheistic. God is held as unique, unlimited, self-sufficient and the supreme creator of all things. God never speaks to humans directly; his word is instead conveyed through messengers called prophets, who are never themselves divine. The religion has two prominent sects, the minority Shiites (originating from Mohammed's descendants) and the majority Sunnis, who split soon after the death of Mohammed owing to political differences, and have since gone on to establish their own interpretations and rituals. The most important pilgrimage site for Muslims in Rajasthan is the extraordinary dargah (burial place) of the Sufi saint Khwaja Muin-ud-din Chishti at Ajmer.

Sufism is a mystic tradition derived from Islam, which originated in medieval times. Being largely secular, it has attracted followers from other religions and is widely practised in North India.

Sikhism

Now among the world's largest religions, Sikhism was founded on the sermons of 10 Sikh gurus, beginning with Guru Nanak Dev (1469–1539). The core values and ideology of Sikhism are embodied in the Guru Granth Sahib, the holy book of the Sikhs, which is also considered the eternal guru of Sikhism. The Sikhs evolved as an organised community over time, and devoted themselves to the creation of a standing militia called the Khalsa, which carried out religious, political and martial duties, and protected the Sikhs from foreign threats. The religion, on its part, grew around the central concept of Vaheguru, the universal lord, with whom an eventual union is believed to result in salvation. The Sikhs believe that salvation is achieved through rigorous discipline and meditation, which help them overcome the five evils – ego, greed, attachment, anger and lust.

Guru Nanak introduced five symbols, or articles of faith, to bind Sikhs together and display their religious devotion, and are the most obvious public elements of Sikhism that people encounter. These are: *kesh* (uncut hair, which men cover by a turban); *kangha* (a wooden comb, for cleanliness); *kara* (a steel bracelet, for the bonds of faith and community); *kaccha* (breeches, for self-control and chastity); and *kirpan* (a ceremonial sword, to defend against injustice).

Jainism

The Jain religion was founded around 500 BC by Mahavira, the 24th and last of the Jain *tirthankars* (path finders). Jainism evolved as a reformist movement against the dominance of priests in Hindu society. It steered clear of complicated rituals, rejected the caste system, and believed in reincarnation and eventual moksha by following the example of the *tirthankars*.

Jains are strict vegetarians and revere all forms of life. The religion has two main sects. The Svetambaras (White Clad) wear unstitched white garments; the monks cover their mouths so as not to inhale insects and brush their path before they walk to avoid crushing small creatures. The monks belonging to the Digambaras (Sky Clad), in comparison, go naked. Jainism preaches nonviolence, and its followers are markedly successful in banking and business, which they consider nonviolent professions.

Rajasthani Food

Wherever you go in this region of India, you'll never be far away from something tempting and delicious. From the sweet, decadent deep-fry of a Jaipur street-food stall, to the bliss of a hot cardamom-scented chai (tea) on a freezing Delhi January morning, food is all around you. Moreover, food is never just food here – it marks celebrations and festivals, honours guests, and accompanies births, marriages and deaths.

Making a Meal of It

Rajasthan's cuisine has developed in response to its harsh climate. Fresh fruit and vegetables are rare commodities in desert zones, but these parts of the state overcome the land's shortcomings by serving up an amazing and creative variety of regional dishes, utilising cereals, pulses, spices, milk products and unusual desert fruits in myriad ways. Rajasthan, Delhi and Agra's regal feasts, meanwhile, are the stuff of legend. And modern Delhi ranks as one of the best restaurant destinations in the country, with scores of establishments serving up everything from butter chicken to international fusion cuisine.

Spotlighting rice, *Finest Rice Recipes,* by Sabina Sehgal Saikia, shows just how versatile this humble grain is, with classy creations such as rice-crusted crab cakes.

Bread of Life

A meal is not complete in north India unless it comes with a bountiful supply of roti, little round circles of unleavened bread (also known as chapati), made with fine wholemeal flour and cooked on a *tawa* (hotplate). In Rajasthan you'll also find *sogra,* a thick, heavy chapati made from millet; *makki ki* roti, a fat cornmeal chapati; and *dhokla,* yummy balls of steamed maize flour cooked with coriander, spinach and mint, and eaten with chutney. Yet another kind of roti is a pastry-like *purat* roti, made by repeatedly coating the dough in oil, then folding it to produce a light and fluffy result. *Cheelre,* meanwhile, is a chapati made with gram (chickpea) powder paste, while *bhakri* is a thick roti made from barley, millet or corn, eaten with pounded garlic, red chilli and raw onions by working-class Rajasthanis, and said to prevent sunstroke.

Alongside the world of roti come *puris, parathas* and naans. A *puri* is a delicious North Indian snack of deep-fried wholemeal dough that puffs up like a soft, crispy balloon. Kachori is similar, but here the dough is pepped up with potato, corn or dhal masala. Flaky *paratha* is a soft, circular bread, deliciously substantial and mildly elastic, which makes for a scrumptious early morning snack, and is often jazzed up with a small bowl of pickle and a stuffing of paneer (unfermented cheese), *aloo* (potato) or grated vegetables. Naan bread, made with leavened white flour, is distinguished from roti by being larger, thicker and doughier, and cooked on the inner walls of a tandoor (oven) rather than on a *tawa.* Best plain, it is also delicious when laced with garlic and lashings of butter, and filled with paneer, *aloo,* or coconut and raisins.

Rice

Basmati rice is considered the cream of India's crop, its name stemming from the Hindi phrase for 'queen of fragrance'. Aside from the plain

VEGETARIANS & VEGANS

Vegetarians will have no problem maintaining a varied and exciting diet in India.

Vegetarian food is sometimes divided up in India into 'veg' and 'pure veg', a frequently blurred and confusing distinction. As a general rule of thumb, 'veg' usually means the same as it does in the West: without meat, fowl or seafood, but possibly containing butter (in India's case, ghee), dairy products, eggs or honey. 'Pure veg' often refers to what the West knows as vegan food: dishes containing no dairy products, eggs or honey. Other times, 'pure veg' might also mean no onions, garlic or mushrooms (which some Hare Krishna believe can have a negative effect on one's state of consciousness), or even no root vegetables or tubers (since many Jains, according to the principles of ahimsa, are loath to damage plants).

Though it's extremely easy to be vegetarian in India, finding vegan food – outside 'pure veg' restaurants – can be trickier. Many basic dishes include a small amount of ghee, so ask whether a dish is 'pure veg', even in a vegetarian restaurant.

steamed rice variety, you'll find pilau (aka pilaf), a tasty, buttery rice dish, whose Rajasthani incarnations frequently include cinnamon, cardamom, cloves and a handful or two of almonds and pistachios.

Dhal & Cereals

India has around 60 different varieties of dhal. In Rajasthan, the dhal of choice is *urad,* black lentils boiled in water, then cooked with *garam masala,* red chillies, cumin seeds, salt, oil and fresh coriander.

> Even deities have their favourite dishes. Krishna likes milk products, and Ganesh is rarely seen without a bowl of *modak* (sweet rice-flour dumplings).

The state's most popular dhal-based dish is *dhal-bati-choorma,* which mixes dhal with *bati,* buttery hard-baked balls of wholemeal flour, and *choorma,* sweet fried wholemeal-flour balls mixed with sugar and nuts.

Gram-flour dumplings known as *gatta* are a delicious dish usually cooked in yoghurt or masala and *mangodi* are lentil-flour dumplings served in an onion or potato gravy. A speciality of Jodhpur is *kabuli Jodhpuri,* a dish made with meat, vegetables and yet more fried gram-flour balls. *Govind gatta* offers a sweet alternative: lentil paste with dried fruit and nuts rolled into a sausage shape, then sliced and deep-fried. *Pakora* (fritters), *sev* (savoury nibbles) and other salted snacks generally known as *farsan* are all equally derived from chickpea gram.

Meat Matters

While Rajasthan's Brahmins and traders stuck to a vegetarian diet, the Rajputs have a far more carnivorous history. Goat (known as 'mutton' since the days of the British Raj), lamb and chicken are the mainstays; religious taboos make beef forbidden to Hindus, and pork to Muslims.

In the deserts of Jaisalmer, Jodhpur and Bikaner, meats are often cooked without the addition of water, instead using milk, curd, buttermilk and plenty of ghee. Cooked this way, dishes keep for days without refrigeration, a practical advantage in the searing heat of the desert. *Murg ko khaato* (chicken cooked in a curd gravy), *achar murg* (pickled chicken), *kacher maas* (dry lamb cooked in spices), *lal maas* (a rich red dish, usually mutton) and *soor santh ro sohito* (pork with millet dumplings) are all classic desert dishes.

> There's really no such thing, in India, as a 'curry'. The term is thought to be an anglicisation of the Tamil word *kari* (black pepper), coined by bewildered Brits for any dish that included spices.

Maas ka sule, a Rajput favourite, is a dry dish that can be made from partridge, wild boar, chicken, mutton or fish. Marinated chunks of meat are cooked on skewers in a tandoor, then glazed with melted butter and a tangy masala spice mix. Mughlai meat dishes, meanwhile, include rich korma and rogan josh, the former mild, the latter cooked with tomatoes and saffron, and both generously spiked with thick, creamy curd.

Fruit & Vegetables

Rajasthan's delicious *sabji* (vegetable) dishes have to be admired for their inventiveness under frequently hostile growing conditions. Dishes you might come across include *papad ki sabzi*, a simple pappadam made with vegetables and masala (a mixture of spices), and *aloo mangori*, ground lentil paste sun-dried then added with potato to a curry. Once rolled by hand, the paste is now often forced through a machine in a similar way to making pasta. A common vegetarian snack is *aloo* samosa, triangular pastry cones stuffed with spicy potato, while another scrumptious local snack is *mirch bada*, a large chilli coated in a thick layer of deep-fried potato and wheatgerm.

There are a few vegetables specific to the deserts of Rajasthan. These include *mogri*, a type of desert bean, which is made into *mogri mangori* (similar to *aloo mangori*), or a sweeter version known as *methi mangori* – *methi* being the leaf of a green desert vegetable. Another use for these *methi* leaves is in *dana methi*, where they are boiled with *dana* (small pea-shaped vegetables) and mixed with sugar, masala and dried fruit.

With developments in infrastructure, more vegetable dishes are now available in Rajasthan than during its barren, warrior-filled past. Heads of cauliflower are usually cooked dry on their own, with potatoes to make *aloo gobi*. Fresh green peas turn up stir-fried with other vegetables in pilaus and biryanis, in samosas along with potato, and in one of North India's signature dishes, *mattar paneer* (peas and fresh, firm white cheese). Brinjal (eggplant or aubergine), *bhindi* (okra or ladies' fingers) and *saag* (a generic term for leafy greens) are all popular choices.

The desert bears a handful of fruits, too. The small, round *kair* is a favourite of camels as well as people, to whom it is usually served with mango pickle; *kachri* is frequently made into chutney. If you order something that arrives looking like a plate of dry sticks, these are *sangri* (dried wild desert beans). The seeds and beans are soaked overnight in water, boiled, and then fried in oil with masala, dried dates, red chillies, turmeric powder, shredded dried mango, salt, coriander and cumin seeds.

Pickles, Chutneys & Relishes

You're in a pickle without a pickle, or *achar:* no Indian meal is complete without one or two *chatnis* (chutneys) and relishes on the side. A relish can be anything from a roughly chopped onion to a delicately crafted fusion of fruit, nuts and spices. The best known is raita (mildly spiced yoghurt or curd often containing cucumber, tomato or pineapple), which makes a refreshing counter to spicy meals.

Other regional variations include *goonde achar, goonde* being a green fruit that is boiled and mixed with mustard oil and masala. *Kair achar* is a pickle with desert fruit as its base, while *lahsun achar* is an onion pickle. *Lal mirch* is a garlic-stuffed red chilli and *kamrak ka achar* is a pickle made from *kamrak,* a type of desert vegetable with a pungent, sour taste.

To find out more about veganism in India, take a look at www.indianvegan.com. For recipe ideas, pick up a copy of *Spicy Vegan* by Sudha Raina.

Gorge yourself by reading about the extravagant royal recipes of Rajasthan in *Royal Indian Cookery,* by Manju Shivraj Singh, the niece of the late Maharaja Bhawani Singh of Jaipur.

TERRIFIC THALIS

Thalis are the traditional cheap and filling meals made up of a combination of curried dishes, served with relishes, pappadams, yoghurt, *puris* and rice. The term 'thali' also covers the characteristic metal tray-plate on which the meal is frequently served. If you're strapped for cash, thalis are a saviour, especially at local hole-in-the-wall restaurants and railway-station dining halls, since they're far heavier on the stomach than the wallet. In southern Rajasthan, many restaurants serve more sophisticated, sweet and lightly spiced Gujarati thalis – one of the best ways to sample a taste of Gujarati cuisine.

The most widely served are made of raw mango, mixed with spices and mustard oil, with lime, shredded ginger, or with tiny whole shallots.

Dairy

For a taste of the desert, try out a few dishes from the recipe collection, *Classic Cooking of Rajasthan*, by Kaira Jiggs and Raminder Malhotra.

Milk and milk products make a staggering contribution to Indian cuisine (hence the sanctity of the cow), and in Rajasthan they're even more important: *dahi* (curd) is served with most meals and is handy for countering heat in terms of both temperature and spiciness of dishes; firm, unmeltable paneer cheese is a godsend for the vegetarian majority and is used in apparently endless permutations; popular lassi (yoghurt-and-iced-water drink) is just one in a host of nourishing sweet or savoury drinks, often with fruit such as banana or mango added; ghee (clarified butter) is the traditional and pure cooking medium; and the best sweets are made with plenty of condensed, sweetened milk or cream.

Sweets & Desserts

Indians have a heady range of tooth-achingly sweet *mithai* (sweets), made from manifold concoctions of sugar, milk, ghee, nuts and yet more sugar. Rajasthani varieties include *badam ki barfi,* a type of fudge made from sugar, powdered milk, almonds and ghee, and *chakki,* a *barfi* (fudge) made from gram flour, sugar and milk. Gram flour, sugar, cardamom, ghee and dried fruits combined make *churma,* while *ladoo* comes in ball form.

Ghewar is a paste based on *urad* (a mung-bean-type pulse) that's crushed, deep-fried and dipped in sugar syrup flavoured with cardamom, cinnamon and cloves. It's served hot, topped with a thick layer of unsweetened cream and garnished with rose petals.

Kheer is perhaps India's favourite dessert, a delectable, fragrant rice pudding with a light flavour of cardamom, saffron, pistachios, flaked almonds, and cashews or dried fruit. *Gulab jamun* are spongy deep-fried balls of milk dough soaked in rose-flavoured syrup. *Kulfi* is addictive once experienced: delicious, substantially firm-textured, made with reduced milk and flavoured with nuts, fruits and berries, and especially tasty in its pale-green pistachio incarnation, *pista kulfi.*

For the full foodie experience while in Delhi, pick up the *Times Food Guide,* published by the *Times of India* .

Alongside these more sophisticated offerings are food-stall sweets such as *jalebis* (orange-coloured whirls of fried batter dipped in syrup), which melt in the mouth and hang heavy on the conscience.

Drinks

Tea & Coffee

India runs on chai (tea). It's a unique and addictive brew: more milk than water, stewed for a long time and frequently sugary enough to give you an energy boost. A glass of steaming, sweet chai is the perfect antidote to the heat and stress of Indian travel.

PAAN

Meals are often rounded off with *paan,* a fragrant mixture of betel nut (also called areca nut), lime paste, spices and condiments wrapped in an edible, silky *paan* leaf. Peddled by *paan*-wallahs, *paan* is a digestive and mouth-freshener. The betel nut is mildly narcotic and some aficionados eat *paan* the same way heavy smokers consume cigarettes, which can cause these people's teeth to rot.

There are two basic types of *paan:* mitha (sweet) and *saadha* (with tobacco). A parcel of *mitha paan* is a splendid way to finish a satisfying meal – pop the whole parcel in your mouth and chew slowly.

BEWARE OF THOSE BHANG LASSIS!

It's rarely printed in menus, but some restaurants in Rajasthan clandestinely whip up bhang lassi, a yoghurt-and-iced-water beverage laced with bhang, a derivative of marijuana. This 'special lassi' can be a potent concoction – some travellers have been stuck in bed for several miserable days after drinking it; others have become delirious.

If you just crave a simple cuppa, many cafes and restaurants can serve up 'tray tea' or 'English tea'. Coffee used to be fairly unusual in the region, but Delhi and the well-travelled parts of Rajasthan have caught up with the double-mocha-latte ways of the West. At bus and train stations, coffee is still almost indistinguishable from chai: the same combination of water, boiled milk and sugar, but with a dash of instant-coffee powder.

Cooling Off

Aside from the usual gamut of Pepsis and 7Ups, India has a few of its own sugary bottled drinks: the vaguely lemonish Limca and orange Mirinda. *Masala soda* is the quintessential Indian soft drink, but it's an acquired taste. Freshly squeezed orange juice is also widely available, though the most popular street juices are made from sweet lemon and sugar cane, pressed in front of you by a mechanised wheel complete with jingling bells.

Jal jeera is made with lime juice, cumin, mint and rock salt and is sold in large earthenware pots by street vendors as well as in restaurants. *Falooda* is a sweet rose-flavoured Muslim speciality made with milk, cream, nuts and strands of vermicelli.

By far the most popular of all Indian cold drinks, however, is a refreshing sweet or salty lassi (yoghurt drink). Jodhpur is famous for its sweet *makhania* lassis, flavoured with saffron and hearty enough to stand in for a meal. *Chach* is a thin, salted lassi and *kairi chach* is unripe mango juice with water and salt added, widely available in summer and allegedly a good remedy for sunstroke.

Cheers

Most travellers champion Kingfisher beer; other brands here include Royal Challenge, Foster's, Dansberg, London Pilsner and Sandpiper. Served ice-cold, all are equally refreshing. But if you can find draught beer, such as Kingfisher and Golden Peacock, you will certainly notice the better taste over the bottled beer, which has glycerine added as a preservative.

Though the Indian wine industry is still in its infancy, there are signs that Indian wines are slowly being accepted into local markets. One of the best-known Indian wine producers is Sula Wines, which creates a whole slew of different varieties with grapes grown in northern Maharashtra. Meanwhile, Grover Vineyards, established in 1988 near Bengaluru (Bangalore), also has a solid reputation, with a smaller range of wines than Sula.

At the other end of the scale, arak, poignantly called *asha* (hope) in the north of India, is what the poor drink to get blotto. The effects of this distilled rice liquor creep up on you quickly and without warning. Only ever drink this from a bottle produced in a government-controlled distillery. *Never* drink it otherwise – hundreds of people die or are blinded every year in India as a result of drinking arak produced in illicit stills.

Learn more about Sula Wines and their environmentally friendly sustainable agriculture programs at their website, www.sulawines.com.

Arts, Crafts & Architecture

The Rajputs knew how to fight, but they also knew how to create. Rajasthan's culture is a celebration of beauty, manifested through its literature, poetry, music, dance, painting and architecture. The state also has a rich legacy of handicrafts, which are prized the world over, both for their intricate craftsmanship and ornamental appeal.

Arts

Ghungroos are anklets made of metallic bells strung together, worn by Indian classical dancers to accentuate their complex footwork during performances.

Dance

Folk dance forms in Rajasthan are generally associated with indigenous tribes and communities of nomadic gypsies. Each region has its own dance specialities. The *ghoomer* (pirouette) is performed by Bhil women at festivals or weddings, and its form varies from one village to another. The Bhils are also known for *gair,* a men-only dance, that's performed at springtime festivities. Combine the two, and you get *gair-ghoomer,* where women, in a small inner circle, are encompassed by men in a larger circle, who determine the rhythm by beating sticks and striking drums.

Among other popular forms, the *kachhi ghori* dance of eastern Rajasthan resembles a battle performance, where dancers ride cloth or paper horses and spar with swords and shields. To the south, the *neja* is danced by the Minas of Kherwara and Dungarpur just after Holi. A coconut is placed on a large pole, which the men try to dislodge, while the women strike the men with sticks and whips to foil their attempts. A nomadic community called the Kalbelias, traditionally associated with snake charming, performs swirling dances such as the *shankaria,* while the Siddha Jats of Bikaner are renowned for their spectacular fire dance, performed on a bed of hot coals, which supposedly leaves no burns.

Painting & Sculpture
Miniatures

Get arty with *Indian Art* by Roy Craven, *Contemporary Indian Art: Other Realities* edited by Yashodhara Dalmia, and *Indian Miniature Painting* by Dr Daljeet and Professor PC Jain.

Rajasthan is famed for its miniatures – small-scale paintings that are executed on small surfaces, but cram in a surprising amount of detail by way of delicate brushwork. Originating in the 16th and 17th centuries, they led to eminent schools such as Marwar, Mewar, Bundi-Kota, Amber and Kishangarh, among others. Each school had its own identity; while paintings from the Mewar school depicted court life, festivals, ceremonies, elephant fights and hunts, those from the Marwar school featured vivid colours and heroic, whiskered men accompanied by dainty maidens. Miniatures gained immense value as souvenirs with the coming of the tourism boom.

Crafts

Paper Making

Paper making is centred in Sanganer, near Jaipur, whose paper has traditionally been the most celebrated in India. The process makes environmentally friendly use of discarded fabric rags, which are soaked, pulped, strained, beaten and then spread out to dry on frames. Though some of

CINEMA IN INDIA

India has the world's biggest film industry. Films come in all languages, the majority pumped out by the Hindi tinsel town of Bollywood in Mumbai, and Mollywood, its Tamil counterpart, in Chennai (Madras). Most productions, however, are formulaic flicks that seize mass attention with hackneyed motifs – unrequited love, action that verges on caricature, slapstick humour, wet saris and plenty of sexual innuendo. Nonetheless, the past 10 years have seen upscale productions aimed at a burgeoning multiplex audience. Check out the cricket extravaganza *Lagaan*, the patriotic *Rang De Basanti*, or Shakespearean adaptations such as *Maqbool* (Macbeth) and *Omkara* (Othello). Although it garnered a bit of criticism from the local industry, the British-Indian production and huge international hit, *Slumdog Millionaire*, finally won over the locals with its Hindi-dubbed version, *Slumdog Crorepati*.

India also has an acclaimed art-house movement. Pioneered by Satyajit Ray, Adoor Gopalakrishnan, Ritwik Ghatak and Shyam Benegal, it now boasts directors such as Mira Nair (*Salaam Bombay, Monsoon Wedding, The Namesake*) and Deepa Mehta (*Fire, Earth, Water*).

the town's factories nowadays use machines, there are places that still perform the process by hand – view the racks of paper spread out to dry along Sanganer's river, or pop in for a visit at one of the town's 10 or so paper-making factories.

Jewellery, Gems & Enamelwork

Two jewellery-making styles particularly prevalent in Rajasthan are *kundan* and *meenakari* work. *Kundan* involves setting gemstones into silver or gold pieces; one symbolic variation is known as *navratan*, in which nine different gems are set into an item of jewellery, corresponding to the nine planets of Indian astrology. This way, it's an eternally lucky item to have about your person, since you will always be wearing, at any given time, the symbol of the ruling planetary body. *Meenakari*, meanwhile, is a gorgeous type of enamelwork, usually applied to a base of silver or gold. Jaipur's pieces of *meenakari* are valued for their vibrant tones; a fantastic selection can be found on sale at the city's Johari Bazaar.

Leatherwork

Leatherworking has a long history in Rajasthan. Leather shoes known as jootis are produced in Jodhpur and Jaipur, often featuring *kashida* (ornate embroidery). Strange to Western eyes and feet, there is no 'right' or 'left': both shoes are identical, but after a few wears they begin to conform to the wearer's feet. Jaipur is the best place to buy jootis; try the marvellous UN-supported Mojari (p119).

Textiles

Rajasthan is renowned for the blazing colour of its textiles. Riotously woven, dyed, block- or resist-printed and embroidered, they are on sale almost everywhere you look throughout the state.

During the Mughal period, embroidery workshops known as kaarkhanas were established to train artisans so that the royal families were ensured an abundant supply of richly embroidered cloth. Finely stitched tapestries, inspired by miniature paintings, were also executed for the royal courts.

Today, Bikaner specialises in embroidery with double stitching, which results in the pattern appearing on both sides of the cloth. In the Shekhawati district, the Jat people embroider motifs of animals and birds on their *odhnis* (headscarves) and *ghaghara* (long cotton skirts), while tiny mirrors are stitched into garments in Jaisalmer. Beautifully embroidered cloth is also produced for domestic livestock, and ornately bedecked camels are a wonderfully common sight, especially at the Pushkar Camel Fair.

Intricate *bandhani* (tie-dye) often carries symbolic meanings when used to make *odhnis* (head-scarves). A yellow background indicates that the wearer has recently given birth, while red circles on that background means she's had a son.

Carpets & Weaving

Carpet weaving took off in the 16th century under the patronage of the great Mughal emperor Akbar, who commissioned the establishment of various carpet-weaving factories, including one in Jaipur. In the 19th century Maharaja Ram Singh II of Jaipur established a carpet factory at the Jaipur jail, and soon other jails introduced carpet-making units. Some of the most beautiful *dhurries* (flat-woven rugs) were produced by prisoners, and Bikaner jail is still well known for the excellence of its *dhurries*. Recent government training initiatives have seen the revival of this craft, and fine-quality carpets are once again being produced across Rajasthan.

Pottery

Of all the arts of Rajasthan, pottery has the longest lineage, with fragments recovered in Kalibangan dating from the Harappan era (around 3000 BC). Before the beginning of the 1st millennium, potters in Bikaner were already decorating red pottery with black designs.

Today, different regions of Rajasthan produce different types of pottery, and most villages in Rajasthan have their own resident potter. The most famous of Rajasthan's pottery is the blue pottery of Jaipur. The blue-glazed work was first evident in tiling on Mughal palaces and cenotaphs, and later applied to pottery.

Architecture

The magnificence of Delhi, Agra and Rajasthan's architectural heritage is astounding, and the province is home to some of India's best-known buildings. From temples and mosques to mansions and mausoleums, the region has it all. Most spectacular, however, are the fairy-tale forts and palaces built by Rajputs and Mughals, which bear testimony to the celebrated history of North India.

Temples

Rajasthan's earliest surviving temples date from the Gupta period. Built between the 4th and 6th century, these temples are small and their architecture restrained – the Sheetaleshvara Temple at Jhalrapatan is a notable example. Temple architecture (both Hindu and Jain) developed through the 8th and 9th centuries, and began to incorporate stunning sculptural work, which can be seen on temples at Osiyan and Chittorgarh. Structurally, the temples usually tapered into a single *sikhara* (spire) and had a *mandapa* (pillared pavilion before the inner sanctum). The Delwara complex (p163) at Mt Abu epitomises the architecture of this era. Built in the 11th century, it has marble carvings that reach unsurpassed heights of virtuosity.

Delhi, traditionally an Islamic stronghold, has few ancient temples to boast of. Nevertheless, the city is known for two spectacular modern structures. The Lotus Temple (p51), built in 1986 as a place of worship for the Bahai community, is a magnificent modern building mimicking a nine-sided lotus with marble-clad petals. It has won several architectural awards for its design. In 2005, Delhi got its second grand temple, Akshardham Temple (p52), which holds a Guinness record for being the world's largest comprehensive Hindu temple.

Forts & Palaces

The fabulous citadels of Rajasthan were built for a whole slew of different reasons ranging from protection from invading armies to the realisation of extravagant royal whims.

Most of Rajasthan's forts and palaces were built between the 15th and 18th centuries, during the Mughal reign in Delhi, seeing the Rajputs borrowing architectural motifs from the Mughals, including the use of

Antique Shopping Rules

Be careful when purchasing items that include delivery to your home country – you may well be given assurances that the price includes all charges, but this is not always the case.

Avoid buying products that further endanger threatened species and habitats. It's illegal to export ivory products or any artefact made from wild animals.

Articles over 100 years old cannot be exported from India without an export clearance certificate. Check with the Director of Antiquities at the Archaeological Survey of India (p45) in Agra

PUPPETRY

Puppetry is one of Rajasthan's most acclaimed, yet endangered, performing arts. Puppeteers first emerged in the 19th century, and would travel from village to village like wandering minstrels, relaying stories through narration, music and an animated performance that featured wooden puppets on strings called *kathputlis*. Puppetry is now a dying art; waning patronage and lack of paying audiences has forced many puppeteers to give up the art form and switch to agriculture or menial labour. Those who frequent tourist hotels in the evening usually have a 'day job' and are not paid by the hotel but rather hope for donations after the performance and maybe to sell a puppet or two. The colourful puppets have certainly retained their value as souvenirs. Organisations such as the Barefoot College now make use of puppetry as a medium to spread useful information on health, education and human rights.

pillared arches and the *sheesh mahal* (hall of mirrors). Another ornamentation widely used across Rajasthan was the spired Bengal roof, shaped like an inverted boat. Magnificent examples of Rajput architecture across the state include Amber Fort (p122), Jaipur's Hawa Mahal (p109), and the City Palace (p149) in Udaipur.

The forts and palaces of Delhi and Agra, conversely, adhere to the Islamic style, with marblework, pietra dura (stone inlay) panels, arched entrances and four-square gardens. Mausoleums and mosques, such as the Taj Mahal (p80) and the Jama Masjid (p40), are capped by onion-shaped domes and flanked by minarets. Almost every dynasty that ruled in Delhi built its own fort and monuments in the city. Though they all follow Islamic architectural style, subtle differences exist among these structures due to their having been built centuries apart from each other.

Towards the end of the British era, an architectural style called the Indo-Saracenic school emerged in India, which blended Victorian and Islamic elements into a highly wrought, frilly whole. Striking buildings were produced in this style, including Albert Hall in Jaipur and Lallgarh Palace in Bikaner.

The Kumbhalgarh Fort, a former Mewar stronghold in the Rajsamand district of Rajasthan, has the second-longest fortification in the world after the Great Wall of China.

Havelis

Rajasthani merchants built ornately decorated residences called *havelis*, and commissioned masons and artists to ensure they were constructed and decorated in a manner befitting the owners' importance and prosperity. The Shekhawati district of northern Rajasthan is riddled with such mansions that are covered with extraordinarily vibrant murals. There are other beautiful *havelis* in Jaisalmer, constructed of sandstone, featuring the fine work of renowned local *silavats* (stone carvers).

Step-Wells & Chhatris

Given the importance of water in Rajasthan, it's unsurprising that the architecture of wells and reservoirs rivals other structures in the region. The most impressive regional *baoris* (step-wells) are Raniji-ki-Baori in Bundi and the extraordinary Chand Baori near Abhaneri.

Chhatris (cenotaphs) are a statewide architectural curiosity, built to commemorate maharajas, nobles, and, as is the case in the Shekhawati district, wealthy merchants. In rare instances, *chhatris* also commemorate women, such as the Chhatri of Moosi Rani at Alwar. Translating to 'umbrella', a *chhatri* comprises a central dome, supported by a series of pillars on a raised platform, with a sequence of small pavilions on the corners and sides.

The most famous marble quarries were located in Makrana, from where the marble used in the Taj Mahal and the Delwara temples was sourced.

1. Peacock carving, City Palace (p107), Jaipur **2.** Weaving rugs, Salawas (p179) **3.** City Palace (p149), Udaipur **4.** Textile printing, Jaipur (p103)

Rajasthani Colour

The most vivid impression on visitors to Rajasthan is that of colour: brilliant, bright tribal dress, glittering gold jewellery and rainbow-coloured bangles adorn the locals and illuminate the bazaars. Inside the palaces, *havelis* and even humble homes, this trend continues.

The people of Rajasthan have a passion for decoration, having taken advantage of their position on trade routes to acquire artistic skills from many lands. This passion is evident in the manifold variations of Rajasthani turbans and in the attire of the state's women, from their block-printed *odhnis* (headscarves) right down to their brilliantly embroidered jootis (leather shoes). Utilitarian items are transported into the world of art with ceramics such as the famous blue-glazed pottery from Jaipur.

Tie-dyed, block-printed and embroidered textiles and hand-woven carpets are functional yet decorative and colourful. Traditionally, all Rajasthan's textile colours were derived from natural sources such as vegetables, minerals and even insects. Yellow, for instance, came from turmeric and buttermilk; green from banana leaves; orange from saffron and jasmine; blue from the indigo plant; and purple from the kermes insect. Today, however, the majority are synthetically dyed; while they may not possess the subtlety of the traditional tones, they will, at least, stand a better chance in a 40°C machine wash.

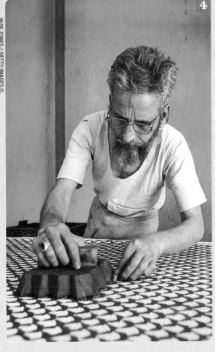

BEST PLACES TO SEE...

- **Block-printed textiles** Sanganer
- **Blue pottery** Jaipur
- **Carpets** Jaipur
- **Embroidery** Jaisalmer
- **Jewellery** Jaipur
- **Miniature Paintings** Udaipur

DANITA DELIMONT / GETTY IMAGES ©

BARTOSZ HADYNIAK / GETTY IMAGES ©

1. Traditional attire
Rajasthani woman in vibrant traditional attire and henna-painted hands.

2. Udaipur
Handicrafts for sale in Udaipur (p148).

3. Puppets
Traditional Rajasthani puppets have carved wooden heads and large painted eyes.

4. Rajasthani textiles
Colourful patchwork quilts for sale, Jaisalmer (p180).

BRENT WINEBRENNER / GETTY IMAGES ©

Naturally Rajasthan

Rajasthan is the India of the hot, dry plains. Dominated by desert and scrub, and punctuated by low hills, it's nevertheless home to a rich variety of flora and fauna. Some are easy to spot, such as the monkeys that remain ubiquitous even in the cities, while others require a little more tracking, like the tiger – king of India's big cats – which persists in several of the region's national parks.

Landscape

The Thar Desert is the most densely populated desert in the world, with an average of over 60 people per square kilometre.

The rugged Aravalli Range splits Rajasthan like a bony spine, running from the northeast to the southwest. These irregular mountains form a boundary between the Thar Desert to the west and the relatively lusher vegetation to the east. With an average height of 600m, in places the range soars to over 1050m; the highest point, Guru Shikhar (1722m), is near Mt Abu. It's thought to be the oldest mountain range in the world. A second hilly spur, the Vindhya Range, splays around the southernmost regions of Rajasthan.

The state's sole perennial river is the wide, life-giving swell of the Chambal. Rising in Madhya Pradesh from the northern slopes of the Vindhyas, the river enters Rajasthan at Chaurasigarh and forms part of Rajasthan's eastern border with Madhya Pradesh. The south is drained by the Mahi and Sabarmati Rivers; the Luni, which rises about 7km north of Ajmer in the Aravalli, is the only river in western Rajasthan. Seasonal and comparatively shallow, the Luni sometimes billows out to over 2km wide.

The arid region in the west of the state is known as Marusthali or Marwar (the Land of Death), which gives some idea of the terrain. Sprawling from the Aravallis in the east to the Sulaiman Kirthar Range in the west is the Thar Desert, which covers almost three-quarters of the state. It's a dry, inhospitable expanse – the eastern extension of the great Saharo-Tharian Desert – forming 61% of the area covered by desert in India.

Low, rugged hills punctuate the parched plains. About 60% of the region is also made up of sand dunes, which are formed by the erosion of these hills and from sand blown from Gujarat's vast desert, the Great Rann of Kutch.

It's hard to believe, but this desolate region was once covered by massive forests and populated by huge animals. In 1996 two palaeontologists working in the Thar Desert discovered 300-million-year-old animal fossils, that included dinosaur fossils. At the Akal Wood Fossil Park, near Jaisalmer, you can visit the incredible remains of fossilised trees that are around 180 million years old. Plant fossils from 45 million years ago show that Rajasthan's metamorphosis into desert is relatively recent – and ongoing.

It's difficult to make out where the desert ends and becomes semiarid. The semiarid zone nestles between the Aravallis and the Thar Desert, extending west from the Aravallis and encompassing the Ghaggar River Plain, parts of Shekhawati and the Luni River Basin.

Delhi lies on the vast flatlands of the Indo-Gangetic Plain, though the northernmost pimples of the Aravallis amount to the Ridge, which lies west of the city centre. The Yamuna River flows southwards along the eastern edge of the city. To the south, Agra lies on the banks of the Yamuna, in the neighbouring state of Uttar Pradesh.

DESERT – JUST ADD WATER

It sounds too simple and it probably is. Irrigating India's vast arid lands has long been the dream of rulers and politicians. The Indira Gandhi Canal was initiated in 1957 and, though still incomplete, it includes an amazing 9709km of canals, with the main canal stretching 649km. Critics suggest that the massive project, connected with Bhakra Dam in Punjab, was concerned with short-term economics and politics to the detriment of the long-term ecology of the region.

The canal has opened up large tracts of the arid western region for cash crops, but these tracts are managed by wealthy landowners rather than the rural poor. Environmentalists say that soil has been destroyed through over-irrigation, and indigenous plants have suffered, adding to the degeneration of the arid zone. Furthermore, sections of the Indira Gandhi Canal are built on traditional grazing grounds, to which graziers are now denied access. The canal has also been blamed for breeding malaria-carrying mosquitoes.

In 2008, the waters from India's largest westward flowing river, the Narmada, which were dammed in highly controversial circumstances, trickled into Rajasthan's drought-ravaged regions of Jalore and Barmer. The miraculous appearance of the water brought untold joy to the long-suffering villagers. However, the entire Narmada River project has been heavily criticised both on environmental grounds and for displacing a large number of tribal people in the Narmada Valley. The search is underway for the next river to dam and tap.

Desert Plants

Vegetation in the desert zone is sparse – only a limited range of grasses and slow-growing thorny trees and shrubs can grow here. The most common tree species are the ubiquitous khejri *(Prosopis cineraria)* and varieties of acacia. Rajasthan also has some dry teak forest, dry mixed deciduous forest, bamboo brakes and subtropical hill forests. Forest stocks are dwindling as inhabitants scour the landscape for fuel and fodder.

The hardy khejri, which is held sacred by the Bishnoi tribes of Jodhpur district, is drought resistant on account of its very deep roots and is heavily utilised. No part of the plant goes to waste: the thorny twigs are used to build barriers to keep sheep and goats away from crops, the leaves are dried and used for fodder, and the bean-shaped fruit can be eaten. The fruit, when cooked, is known as *sangri*. The wood is used to make furniture and the branches are burnt for fuel. The khejri twigs are used in the sacred fire that's lit during marriage ceremonies. When you see the heavily pruned khejri trees around Jodhpur you will be amazed by their staying power.

Wild Rajasthan

For a place apparently so inhospitable, Rajasthan hosts an incredible array of animals and birds; the stars are the dwindling numbers of tigers now virtually restricted to Ranthambhore National Park and the magnificent migratory bird show of Keoladeo Ghana National Park.

Animals

Arid-zone mammals have adapted to the lack of water in various resourceful ways. For example, some top up their fluids with insects that are composed of between 65% and 80% water, and water-bearing plants, while others retain water for longer periods. Faced with the incredible heat, many creatures burrow in the sand or venture out only at night.

The website of India's premier wildlife magazine, *Sanctuary* (www.sanctuaryasia.com) highlights the latest conservation issues and has numerous related links.

Antelopes & Gazelles

Blackbuck antelopes, with their amazing long spiralling horns, are most common around Jodhpur, where they are protected by local Bishnoi tribes. Bishnoi conservation has also helped the chinkaras (Indian gazelles); these delicate, small creatures are extremely fast and agile and are seen in small family herds.

Also notable is the extraordinary nilgai (or blue bull), which is the largest of the antelope family – only the males attain the blue colour. It's a large, muscular animal whose front legs appear longer than its rear legs, giving it a rather ungainly stance.

A Guide to the Wildlife Parks of Rajasthan, by Dr Suraj Ziddi, with photographs by Subhash Bhargava, is a comprehensive guide to Rajasthan's reserves.

Big Cats

Tigers were once found along the length of the Aravallis. However, royal hunting parties, poachers and habitat destruction have decimated the population, and the only viable tiger populations in Rajasthan can be found in Ranthambhore National Park and, to a much lesser extent the Sariska Tiger Reserve. According to a survey released in January 2015, the parks contained adult populations of 43 and nine tigers respectively.

The mainly nocturnal and rarely seen leopard (panther) inhabits rocky declivities in the Aravallis, and parts of the Jaipur and Jodhpur districts.

Dogs

Jackals are renowned for their unearthly howling. Once common throughout Rajasthan, they would lurk around villages, where they scavenged and preyed on livestock. Habitat encroachment and hunting (for their skins) have reduced their numbers, though they are still a very common sight in Keoladeo Ghana, Ranthambhore and Sariska parks.

Wolves used to roam in large numbers in the desert, but farmers hunted them almost to the point of extinction. They have begun to reappear over recent decades, due to concerted conservation efforts. The wildlife sanctuary at Kumbhalgarh is known for its wolves.

TOP NATIONAL PARKS & WILDLIFE SANCTUARIES

PARK	LOCATION	FEATURES	BEST TIME TO VISIT
Desert National Park	western Rajasthan	great Indian bustards, blackbuck, nilgai, wolves, desert foxes, crested porcupines	Sep–Mar
Keoladeo Ghana National Park	eastern Rajasthan	400 bird species, including migratory birds & waterbirds (wetlands)	Oct–Mar, Jul & Aug
Kumbhalgarh Wildlife Sanctuary	southern Rajasthan	wolves in packs of up to 40, chowsinghas (four-horned antelopes), leopards, horse riding	Oct–Jun
Mt Abu Wildlife Sanctuary	southern Rajasthan	forest, sloth bears, wild boar, sambars, leopards	Mar–Jun
Ranthambhore National Park	eastern Rajasthan	tigers, chitals, leopards, nilgai, chinkaras, bird life, ancient fort	Oct–Apr
Sariska Tiger Reserve	eastern Rajasthan	leopards, chitals, chinkaras, bird life, fort, deserted city & temples	Nov–Jun
Tal Chhapar Wildlife Sanctuary	northern Rajasthan	blackbuck, chinkaras, desert foxes, antelopes, harriers, eagles, sparrowhawks	Sep–Mar

GOING, GOING, GONE...

Some of Rajasthan's endangered wildlife is disappearing due to ongoing encroachment on its habitat, but poaching is also a serious problem.

From numbers in excess of 40,000 in the early 20th century, wild tigers in India had crashed as low as 1400 by 2010, although a new survey using camera traps and other techniques estimated that the population had rebounded to 2226 in 2014. Of these, Rajasthan's tiger parks, Ranthambhore and Sariska, are thought to hold 52 adult tigers. Both have been badly hit by poaching in recent decades, and Sariska's tigers had to be reintroduced after becoming locally extinct in 2010.

Numbers of the great Indian bustard have also dwindled alarmingly due to hunting and because the bird's eggs are trampled by livestock. However, in Rajasthan, where the bird is the emblem of the state, there is no program for conservation and this has led to calls for a national program similar to Project Tiger to protect this majestic bird.

Three types of vulture have become endangered in recent years. Once common, they joined the endangered ranks after the population in south Asia fell by 95%. The cause was exposure to a veterinary drug, which the vultures absorbed while feeding from livestock carcasses. The reduction in numbers has had knock-on ecological and health effects, as the birds once disposed of many carcasses, thus reducing risks of disease.

The sandy-coloured desert fox is a subspecies of the red fox and was once prolific in the Thar Desert. As with wolves, the fox population has shrunk due to human endeavours. Keep your eyes open for them scavenging roadkill on the highway near Jaisalmer.

Monkeys

Monkeys seem to be everywhere in Rajasthan. There are two common types: the red-faced and red-rumped rhesus macaque and the shaggy grey, black-faced langur, with prominent eyebrows and long tails. Both types are keen on hanging around human settlements, where they can find easy pickings. Both will steal food from your grasp at temples, but the macaque is probably the more aggressive and the one to be particularly wary of.

Bears

In forested regions you might see a sloth bear – a large creature covered in long black hair with a prominent white V on its chest and a peculiar muzzle with an overhanging upper lip. That lip helps it feed on ants and termites dug out with those dangerous-looking claws on its front paws. Sloth bears feed mostly on vegetation and insects, but aren't averse to a bit of carrion. The bears are reasonably common around Mt Abu and elsewhere on the western slopes of the Aravalli Range.

Birds

Keoladeo Ghana National Park (p124), a wetland in eastern Rajasthan, is internationally renowned for birdwatching. Resident and winter migrants put on an amazing feathery show. Migratory species include several varieties of storks, spoonbills, herons, cormorants, ibis and egrets. Wintering waterfowl include the common, marbled, falcated and Baikal teal; pintail, gadwall, shoveler, coot, wigeon, bar-headed and greylag geese; common and brahminy pochards; and the beautiful demoiselle crane. Waders include snipe, sandpipers and plovers. Species resident throughout the year include the monogamous sarus crane, moorhens, egrets, herons, storks and cormorants. Birds of prey include many types of eagles (greater spotted, steppe, imperial, Spanish imperial and fishing), vultures (white-backed and scavenger), owls (spotted, dusky horned and mottled wood), marsh harriers, sparrowhawks, kestrels and goshawks.

If you want to put names to feathers on your travels, pick up a copy of *A Field Guide to Birds of the Indian Subcontinent* by Krys Kazmierczak, with illustrations by Ber van Perlo.

The remaining forests and jungles that cling to the rugged Aravalli Ranges harbour orioles, hornbills, kingfishers, swallows, parakeets, warblers, mynahs, robins, flycatchers, quails, doves, peacocks, barbets, bee-eaters, woodpeckers and drongos, among others. Birds of prey include numerous species of owls (great horned, dusky, brown fishing and collared scops, and spotted owlets), eagles (spotted and tawny), white-eyed buzzards, black-winged kites and shikras.

Common birds of the open grasslands include various species of lark. Quails can also be seen, as can several types of shrike, mynahs, drongos and partridges. Migratory birds include the lesser florican, seen during the monsoon, and the Houbara bustard, which winters at the grasslands. Birds of prey include falcons, eagles, hawks, kites, kestrels and harriers.

The Thar Desert also has a prolific variety of bird life. At the small village of Kheechan, about 135km from Jodhpur, you can see vast flocks of demoiselle cranes descending on fields from the end of August to the end of March. Other winter visitors to the desert include Houbara bustards and common cranes. As water is scarce, waterholes attract large flocks of imperial, spotted, pintail and Indian sandgrouse in the early mornings. Other desert dwellers include drongos, common and bush quail, blue-tailed and little green bee-eaters, and grey partridges. Desert birds of prey include eagles (steppe and tawny), buzzards (honey and long-legged), goshawks, peregrine falcons and kestrels. The most notable of the desert and dry grassland dwellers is the impressive Indian bustard.

Survival Guide

Scams

India has a deserved reputation for scams. Of course, most can be easily avoided with a little common sense and an appropriate amount of caution. Scams tend to be more of a problem in the big cities of arrival (such as Delhi or Mumbai), or very touristy spots (such as Rajasthan), though in Goa and Kerala they are rare. Chat with fellow travellers to keep abreast of the latest cons. Look at the India branch of Lonely Planet's Thorn Tree Travel Forum (www.lonelyplanet.com/thorntree), where travellers post warnings about problems they have encountered on the road.

Contaminated Food & Drink

➡ The late 1990s saw a scam in North India where travellers died after consuming food laced with dangerous bacteria from restaurants linked to dodgy medical clinics; we've heard no recent reports but the scam could resurface. In unrelated incidents, some clinics have also given more treatment than necessary to procure larger payments.

➡ Most bottled water is legit, but ensure the seal is intact and the bottom of the bottle hasn't been tampered with. While in transit, try to carry packed food. If you eat at bus or train stations, buy cooked food only from fast-moving places.

Credit-Card Con

Be careful when paying for souvenirs with a credit card. While government shops are usually legitimate, private souvenir shops have been known to run off extra copies of the credit-card imprint slip and use them for phoney transactions later. Ask the trader to process the transaction in front of you. Memorising the CVV/CVC2 number and scratching it off the card is also a good idea, to avoid misuse. In some restaurants, waiters will ask you for your PIN with the intention of taking your credit card to the machine – never give your PIN to anyone, and ask to use the machine in person.

Druggings

Occasionally, tourists (especially solo travellers) are drugged and robbed during train or bus journeys. A spiked drink is the most commonly used method for sending them off to sleep – chocolates, chai from a co-conspiring vendor and 'homemade' Indian food are also known to be used. Use your instincts, and if you're unsure, politely decline drinks or food offered.

Gem Scams

This classic scam involves charming con artists who promise foolproof 'get rich quick' schemes. Travellers are asked to carry or mail gems home and then sell them to the trader's (nonexistent) overseas representatives at a profit. Without exception, the goods – if they arrive at all – are worth a fraction of what you paid, and the 'representatives' never materialise.

KEEPING SAFE

➡ A good travel-insurance policy is essential.

➡ Email copies of your passport identity page, visa and airline tickets to yourself, and keep copies on you.

➡ Keep your money and passport in a concealed money belt or a secure place under your shirt.

➡ Store at least US$100 separately from your main stash.

➡ Don't publicly display large wads of cash when paying for services or checking into hotels.

➡ If you can't lock your hotel room securely from the inside, stay somewhere else.

Don't believe hard-luck stories about an inability to obtain an export licence, or the testimonials they show you from other travellers – they are fake. Travellers have reported this con happening in Agra, Delhi, and Jaisalmer among other places, but it's particularly prevalent in Jaipur. Carpets, curios and *pashminas* are other favourites for this con.

Overpricing

Always agree on prices beforehand while availing services that don't have regulated tariffs. This particularly applies to friendly neighbourhood guides, snack bars at places of touristy interest, and autorickshaws and taxis without meters.

Photography

Use your instincts (better still, ask for permission) while photographing people. The common argument – sometimes voiced after you've snapped your photos – is you're going to sell them to glossy international magazines, so it's only fair that you pay a fee.

Theft

Theft is a risk in India, as anywhere else. Keep luggage locked and chained on buses and trains. Remember that snatchings often occur when a train is pulling out of the station, as it's too late for you to give chase.

Touts & Commission Agents

➡ Touts come in many avatars and operate in mysterious ways. Cabbies and autorickshaw drivers will often try to coerce you to stay at a budget hotel of their choice, only to collect a commission (included within your room tariff) from the receptionists afterward.

➡ Wherever possible, arrange hotel bookings (if only for

OTHER TOP SCAMS

➡ Gunk (dirt, paint, poo) suddenly appears on your shoes, only for a shoe cleaner to magically appear and offer to clean it off – for a price.

➡ Some shops are selling overpriced SIM cards and not activating them; it's best to buy your SIM from an official shop (Airtel, Vodafone etc) and check it works before leaving the area (activation can take 24 hours).

➡ Shops and restaurants 'borrow' the name of their more successful and popular competitor.

➡ Touts claim to be 'government-approved' guides or agents, and sting you for large sums of cash. Enquire at the local tourist office about licensed guides and ask to see identification from guides themselves.

➡ Artificial 'tourist offices' that are actually dodgy travel agencies whose aim is to sell you overpriced tours, tickets and tourist services.

the first night), and request a hotel pick-up. You'll often hear stories about hotels of your choice being 'full' or 'closed' – check things out yourself. Reconfirm and double-check your booking the day before you arrive.

➡ Be very sceptical of phrases like 'my brother's shop' and 'special deal at my friend's place'. Many fraudsters operate in collusion with souvenir stalls, so be careful while making expensive purchases in private stores.

➡ Avoid friendly people and 'officials' in train and bus stations who offer unsolicited help, then guide you to a commission-paying travel agent. Look confident, and if anyone asks if this is your first trip to India, say you've been here several times, even if you haven't. Telling touts that you have already prepaid your transfer/tour/onward journey may help dissuade them.

Transport Scams

➡ Upon arriving at train stations and airports, if you haven't prearranged pick-up, book transport from government-approved booths. All major airports now have radio cab, prepaid taxi and

airport shuttle bus counters in the arrival lounge. Never go with a loitering cabbie who offers you a cheap ride into town, especially at night.

➡ While booking multiday sightseeing tours, stick to itineraries offered by tourism departments, or those that come recommended either in this guidebook or by friends who've personally used them. Be extremely wary of anyone in Delhi offering houseboat tours to Kashmir – we've received many complaints over the years about dodgy deals.

➡ When buying a bus, train or plane ticket anywhere other than the registered office of the transport company, make sure you're getting the ticket class you paid for. Use official online booking facilities where possible.

➡ Some tricksters pose as Indian Railways officials and insist you pay to have your e-ticket validated on the platform; ignore them.

➡ Train station touts (even in uniform or with 'official' badges) may tell you that your intended train is cancelled/flooded/broken down or that your ticket is invalid. Do not respond to any 'official' approaches at train stations.

Women & Solo Travellers

There are extra considerations for women and solo travellers when visiting India – from cost to safety. As with anywhere else in the world, it pays to be prepared.

Women Travellers

Although Bollywood might suggest otherwise, India remains a conservative society. Female travellers should be aware that their behaviour and attire choice are likely to be under constant scrutiny.

Unwanted Attention

Unwanted attention from men is a common problem.

➧ Be prepared to be stared at; it's something you'll simply have to live with, so don't allow it to get the better of you.

➧ Refrain from returning male stares; this can be considered encouragement.

➧ Dark glasses, phones, books or electronic tablets are useful props for averting unwanted conversations.

Clothing

Avoiding culturally inappropriate clothing will help avert undesirable attention.

➧ Steer clear of sleeveless tops, shorts, short skirts (ankle-length skirts are recommended) and anything else that's skimpy, see-through or tight-fitting.

➧ Wearing Indian-style clothes is viewed favourably.

➧ Draping a dupatta (long scarf) over T-shirts is another good way to avoid stares – it's shorthand for modesty, and also handy if you visit a shrine that requires your head to be covered.

➧ Wearing a salwar kameez (traditional dresslike tunic and trousers) will help you blend in; a smart alternative is a kurta (long shirt) worn over jeans or trousers.

➧ Avoid going out in public wearing a choli (sari blouse) or a sari petticoat (which some foreign women mistake for a skirt); it's like strutting around half-dressed.

➧ Aside from at pools, many Indian women wear long shorts and a T-shirt when swimming in public view; it's wise to wear a sarong from the beach to your hotel.

Health & Hygiene

➧ Sanitary pads are widely available but tampons are usually restricted to pharmacies in big cities and tourist towns (even then, the choice may be limited). Carry additional stocks for travel off the beaten track.

Sexual Harassment

Many female travellers have reported some form of sexual harassment while in India, such as lewd comments, invasion of privacy and even groping. Serious sexual assaults do happen but are rare; follow similar safety precautions as you would at home.

➧ Women travellers have experienced provocative gestures, jeering, getting 'accidentally' bumped into on the street and being followed.

➧ Incidents are common at exuberant (and crowded) public events such as the Holi festival. If a crowd is gathering, make yourself scarce or find a safer place overlooking the event so that you're away from wandering hands.

➧ Women travelling with a male partner will receive far less hassle.

Staying Safe

The following tips will help you avoid uncomfortable or dangerous situations during your journey:

➧ Always be aware of your surroundings. If it feels wrong, trust your instincts. Tread with care. Don't be scared, but don't be reckless either.

➧ If travelling after 9pm, use a recommended, registered taxi service.

➧ Don't organise your travel in such a way that means you're hanging out at bus/train stations or arriving late at night. Arrive in towns before dark.

➧ Keep conversations with unknown men short – getting involved in an inane conversation with someone you barely know can be misinterpreted as a sign of sexual interest.

→ Some women wear a pseudo wedding ring, or announce early on in the conversation that they're married or engaged (regardless of the reality).

→ If you feel that a guy is encroaching on your space, he probably is. A firm request to keep away usually does the trick, especially if your tone is loud and curt enough to draw the attention of passers-by.

→ The silent treatment can also be very effective.

→ Follow local women's cues and instead of shaking hands say *namaste* – the traditional, respectful Hindu greeting.

→ Avoid wearing expensive-looking jewellery and carrying flashy accessories.

→ Check the reputation of any teacher or therapist before going to a solo session (get recommendations from travellers). Some women have reported being molested by masseurs and other therapists. If you feel uneasy at any time, leave.

→ Female filmgoers may attract less attention and lessen the chances of harassment by going to the cinema with a companion.

→ Lone women may want to invest in a good-quality hotel in a better neighbourhood.

→ At hotels keep your door locked, as staff (particularly at budget and midrange places) can knock and walk in without waiting for your permission.

→ Avoid wandering alone in isolated areas even during daylight. Steer clear of gallis (narrow lanes) and deserted roads.

→ When on rickshaws alone, call/text someone, or pretend to, to indicate someone knows where you are.

→ Act confidently in public; to avoid looking lost (and thus more vulnerable) consult maps at your hotel (or at a restaurant) rather than on the street.

Taxis & Public Transport

Being female has some advantages; women can usually queue-jump for buses and trains without consequence and on trains there are special ladies-only carriages. There are also women-only waiting rooms at some stations.

→ Solo women should prearrange an airport pick-up from their hotel, especially if their flight is scheduled to arrive after dark.

→ Delhi and some other cities have licensed prepaid radio cab services such as Easycabs – they're more expensive than the regular prepaid taxis, but promote themselves as being safe, with drivers who have been vetted as part of their recruitment.

→ If you do catch a regular prepaid taxi, make a point of writing down the registration and driver's name – in front of the driver – and giving it to one of the airport police.

→ Avoid taking taxis alone late at night and never agree to have more than one man (the driver) in the car – ignore claims that this is 'just my brother' etc.

→ Solo women have reported less hassle by choosing more expensive classes on trains.

→ If you're travelling overnight in a three-tier carriage, try to get the uppermost berth, which will give you more privacy (and distance from potential gropers).

→ On public transport, don't hesitate to return any errant limbs, put an item of luggage between you and others, be vocal (attracting public attention, thus shaming the pest), or simply find a new spot.

Solo Travellers

One of the joys of travelling solo in India is that you're more likely to be 'adopted' by families, especially if you're commuting together on a long rail journey. It's a great opportunity to make friends and get a deeper understanding of local culture. If you're keen to hook up with fellow travellers, tourist hubs such as Goa, Rajasthan, Kerala, Manali, McLeod Ganj, Leh, Agra and Varanasi are some popular places to do so. You may also be able to find travel companions on Lonely Planet's **Thorn Tree Travel Forum** (www.lonelyplanet. com/thorntree).

Cost

The most significant issue facing solo travellers is cost.

→ Single-room accommodation rates are sometimes not much lower than double rates.

→ Some midrange and top-end places don't even offer a single tariff.

→ It's always worth trying to negotiate a lower rate for single occupancy.

Safety

Most solo travellers experience no major problems in India but, like anywhere else, it's wise to stay on your toes in unfamiliar surroundings.

→ Some less honourable souls (locals and travellers alike) view lone tourists as an easy target for theft and sexual assault.

→ Single men wandering around isolated areas have been mugged, even during the day.

Transport

→ You'll save money if you find others to share taxis and autorickshaws, as well as when hiring a car for longer trips.

→ Solo bus travellers may be able to get the 'co-pilot' (near the driver) seat on buses, which not only has a good view out front, but is also handy if you've got a big bag.

Directory A–Z

Accommodation

Accommodation ranges from grungy backpacker hostels with concrete floors and cold 'bucket' showers to opulent palaces fit for a maharaja.

Categories

As a general rule, budget ($) covers everything from basic hostels and railway retiring rooms to simple guesthouses in traditional village homes.

Midrange ($$) hotels tend to be modern-style concrete blocks that usually offer extras such as cable/satellite TV and air-conditioning (although some just have noisy 'air-coolers' that simply cool air by blowing it over water).

Top-end ($$$) places stretch from gorgeous heritage hotels to luxury five-star international chains.

Reservations

➡ It's a good idea to book ahead, online or by phone, especially when travelling to more popular destinations. Some hotels require a credit-card deposit at the time of booking.

➡ Some budget options won't take reservations as they don't know when people are going to check out. Call ahead to check.

➡ Other places may ask for a deposit at check-in – ask for a receipt and be wary of any request to sign a blank impression of your credit card. If the hotel insists, pay cash and get a receipt.

➡ Verify the check-out time when you check in – some hotels have a fixed check-out time (usually 10am or noon), while others give you 24-hour check-out.

Seasons

➡ Rates are full price in high season, which coincides with the best weather (October to mid-February). In areas popular with foreign tourists there's an additional peak period over Christmas and New Year – make reservations well in advance. At other times you may find significant discounts; if the hotel seems quiet, ask for a discount.

➡ Many temple towns (such as Pushkar) have additional peak seasons around major festivals and pilgrimages.

Taxes & Service Charges

➡ At midrange and top-end accommodation, you usually have to pay a 10% 'luxury' tax on rooms over ₹1000 plus 12.5% on food and beverages in hotels that attract the luxury tax on their rooms.

➡ Many midrange and upmarket hotels also add 'service charge' (usually 10%).

➡ Rates quoted include taxes unless noted.

Accommodation Types

BUDGET & MIDRANGE HOTELS

➡ Room quality can vary considerably within hotels so try to inspect a few rooms first, and avoid carpeted rooms at cheaper hotels unless you like the smell of mouldy socks.

➡ Shared bathrooms (often with squat toilets) are usually only found at the cheapest lodgings.

➡ Most rooms have ceiling fans, and better rooms have electric mosquito-killers and/or window nets, though cheaper rooms may lack windows altogether.

➡ If staying at the very cheapest of hotels bring your

BOOK YOUR STAY ONLINE

For more accommodation reviews by Lonely Planet authors, check out http://lonelyplanet.com/hotels. You'll find independent reviews, as well as recommendations on the best places to stay. Best of all, you can book online.

own sheet or sleeping-bag liner along with a towel.

➡ Sound pollution can be irksome (especially in urban hubs); pack good-quality earplugs and request a room that doesn't face a busy road.

➡ It's wise to keep your door locked, as some staff (particularly in budget accommodation) may knock and automatically walk in without first seeking your permission.

➡ Note that some hotels lock their doors at night. Members of staff may sleep in the lobby but waking them up can be a challenge. Let the hotel know in advance if you'll be arriving or returning to your room late in the evening.

➡ Away from tourist areas, cheaper hotels may not take foreigners because they don't have the necessary foreigner-registration forms.

DORMITORY ACCOMMODATION

➡ A number of hotels have cheap dormitories though these may be mixed and, in less touristy places, full of drunken drivers – not ideal conditions for women. More traveller-friendly dorms are found at the handful of hostels run by the YMCA, YWCA and Salvation Army as well as at HI-associated hostels.

PAYING GUEST HOUSE SCHEME (HOMESTAYS)

➡ Rajasthan pioneered the Paying Guest House Scheme, so it's well developed in the state. Prices range from budget to upper midrange – contact the local Rajasthan Tourism Development Corporation (RTDC) tourist reception centres for details.

RAILWAY RETIRING ROOMS

➡ Most large train stations have basic rooms for travellers holding an ongoing train ticket or Indrail Pass.

> ## SLEEPING PRICE RANGES
>
> The following price ranges refer to the cost of a double room, including private bathroom, unless otherwise noted.
>
> **$** less than ₹1000
>
> **$$** ₹1000–5000
>
> **$$$** more than ₹5000

Some are grim, others are surprisingly pleasant, but all are noisy from the sound of trains and passengers. Nevertheless, they're useful for early-morning train departures and there's usually a choice of dormitories or private rooms (24-hour check-out).

PALACES, FORTS & HAVELIS

➡ Rajasthan is famous for its wonderful heritage hotels created from palaces, forts and *havelis*. There are hundreds, and it often doesn't cost a fortune: some are the height of luxury and priced accordingly, but many are simpler, packed with character and set in stunning locations.

➡ You can browse members of the Indian Heritage Hotels Association online on the tourist board website **Incredible India** (www. incredibleindia.org).

TOP-END HOTELS

➡ As major tourist centres, Rajasthan, Delhi and Agra have a bevy of top-end hotels. If you're staying at a top-end hotel, it's often cheaper to book it online. Nevertheless, unless the hotel is busy, you can nearly always score a discount from the rack rates.

Customs Regulations

➡ Technically you're supposed to declare any amount of cash over US$5000, or total amount of currency over US$10,000 on arrival. Indian rupees shouldn't be taken out of India.

➡ Officials very occasionally ask tourists to enter expensive items such as video cameras and laptop computers on a 'Tourist Baggage Re-export' form to ensure they're taken out of India at the time of departure.

➡ Exporting antiques (defined as objects of historical interest not less than 100 years old) from India is explicitly prohibited. Reputable antique dealers know the laws and can make arrangements for an export-clearance certificate for old items that are OK to export, but it's best to look for quality reproductions instead.

Electricity

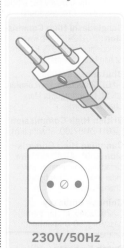

230V/50Hz

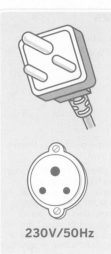

230V/50Hz

Embassies & Consulates

Many foreign diplomatic missions have certain timings for visa applications (usually mornings), so phone for details. These consulates are all based in Delhi.

Australian High Commission (☏011-41399900011-41399900; www.india.highcommission.gov.au; 1/50G Shantipath, Chanakyapuri)

Bangladeshi High Commission (☏011-24121394; www.bdhcdelhi.org; EP39 Dr Radakrishnan Marg, Chanakyapuri)

Bhutanese Embassy (☏011-26889230; www.bhutan.gov.bt; Chandragupta Marg, Chanakyapuri)

British High Commission (☏011-24192100; Shantipath)

Canadian High Commission (☏011-41782000; www.canadainternational.gc.ca/india-inde; 7/8 Shantipath, Chanakyapuri)

Chinese Embassy (☏26112345; in.china-embassy.org; 50-D Shantipath, Chanakyapuri)

Dutch Embassy (☏011-24197600; http://india.nlembassy.org; 6/50F Shantipath, Chanakyapuri)

French Embassy (☏011-24196100; http://ambafrance-in.org; 2/50E Shantipath, Chanakyapuri)

German Embassy (☏011-44199199; www.new-delhi.diplo.de; 6/50G Shantipath, Chanakyapuri)

Irish Embassy (☏011-24940 3200; www.irelandindia.com; C17 Malcha Marg, Chanakyapuri)

Israeli Embassy (☏011-30414500011-30414500; http://delhi.mfa.gov.il; 3 Aurangzeb Rd)

Japanese Embassy (☏011-26876581; www.in.emb-japan.go.jp; 50G Shantipath, Chanakyapuri)

Malaysian High Commission (☏011-26111291/97; www.kln.gov.my/web/ind_new-delhi/home; 50M Satya Marg, Chanakyapuri)

Myanmar Embassy (☏011-24678822; http://myanmedelhi.com; 3/50F Nyaya Marg)

Nepali Embassy (☏011-23476200; www.nepalembassy.in; Mandi House, Barakhamba Rd)

New Zealand High Commission (☏011-46883170011-46883170; www.nzembassy.com/india; Sir Edmund Hillary Marg, Chanakyapuri)

Pakistani Embassy (☏011-24676004; www.mofa.gov.pk/india; 2/50G Shantipath, Chanakyapuri)

Singaporean High Commission (☏011-46000915011-46000915; www.mfa.gov.sg/newdelhi; E6 Chandragupta Marg, Chanakyapuri)

Sri Lankan High Commission (☏011-23010202; www.slhcindia.org; 27 Kautilya Marg, Chanakyapuri)

Thai Embassy (☏011-4977 4100; www.thaiemb.org.in; 56N Nyaya Marg, Chanakyapuri)

US Embassy (☏011-24198000; http://newdelhi.usembassy.gov; Shantipath)

Food

See the Rajasthani Food chapter (p221) for details on this region's cuisine.

Gay & Lesbian Travellers

Homosexuality was made illegal in India in 2013, having only been decriminalised since 2009. Gay and lesbian visitors should be discreet in this conservative country. Public displays of affection are frowned upon for both homosexual and heterosexual couples.

Despite the ban there are are low-key gay scenes in many larger cities, including Delhi.

Gay Delhi (www.gaydelhi.org) LGBT support group, organising social events in Delhi.

Gaysi Zine (http://gaysifamily.com) A thoughtful monthly magazine and website featuring gay writing and issues.

Indian Dost (www.indiandost.com/gay.php) News and information including contact groups in India.

Queer Ink (www.queer-ink.com) Online bookstore specialising in gay- and lesbian-interest books from the subcontinent.

EATING PRICE RANGES

The following price ranges refer to a standard main course.

$ less than ₹100

$$ ₹100–300

$$$ more than ₹300

Insurance

➡ Comprehensive travel insurance to cover theft, loss and medical problems (as well as air evacuation) is strongly recommended.

➡ Some policies specifically exclude potentially dangerous activities such as scuba diving, skiing, motorcycling, paragliding and trekking – read the fine print.

➡ If you plan to hire a motorcycle in India make sure the rental policy includes at least third-party insurance.

➡ Check in advance if your insurance policy will pay doctors and hospitals directly or reimburse you later for overseas health expenditures (keep all documentation for your claim).

➡ It's crucial to get a police report in India if you've had anything stolen; insurance companies may refuse to reimburse you without one.

➡ Worldwide travel insurance is available at www.lonelyplanet.com/travel-insurance. You can buy, extend and claim online anytime – even if you're already on the road.

Internet Access

Internet cafes are widespread and connections are usually decent, except in more remote areas. Wi-fi access is widely available; it's usually free but some places charge.

Practicalities

➡ Internet charges vary regionally, falling anywhere between ₹15 and ₹80 per hour and often with a 15-to-30-minute minimum.

➡ Bandwidth load tends to be lowest in the early morning and early afternoon.

➡ Some internet cafes may ask to see your passport.

Security

➡ Be wary of sending sensitive financial information from internet cafes; some places can use keystroke-capturing technology to access passwords and emails.

➡ Avoid sending credit-card details or other personal data over a wireless connection; using online banking on any nonsecure system is generally unwise.

Laptops

The simplest way to connect to the internet when away from a wi-fi connection is to use your smartphone as a personal wi-fi hotspot (use a local SIM to avoid roaming charges). However, if this isn't an option, companies that offer prepaid wireless 2G/3G modem sticks (dongles) include Reliance, Airtel, Tata Docomo, MTS and Vodafone. Getting online is a lesson in Indian bureaucracy: you have to submit your proof of identity and address in India (get a letter from your hotel), and often provide a passport photo. A local phone number is also essential to receive the modem activation code – the whole thing can take up to 24 hours. Costs are around ₹2000, which includes about 10GB of data (20GB recharges cost around ₹1000). Make sure the areas you're travelling to are covered by your service provider.

Consider purchasing a fuse-protected universal AC adaptor to protect your device from power surges. Plug adaptors are widely available throughout India, but bring spare plug fuses from home.

Legal Matters

If you're in a sticky legal situation, contact your embassy as quickly as possible. However, be aware that all your embassy may be able to do is monitor your treatment in custody and arrange a lawyer. In the Indian justice system, the burden of proof can often be on the accused, and stints in prison before trial are not unheard of. Travellers should note that they can be prosecuted under the law of their home country regarding age of consent, even when abroad.

Antisocial Behaviour

➡ Smoking in public places is illegal throughout India but this is very rarely enforced; if caught you'll be fined ₹200 (or even ₹20,000 if proposed changes go ahead).

➡ People can smoke inside their homes and in most open spaces such as streets (heed any signs stating otherwise).

➡ A number of Indian cities have banned spitting and littering, but this is also variably enforced.

Drugs

➡ Indian law doesn't distinguish between 'hard' and 'soft' drugs; possession of any illegal drug is regarded as a criminal offence, which will result in a custodial sentence.

➡ Sentences may be up to a year for possession of a small amount for personal use, to a minimum of 10 years if it's deemed the purpose was for sale or distribution.

➡ Cases can take months, even several years, to appear before a court while the accused may have to wait in prison. There's also usually a hefty monetary fine on top of any custodial sentence.

➡ Be aware that travellers have been targeted in sting operations in some backpacker enclaves.

➡ Marijuana grows wild in various parts of India, but consuming it is still an offence, except in towns where bhang is legally sold for religious rituals.

➡ Police are getting particularly tough on foreigners who use drugs, so you should take this risk very seriously.

Police

➡ You should always carry your passport; police are entitled to ask you for identification at any time.

➡ If you're arrested for an alleged offence and asked for a bribe, note that it is illegal to pay a bribe in India. Many people deal with an on-the-spot fine by just

paying it to avoid trumped-up charges.

➡ Corruption is rife, so the less you have to do with local police the better; try and avoid potentially risky situations in the first place.

Maps

Maps available inside India are of variable quality. Throughout Rajasthan, most state-government tourist offices stock basic local maps. The following maps are available at good bookshops:

Eicher (http://maps.eicher-world.com/) Road, state and city maps.

Nelles (www.nelles-verlag.de) Western India.

Survey of India (www.survey-ofindia.gov.in) Decent city, state and country maps but some titles are restricted for security reasons.

Money

The Indian rupee (₹) is divided into 100 paise, but paise coins are becoming increasingly rare. Coins come in denominations of ₹1, ₹2 and ₹5; and notes in ₹5, ₹10, ₹20, ₹50, ₹100, ₹500 and ₹1000. The Indian rupee is linked to a basket of currencies and has been subject to fluctuations in recent years.

ATMs

➡ ATMs are found in most urban centres. Visa, MasterCard, Cirrus, Maestro and Plus are the most commonly accepted debit cards.

➡ Some banks in India that accept foreign cards include Citibank, HDFC, ICICI, Standard Chartered, HSBC, State Bank of India (SBI) and State Bank of Bikaner & Jaipur (SBBJ).

➡ Before your trip, check whether your card can reliably access banking

networks in India and ask for details of charges. Most ATMs have withdrawal limits of ₹10,000 to ₹15,000.

➡ Notify your bank that you'll be using your card in India (provide dates) to avoid having your card blocked; take along your bank's phone number just in case.

➡ Always keep the emergency lost-and-stolen numbers for your credit cards in a safe place, separate from your cards, and report any loss or theft immediately.

➡ Away from major towns, always carry cash or travellers cheques as back up.

Black Market

➡ Black-market moneychangers exist but legal moneychangers are so common that there's no reason to use them.

➡ As a rule, if someone approaches you on the street and offers to change money, you're probably being set up for a scam.

Cash

➡ Major currencies such as US dollars, British pounds and Euros are easy to change throughout India, although some bank branches insist on travellers cheques only. Some banks also accept other currencies such as Australian and Canadian dollars, and Swiss francs.

➡ Private moneychangers deal with a wider range of currencies.

➡ When travelling off the beaten track, always carry an adequate stock of rupees.

➡ Whenever changing money, check every note. Don't accept any filthy, ripped or disintegrating notes, as these may be difficult to use.

→ It can be tough getting change in India: jealously hoard your ₹10, ₹20 and ₹50 notes.

→ Officially, you cannot take rupees out of India, but this rule is laxly enforced. You can change any leftover rupees back into foreign currency, most easily at the airport (some banks have a ₹1000 minimum). You may be required to present your encashment certificates or credit-card/ATM receipts, and show your passport and airline ticket.

Credit Cards

→ Credit cards are accepted at a growing number of shops, upmarket restaurants, and midrange and top-end hotels, and they can usually be used to pay for flights and train tickets.

→ Cash advances on major credit cards are also possible at some banks.

→ MasterCard and Visa are the most widely accepted cards.

Encashment Certificates

→ Indian law states that all foreign currency must be changed at official moneychangers or banks.

→ For every (official) foreign-exchange transaction, you'll receive an encashment certificate (receipt), which will allow you to exchange rupees back into foreign currency when departing India.

→ Encashment certificates should total the amount of rupees you intend changing back to foreign currency.

→ Printed receipts from ATMs are also accepted as evidence of an international transaction at most banks.

International Transfers

→ If you run out of money, someone back home can wire you cash via moneychangers affiliated with **Moneygram** (www.moneygram.com) or **Western Union** (www.westernunion.com). A fee is added to the transaction. To collect cash, bring your passport and the name and reference number of the person who sent the funds.

Moneychangers

→ Private moneychangers are usually open for longer hours than banks, and are found almost everywhere (many also double as internet cafes and travel agents). Upmarket hotels may also change money, but their rates are usually not as competitive.

Tipping, Baksheesh & Bargaining

→ In tourist restaurants or hotels, a service fee is usually already added to your bill and tipping is optional. Elsewhere, a tip is appreciated.

→ Hotel bellboys and train/airport porters appreciate anything from around ₹20 to ₹50, and hotel staff should be given similar gratuities for services above and beyond the call of duty.

→ It's not mandatory to tip taxi or rickshaw drivers, but it's good to tip the drivers who are honest about the fare.

→ If you hire a car with driver for more than a couple of days, a tip is recommended if you receive good service from the driver.

→ Baksheesh can loosely be defined as a 'tip'; it covers everything from alms for beggars to bribes.

→ Many Indians implore tourists not to hand out sweets, pens or money to children, as it encourages them to beg. To make a lasting difference, instead donate to a reputable school or charitable organisation.

→ Unless you are shopping in fixed-price shops (such as government emporiums and fair-trade cooperatives), bargaining is the norm.

Travellers Cheques

→ All major brands are accepted, but some banks may only accept cheques that are from American Express (Amex) and Thomas Cook.

→ Pounds sterling and US dollars are the safest currencies, especially in smaller towns.

→ Keep a record of the cheques' serial numbers separate from your cheques, along with the proof-of-purchase slips, encashment vouchers and photocopied passport details. If you lose your cheques, contact the Amex or Thomas Cook office in Delhi.

→ To replace lost travellers cheques, you need the proof-of-purchase slip and the numbers of the missing cheques (some places require a photocopy of the police report and a passport photo). If you don't have the numbers of your missing cheques, the company that issued them will contact the place where you bought them.

Opening Hours

→ Official business hours are from 10am to 5.30pm Monday to Friday.

→ Most offices have an official lunch hour from around 1pm.

→ Bank opening hours vary from town to town, so check locally; foreign-exchange offices may open longer and operate daily.

→ Some larger post offices operate for a full day on Saturday and a half-day on Sunday.

BUSINESS	OPENING HOURS
airline offices	9.30am-5.30pm Mon-Sat
banks	9.30am or 10am-2pm or 4pm Mon-Fri, to noon or 1pm Sat
government offices	9.30am-1pm & 2-5.30pm Mon-Fri, to noon Sat, closed alternative Sat (usually 2nd & 4th)
post offices	10am-4pm Mon-Fri, to noon Sat
museums	10am-5pm Tue-Sun
restaurants	lunch: noon-2.30pm or 3pm; dinner: 7-10pm or 11pm
sights	10am-5pm or dawn-dusk
shops	10am-7pm, some closed Sun

Photography

For useful tips and techniques on travel photography, read Lonely Planet's guide to *Travel Photography*.

Digital

➡ Memory cards for digital cameras are available from photographic shops in most large cities and towns. Expect to pay upwards of ₹200 for a 4GB card.

➡ To be safe, regularly back up your memory cards. If you don't have Cloud storage or a card-reader, many internet cafes will burn your pictures to a CD.

➡ Some photographic shops make prints from digital photographs for roughly the standard print-and-processing charge.

Restrictions

➡ India is touchy about anyone taking photographs of military installations – this can include train stations, bridges, airports, military sites and sensitive border regions.

➡ Photography from the air is officially prohibited, although airlines rarely enforce this.

➡ Many places of worship, such as monasteries, temples and mosques, also prohibit photography. Taking photos inside a shrine, at a funeral, at a religious ceremony or of people publicly bathing (including rivers) can also be offensive. Always ask first.

➡ Flash photography may be prohibited in certain areas of a shrine, or may not be permitted at all.

➡ Exercise sensitivity when taking photos of people, especially women, who may find it offensive – obtain permission in advance.

➡ When photographing people, use your instincts; some people may demand money afterwards.

Post

India has the biggest postal network in the world, with over 155,000 post offices. Mail and poste-restante services are generally good, although the speed of delivery will depend on the efficiency of any given office. Airmail is faster and more reliable than sea mail, although it's best to use courier services (such as DHL) to send and receive items of value – expect to pay around ₹3000 per kilogram to Europe, Australia or the USA. Private couriers are often cheaper, but goods may be repacked into large packages to cut costs and things sometimes go missing.

Receiving Mail

➡ Ask senders to address letters to you with your surname in capital letters and underlined, followed by poste restante, GPO (main post office), and the city or town in question. To claim mail you'll need to show your passport.

➡ Many 'lost' letters are simply misfiled under given/first names, so check under both your names and ask senders to provide a return address.

➡ Letters sent via poste restante are generally held for around one to two months before being returned.

➡ It's best to have any parcels sent to you by registered post.

Sending Mail
LETTERS

➡ Posting letters/aerogrammes to anywhere overseas costs ₹25/15.

➡ International postcards cost around ₹12.

➡ For postcards, stick on the stamps *before* writing on them, as post offices can give you as many as four stamps per card.

➡ Sending a letter overseas by registered post adds ₹50 to the cost.

PARCELS

➡ Posting parcels can be relatively straightforward or involve multiple counters and a fair amount of queuing; get to the post office in the morning.

➡ Prices vary depending on weight (including packing material).

➡ An (unregistered) airmail package costs around ₹400 to ₹850 (up to 250g) to any country and ₹50 to ₹150 per additional 250g (up to a maximum of 2000g; different charges apply for higher weights).

➡ Parcel post has a maximum of 20kg to 30kg depending on the destination.

➡ There is the choice of airmail (delivery in one to three weeks); sea mail (two to four months); or Surface Air-Lifted (SAL), a curious hybrid where parcels travel by both air and sea (around one month). Another option is EMS (express mail service; delivery within three days) for around 30% more than the normal airmail price.

➡ Parcels must be stitched up in white linen and the seams sealed with wax – agents at the post office offer this service for a fee. It's a joy to watch.

➡ The post office can provide the necessary customs declaration forms and these must be stitched or pasted to the parcel. If the contents are a gift under the value of ₹1000, you won't be required to pay duty at the delivery end.

➡ Carry a permanent marker to write any information requested by the desk on the parcel.

➡ Books or printed matter can go by international book post for ₹350 (maximum 5kg), the parcel has to be packed with an opening so it may be checked by customs.

➡ **India Post** (www.indiapost. gov.in) has an online calculator for domestic and international postal tariffs.

Public Holidays

There are officially three national public holidays – Republic and Independence Days and Gandhi's birthday (Gandhi Jayanti). Every state celebrates its own official holidays, which cover bank holidays for government workers as well as major religious festivals. Most businesses (offices, shops etc) and tourist sites close on public holidays, but transport is usually unaffected. It's

wise to make transport and hotel reservations well in advance if you intend visiting during major festivals.

Republic Day 26 January

Holi (Hindu) February/March

Mahavir Jayanti (Jain) March/April

Easter (Christian) March/April

Buddha Jayanti (Buddhist) April/May

Eid al-Fitr (Muslim) June/July

Independence Day 15 August

Dussehra (Hindu) September/October

Gandhi Jayanti 2 October

Diwali (Hindu) October/November

Nanak Jayanti (Sikh) November

Christmas (Christian) 25 December

Safe Travel

Travellers to India's major cities may fall prey to petty and opportunistic crime. Also have a look at the India branch of Lonely Planet's Thorn Tree travel forum (www.lonelyplanet.com/thorntree), where travellers often post timely warnings about problems they've encountered on the road.

Indian cities have occasionally been targeted by

bombers, typically associated with the situation in Kashmir. However rare such attacks may be, it makes sense to check the security situation with embassy travel advisories and local newspapers. Always check your government's travel advisory warnings.

Telephone

➡ Private PCO/STD/ISD call booths offer inexpensive local, interstate and international calls at lower prices than calls made from hotel rooms.

➡ A digital meter displays how much the call is costing and usually provides a printed receipt when the call is finished.

➡ Costs vary depending on the operator and destination, but can range from ₹1 per minute for local calls and between ₹5 and ₹10 for international calls.

➡ Some booths also offer a 'call-back' service – you ring home, provide the phone number of the booth and wait for people at home to call you back, for a fee of around ₹10 on top of the cost of the preliminary call.

SECURE IT OR LOSE IT

➡ The safest place for your money and your passport is next to your skin, in a concealed moneybelt or pouch. Never, ever carry these things in your luggage or a shoulder bag. Bum bags are not recommended either, as they advertise that you have a stash of goodies.

➡ Never leave your valuable documents and travellers cheques in your hotel room (including under your mattress). If the hotel is a reputable one, you should be able to use the hotel safe.

➡ It's wise to peel off at least US$100 and keep it stashed away separately from your main horde, for emergencies.

➡ Separate your big notes from your small ones so you don't display large wads of cash when paying for things.

➡ Useful online resources include the **Yellow Pages** (www.indiayellowpages.com) and **Justdial** (www.justdial.com).

Mobile Phones

➡ Indian mobile phone numbers usually have 10 digits typically beginning with 9 (sometimes also 7 or 8)

➡ There's roaming coverage for international GSM phones in most cities and large towns.

➡ To avoid expensive roaming costs (often highest for incoming calls), get hooked up to the local mobile-phone network. You'll need to have an unlocked phone to use an Indian SIM card, or buy a local handset (from ₹2000).

GETTING CONNECTED

➡ Getting connected is inexpensive and fairly straightforward in many areas. It's easiest to obtain a local SIM card when you arrive if you're flying into a large city.

➡ Foreigners must supply between one and five passport photos, their passport, and photocopies of their passport identity and visa pages. Often mobile shops can arrange all this for you, or you can ask your hotel to help you. It's best to try to do this in tourist centres and cities.

➡ You must also supply a residential address, which can be the address of your hotel. Usually the phone company will call your hotel (warn the hotel a call will be coming through) any time up to 24 hours after your application to verify that you are staying there.

➡ It's a good idea to obtain the SIM card somewhere you're staying for a day or two so that you can return to the vendor if there's any problem. Only obtain your SIM card from a reputable branded phone store in order to avoid scams.

➡ Another option is to get a friendly local to register the phone using their local ID.

➡ Prepaid mobile-phone kits (SIM card and phone number, plus an allocation of calls) are available in most Indian towns from around ₹200 from a phone shop or local PCO/STD/ISD booth, internet cafe or grocery store.

➡ Credit must usually be used within a set time limit and costs vary with the amount of credit on the card.

➡ The amount you pay for a credit top-up is not the amount you get on your phone – state taxes and service charges come off first.

CHARGES

➡ Calls made within the state or city in which you bought the SIM card are cheap – ₹1 per minute – and you can call internationally for less than ₹10 per minute.

➡ SMS messaging is even cheaper. Usually, the more credit you have on your phone, the cheaper the call rate. Most SIM cards are state specific; they can be used in other states, but you pay for calls at roaming rates and you'll be charged for incoming calls as well as outgoing calls.

➡ The leading service providers include Airtel, Vodafone and Reliance. Coverage varies from region to region.

Phone Codes

Note that the government is slowly trying to bring all numbers in India onto the same system, so area codes may change and new digits may be added to numbers with limited warning.

Calling India from abroad Dial your country's international access code, then ☑91 (India's country code), then the area code (without the initial zero), then the local number.

Calling internationally from India Dial ☑00 (the international access code), then the country code of the country you're calling, then the area code (without the initial zero if there is one) and the local number.

Toll-free numbers These begin with ☑1800.

Time

India uses the 12-hour clock and the local standard time is known as IST (Indian Standard Time). IST is 5½ hours ahead of GMT/UTC. The floating half-hour was added to maximise daylight hours over such a vast country.

CITY	NOON IN DELHI
Beijing	2.30pm
Dhaka	12.30pm
Islamabad	11.30am
London	6.30am
Kathmandu	12.15pm
New York	1.30am
San Francisco	10.30pm
Sydney	5.30pm
Tokyo	3.30pm

Toilets

Public toilets are most easily found in major cities and tourist sites and the cleanest toilets (usually with sit-down and squat choices) are most reliably found at modern restaurants, shopping complexes and cinemas. Beyond urban centres toilets are of the squat variety and locals will use the 'hand-and-water' technique, which involves performing ablutions with a small jug of water and the left hand. It's always a good idea to carry your own toilet paper and hand sanitiser, just in case.

Tourist Information

In addition to the Government of India tourist offices (also known as 'India Tourism') each state maintains its own network of tourist offices. In Rajasthan, the Rajasthan Tourism Development Corporation (RTDC) operates Tourist Reception Centres in most places of interest. These vary in their efficiency and usefulness – some are run by enthusiastic souls who go out of their way to help, others are little more than a means of drumming up business for RTDC tours.

Most have free brochures and often a free (or inexpensive) local map.

The first stop for information should be the tourism website of the Government of India, **Incredible India** (www.incredibleindia.org). For details of its regional offices around the country, click on the 'Help Desk' tab at the top of the homepage.

Travellers with Disabilities

India's crowded public transport, hectic urban life and variable infrastructure can test even the hardiest able-bodied traveller. If you have a physical disability or you are vision impaired, these factors can pose even more of a challenge. If your mobility is considerably restricted you may like to ease the stress by travelling with an able-bodied companion.

Accommodation Wheelchair-friendly hotels are almost exclusively top end. Make pre-trip enquiries and book ground-floor rooms at hotels that lack adequate facilities.

Accessibility Some restaurants and offices have ramps; most tend to have at least one step. Staircases are often steep; lifts frequently stop at mezzanines between floors.

Footpaths Where pavements exist, they can be riddled with holes, littered with debris and packed with pedestrians. If using crutches, bring along spare rubber caps.

Transport Hiring a car with a driver will make moving around a lot easier; if you use a wheelchair, make sure the car-hire company can provide an appropriate vehicle to carry it.

Further advice Consult your doctor about your specific requirements before heading to India.

Internet Resources

Access-Able Travel Source (www.access-able.com)

Accessible Journeys (www.disabilitytravel.com)

Global Access News (www.globalaccessnews.com)

Mobility International USA (MIUSA; www.miusa.org)

Visas

Visa on Arrival

Citizens of Australia, Brazil, Cambodia, Cook Islands, Djibouti, Fiji, Finland, Germany, Guyana, Indonesia, Israel, Japan, Jordan, Kenya, Kiribati, Laos, Luxembourg, Marshall Islands, Mauritius, Mexico, Micronesia, Myanmar, Nauru, New Zealand, Niue Island, Norway, Oman, Palau, Palestine, Papua New Guinea, Philippines, Republic of Korea, Russia, Samoa, Singapore, Solomon Islands, Thailand, Tonga, Tuvalu, UAE, Ukraine, USA, Vanuatu and Vietnam are currently granted a 30-day single-entry visa on arrival (VOA) at Delhi airport, as well as at Bengaluru (Bangalore), Chennai (Madras), Kochi (Cochin), Goa, Hyderabad, Kolkata (Calcutta), Mumbai (Bombay) and Thiruvananthapuram (Trivandrum).

However, to participate in the scheme, you need to apply online at https://indianvisaonline.gov.in for an Electronic Travel Authority (ETA), a minimum/maximum four/30 days before you are due to travel. The fee is US$60, and you have to upload a photograph as well as a copy of your passport. Travellers have reported being asked for documentation showing their hotel confirmation at the airport, though this is not specified on the VOA website. The VOA is valid from the date of arrival.

It's intended that the scheme will be rolled out to 180 nations, including the UK and China, so check online for any updates.

Other Visas

If you want to stay longer than 30 days, or are not covered by the VOA scheme, you must get a visa before arriving in India (apart from Nepali or Bhutanese citizens). Visas are available at Indian missions worldwide, though in many countries, applications are processed by a separate private company. In some countries, including the UK, you must apply in person at the designated office as well as filing an application online.

Note that your passport needs to be valid for at least six months beyond your intended stay in India, with at least two blank pages. Most people are issued with a standard six-month tourist visa, which for most nationalities permits multiple entry.

→ Student, business and journalist visas have strict conditions (consult the Indian embassy for details).

→ Tourist visas are valid from the date of issue, not the date you arrive in India.

→ Five- and 10-year tourist visas are available to US citizens only under a bilateral arrangement; however, you can still only stay in the country for up to 180 days continuously.

→ Currently you are required to submit two passport photographs with your visa application; these must be in colour and must be 5.08cm by 5.08 cm (2in by 2in; larger than regular passport photos).

→ An onward travel ticket is a requirement for some visas, but this isn't always enforced (check in advance).

→ Additional restrictions apply to travellers from Bangladesh and Pakistan, as well as certain eastern European, African and central Asian countries. Check any special conditions for your nationality with the Indian embassy in your country.

→ Visas are priced in the local currency and may have an added service fee.

→ Extended visas are possible for people of Indian origin (excluding those in Pakistan and Bangladesh) who hold a non-Indian passport and live abroad.

→ For visas lasting more than six months, you're supposed to register at the **Foreigners' Regional Registration Office** (FRRO; ☎011-26711443; frrodil@nic.in; Level 2, East Block 8, Sector 1, Rama Krishna (RK) Puram, Delhi; ⏰9.30am-3pm Mon-Fri) in Delhi within 14 days of arriving in India; enquire about these special conditions when you apply for your visa.

Visa Extensions

At the time of writing, the **Ministry of Home Affairs** (☎011-23385748; 26 Man Singh Rd, Jaisalmer House, Delhi; ⏰enquiries 9-11am Mon-Fri) was not granting visa extensions. The only circumstances where this might conceivably happen are in *extreme* medical emergencies or if you were robbed of your passport just before you planned to leave the country (at the end of your visa).

In such cases, you should contact the Foreigners' Regional Registration Office, just around the corner from the Hyatt Regency hotel in Delhi. This is also the place to come for a replacement visa if you need your lost/stolen passport replaced (required before you can leave the country). Note that regional FRROs are even less likely to grant an extension.

Assuming you meet the stringent criteria, the FRRO is permitted to issue an extension of 14 days (free for nationals of most countries; enquire on application). You must bring your confirmed air ticket, one passport photo (take two, just in case) and a photocopy of your passport identity and visa pages. Note that this system

is designed to get you out of the country promptly with the correct official stamps, not to give you two extra weeks of travel.

Volunteering

Many charities and international aid agencies work in India and there are numerous opportunities for volunteers. It may be possible to find a placement after you arrive in India, but charities and NGOs normally prefer volunteers who have applied in advance and been approved for the kind of work involved.

Lonely Planet does not endorse any organisations that we do not work with directly, so it is essential that you do your own thorough research before agreeing to volunteer with any organisation.

The website www.ethicalvolunteering.org has useful tips on choosing an ethical volunteer organisation.

There are some excellent local charities and NGOs, some of which have opportunities for volunteers; for listings see www.indianngos.com.

The **Concern India Foundation** (☎011-26224482, 011-26224483; www.concern indiafoundation.org; Lajpat Nagar 4, Room A52, 1st fl, Amar Colony) may be able to link volunteers with current projects around the country; contact them well in advance for information. Delhi's *First City* magazine lists various local NGOs that welcome volunteers and financial aid.

Overseas Volunteer Placement Agencies

For long-term posts and information on volunteering check out the following organisations:

Action Without Borders (www.idealist.org)

AidCamps International (www.aidcamps.org)

Coordinating Committee for International Voluntary Service (www.ccivs.org)

Global Volunteers (www.globalvolunteers.org)

Indicorps (www.indicorps.org)

Voluntary Service Overseas (www.vso.org.uk)

Volunteer Abroad (www.volunteerabroad.com)

Working Abroad (www.workingabroad.com)

World Volunteer Web (www.worldvolunteerweb.org)

Worldwide Volunteering (www.worldwidevolunteering.org.uk)

Aid Programs

The following programs may have opportunities for volunteers with specific skills.

DELHI
Missionaries of Charity (☎011-33237839; www.motherteresa.org; 1 Magazine Rd) Welcomes volunteers (weekdays only).

Salaam Baalak Trust (☎011-23681803; www.salaambaalaktrust.com; Chandiwalan, Main Bazaar, Paharganj) Provides shelter, food, education and other support to Delhi's homeless street children. There's opportunities to sponsor a child for ₹28,500 per year, fund individual projects or donate clothes, toys, blankets, books and computers. Volunteer English teachers, doctors and computer experts are welcome.

RAJASTHAN
Action Formation Education Voyage (AFEV; ☎9829867323; www.afevinde.com; KEM Rd, Pause Café) An NGO working on projects in and around Bikaner including plastic-bag recycling, a small

orphanage, street cleaning and equitable tourism. It's run by a local French resident and foreign volunteers can work with children, on information services or other projects, with food and accommodation provided.

Animal Aid Unlimited (☎9950531639, 9352511435; www.animalaidunlimited.com; Badi Village) Volunteers can help rescue, treat and care for injured, abandoned or stray animals (mostly dogs, cows and donkeys) at its spacious premises a few kilometres outside Udaipur. Make an appointment before going to see them. There's no minimum period, but volunteers are encouraged to stay long enough to learn the routines and develop relationships with individual animals.

Help in Suffering (☎0141-3245673; www.his-india.org.au; Maharani Farm, Durgapura, Jaipur) Jaipur-based animal welfare charity. Welcomes qualified voluntary vets (three-/six-/12-month commitments). Apply first in writing.

Ladli (☎9829011124; www.ladli.org; 74 Govindpuri, Rakdi, Sodala, Jaipur) Vocational training for abused, orphaned and destitute children. Volunteers work in child care and teach English; placements last up to a year.

Marwar Medical & Relief Society (☎0291-2545210; www.mandore.com; Mandore Guesthouse, Dadwari Lane) Runs educational, health, environmental and other projects in villages in the Jodhpur district. Guests at its guesthouse in Mandore and other short- or long-term volunteers are welcomed.

Sambhali Trust (☎0291-2512385; www.sambhali-trust.org; Durag Niwas Guest House, 1st Old Public Park, Raika Bagh, Jodhpur) Organisation aiming to empower disadvantaged women and girls in Jodhpur city and Setrawa village, primarily through textile production, literacy and English-language learning. Volunteers can teach and help organise workshops on topics such as health, women's rights and nutrition.

Seva Mandir (☎0294-2451041; www.sevamandir.org; Old Fatehpura, Udaipur) A long-established NGO working with rural and tribal people in southern Rajasthan on a host of projects including afforestation, water resources, health, education and empowerment of women and village institutions. Volunteers and interns can get involved in a wide range of activities.

Shikshantar (☎0294-2451303; www.swaraj.org/shikshantar; 83 Adinath Nagar, Kharol Colony) Volunteers can work on issues such as slow food, healthy lifestyles, herbal medicines, urban and organic farming, alternative technologies and zero-waste design.

URMUL Trust (www.urmul.org; Ganganagar Rd, Urmul Bhawan, Bikaner) Provides primary health care and education to desert dwellers in arid western Rajasthan, as well as promoting their handicrafts and women's rights. Volunteer placements (minimum one month) are available in English-teaching, health care, documentation and other work.

Transport

GETTING THERE & AWAY

Plenty of international airlines service India and overland routes are open to and from Nepal, Bangladesh, Bhutan and Pakistan. Flights, tours and other tickets may be booked online at www. lonelyplanet.com/bookings.

Entering India

Entering India by air or land is relatively straightforward, with standard immigration and customs procedures. A frustrating law barring re-entry into India within two months of the previous date of departure has now been done away with (except for citizens of some Asian countries), thus allowing most travellers to combine their India tour with side trips to neighbouring countries.

Passport

To enter India you need a valid passport and an on-ward/return ticket. You'll also need a visa (p253), which some nationalities can now obtain on arrival. Other nationalities or those wishing to stay more than 30 days need to get their visa beforehand. Your passport should be valid for at least six months beyond your intended stay in India. If your passport is lost or stolen, immediately contact your country's representative. Keep photocopies of your airline ticket and the identity and visa pages of your passport in case of emergency. Better yet, scan and email copies to yourself. Check with the Indian embassy in your home country for any special conditions that may exist for your nationality.

Air

Airports & Airlines

India has six main gateways for international flights. Most Rajasthan-bound travellers fly into Delhi or Mumbai. A small number of international flights, mostly from the Middle East, serve Jaipur – for details, inquire at travel agencies and see www.aai.aero.

India's national carrier is **Air India** (www.airindia.com), of which the former state-owned domestic carrier, Indian Airlines, is now a part, following a merger deal. Air India has had a relatively decent air safety record in recent years.

Indira Gandhi International Airport (91-1243376000; www. newdelhiairport.in; Delhi)

Kolkata (CCU; 033-25118036; www.aai.aero/kolkata; Kolkata, Netaji Subhash Chandra Bose International Airport)

Chhatrapati Shivaji International Airport (022-2626 4000; www.csia. in; Mumbai)

Tickets

Departure tax and other charges are included in airline tickets. You are required to show a copy of your

---

CLIMATE CHANGE & TRAVEL

Every form of transport that relies on carbon-based fuel generates CO_2, the main cause of human-induced climate change. Modern travel is dependent on aeroplanes, which might use less fuel per kilometre per person than most cars but travel much greater distances. The altitude at which aircraft emit gases (including CO_2) and particles also contributes to their climate change impact. Many websites offer 'carbon calculators' that allow people to estimate the carbon emissions generated by their journey and, for those who wish to do so, to offset the impact of the greenhouse gases emitted with contributions to portfolios of climate-friendly initiatives throughout the world. Lonely Planet offsets the carbon footprint of all staff and author travel.

ticket (or e-ticket) and your passport in order to enter the airport, whether flying internationally or within India.

Land
Rajasthan to Pakistan
Given the rocky relationship between India and Pakistan, crossing by land depends on the current state of relations between the two countries – check locally. If the crossings are open, you can travel from Rajasthan to Pakistan by train from Jodhpur, on a weekly train to Karachi.

You must have a visa to enter Pakistan. It's easiest to obtain this from the Pakistan mission in your home country. At the time of research, the **Pakistan Embassy** (☑011-24676004; www.mofa.gov.pk/india; 2/50G Shantipath, Chanakyapuri) in Delhi was not issuing tourist visas for most nationalities, but this could change.

GETTING AROUND

Air
Within Rajasthan, there are airports in Jaipur, Jaisalmer, Jodhpur and Udaipur. However, Jaisalmer is occasionally closed if tensions are high along the Pakistan border.

Security at airports is stringent. In smaller airports, all hold baggage must be X-rayed prior to check-in (major airports now have in-line baggage screening facilities). Every item of cabin baggage needs a label, which must be stamped as part of the security check (don't forget to collect tags at the check-in counter). You may also have to allow for a spot-check of your cabin baggage on the tarmac before you board.

Keeping peak hour congestion in mind, the recommended check-in time for domestic flights is two hours before departure – the dead-

---

DELHI TO KATHMANDU
For those on tight budgets and with a lot of stamina, it's possible to travel overland from Delhi to Kathmandu in Nepal in a single shot. Luxury buses run daily from near Delhi Gate, taking a whopping 30 hours. Tickets (₹2300) are sold by agencies in Paharganj and other areas popular with travellers. You cross at Sunauli border (Bhairahawa on the Nepali side). At the time of research, visas on arrival were available for most nationalities, but check the current situation before travelling.

---

line is 45 minutes. The usual baggage allowance is 20kg (10kg for smaller aircraft) in economy class.

Airlines in India
Transporting vast numbers of passengers each year, India has a very competitive domestic airline industry. But in a crowded marketplace, many players have suffered huge financial losses and run into trouble, and at the time of research, the future of SpiceJet was uncertain. Established carriers with flights in Rajasthan are Air India, Kingfisher and Jet Airways.

Airline seats can be booked cheaply over the internet or through travel agencies. Apart from airline sites, bookings can be made through reliable ticketing portals such as **Cleartrip** (www.cleartrip.com), **Make My Trip** (www.makemytrip.com) and **Yatra** (www.yatra.com). Domestic airlines set rupee fares for Indian citizens, while foreigners may be charged US dollar fares (usually payable in rupees).

At the time of research, the following airlines were operating across various destinations in India.

Air India (☑1800-1801407; www.airindia.com) India's national carrier operates many domestic and international flights.

Jet Airways (☑011-39893333; www.jetairways.com) Rated by many as India's best airline, with growing domestic and international services.

Kingfisher Airlines (☑1800-2093030; www.flykingfisher.com) Domestic and international flights; Kingfisher Red is their low-cost option.

SpiceJet (☑1800-1803333; www.spicejet.com)

Bicycle
Rajasthan offers an immense array of experiences for a long-distance cyclist. Nevertheless, long-distance cycling is not for the faint of heart or weak of knee. You'll need physical endurance to cope with the roads, traffic and climate.

There are no restrictions on bringing a bicycle into the country. However, bicycles sent by sea can take a few weeks to clear customs in India, so it's better to fly bikes in. It may actually be cheaper (and less hassle) to hire or buy a bicycle in India itself. Read up on bicycle touring before you travel – Rob Van Der Plas' *The Bicycle Touring Manual* and Stephen Lord's *Adventure Cycle-Touring Handbook* are good places to start. Consult local cycling magazines and cycling clubs for useful information and advice. The **Cycling Federation of India** (☑011-23753529; www.cyclingfederationofindia.org; 12 Pandit Pant Marg; ⊙10am-5pm Mon-Fri) can provide local information.

Hire
➡ Tourist centres and traveller hang-outs are the easiest spots to find bicycles for hire.

→ Prices vary between ₹40 and ₹100 per day for roadworthy, Indian-made bicycles. Mountain bikes are usually upwards of ₹400 per day.

→ Hire places may require a cash security deposit (avoid leaving your airline ticket or passport).

Practicalities

→ Roadside cycle mechanics abound but you should still bring spare tyres and brake cables, lubricating oil and a chain repair kit, and plenty of puncture-repair patches.

→ Bikes can often be carried for free, or for a small luggage fee, on the roof of public buses – handy for uphill stretches.

→ Contact your airline for information about transporting your bike and customs formalities in your home country.

Purchase

→ Delhi's Jhandewalan Cycle Market has new and second-hand bikes and spare parts.

→ Indian mountain bikes such as Hero and Atlas start at around ₹7000.

→ Reselling is easy – ask at local cycle or hire shops or put up an advert on travel noticeboards. If you purchased a new bike and it's still in reasonable condition, you should be able to recoup around 50% of what you originally paid.

On the Road

→ Vehicles drive on the left side in India but otherwise road rules are virtually nonexistent. Cities and national highways can be hazardous places to cycle, so, where possible, stick to the back roads.

→ Be conservative about the distances you expect to cover – an experienced cyclist can manage around 60km to 100km a day on the plains and 40km or less on dirt roads.

Bus

→ The Rajasthan state government bus service is **Rajasthan State Road Transport Corporation** (http://rsrtc.rajasthan.gov.in), sometimes still known as Rajasthan Roadways.

→ Often there are privately owned local bus services as well as luxury private coaches running between major cities – these can be booked through travel agencies.

→ Avoid night buses unless there's no alternative, as driving conditions are more hazardous and drivers may be suffering from lack of sleep.

→ All buses make snack and toilet stops (some more frequently than others), providing a break but possibly adding hours to journey times.

Bus Types & Classes

→ On the main routes in Rajasthan you have a choice of ordinary, express and deluxe. Express and deluxe buses make fewer stops than ordinary buses – they're still usually crowded though. The fare is marginally higher than ordinary buses, but worth every rupee.

→ On selected routes there are RSRTC Gray Line (sleeper) buses – these have beds and make overnight trips more comfortable. Beds have a bunk-bed arrangement, with rows of single beds, each with a curtain for privacy.

→ Silver Line is a so-called superdeluxe service and the buses have a reasonable level of comfort.

→ Air-conditioned Volvo and Gold Line buses are the best bus options and serve the Jaipur–Delhi and Agra–Udaipur routes.

→ Private buses also operate on most Rajasthani routes; apart from often being quicker and usually more comfortable, the booking procedure is much simpler than for state-run buses. However, private companies can often change schedules at the last minute to get as many bums on seats as possible.

Luggage

→ Luggage is either stored in compartments underneath the bus (sometimes for a small fee) or it can be carried on the roof.

→ Arrive at least an hour ahead of the scheduled departure time – some buses cover the roof-stored bags with a large sheet of canvas, making it inconvenient/impossible for last-minute additions.

→ If your baggage is stored on the roof, make sure it is securely locked, and tied tightly to the metal baggage rack – some unlucky travellers have seen their belongings go bouncing off the roof on bumpy roads!

→ Theft is a risk – keep an eye on your bags at snack and toilet stops and *never* leave your daypack or valuables unattended inside the bus.

Reservations

→ Most deluxe buses can be booked in advance – usually up to a month in advance for government buses – at bus stations or local travel agencies.

→ Online bookings for many routes can be made through the portals **Cleartrip** (www.cleartrip.com) and **Redbus** (www.redbus.in).

→ Reservations are rarely possible on 'ordinary' buses and travellers often get left behind in the mad rush for a seat. To maximise your chances of securing a spot, either send a travelling companion ahead to grab some space, or pass a book or article of clothing through an open window and place it on an empty seat.

→ Many buses only depart when full – you may find your bus suddenly empties to join another bus that's ready to leave before yours.

➡ At many bus stations there's a separate women's queue, although this isn't always obvious because signs are often in Hindi and men frequently join the melee. Women travellers should sharpen their elbows and make their way to the front, where they will get almost immediate service.

Car

Few people bother with self-drive car rental – not only because of the hair-raising driving conditions, but also because hiring a car with a driver is wonderfully affordable in India, particularly if several people share the cost. International rental companies with representatives in India include **Budget** (www.budget.com) and **Hertz** (www.hertz.com).

Hiring a Car & Driver

➡ Most towns have taxi stands or car-hire companies where you can arrange short or long tours.

➡ Use your hotel to find a car and driver – this achieves a good level of security and reliability and a better rate.

➡ Not all hire cars are licensed to travel beyond their home state. Even those vehicles that are licensed to enter different states have to pay extra (often hefty) state taxes, which will add to the rental charge.

➡ Ask for a driver who speaks some English and knows the region you intend visiting, and try to see the car and meet the driver before paying any money.

➡ Ambassador cars look great but are rather slow and uncomfortable if travelling long distances – consider them for touring cities.

➡ For multiday trips, the charge should cover the driver's meals and accommodation. Drivers should make their own sleeping and eating arrangements.

➡ It is essential to set the ground rules with the driver from day one, in order to avoid anguish later.

Costs

➡ The price depends on the distance and sometimes the terrain (driving on mountain roads uses more petrol, hence the 'hill charges').

➡ One-way trips usually cost the same as return ones (to cover the petrol and driver charges for getting back).

➡ To avoid potential misunderstandings, ensure you get in writing what you've been promised (quotes should include petrol, sightseeing stops, all your chosen destinations, and meals and accommodation for the driver).

➡ If a driver asks you for money to pay for petrol en route (reasonable on long trips), keep a record (he will do the same).

➡ Operators usually charge from ₹7 to ₹10 per kilometre per day (depending on the car and if it has AC), with a 250km minimum per day and an overnight charge of up to ₹300.

➡ For sightseeing day trips around a single city, expect to pay anywhere upwards of ₹1000/1200 for a non-AC/AC car with an eight-hour, 80km limit per day (extra charges apply beyond this).

➡ A tip is customary at the end of your journey; ₹150 to ₹200 per day is fair.

Local Transport

➡ Buses, cycle-rickshaws, autorickshaws, taxis and urban trains provide transport around cities.

➡ On any form of transport without a fixed fare, agree on the price *before* you start your journey and make sure that it covers your luggage and every passenger.

➡ Fares usually increase at night (by up to 100%) and some drivers charge a few rupees extra for luggage.

➡ Carry plenty of small bills for taxi and rickshaw fares as drivers rarely have change.

➡ Carry a business card of the hotel in which you are staying, as your pronunciation of streets, hotel names etc may be incomprehensible to drivers. Some hotel cards even have a sketch map clearly indicating their location.

➡ Some taxi/autorickshaw drivers are involved in the commission racket.

Autorickshaw & Tempo

➡ The Indian autorickshaw is basically a three-wheeled motorised contraption with a tin or canvas roof and sides, providing room for two passengers (although you'll often see many more bodies squeezed in) and limited luggage.

➡ They are also referred to as autos, tuk-tuks, Indian helicopters, or Ferraris.

➡ Autorickshaws are mostly cheaper than taxis and are often metered, although getting the driver to turn on the meter can be a challenge.

➡ Tempos and *vikrams* (large tempos) are outsized autorickshaws with room for more than two passengers, running on fixed routes for a fixed fare.

Bus

➡ Urban buses, particularly in the big cities, are fume-belching, human-stuffed mechanical monsters that travel at breakneck speed (except during morning and evening rush hours, when they can be endlessly stuck in traffic). It's usually far more convenient and comfortable to opt for an autorickshaw or taxi.

Cycle-Rickshaw

➡ A cycle-rickshaw is a pedal cycle with two rear wheels, supporting a bench seat for

PREPAID TAXIS

Most Indian airports and many train stations have a prepaid taxi booth, normally just outside the terminal building. Here, you can book a taxi for a fixed price (which will include baggage) and thus avoid commission scams. However, officials advise holding on to the payment coupon until you reach your chosen destination, in case the driver has any other ideas. Smaller airports and stations may have prepaid autorickshaw booths instead.

passengers. Most have a canopy that can be raised in wet weather, or lowered to provide extra space for luggage.

➡ Many of the big cities have phased out (or reduced) the number of cycle-rickshaws, but you can still find them in Delhi and Jaipur, and they remain a major means of local transport in many smaller towns.

➡ Fares must be agreed upon in advance – speak to locals to get an idea of what is a fair price. Remember this is extremely strenuous work and the wallahs are among India's poorest, so a tip is appreciated and haggling over a few rupees unnecessary.

Share Jeep

➡ Share jeeps supplement the bus service in many parts of Rajasthan, especially in areas off the main road routes, such as many of the towns in Shekhawati.

➡ Jeeps leave when (very) full, from well-established 'passenger stations' on the outskirts of towns and villages; locals should be able to point you in the right direction.

Taxi

➡ Taxis are usually metered, but drivers often claim that the meter is broken and proceed to request an elevated 'fixed' fare instead – threatening to get another taxi will often miraculously fix the meter.

➡ Meters are almost always outdated, so fares are calculated using a combination

of the meter reading and a complicated 'fare adjustment card'. Predictably, this system is open to abuse.

➡ In tourist areas in particular, some taxis flatly refuse to use the meter – if this happens, get out and find another cab.

➡ To avoid fare-setting shenanigans, only use prepaid taxis where possible.

Motorcycle

Cruising solo around India by motorcycle offers the freedom to go when and where you desire. There are also some excellent motorcycle tours available, which take the hassle out of doing it alone.

Helmets, leathers, gloves, goggles, boots, waterproofs and other protective gear are best brought from your home country, as they're either unavailable in India or are of variable quality.

Driving Licence

➡ To hire a motorcycle in India, you're required to have a valid international drivers' permit in addition to your domestic licence.

➡ In tourist areas, some places may rent out a motorcycle without asking for a driving permit/licence, but you won't be covered by insurance and may also face a fine.

Hire

➡ The classic way to motorcycle round India is on an Enfield Bullet, still built to many of the original 1940s

specifications. As well as making a satisfying sound, these bikes are easy to repair (parts can be found almost everywhere in India). On the other hand, Enfields are less reliable than the newer, Japanese-designed bikes.

➡ Plenty of places rent out motorcycles for local trips and longer tours. Japanese- and Indian-made bikes in the 100cc to 150cc range are cheaper than the big 350cc and 500cc Enfields.

➡ As a deposit, you'll need to leave a large cash lump sum (ensure you get a receipt that also stipulates the refundable amount), your passport or your air ticket. It's strongly advisable to avoid leaving your passport, which you'll need to check in at hotels and which the police can demand to see at any time.

➡ For three weeks' hire, a 500cc Enfield costs from ₹22,000; a 350cc costs ₹15,000. The price can include excellent advice and an invaluable crash course in Enfield mechanics and repairs.

Purchase

Second-hand bikes are widely available and the paperwork is a lot easier than buying a new machine.

Finding a second-hand motorcycle is a matter of asking around, checking travellers' noticeboards and approaching local motorcycle mechanics.

A looked-after, second-hand 350cc Enfield will cost anywhere from ₹50,000 to ₹100,000. The 500cc model costs anywhere from ₹85,000 to ₹140,000. You will also have to pay for insurance. It's advisable to get any second-hand bike serviced before you set off.

When reselling your bike, expect to get between half and two-thirds of the price you paid if the bike is still in reasonable condition. Shipping an Indian bike overseas is complicated and expensive – ask the shop you bought the bike from to explain the process.

Helmets are available for ₹500 to ₹2000 and extras like panniers, luggage racks, protection bars, rear-view mirrors, lockable fuel caps, petrol filters and extra tools are easy to come by. One useful extra is a customised fuel tank, which will increase the range you can cover between fuel stops. An Enfield 500cc gives about 25km/L: the 350cc model gives slightly more.

The following dealers come recommended:

➡ **Delhi** Run by the knowledgable Lalli Singh, **Lalli Motorbike Exports** (☑011-28750869; www.lallisingh.com; 1740-A/55 Hari Singh Nalwa St, Abdul Aziz Rd; Ⓜ Karol Bagh) sells and rents out Enfields and parts, and buyers get a crash course in running and maintaining these lovable but temperamental machines. He can also recommend other reputable dealers in the area.

➡ **Jaipur** For hiring, fixing or purchasing a motorcycle, visit **Rajasthan Auto Centre** (☑2568074, 9829188064; www.royalenfieldsalim.com; Sanganeri Gate, Sanjay Bazaar; ◷10am-8pm, to 2pm Sun). To hire a 350cc Bullet costs ₹500 per day (including helmet); if you take the bike outside Jaipur, it costs ₹600 per day. Ask for Saleem, the Bullet specialist.

OWNERSHIP PAPERS

There's plenty of paperwork associated with owning a motorcycle; the registration papers are signed by the local registration authority when the bike is first sold and you'll need these papers when you buy a second-hand bike.

Foreign nationals cannot change the name on the registration. Instead, you must fill out the forms for a change of ownership and transfer of insurance. If you buy a new bike, the company selling it must register the machine for you, adding to the cost.

For any bike, the registration must be renewed every 15 years (for around Rs5000)

and you must make absolutely sure that it states the 'fitness' of the vehicle, and that there are no outstanding debts or criminal proceedings associated with the bike.

The process is complicated and it makes sense to seek advice from the company selling the bike – allow two weeks to tackle the paperwork and get on the road.

Fuel, Spare Parts & Extras

➡ If you're going to remote regions it's also important to carry basic spares (valves, fuel lines, piston rings etc).

➡ Spare parts for Indian and Japanese machines are widely available in cities and larger towns and Delhi's Karol Bagh is a good place to find parts.

➡ Make sure you regularly check and tighten all nuts and bolts, as Indian roads and engine vibration tend to work things loose quite quickly.

➡ Check the engine and gearbox oil level regularly (at least every 500km) and clean the oil filter every few thousand kilometres.

➡ Given the road conditions, the chances are you'll make at least a couple of visits to a puncture-wallah – start your trip with new tyres and carry spanners to remove your own wheels.

Insurance

➡ Only hire a bike with third-party insurance – if you hit someone without insurance, the consequences can be very costly. Reputable companies will include third-party cover in their policies; those that don't probably aren't trustworthy.

➡ You must also arrange insurance if you buy a motorcycle (usually you can organise this through the person selling the bike).

➡ The minimum level of cover is third-party insurance – available for ₹300 to ₹600

per year. This will cover repair and medical costs for any other vehicles, people or property you might hit, but no cover for your own machine. Comprehensive insurance (recommended) costs upwards of ₹800 per year.

Road Conditions

➡ Given the varied road conditions, India can be challenging for novice riders.

➡ Hazards range from cows and chickens crossing the carriageway to broken-down trucks, pedestrians on the road, and perpetual potholes and unmarked speed humps. Rural roads sometimes have grain crops strewn across them to be threshed by passing vehicles – a serious sliding hazard for bikers.

➡ Try not to cover too much territory in one day and avoid travelling after dark – many vehicles drive without lights and dynamo-powered motorcycle headlamps are useless at low revs while negotiating potholes.

➡ On busy national highways expect to average 45km/h without stops; on winding back roads and dirt tracks this can drop to 10km/h.

Organised Motorcycle Tours

Dozens of companies offer organised motorcycle tours around India with a support vehicle, mechanic and guide. Below are some reputable outfits (see websites for contact details, itineraries and prices):

Blazing Trails (www.blazing-trailstours.com)

Classic Bike Adventure (www.classic-bike-india.com)

Ferris Wheels (www.ferriswheels.com.au)

H-C Travel (www.hctravel.com)

Indian Motorcycle Adventures (www.indianmotorcycleadventures.com)

Lalli Singh Tours (www.lallisingh.com)

Moto Discovery (www.moto discovery.com)

Royal Expeditions (www. royalexpeditions.com)

Saffron Road Motorcycle Tours (www.saffronroad.com)

Wheel of India (www.wheelof india.com)

Tours

Organised tours can be a cheap way to see several places on one trip, although you rarely get much time at each place. If you arrange a tailor-made tour, you'll have more freedom about where you go and how long you stay.

Drivers may double as guides, or you can hire a qualified local guide for a fee. In tourist towns, be wary of touts claiming to be professional guides.

Train

Travelling by train is one of the quintessential Indian experiences. Trains offer a smoother ride than buses, and are especially recommended for long journeys that include overnight travel. India's rail network is one of the largest and busiest in the world and Indian Railways is the largest utility employer on earth, with roughly 1.5 million workers.

Although we list the most useful, there are hundreds of train services. The best way of sourcing updated railway information is to use relevant internet sites such as **Indian Railways** (www.indianrail.gov. in) and the useful www.seat61. com/India.htm. There's also *Trains at a Glance* (₹45), available at many train station bookstands and good bookshops or newsstands, but it's published annually so it's not as up to date as websites. Nevertheless, it offers comprehensive timetables covering all the main lines.

Booking Tickets in India

You can either book tickets through a travel agency or hotel (for a commission), or in person at the train station. You can also book online through **IRCTC** (www.irctc. co.in), the e-ticketing division of Indian Railways, or portals such as **Cleartrip** (www. cleartrip.com), **Make My Trip** (www.makemytrip.com) and **Yatra** (www.yatra.com). Remember, however, that online booking of train tickets has its share of glitches: travellers have reported problems with registering themselves on some portals and using certain overseas credit cards; you may also need an Indian phone number to register. Big stations often have

English-speaking staff who can help with reservations.

At smaller stations, the stationmaster and his deputy usually speak English.

➡ To book at the station, get a reservation slip from the information window, fill in the name of the departure station, destination station, the class you want to travel and the name and number of the train. Join the long queue to the ticket window where your ticket will be printed. Women should use the separate women's queue – if there isn't one, go to the front of the regular queue. Larger stations often have a counter for foreigners.

➡ Larger cities and major tourist centres have an International Tourist Bureau, which allows you to book tickets in relative peace – check www.indianrail.gov.in for a list of these stations.

Reservations

Bookings open 90 days before departure and you must make a reservation for all chair-car, sleeper, and 1AC, 2AC and 3AC carriages. No reservations are required for general (2nd class) compartments. Trains are always busy in India so it's wise to book as far in advance as possible; advanced booking for overnight trains is strongly recommended. Train services

---

TRAIN CLASSES

Air-Conditioned 1st Class (1AC) The most expensive class of train travel; two- or four-berth compartments with locking doors and meals included.

Air-Conditioned 2-Tier (2AC) Two-tier berths arranged in groups of four and two in an open-plan carriage. The bunks convert to seats by day and there are curtains for some semblance of privacy.

Air-Conditioned 3-Tier (3AC) Three-tier berths arranged in groups of six in an open-plan carriage; no curtains.

AC Executive Chair Comfortable, reclining chairs and plenty of space; usually found on Shatabdi express trains.

AC Chair Similar to the Executive Chair carriage but with less-fancy seating.

Sleeper Class Open-plan carriages with three-tier bunks and no AC; the open windows afford great views.

Unreserved 2nd Class Wooden or plastic seats and a lot of people – but cheap!

to certain destinations are often increased during major festivals but it's still worth booking well in advance.

Reserved tickets show your seat/berth number and the carriage number. When the train pulls in, keep an eye out for your carriage number written on the side of the train (station staff and porters can also point you in the right direction). A list of names and berths is also posted on the side of each reserved carriage.

Be aware that train trips can be delayed at any time of the journey, so, to avoid stress, factor some leeway into your travel plans.

If the train you want to travel on is sold out, be sure to enquire about the following:

Reservation Against Cancellation (RAC) Even when a train is fully booked, Indian Railways sells a handful of RAC seats in each class. This means that if you have an RAC ticket and someone cancels before the departure date, you will get that seat (or berth). You'll have to check the reservation list at the station on the day of travel to see where you've been allocated to sit. Even if no one cancels, as an RAC ticket holder you can still board the train, and even if you don't get a seat you can still travel.

Taktal Tickets Indian Railways holds back a limited number of tickets on key trains and releases them at 8am two days before the train is due to depart. A charge of ₹10 to ₹400 is added to each ticket price. 1AC and Executive Chair tickets are excluded from the scheme.

Tourist Quota A special (albeit small) tourist quota is set aside for foreign tourists travelling between popular stations. These seats can only be booked at dedicated reservation offices in major cities, and you need to show your passport and visa as ID. Tickets can be paid for in rupees (some offices may ask to see foreign exchange certificates – ATM receipts will suffice).

Wait List (WL) Trains are frequently overbooked, but many passengers cancel and there are regular no-shows. So if you buy

PALACES ON WHEELS

To travel maharaja style, try the RTDC Palace on Wheels and Royal Rajasthan on Wheels train services.

The **Palace on Wheels** (www.palaceonwheels.net) operates one-week tours of Rajasthan, departing from Delhi. The itinerary includes Jaipur, Jaisalmer, Jodhpur, Ranthambhore National Park, Chittorgarh, Udaipur, Keoladeo Ghana National Park and Agra. Fit-for-a-maharaja carriages are sumptuously decked out and there are dining cars, a bar, a lounge and a library. The train runs from September to April and the fare (seven nights) per person per night is from US$615/451/411 for single/double/triple cabins. Book ahead – tickets can sell out 10 months in advance for peak periods.

The **Royal Rajasthan on Wheels** (www.royalrajasthanonwheels.co.in) is even more luxurious and runs one-week trips from October to March starting and finishing in Delhi. The route takes in Jodhpur, Udaipur, Chittorgarh, Ranthambhore National Park, Jaipur, Khajuraho, Varanasi and Agra. The nightly fare (seven nights) per person is US$875/625 for single/twin occupancy of deluxe suites.

a ticket on the waiting list you're quite likely to get a seat, even if there are a number of people ahead of you on the list. Check your booking status at http://www.indianrail.gov.in/pnr_Enq.html by entering the PNR number of your ticket. A refund is available if you fail to get a seat.

Refunds

Tickets are refundable but fees apply. If you present more than one day in advance, a fee of ₹20 to ₹70 applies. Steeper charges apply if you seek a refund less than four hours prior to departure, but you can get some sort of refund as late as 12 hours afterwards.

Classes & Costs

Shatabdi express trains are same-day services between major and regional cities. These are the fastest and most expensive trains, with only two classes; AC Executive Chair and AC Chair. Shatabdis are comfortable, but the glass windows cut the views considerably compared to non-AC classes on slower trains, which have barred windows and fresh air.

Rajdhani express trains are long-distance express services running between Delhi and the state capitals, and offer 1AC, 2AC, 3AC and 2nd class. Two-tier means there are two levels of bunks in each compartment, which are a little wider and longer than their counterparts in 3-tier. Costing respectively a half and a third as much as 1AC, the classes 2AC and 3AC are perfectly adequate for an overnight trip.

For an excellent description of the various train classes (including pictures) see www.seat61.com/India.htm.

Fares are calculated by distance and class of travel; Rajdhani and Shatabdi trains are slightly more expensive, but the price includes meals. Most air-conditioned carriages have a catering service (meals are brought to your seat). In unreserved classes it's a good idea to carry portable snacks. Seniors (those over 60) get 30% off all fares in all classes on all types of trains. Children below the age of five travel for free; those aged between five and 12 years are charged half price.

Health

Hygiene is generally poor in most regions so food and water-borne illnesses are fairly common. A number of insect-borne diseases are present, particularly in tropical areas. Medical care is basic in various areas (especially beyond the larger cities) so it's essential to be well prepared.

Pre-existing medical conditions and accidental injury (especially traffic accidents) account for most that are life-threatening. Becoming ill in some way, however, is common. Fortunately, most travellers' illnesses can be prevented with some common-sense behaviour or treated with a well-stocked travellers' medical kit – however, never hesitate to consult a doctor while on the road, as self-diagnosis can be hazardous.

The following information is a general guide only and certainly does not replace the advice of a doctor trained in travel medicine.

BEFORE YOU GO

You can buy many medications over the counter in India without a doctor's prescription, but it can be difficult to find some of the newer drugs, particularly the latest antidepressant drugs, blood-pressure medications and contraceptive pills. Bring the following:

➡ medications in their original, labelled containers

➡ a signed, dated letter from your doctor describing your medical conditions and medications, including generic names

➡ a doctor's letter documenting the necessity of any syringes you bring

➡ if you have a heart condition, a copy of your ECG taken just prior to travelling

➡ any regular medication (double your ordinary needs)

Insurance

Don't travel without health insurance. Emergency evacuation is expensive. Consider the following when buying insurance:

➡ You may require extra cover for adventure activities such as rock climbing.

➡ In India, doctors usually require immediate payment in cash. Your insurance plan may make payments directly to providers or it will reimburse you later for overseas health expenditures. If you do have to claim later, make sure you keep all relevant documentation.

➡ Some policies ask that you telephone back (reverse charges) to a centre in your home country where an immediate assessment of your problem will be made.

Vaccinations

Specialised travel-medicine clinics are your best source of up-to-date information; they stock all available vaccines and can give specific recommendations for your trip. Most vaccines don't give immunity until *at least* two weeks after they're given, so visit a doctor well before de-parture. Ask your doctor for an International Certificate of Vaccination (sometimes known as the 'yellow booklet'), which will list all the vaccinations you've received.

Medical Checklist

Recommended items for a personal medical kit:

➡ Antifungal cream, eg clotrimazole

➡ Antibacterial cream, eg mupirocin

➡ Antibiotic for skin infections, eg amoxicillin/ clavulanate or cephalexin

➡ Antihistamine – there are many options, eg cetrizine for daytime and promethazine for night

➡ Antiseptic, eg Betadine

➡ Antispasmodic for stomach cramps, eg Buscopam

➡ Contraceptive

➡ Decongestant, eg pseudoephedrine

➡ DEET-based insect repellent

➡ Diarrhoea medication – consider an oral rehydration solution (eg Gastrolyte), diarrhoea 'stopper' (eg loperamide) and antinausea medication (eg prochlorperazine). Antibiotics for diarrhoea include ciprofloxacin; for bacterial diarrhoea azithromycin; for giardia or amoebic dysentery tinidazole

➡ First-aid items such as elastoplasts, bandages, gauze, thermometer (but not mercury), sterile needles and syringes, and tweezers

➡ Ibuprofen or another anti-inflammatory

➡ Iodine tablets (unless you're pregnant or have a thyroid problem) to purify water

➡ Migraine medication if you suffer from migraines

➡ Paracetamol

➡ Pyrethrin to impregnate clothing and mosquito nets

➡ Steroid cream for allergic or itchy rashes, eg 1% to 2% hydrocortisone

➡ High-factor sunscreen

➡ Throat lozenges

➡ Thrush (vaginal yeast infection) treatment, eg clotrimazole pessaries or Diflucan tablet

➡ Ural or equivalent if prone to urine infections

Websites

There is lots of travel-health advice on the internet; www.lonelyplanet.com is a good place to start. Other options:

Centers for Disease Control and Prevention (CDC; www.cdc.gov) Travel health advice.

MD Travel Health (www.mdtravelhealth.com) Travel-health recommendations for every country, updated daily.

World Health Organization (WHO; www.who.int/ith) Its helpful book *International Travel & Health* is revised annually and is available online.

Further Reading

Lonely Planet's *Healthy Travel – Asia & India* is pocket sized with useful information, including pre-trip planning, first aid, immunisation

REQUIRED & RECOMMENDED VACCINATIONS

The only vaccine required by international regulations is **yellow fever**. Proof of vaccination will only be required if you have visited a country in the yellow-fever zone within the six days prior to entering India. If you are travelling to India from Africa or South America, you should check to see if you require proof of vaccination.

The World Health Organization (WHO) recommends the following vaccinations for travellers to India (as well as being up to date with measles, mumps and rubella vaccinations):

Adult diphtheria & tetanus Single booster recommended if none in the previous 10 years. Side effects include sore arm and fever.

Hepatitis A Provides almost 100% protection for up to a year; a booster after 12 months provides at least another 20 years' protection. Mild side effects such as headache and sore arm occur in 5% to 10% of people.

Hepatitis B Now considered routine for most travellers. Given as three shots over six months. A rapid schedule is also available, as is a combined vaccination with Hepatitis A. Side effects are mild and uncommon, usually headache and sore arm. In 95% of people lifetime protection results.

Polio Only one booster is required as an adult for lifetime protection. Inactivated polio vaccine is safe during pregnancy.

Typhoid Recommended for all travellers to India, even those only visiting urban areas. The vaccine offers around 70% protection, lasts for two to three years and comes as a single shot. Tablets are also available, but the injection is usually recommended as it has fewer side effects. Sore arm and fever may occur.

Varicella If you haven't had chickenpox, discuss this vaccination with your doctor.

These immunisations are recommended for long-term travellers (more than one month) or those at special risk (seek further advice from your doctor):

Japanese B Encephalitis Three injections in all. Booster recommended after two years. Sore arm and headache are the most common side effects. In rare cases, an allergic reaction comprising hives and swelling can occur up to 10 days after any of the three doses.

Meningitis Single injection. There are two types of vaccination: the quadravalent vaccine gives two to three years' protection; meningitis group C vaccine gives around 10 years' protection. Recommended for long-term backpackers aged under 25.

Rabies Three injections in all. A booster after one year will then provide 10 years' protection. Side effects are rare – occasionally headache and sore arm.

Tuberculosis (TB) Adult long-term travellers are usually recommended to have a TB skin test before and after travel, rather than vaccination. Only one vaccine given in a lifetime.

information, and what to do if you get sick on the road. Other good references include *Travellers' Health* by Dr Richard Dawood and *Travelling Well* by Dr Deborah Mills – check out the website (www.travellingwell.com.au) too.

IN INDIA

Availability of Health Care

Medical care is hugely variable in India. Some cities now have clinics catering specifically to travellers and expatriates; these clinics are usually more expensive than local medical facilities, and offer a higher standard of care. Additionally, they know the local system, including reputable local hospitals and specialists. They may also liaise with insurance companies should you require evacuation. It is usually difficult to find reliable medical care in rural areas.

Self-treatment may be appropriate if your problem is minor (eg traveller's diarrhoea), you are carrying the relevant medication, and you cannot attend a recommended clinic. If you suspect a serious disease, especially malaria, travel to the nearest quality facility.

Before buying medication over the counter, check the use-by date, and ensure the packet is sealed and properly stored (eg not exposed to the sunshine).

Infectious Diseases

Malaria

This is a potentially deadly disease. Before you travel, seek expert advice according to your itinerary (rural areas are especially risky) and on medication and side effects.

Malaria is caused by a parasite transmitted by the bite of an infected mosquito. The most important symptom of malaria is fever, but general symptoms, such as headache, diarrhoea, cough or chills, may also occur. Diagnosis can only be properly made by taking a blood sample.

Two strategies should be combined to prevent malaria: mosquito avoidance and antimalarial medications. Most people who catch malaria are taking inadequate or no antimalarial medication.

Travellers are advised to prevent mosquito bites by taking these steps:

➡ Use a DEET-based insect repellent on exposed skin. Wash this off at night – as long as you are sleeping under a mosquito net. Natural repellents such as citronella can be effective, but must be applied more frequently than products containing DEET.

➡ Sleep under a mosquito net impregnated with pyrethrin.

➡ Choose accommodation with proper screens and fans (if not air-conditioned).

➡ Impregnate clothing with pyrethrin in high-risk areas.

➡ Wear long sleeves and trousers in light colours.

➡ Use mosquito coils.

➡ Spray your room with insect repellent before going out for your evening meal.

There are a variety of medications available:

Chloroquine & Paludrine combination Limited effectiveness in many parts of South Asia. Common side effects include nausea (40% of people) and mouth ulcers.

Doxycycline (daily tablet) A broad-spectrum antibiotic that helps prevent a variety of tropical diseases, including leptospirosis, tick-borne disease and typhus. Potential side effects include photosensitivity (a tendency to sunburn), thrush (in women), indigestion, heartburn, nausea and interference with the contraceptive pill. More serious side effects include ulceration of the oesophagus – take your tablet with a meal and a large glass of water, and never lie down within half an hour of taking it. It must be taken for four weeks after leaving the risk area.

Lariam (mefloquine) This weekly tablet suits many people. Serious side effects are rare but include depression, anxiety, psychosis and seizures. Anyone with a history of depression, anxiety, other psychological disorders or epilepsy should not take Lariam. It is considered safe in the second and third trimesters of pregnancy. Tablets must be taken for four weeks after leaving the risk area.

Malarone A combination of atovaquone and proguanil. Side effects are uncommon and mild, most commonly nausea and headache. It is the best tablet for scuba divers and for those on short trips to high-risk areas. It must be taken for one week after leaving the risk area.

Other diseases

Avian Flu 'Bird flu' or Influenza A (H5N1) is a subtype of the type A influenza virus. Contact with dead or sick birds is the principal source of infection and bird-to-human transmission does not

---

HEALTH ADVISORIES

It's a good idea to consult your government's travel-health website before departure, if one is available:

Australia (www.smartraveller.gov.au)

Canada (www.travelhealth.gc.ca)

New Zealand (www.mfat.govt.nz/travel)

UK (www.fco.gov.uk/en/travelling-and-living-overseas)

US (www.cdc.gov/travel)

easily occur. Symptoms include high fever and flu-like symptoms with rapid deterioration, leading to respiratory failure and death in many cases. Immediate medical care should be sought if bird flu is suspected. Check www.who.int/en/ or www.avianinfluenza.com.au.

Dengue Fever This mosquito-borne disease is becomingly increasingly problematic, especially in the cities. As there is no vaccine available it can only be prevented by avoiding mosquito bites at all times. Symptoms include high fever, severe headache and body ache and sometimes a rash and diarrhoea. Treatment is rest and paracetamol – do not take aspirin or ibuprofen as it increases the likelihood of haemorrhaging. Make sure you see a doctor to be diagnosed and monitored.

Hepatitis A This food- and water-borne virus infects the liver, causing jaundice (yellow skin and eyes), nausea and lethargy. There is no specific treatment for hepatitis A; just allow time for the liver to heal. All travellers to India should be vaccinated against hepatitis A.

Hepatitis B This sexually transmitted disease is spread by body fluids and can be prevented by vaccination. The long-term consequences can include liver cancer and cirrhosis.

Hepatitis E Transmitted through contaminated food and water, hepatitis E has similar symptoms to hepatitis A, but is far less common. It is a severe problem in pregnant women and can result in the death of both mother and baby. There is no commercially available vaccine, and prevention is by following safe eating and drinking guidelines.

HIV Spread via contaminated body fluids. Avoid unsafe sex, unsterile needles (including in medical facilities) and procedures such as tattoos. The growth rate of HIV in India is one of the highest in the world.

Influenza Present year-round in the tropics, influenza (flu) symptoms include fever, muscle aches, a runny nose, cough and sore throat. It can be severe in people over the age of 65 or in those with medical conditions such as heart disease or diabetes – vaccination is recommended for these individuals. There is no specific treatment, just rest and paracetamol.

Japanese B Encephalitis This viral disease is transmitted by mosquitoes and is rare in travellers. Most cases occur in rural areas and vaccination is recommended for travellers spending more than one month outside of cities. There is no treatment, and it may result in permanent brain damage or death. Ask your doctor for further details.

Rabies This fatal disease is spread by the bite or possibly even the lick of an infected animal – most commonly a dog or monkey. You should seek medical advice immediately after any animal bite and commence postexposure treatment. Having pretravel vaccination means the postbite treatment is greatly simplified. If an animal bites you, gently wash the wound with soap and water, and apply iodine-based antiseptic. If you are not prevaccinated you will need to receive rabies immunoglobulin as soon as possible, and this is very difficult to obtain in much of India.

Tuberculosis While TB is rare in travellers, those who have significant contact with the local population (such as medical and aid workers and long-term travellers) should take precautions. Vaccination is usually only given to children under the age of five, but adults at risk are recommended to have pre- and post-travel TB testing. The main symptoms are fever, cough, weight loss, night sweats and fatigue.

Typhoid This bacterial infection is spread via food and water. It gives a high and progressive fever and headache, and may be accompanied by a dry cough and stomach pain. It is diagnosed by blood tests and treated with antibiotics. Vaccination recommended for travellers who are spending more than a week in India. Vaccination is not 100% effective, so you must still be careful with what you eat and drink.

Travellers' Diarrhoea

This is by far the most common problem affecting travellers in India – between 30% and 70% of people will suffer from it within two weeks of starting their trip. It's usually caused by a bacteria, and thus responds promptly to treatment with antibiotics.

Travellers' diarrhoea is defined as the passage of more than three watery bowel actions within 24 hours, plus at least one other symptom, such as fever, cramps, nausea, vomiting or feeling generally unwell.

Treatment consists of staying well hydrated; rehydration solutions like Gastrolyte are the best for this. Antibiotics such as ciprofloxacin or azithromycin should kill the bacteria quickly. Seek medical attention quickly if you do not respond to an appropriate antibiotic.

Loperamide is just a 'stopper' and doesn't get to the cause of the problem. It can be helpful, though (eg if you have to go on a long bus ride). Don't take loperamide if you have a fever or blood in your stools.

Amoebic Dysentery Amoebic dysentery is very rare in travellers but is quite often misdiagnosed by poor-quality labs. Symptoms are similar to bacterial diarrhoea: fever, bloody diarrhoea and generally feeling unwell. You should always seek reliable medical care if you have blood in your diarrhoea. Treatment involves two drugs: tinidazole or metronidazole to kill the parasite in your gut and then a second drug to kill the cysts. If left untreated complications such as liver or gut abscesses can occur.

Giardiasis Giardia is a parasite that is relatively common in travellers. Symptoms include nausea, bloating, excess gas, fatigue and intermittent diarrhoea. The parasite will eventually go away if left untreated but this can take months; the best advice is to seek medical treatment. The treatment of choice is tinidazole, with metronidazole being a second-line option.

Environmental Hazards

Air Pollution

Air pollution, particularly vehicle pollution, is an increasing problem in most of India's urban hubs. If you have severe respiratory problems, speak with your doctor before travelling to India.

Diving & Surfing

Divers and surfers should seek specialised advice before they travel to ensure their medical kit contains treatment for coral cuts and tropical ear infections. Divers should ensure their insurance covers them for decompression illness – get specialised dive insurance through an organisation such as Divers Alert Network (www.danasiapacific.org). Certain medical conditions are incompatible with diving; check with your doctor.

Food

Dining out brings with it the possibility of contracting diarrhoea. Ways to help avoid food-related illness:

➡ eat only freshly cooked food

➡ avoid shellfish and buffets

➡ peel fruit

➡ cook vegetables

➡ soak salads in iodine water for at least 20 minutes

➡ eat in busy restaurants with a high turnover of customers

Heat

Many parts of India, especially down south, are hot and humid throughout the year. For most visitors it takes around two weeks to comfortably adapt to the hot climate. Swelling of the feet and ankles is common, as are muscle cramps caused by excessive sweating. Prevent these by avoiding dehydration and excessive activity in the heat. Don't eat salt tablets (they aggravate the gut); drinking rehydration solution or eating salty food helps. Treat cramps by resting, rehydrating with double-strength rehydration solution and gently stretching.

Dehydration is the main contributor to heat exhaustion. Recovery is usually rapid and it is common to feel weak for some days afterwards. Symptoms include:

➡ feeling weak

➡ headache

➡ irritability

➡ nausea or vomiting

➡ sweaty skin

➡ a fast, weak pulse

➡ normal or slightly elevated body temperature.

Treatment:

➡ get out of the heat

➡ fan the sufferer

➡ apply cool, wet cloths to the skin

➡ lay the sufferer flat with their legs raised

➡ rehydrate with water containing one-quarter teaspoon of salt per litre.

Heat stroke is a serious medical emergency. Symptoms include:

➡ weakness

➡ nausea

➡ a hot dry body

➡ temperature of over 41°C

➡ dizziness

➡ confusion

➡ loss of coordination

➡ seizures

➡ eventual collapse.

Treatment:

➡ get out of the heat

➡ fan the sufferer

➡ apply wet cloths to the skin or ice to the body, especially to the groin and armpits.

Prickly heat is a common skin rash in the tropics, caused by sweat trapped under the skin. Treat it by moving out of the heat for a few hours and by having cool showers. Creams and ointments clog the skin so they should be avoided. Locally bought prickly-heat powder can be helpful.

Altitude Sickness

If you are going to altitudes above 3000m, Acute Mountain Sickness (AMS) is an issue. The biggest risk factor is going too high too quickly – follow a conservative acclimatisation schedule found in good trekking guides, and *never* go to a higher altitude when you have any symptoms that could be altitude related. There is no way to

---

DRINKING WATER

➡ Never drink tap water.

➡ Bottled water is generally safe – check the seal is intact at purchase.

➡ Avoid ice unless you know it has been made hygienically.

➡ Be careful of fresh juices served at street stalls in particular – they may have been watered down or may be served in unhygienic jugs/glasses.

➡ Boiling water is the most efficient method of purifying it.

➡ The best chemical purifier is iodine. It should not be used by pregnant women or those with thyroid problems.

➡ Water filters should also filter out most viruses. Ensure your filter has a chemical barrier such as iodine and a small pore size (less than four microns).

predict who will get altitude sickness and it is quite often the younger, fitter members of a group who succumb.

Symptoms usually develop during the first 24 hours at altitude but may be delayed up to three weeks. Mild symptoms include:

➡ headache

➡ lethargy

➡ dizziness

➡ difficulty sleeping

➡ loss of appetite.

AMS may become more severe without warning and can be fatal. Severe symptoms include:

➡ breathlessness

➡ a dry, irritative cough (which may progress to the production of pink, frothy sputum)

➡ severe headache

➡ lack of coordination and balance

➡ confusion

➡ irrational behaviour

➡ vomiting

➡ drowsiness

➡ unconsciousness.

Treat mild symptoms by resting at the same altitude until recovery, which usually takes a day or two. Paracetamol or aspirin can be taken for headaches. If symptoms persist or become worse, immediate descent is necessary; even 500m can help. Drug treatments should never be used to avoid descent or to enable further ascent.

The drugs acetazolamide and dexamethasone are recommended by some doctors for the prevention of AMS; however, their use is controversial. They can reduce the symptoms, but they may also mask warning signs; severe and fatal AMS has occurred in people taking these drugs.

To prevent acute mountain sickness:

➡ ascend slowly – have frequent rest days, spending

CARBON-MONOXIDE POISONING

Some mountain areas rely on charcoal burners for warmth, but these should be avoided due to the risk of fatal carbon-monoxide poisoning. The thick, mattress-like blankets used in many mountain areas are amazingly warm once you get beneath the covers. If you're still cold, improvise a hot-water bottle by filling your drinking-water bottle with boiled water and covering it with a sock.

---

two to three nights at each rise of 1000m

➡ sleep at a lower altitude than the greatest height reached during the day, if possible. Above 3000m, don't increase sleeping altitude by more than 300m daily

➡ drink extra fluids

➡ eat light, high-carbohydrate meals

➡ avoid alcohol and sedatives

Insect Bites & Stings

Bedbugs Don't carry disease but their bites can be very itchy. They usually live in furniture and walls and then migrate to the bed at night. You can treat the itch with an antihistamine.

Lice Most commonly appear on the head and pubic areas. You may need numerous applications of an antilice shampoo such as pyrethrin. Pubic lice are usually contracted from sexual contact.

Ticks Contracted walking in rural areas. Ticks are commonly found behind the ears, on the belly and in armpits. If you have had a tick bite and have a rash at the site of the bite or elsewhere, fever or muscle aches, you should see a doctor. Doxycycline prevents tick-borne diseases.

Leeches Found in humid rainforest areas. They do not transmit any disease but their bites are often intensely itchy for weeks and can easily become infected. Apply an iodine-based antiseptic to any leech bite to help prevent infection.

Bee and wasp stings Anyone with a serious bee or wasp allergy should carry an injection of adrenalin (eg an Epipen). For others pain is the main problem –

apply ice to the sting and take painkillers.

Skin Problems

Fungal rashes There are two common fungal rashes that affect travellers. The first occurs in moist areas, such as the groin, armpits and between the toes. It starts as a red patch that slowly spreads and is usually itchy. Treatment involves keeping the skin dry, avoiding chafing and using an antifungal cream such as clotrimazole or Lamisil. The second, *Tinea versicolor,* causes light-coloured patches, most commonly on the back, chest and shoulders. Consult a doctor.

Cuts and scratches These become easily infected in humid climates. Immediately wash all wounds in clean water and apply antiseptic. If you develop signs of infection (increasing pain and redness), see a doctor.

Women's Health

For gynaecological health issues, seek out a female doctor.

Birth control Bring adequate supplies of your own form of contraception.

Sanitary products Pads, rarely tampons, are readily available.

Thrush Heat, humidity and antibiotics can all contribute to thrush. Treatment is with antifungal creams and pessaries such as clotrimazole. A practical alternative is a single tablet of fluconazole (Diflucan).

Urinary-tract infections These can be precipitated by dehydration or long bus journeys without toilet stops; bring suitable antibiotics.

Language

India's linguistic landscape is varied – 23 languages (including English) are recognised in the constitution, and more than 1600 minor languages are spoken. This large number of languages certainly helps explain why English is still widely spoken in India and why it's still in official use. Despite major efforts to promote Hindi as the national language of India, phasing out English, many educated Indians speak English as virtually their first language. For the large number of Indians who speak more than one language, it's often their second tongue. Although you'll find it very easy to get around India with English, it's always good to know a little of the local language.

While the locals in Rajasthan, Agra and Delhi may speak Punjabi, Urdu, Marwari, Jaipuri, Malvi or Mewati to each other, for you, Hindi will be the local language of choice. Hindi has about 600 million speakers worldwide, of which 180 million are in India. It developed from Classical Sanskrit, and is written in Devanagari script. In 1947 it was granted official status along with English.

Pronunciation

Most Hindi sounds are similar to their English counterparts. The main difference is that Hindi has both 'aspirated' consonants (pronounced with a puff of air, like saying 'h' after the sound) and unaspirated ones, as well as 'retroflex' (pronounced with the tongue bent backwards) and nonretroflex consonants.

WANT MORE?

For in-depth language information and handy phrases, check out Lonely Planet's *India Phrasebook*. You'll find them at **shop.lonelyplanet.com**, or you can buy Lonely Planet's iPhone phrasebooks at the Apple App Store.

Our simplified pronunciation guides don't include these distinctions – read them as if they were English and you'll be understood.

Pronouncing the vowels correctly is important, especially their length (eg a and aa). The consonant combination ng after a vowel indicates nasalisation (ie the vowel is pronounced 'through the nose'). Note also that au is pronounced as the 'ow' in 'how'. Word stress is very light – we've indicated the stressed syllables with italics.

Basics

Hindi verbs change form depending on the gender of the speaker (or the subject of the sentence in general), so it's the verbs, not the pronouns 'he' or 'she' (as is the case in English) which show whether the subject of the sentence is masculine or feminine. In these phrases we include the options for male and female speakers, marked 'm' and 'f' respectively.

Hello./Goodbye.	नमस्ते ।	na·ma·*ste*
Yes.	जी हाँ ।	jee haang
No.	जी नहीं ।	jee na·*heeng*
Excuse me.	सुनिये ।	su·ni·*ye*
Sorry.	माफ़ कीजिये ।	maaf *kee*·ji·ye
Please ...	कृपया ...	kri·pa·*yaa* ...
Thank you.	थैंक्यू ।	*thayn*·kyoo
You're welcome.	कोई बात नहीं ।	*ko*·ee baat na·*heeng*

How are you?
आप कैसे/कैसी हैं?

aap *kay*·se/*kay*·see hayng (m/f)

Fine. And you?
मैं ठीक हूँ ।
आप सुनाइये ।

mayng teek hoong
aap su·*naa*·i·ye

What's your name?
आप का नाम क्या है? — aap kaa naam kyaa hay

My name is ...
मेरा नाम ... है। — me·raa naam ... hay

Do you speak English?
क्या आपको अंग्रेज़ी आती है? — kyaa aap ko an·gre·zee aa·tee hay

I don't understand.
मैं नहीं समझा/समझी। — mayng na·heeng sam·jaa/sam·jee (m/f)

Accommodation

Where's a ...? — ... कहाँ है? — ... ka·haang hay
- **guesthouse** — गेस्ट हाउस — gest haa·us
- **hotel** — होटल — ho·tal
- **youth hostel** — यूथ हास्टल — yoot haas·tal

Do you have a ... room? — क्या ... कमरा है? — kyaa ... kam·raa hay
- **single** — सिंगल — sin·gal
- **double** — डबल — da·bal

How much is it per ...? — ... के लिये कितने पैसे लगते हैं? — ... ke li·ye kit·ne pay·se lag·te hayng
- **night** — एक रात — ek raat
- **person** — हर व्यक्ति — har vyak·ti

- **air-con** — ए॰ सी॰ — e see
- **bathroom** — बाथरूम — baat·room
- **hot water** — गर्म पानी — garm paa·nee
- **mosquito net** — मसहरी — mas·ha·ree
- **washerman** — धोबी — do·bee
- **window** — खिड़की — kir·kee

Directions

Where's ...? — ... कहाँ है? — ... ka·haang hay

How far is it? — वह कितनी दूर है? — voh kit·nee door hay

What's the address? — पता क्या है? — pa·taa kyaa hay

Can you show me (on the map)? — (नक्शे में) दिखा सकते है? — (nak·she meng) di·kaa sak·te hayng

Turn left/right. — लेफ्ट/राइट मुड़िये। — left/raa·it mu·ri·ye

NUMBERS

1	१	एक	ek
2	२	दो	do
3	३	तीन	teen
4	४	चार	chaar
5	५	पाँच	paanch
6	६	छह	chay
7	७	सात	saat
8	८	आठ	aat
9	९	नौ	nau
10	१०	दस	das
20	२०	बीस	bees
30	३०	तीस	tees
40	४०	चालीस	chaa·lees
50	५०	पचास	pa·chaas
60	६०	साठ	saat
70	७०	सत्तर	sat·tar
80	८०	अस्सी	as·see
90	९०	नब्बे	nab·be
100	१००	सौ	sau
1000	१०००	एक हज़ार	ek ha·zaar

- **at the corner** — कोने पर — ko·ne par
- **at the traffic lights** — सिगनल पर — sig·nal par
- **behind ...** — ... के पीछे — ... ke pee·che
- **in front of ...** — ... के सामन — ... ke saam·ne
- **near ...** — ... के पास — ... ke paas
- **opposite ...** — ... के सामने — ... ke saam·ne
- **straight ahead** — सीधे — see·de

Eating & Drinking

What would you recommend?
आपके ख्याल में क्या अच्छा होगा? — aap ke kyaal meng kyaa ach·chaa ho·gaa

Do you have vegetarian food?
क्या आप का खाना शाकाहारी है? — kyaa aap kaa kaa·naa shaa·kaa·haa·ree hay

I don't eat (meat).
मैं (गोश्त) नहीं खाता/खाती। — mayng (gosht) na·heeng kaa·taa/kaa·tee (m/f)

I'll have ...
मुझे ... दीजिये। — mu·je ... dee·ji·ye

That was delicious.
बहुत मज़ेदार हुआ। — ba·hut ma·ze·daar hu·aa

Please bring the menu/bill.
मेन्यू/बिल लाइये। — men·yoo/bil laa·i·ye

Key Words

bottle	बोतल	bo·tal
bowl	कटोरी	ka·to·ree
breakfast	नाश्ता	naash·taa
dessert	मीठा	mee·taa
dinner	रात का खाना	raat kaa kaa·naa
drinks	पीने की चीज़ेष्ठ	pee·ne kee chee·zeng
food	खाना	kaa·naa
fork	काँटा	kaan·taa
glass	गिलास	glaas
knife	चाकू	chaa·koo
local eatery	ढाबा	daa·baa
lunch	दिन का खाना	din kaa kaa·naa
market	बाज़ार	baa·zaar
plate	प्लेट	plet
restaurant	रेस्टोरेष्ट	res·to·rent
set meal	थाली	taa·lee
snack	नाश्ता	naash·taa
spoon	चम्मच	cham·mach

Meat & Fish

beef	गाय का गोश्त	gaai kaa gosht
chicken	मुर्गी	mur·gee
duck	बतख़	ba·tak
fish	मछली	mach·lee
goat	बकरा	bak·raa
lobster	बड़ी झींग्गा	ba·ree jeeng·gaa
meat	गोश्त	gosht
meatballs	कोफ़्ता	kof·taa
pork	सुअर का गोश्त	su·ar kaa gosht
prawn	झींग्गी मछली	jeeng·gee mach·lee
seafood	मछली	mach·lee

Fruit & Vegetables

apple	सेब	seb
apricot	खुबानी	ku·baa·nee
banana	केला	ke·laa
capsicum	मिर्च	mirch

Question Words

How?	कैस?	kay·se
What?	क्या?	kyaa
Which?	कौनसा?	kaun·saa
When?	कब?	kab
Where?	कहाँ?	ka·haang
Who?	कौन?	kaun
Why?	क्यों?	kyong

carrot	गाजर	gaa·jar
cauliflower	फूल गोभी	pool go·bee
corn	मक्का	mak·kaa
cucumber	ककड़ी	kak·ree
date	खज़ूर	ka·joor
eggplant	बैंगन	bayng·gan
fruit	फल	pal
garlic	लहसुन	leh·sun
grape	अंगूर	an·goor
grapefruit	चकोतरा	cha·kot·raa
lemon	निम्बू	nim·boo
lentils	दाल	daal
mandarin	सन्तरा	san·ta·raa
mango	आम	aam
mushroom	खुम्भी	kum·bee
nuts	मेवे	me·ve
orange	नारंगी	naa·ran·gee
papaya	पपीता	pa·pee·taa
peach	आड़ू	aa·roo
peas	मटर	ma·tar
pineapple	अनन्नास	a·nan·naas
potato	आलू	aa·loo
pumpkin	कद्दू	kad·doo
spinach	पालक	paa·lak
vegetables	सब्ज़ी	sab·zee
watermelon	तरबूज़	tar·booz

Other

bread	चपाती/नान/रोटी	cha·paa·tee/naan/ro·tee
butter	मक्खन	mak·kan
chilli	मिर्च	mirch
chutney	चटनी	chat·nee
egg	अंडे	an·de
honey	मधु	ma·dhu
ice	बर्फ़	barf
ice cream	कुल्फ़ी	kul·fee
pappadams	पपड़	pa·par
pepper	काली मिर्च	kaa·lee mirch
relish	अचार	a·chaar
rice	चावल	chaa·val
salt	नमक	na·mak
spices	मिर्च मसाला	mirch ma·saa·laa
sugar	चीनी	chee·nee
tofu	टोफू	to·foo

Drinks

beer	बियर	bi·yar
coffee	काईफ़ी	kaa·fee

milk	दूध	dood
red wine	लाल शराब	laal sha·*raab*
sweet fruit drink	शरबत	*shar*·bat
tea	चाय	chaai
water	पानी	*paa*·nee
white wine	सफ़ेद शराब	sa·*fed* sha·*raab*
yoghurt	लस्सी	*las*·see

Emergencies

Help!
मदद कीजिये! — ma·*dad* kee·ji·ye

Go away!
जाओ! — *jaa*·o

I'm lost.
मैं रास्ता भूल गया/गयी हूँ। — mayng *raas*·taa bool ga·*yaa*/ga·*yee* hoong (m/f)

Call a doctor!
डॉक्टर को बुलाओ! — *daak*·tar ko bu·*laa*·o

Call the police!
पुलिस को बुलाओ! — pu·*lis* ko bu·*laa*·o

I'm ill.
मैं बीमार हूँ। — mayng *bee*·maar hoong

Where is the toilet?
टॉइलेट कहाँ है? — *taa*·i·let ka·*haang* hay

Shopping & Services

I'd like to buy ...
मुझे ... चाहिये। — mu·*je* ... *chaa*·hi·ye

I'm just looking.
सिर्फ़ देखने आया/आयी हूँ। — sirf *dek*·ne aa·*yaa*/aa·*yee* hoong (m/f)

Can I look at it?
दिखाइये। — di·*kaa*·i·ye

How much is it?
कितने का है? — *kit*·ne kaa hay

It's too expensive.
यह बहुत महँगा/महँगी है। — yeh ba·*hut* ma·*han*·gaa/ma·*han*·gee hay (m/f)

There's a mistake in the bill.
बिल में गलती है। — bil meng *gal*·tee hay

bank	बैंक	baynk
post office	डाक ख़ाना	daak *kaa*·naa
public phone	सार्वजनिक फ़ोन	*saar*·va·ja·nik fon
tourist office	पर्यटन ऑफ़िस	*par*·ya·tan *aa*·fis

Time & Dates

What time is it?
टाइम क्या है? — *taa*·im kyaa hay

It's (10) o'clock.
(दस) बजे हैं। — (das) ba·*je* hayng

Half past (10).
साढ़े (दस)। — *saa*·re (das)

morning	सुबह	su·*bah*
afternoon	दोपहर	*do*·pa·har
evening	शाम	shaam

Monday	सोमवार	*som*·vaar
Tuesday	मंगलवार	man·*gal*·vaar
Wednesday	बुधवार	*bud*·vaar
Thursday	गुरुवार	gu·ru·*vaar*
Friday	शुक्रवार	*shuk*·ra·vaar
Saturday	शनिवार	sha·ni·*vaar*
Sunday	रविवार	ra·vi·*vaar*

TRANSPORT

Public Transport

When's the ... (bus)?	... (बस) कब जाती है?	... (bas) kab *jaa*·tee hay
first	पहली	*peh*·lee
last	आख़िरी	*aa*·ki·ree

bicycle rickshaw	साइकिल रिक्शा	*saa*·i·kil *rik*·shaa
boat	जहाज़	ja·*haaz*
bus	बस	bas
plane	हवाई जहाज़	ha·*vaa*·ee ja·*haaz*
train	ट्रेन	tren

At what time does it leave?
कितने बजे जाता/जाती है? — *kit*·ne ba·*je jaa*·taa/*jaa*·tee hay (m/f)

How long does the trip take?
जाने में कितनी देर लगती है? — *jaa*·ne meng *kit*·nee der *lag*·tee hay

How long will it be delayed?
उसे कितनी देर हुई है? — u·*se kit*·nee der hu·*ee* hay

Does it stop at ...?
क्या ... में रुकती है? — kyaa ... meng *ruk*·tee hay

Please tell me when we get to ...

जब ... आता है,	jab ... aa·taa hay
मुझे बताइये।	mu·je ba·taa·i·ye

Please go straight to this address.

इसी जगह को	is·ee ja·gah ko
फ़ौरन जाइए।	fau·ran jaa·i·ye

Please stop here.

यहाँ रुकिये।	ya·haang ru·ki·ye

A ... ticket (to ...).	(...) के लिये ... टिकट दीजिये।	(...) ke li·ye ... ti·kat dee·ji·ye
1st-class	फ़र्स्ट क्लास	farst klaas
2nd-class	सेकन्ड क्लास	se·kand klaas
one-way	एक तरफ़ा	ek ta·ra·faa
return	आने जाने का	aa·ne jaa·ne kaa

I'd like a/an ... seat.	मुझे ... सीट चाहिये।	mu·je ... seet chaa·hi·ye
aisle	किनारे	ki·naa·re
window	खिड़की के पास	kir·kee ke paas

bus stop	बस स्टॉप	bas is·taap
ticket office	टिकटघर	ti·kat·gar
timetable	समय सारणी	sa·mai saa·ra·nee
train station	स्टेशन	ste·shan

Driving & Cycling

I'd like to hire a ...	मुझे ... किराये पर लेना है।	mu·je ... ki·raa·ye par le·naa hay
4WD	फ़ोर व्हील ड्राइव	for vheel draa·iv
bicycle	साइकिल	saa·i·kil
car	कार	kaar
motorbike	मोटर साइकिल	mo·tar saa·i·kil

Is this the road to ...?

क्या यह ... का रास्ता है?	kyaa yeh ... kaa raas·taa hay

Can I park here?

यहाँ पार्क कर सकता/ सकती हूँ?	ya·haang paark kar sak·taa/ sak·tee hoong (m/f)

Where's a service station?

पेट्रोल पम्प कहाँ है?	pet·rol pamp ka·haang hay

I need a mechanic.

मुझे मरम्मत करने वाला चाहिये।	mu·je ma·ram·mat kar·ne vaa·laa chaa·hi·ye

The car/motorbike has broken down at ...

कार/मोटर साइकिल ... मेंष ख़राब हो गयी है।	kaar/mo·tar saa·i·kil ... meng ka·raab ho ga·yee hay

I have a flat tyre.

टायर पंक्चर हो गया है।	taa·yar pank·char ho ga·yaa hay

I've run out of petrol.

पेट्रोल ख़त्म हो गया है।	pet·rol katm ho ga·yaa hay

GLOSSARY

ahimsa – nonviolence and reverence for all life

apsara – celestial maiden

Aryan – Sanskrit word for 'noble'; people who migrated from Persia and settled in northern India

ashram – spiritual community or retreat

autorickshaw – a noisy three-wheeled device that has a motorbike engine and seats for two passengers behind the driver

Ayurveda – the ancient and complex science of Indian herbal medicine and healing

bagh – garden

baithak – salon in a *haveli* where merchants received guests

baksheesh – tip, donation (alms) or bribe

bandhani – tie-dye

baori – well, particularly a step-well with landings and galleries

betel – nut of the betel tree; chewed as a stimulant and digestive in a concoction know as *paan*

bhang – dried leaves and flowering shoots of the marijuana plant

Bhil – tribal people of southern Rajasthan

bindi – forehead mark

Bishnoi – tribe known for their reverence for the environment

Bodhi Tree – *Ficus religiosa*, under which Buddha attained enlightenment

Brahmin – member of the priest caste, the highest Hindu caste

Buddha – Awakened One; the originator of Buddhism, who is also regarded by Hindus as the ninth incarnation of Vishnu

bund – embankment, dyke

chajera – mason employed by Marwari businessmen of Shekhawati to build *havelis*

charpoy – simple bed made of ropes knotted together on a wooden frame

chaupar – town square formed by the intersection of major roads

chhatri – cenotaph (literally 'umbrella')

choli – sari blouse

chowk – town square, intersection or marketplace

chowkidar – caretaker; night watchman

crore – 10 million

cycle-rickshaw – three-wheeled bicycle with seats for two passengers behind the rider

dacoit – bandit

Dalit – preferred term for India's *Untouchable* caste

dalwar – sword

dargah – shrine or place of burial of a Muslim saint

dharamsala – pilgrims guest house

dhobi – laundry

dhurrie – cotton rug

Digambara – Sky Clad; a Jain sect whose monks show disdain for worldly goods by going naked

Diwan-i-Am – hall of public audience

Diwan-i-Khas – hall of private audience

dupatta – long scarf for women often worn with the *salwar kameez*

durbar – royal court; also a government

garh – fort

ghat – steps or landing on a river; range of hills or road up hills

ghazal – Urdu song derived from poetry; sad love theme

ghoomer – dance performed by women during festivals and weddings

gopis – milkmaids; Krishna was very fond of them

guru – teacher or holy person

Harijan – name (no longer considered acceptable) given by Gandhi to India's *Untouchables*, meaning 'children of god'

hathi – elephant

haveli – traditional, ornately decorated rseidence

hijra – eunuch

hookah – water pipe

howdah – seat for carrying people on an elephant's back

jali – carved marble lattice screen; also refers to the holes or spaces produced through carving timber

Jats – traditionally people who were engaged in agriculture; today Jats play a strong role in administration and politics

jauhar – ritual mass suicide by immolation, traditionally performed by *Rajput* women after military defeat to avoid dishonour

jootis – traditional leather shoes of Rajasthan; men's *jootis* often have curled-up toes; also known as *mojaris*

kabas – the holy rats believed to be the incarnations of local families at Karni Mata Temple at Deshnok

Kalbelias – nomadic tribal group associated with snake charming

karma – Hindu, Buddhist and Sikh principle of retributive justice for past deeds

kashida – embroidery on *jootis*

kathputli – puppeteer

khadi – homespun cloth; Mahatma Gandhi encouraged people to spin *khadi* rather than buy English cloth

khadim – Muslim holy servant or mosque attendant

kotwali – police station

Kshatriya – warrior or administrator caste, second in the caste hierarchy; Rajputs claim lineage from the Kshatriyas

kundan – type of jewellery featuring *meenakari* on one side and precious stones on the other

kurta – long cotton shirt with either a short collar or no collar

lakh – 100,000

lingam – phallic symbol; symbol of Shiva

madrasa – Islamic college

Mahabharata – Vedic epic poem of the Bharata dynasty; describes the battle between the Pandavas and the Kauravas

mahal – house, palace

maharaja – literally 'great king'; princely ruler; also known as maharana, maharao and maharawal

maharani – wife of a princely ruler or a ruler in her own right

Mahavir – the 24th and last *tirthankar*

mahout – elephant driver/keeper

mandapa – chamber before the inner sanctum of a temple

mandir – temple

mantra – sacred word or syllable used by Buddhists and Hindus to aid concentration; metric psalms of praise found in the *Vedas*

Marathas – warlike central Indians who controlled much of India at times and fought against the *Mughals* and *Rajputs*

marg – major road

masjid – mosque

Marwar – kingdom of the Rathore dynasty that ruled from Mandore, and later from Jodhpur

meenakari – type of enamel-work used on ornaments and jewellery

mehfilkhana – Islamic building in which religious songs are sung

mehndi – henna; intricate henna designs applied by women to their hands and feet

mela – fair, festival

Mewar – kingdom of the Sisodia dynasty; ruled Udaipur and Chittorgarh

moksha – release from the cycle of birth and death

monsoon – rainy season; June to October

mosar – death feast

Mughal – Muslim dynasty of Indian emperors from Babur to Aurangzeb (16th to 18th centuries)

nawab – Muslim ruling prince or powerful landowner

nilgai – antelope

niwas – house, building

NRI – nonresident Indian

odhni – headscarf

Om – sacred invocation that represents the essence of the divine principle

paan – chewable preparation made from betel leaves, nuts and lime

PCO – public call office

pol – gate

prasad – sacred food offered to the gods

puja – literally 'respect'; offering or prayer

purdah – custom among some conservative Muslims (also adopted by some Hindus, especially the Rajputs) of keeping women in seclusion; veiled

raga – any conventional pattern of melody and rhythm that forms the basis for free composition

raj – rule or sovereignty; British Raj (sometimes just Raj) refers to British rule before 1947

raja – king; also *rana*

Rajputs – Sons of Princes; Hindu warrior caste, former rulers of western India

rana – see *raja*

rani – female ruler; wife of a king

rawal – nobleman

Road – railway town that serves as a communication point to a larger town off the line, eg Mt Abu and Abu Road

RSRTC – Rajasthan State Road Transport Corporation

RTDC – Rajasthan Tourism Development Corporation

sadar – main

sadhu – ascetic, holy person, one who is trying to achieve enlightenment; usually addressed as 'swamiji' or 'babaji'

sagar – lake, reservoir

sahib – respectful title applied to a gentleman

sal – gallery in a palace

salwar kameez – traditional dresslike tunic and trouser combination for women

sambar – deer

sati – suicide by immolation; banned more than a century ago, it is still occasionally performed

Scheduled Tribes – government classification for tribal groups of Rajasthan; the tribes are grouped with the lowest caste-less class, the Dalits

shikar – hunting expedition

Sikh – member of the mono-theistic religion Sikhism, which separated from Hinduism in the 16th century and has a military tradition; Sikh men can be recognised by their beards and turbans

sikhara – temple-spire or temple

silavat – stone carvers

Singh – literally 'lion'; a surname adopted by Rajputs and Sikhs

Sufi – Muslim mystic

tabla – pair of drums

tempo – noisy three-wheeled public transport; bigger than an autorickshaw

thakur – Hindu caste; nobleman

tikka – a mark devout Hindus put on their foreheads with *tikka* powder; also known as a *bor* or *rakhadi*

tirthankars – the 24 great Jain teachers

tonga – two-wheeled passenger vehicle drawn by horse or pony

toran – shield-shaped device above a lintel, which a bride-groom pierces with his sword before claiming his bride

torana – elaborately sculpted gateway before temples

tripolia – triple gateway

Vaishya – merchant caste; the third caste in the hierarchy

Vedas – Hindu sacred books; collection of hymns composed during the 2nd millennium BC and divided into four books: Rig-Veda, Yajur-Veda, Sama-Veda and Atharva-Veda

wallah – man; added onto almost anything, eg *dhobi-wallah*, *chai-wallah*, *taxi-wallah*

yagna – self-mortification

zenana – women's quarters

Behind the Scenes

SEND US YOUR FEEDBACK

We love to hear from travellers – your comments keep us on our toes and help make our books better. Our well-travelled team reads every word on what you loved or loathed about this book. Although we cannot reply individually to postal submissions, we always guarantee that your feedback goes straight to the appropriate authors, in time for the next edition. Each person who sends us information is thanked in the next edition – the most useful submissions are rewarded with a selection of digital PDF chapters.

Visit **lonelyplanet.com/contact** to submit your updates and suggestions or to ask for help. Our award-winning website also features inspirational travel stories, news and discussions.

Note: We may edit, reproduce and incorporate your comments in Lonely Planet products such as guidebooks, websites and digital products, so let us know if you don't want your comments reproduced or your name acknowledged. For a copy of our privacy policy visit lonelyplanet.com/privacy.

OUR READERS

Many thanks to the travellers who used the last edition and wrote to us with helpful hints, useful advice and interesting anecdotes:

A Aanas Ruhomaully, Altien van Steenbergen, Anne Jordan **B** Brendan Moore **C** Chad Pomeroy, Chris Kingsford-Curram, Cristina Vascotto **E** Eize Siegersma, Eva Warner **G** Geeske van der Molen, Giovanni Coudeville **I** Ian Pace **J** Jenny Moffatt, Judy Dunlop, Julia Medori **L** Loa Elaine Bliss **M** Malene Lysdahl, Mandy Dyke, Marc Eymard, Maria Sanchez , Marie Capion, Marilyn Carroll **R** Rebecca Young, Richard Fedje, Rob Turner, Roger Stoffel **S** Sam Chandra, Schoeters Parker, Simon Andersson, Sumit Makhija **V** Vicky Challacombe

AUTHOR THANKS

Paul Clammer

Thanks – and apologies – to everyone I met on the road who helped with research, without realising that Rajasthan is a place best covered anonymously for Lonely Planet. I wish I could have told you what I was doing! It would have been immeasurably harder however if I hadn't had a confidante along the way, so my biggest thanks and love go to Robyn – sidekick and constant companion, in India as she is everywhere else I go. In Fatehpur and Bikaner, thank you Jean for the limericks and the gin, and in Pushkar, Anna Voss for the fairy lights and being a lovely neighbour. Thank you also to fellow authors Sarina Singh, and Daniel McCrohan for the kebabs, Karim's and Kingfishers in Delhi.

Abigail Blasi

Thank you Joe Bindloss and Sarina Singh, DE and CA supreme, and to my wonderful co-authors. Thanks in Delhi to Sarah Fotheringham, to Nicolas Thompson and Danish Abbas, to Dilliwala Mayank Austen Soofi, to Rajinder and Surinder Budhraja, to Nirinjan and Jyoti Desai, my Delhi family, and to Luca for holding the fort.

Kevin Raub

Thanks to my wife, Adriana Schmidt Raub, who gladly ships me off to India without her! Thanks to Joe Bindloss at LP, and, on the road, Anil Whadwa, Mini-Google, Shiron Haider, Shibab Haider, Naghma Haider, Aisha Khan, Mukal Kumar, Guatam Singh, Megha Singh, Naheed Varma, Harish Rijhwani, Malika Rijhwani, Rochikant Mishra, Nicole Seregni, Fernanda Polacow, Marta Delellis, Rashi Rajoria, R.K. Rai, Saptarishi Saigal, Awesh Ali, Eli Rasaero and Ivan and Pixie Lamech.

ACKNOWLEDGMENTS

Climate map data adapted from Peel MC, Finlayson BL & McMahon TA (2007) 'Updated World Map of the Köppen-Geiger Climate Classification', Hydrology and Earth System Sciences, 11, 163344.

Illustrations pp98-9 by Michael Weldon; pp36-7 and pp84-5 by Javier Zarracina.

Cover photograph: City Palace, Jaipur/ Alvaro Leiva/Robert Hardin

THIS BOOK

This 4th edition of Lonely Planet's *Rajasthan, Delhi & Agra* guidebook was researched and written by Paul Clammer, Abigail Blasi and Kevin Raub.

This guidebook was produced by the following:

Destination Editor
Joe Bindloss

Product Editors
Kate Mathews, Alison Ridgway

Book Designer
Katherine Marsh

Assisting Editors Imogen Bannister, Nigel Chin, Paul Harding, Victoria Harrison, Gabrielle Innes, Kellie Langdon, Katie O'Connell, Kathryn Rowan

Cover Researcher
Naomi Parker

Thanks to Carolyn Boicos, Lonely Planet Cartography, Wayne Murphy, Ellie Simpson

Index

NOTES

Map Legend

Sights
- Beach
- Bird Sanctuary
- Buddhist
- Castle/Palace
- Christian
- Confucian
- Hindu
- Islamic
- Jain
- Jewish
- Monument
- Museum/Gallery/Historic Building
- Ruin
- Shinto
- Sikh
- Taoist
- Winery/Vineyard
- Zoo/Wildlife Sanctuary
- Other Sight

Activities, Courses & Tours
- Bodysurfing
- Diving
- Canoeing/Kayaking
- Course/Tour
- Sento Hot Baths/Onsen
- Skiing
- Snorkelling
- Surfing
- Swimming/Pool
- Walking
- Windsurfing
- Other Activity

Sleeping
- Sleeping
- Camping

Eating
- Eating

Drinking & Nightlife
- Drinking & Nightlife
- Cafe

Entertainment
- Entertainment

Shopping
- Shopping

Information
- Bank
- Embassy/Consulate
- Hospital/Medical
- Internet
- Police
- Post Office
- Telephone
- Toilet
- Tourist Information
- Other Information

Geographic
- Beach
- Hut/Shelter
- Lighthouse
- Lookout
- Mountain/Volcano
- Oasis
- Park
- Pass
- Picnic Area
- Waterfall

Population
- Capital (National)
- Capital (State/Province)
- City/Large Town
- Town/Village

Transport
- Airport
- Border crossing
- Bus
- Cable car/Funicular
- Cycling
- Ferry
- Metro station
- Monorail
- Parking
- Petrol station
- Subway station
- Taxi
- Train station/Railway
- Tram
- Underground station
- Other Transport

Note: Not all symbols displayed above appear on the maps in this book

Routes
- Tollway
- Freeway
- Primary
- Secondary
- Tertiary
- Lane
- Unsealed road
- Road under construction
- Plaza/Mall
- Steps
- Tunnel
- Pedestrian overpass
- Walking Tour
- Walking Tour detour
- Path/Walking Trail

Boundaries
- International
- State/Province
- Disputed
- Regional/Suburb
- Marine Park
- Cliff
- Wall

Hydrography
- River, Creek
- Intermittent River
- Canal
- Water
- Dry/Salt/Intermittent Lake
- Reef

Areas
- Airport/Runway
- Beach/Desert
- Cemetery (Christian)
- Cemetery (Other)
- Glacier
- Mudflat
- Park/Forest
- Sight (Building)
- Sportsground
- Swamp/Mangrove

OUR STORY

A beat-up old car, a few dollars in the pocket and a sense of adventure. In 1972 that's all Tony and Maureen Wheeler needed for the trip of a lifetime – across Europe and Asia overland to Australia. It took several months, and at the end – broke but inspired – they sat at their kitchen table writing and stapling together their first travel 'guide, *Across Asia on the Cheap*. Within a week they'd sold 1500 copies. Lonely Planet was born.

Today, Lonely Planet has offices in Franklin, London, Melbourne, Oakland, Beijing and Delhi, with more than 600 staff and writers. We share Tony's belief that 'a great guidebook should do three things: inform, educate and amuse'.

OUR WRITERS

Paul Clammer

Coordinating Author, Rajasthan Paul Clammer has contributed to over 25 Lonely Planet guidebooks, and worked as a tour guide in countries from Turkey to Morocco. In a previous life he may even have been a molecular biologist. He first covered India for LP back in 2004, up in the Himalayas, so jumped at the chance to explore Rajasthan in more depth this time around, staying on to write the chapter in a converted temple in Pushkar, where it was necessary to lock the doors to stop monkeys stealing his notes. Follow @paulclammer on Twitter.

Abigail Blasi

Delhi This is Abigail's sixth India title for Lonely Planet, and she was delighted to return to explore Delhi again, learning to love Paharganj, exploring the city's enclaves, and cycling through the mayhem of Old Delhi. She fell in love with the country on her first visit in 1994, and since then she's explored and written on India from north to south and back again. She's covered plenty of other places for Lonely Planet too, from Mauritania and Mali to Rome and Lisbon. Abigail also wrote the Scams, Women & Solo Travellers and Health chapters.

Kevin Raub

Agra & the Taj Mahal Kevin Raub grew up in Atlanta and started his career as a music journalist in New York, working for *Men's Journal* and *Rolling Stone* magazines. He ditched the rock 'n' roll lifestyle for travel writing and moved to Brazil. On his 8th epic Indian journey, Kevin was only out-spiced by an Indian chef once and never outsmarted by a rickshaw driver. This is Kevin's 30th Lonely Planet guide. Follow him on Twitter (@RaubOnTheRoad).

Read more about Kevin at:
http://auth.lonelyplanet.com/profiles/kraub

Published by Lonely Planet Publications Pty Ltd
ABN 36 005 607 983
4th edition – October 2015
ISBN 978 1 74220 577 9
© Lonely Planet 2015   Photographs © as indicated 2015
10 9 8 7 6 5 4 3 2 1
Printed in China